Self and Liberation

Other Books in the Jung and Spirituality Series

CARL JUNG AND CHRISTIAN SPIRITUALITY
Edited by Robert L. Moore

TRANSFORMING BODY AND SOUL
Therapeutic Wisdom in the Gospel Healing Stories
by Steven A. Galipeau

JUNG AND CHRISTIANITY IN DIALOGUE
Faith, Feminism, and Hermeneutics
Edited by Robert L. Moore
and Daniel J. Meckel

LORD OF THE FOUR QUARTERS
The Mythology of Kingship
by John Weir Perry

THE WEB OF THE UNIVERSE
Jung, the "New Physics," and Human Spirituality
by John Hitchcock

Daniel J. Meckel
Robert L. Moore
editors

Self and Liberation

THE JUNG-BUDDHISM DIALOGUE

Paulist Press
New York ◊ Mahwah

Author photos on back cover by Susan Reich.

Cover Image: Mandala Tanka of the Nor School, inscribed with dedicatory verse to deity listed by epithet rather than name: conqueror at death, c. 1700, Otto Doerring III Fund Purchase. Printed with permission of The Art Institute of Chicago, Department of Graphic Services and Reproductions, Chicago, Illinois.

Library of Congress Cataloging-in-Publication Data

Self and liberation: the Jung-Buddhism dialogue/Daniel J. Meckel and Robert L.
    Moore, editors.
        p.   cm.—(Jung and spirituality series)
    Includes bibliographical references and index.
    ISBN 0-8091-3301-6 (pbk.)
    1. Buddhism—Psychology. 2. Jung, C. G. (Carl Gustav), 1875–1961.
I. Moore, Robert L. II. Meckel, Daniel J. III. Series: Jung and spirituality.
BQ4570.P76S45   1992
294.3'375—dc20   91-40818
                                                                      CIP

Published by Paulist Press
997 Macarthur Blvd.
Mahwah, N.J. 07430

Printed and bound in the United States of America

Contents

Introduction: The Dialogue Between Jungian Psychoanalysis and Buddhist Spirituality 1
D.J. Meckel and R.L. Moore

PART ONE
JUNG ON BUDDHISM

Foreword to Suzuki's "Introduction to Zen Buddhism" 11
C.G. Jung

The Psychology of Eastern Meditation 31
C.G. Jung

Psychological Commentary on *The Tibetan Book of the Great Liberation* 48
C.G. Jung

Psychological Commentary on *The Tibetan Book of the Dead* ... 81
C.G. Jung

PART TWO
JUNG AND HISAMATSU

Editors' Comments 101

Self and Liberation: A Dialogue Between Carl G. Jung and Shin'ichi Hisamatsu 103

Jung's Commentary on the Conversation 114
    C.G. Jung

Hisamatsu's Commentary on the Conversation 116
    S. Hisamatsu

What Is the True Self? A Discussion 119
    K. Sato, H. Kataoka, R. DeMartino, M. Abe,
    H. Kawai

The Self in Jung and Zen 128
    Masao Abe

PART THREE
ON JUNGIAN THOUGHT AND BUDDHISM

Zen Buddhism, Freud, and Jung 143
    Thomas P. Kasulis

Jung, Eastern Religion, and the Language of the Imagination 166
    Peter Bishop

Self-Realization in the Ten Oxherding Pictures 181
    Mokusen Miyuki

The Bodhisattva as Metaphor to Jung's Concept of Self 206
    James D. Thomas

Mechanisms of Self-Deception and True Awareness 232
    Frederick J. Streng

Jung's Commentary on the *Amitāyur Dhyāna Sūtra* 247
    Harold Coward

Jung's Commentary on *The Tibetan Book of the Dead* 261
    Harold Coward

Tantric Buddhism and Jung: Connections, Similarities, Differences 275
> *Radmila Moacanin*

Ḍākinī and Anima—On Tantric Deities and Jungian Archetypes 302
> *Nathan Katz*

Notes on the Contributors 330

Index 334

DEDICATION

With this volume we wish to honor His Holiness, Tenzin Gyatso, the Fourteenth Dalai Lama of Tibet. It is our hope that the *Jung and Spirituality* series will reflect the spirit of ecumenical understanding, mutual compassion, and commitment to world peace which the Dalai Lama embodies.

D.J.M.
R.L.M.

APPRECIATIONS

We wish first to thank Carolyn Dame and Margaret Shanahan for their continuing support and patience during our protracted periods of preoccupation with this book and its companion volumes.

The efforts of several people have been essential to the making of this volume. Professor Isshi Yamada of Northwestern University devoted many hours to translating the Jung-Hisamatsu conversation and Hisamatsu's commentary from the Japanese manuscript. His skillful and meticulous work is greatly appreciated, as is his active interest in the relationship of Western psychology to Zen Buddhism —an interest which stirred many lively conversations throughout the process of translating the texts. Professors Masao Abe and Richard J. DeMartino were also very generous with their time in looking over the translations, revising their own writings, and providing us with information needed for the book. Much appreciation is also due to Jack Kornfield for his help and encouragement.

As usual, the editorial and production staff at Paulist Press has been supportive and helpful at every stretch. Thanks go to Kevin Lynch, Lawrence Boadt, Don Brophy, Bob Byrns, Hugh Lally, Theresa Sparacio, and Karen Scialabba.

Georgia Christo continues to weave together the many strands of detail in the production of this series at the Paulist end, while responding with remarkable patience to our endless inquiries and requests. We're grateful, Georgia! Tim McKeen has inspired us yet again with his creative cover designs for the series, and Elizabeth Burke at the Art Institute of Chicago was very helpful to us in selecting and reproducing the artwork on the cover of this volume.

We are grateful to Noboru Sakano, Editor of *Psychologia*, and Yukie Dan, Secretary of the Eastern Buddhist Society, which publishes *The Eastern Buddhist*. Over the past several decades, these journals have published many valuable articles on Jung and Buddhism, some of which appear here. Princeton University Press has been most kind in allowing us to reprint Jung's essays on Buddhism. Thanks go to the library staffs at Regenstein Library of the University of Chicago, and at the Vanderbilt University Library, for their help in researching and preparing this text.

Finally, we extend our thanks and appreciation to the authors whose writings appear in this volume. It is through their efforts that a creative discourse continues between Jungian psychology and Buddhism.

SERIES FOREWORD

The *Jung and Spirituality* series provides a forum for the critical interaction between Jungian psychology and living spiritual traditions. The series serves two important goals.

The first goal is: *To enhance a creative exploration of the contributions and criticisms which Jung's psychology can offer to religion.* Jungian thought has far-reaching implications for the understanding and practice of spirituality. Interest in these implications continues to expand in both Christian and non-Christian religious communities. People are increasingly aware of the depth and insight which a Jungian perspective adds to the human experiences of the sacred. And yet, the use of Jungian psychoanalysis clearly does not eliminate the need for careful philosophical, theological and ethical reflection or for maintaining one's centeredness in a spiritual tradition.

The second goal is: *To bring the creative insights and critical tools of religious studies and practice to bear on Jungian thought.* Many volumes in the Jung and Spirituality series work to define the borders of the Jungian and spiritual traditions, to bring the spiritual dimensions of Jung's work into relief, and to deepen those dimensions. We believe that an important outcome of the Jung-Spirituality dialogue is greater cooperation of psychology and spirituality. Such cooperation will move us ahead in the formation of a post-modern spirituality, equal to the challenges of the twenty-first century.

Robert L. Moore
Series Editor

Daniel J. Meckel
Managing Editor

ACKNOWLEDGMENTS

The Publisher gratefully acknowledges use of the following materials: "Mechanisms of Self-Deception and True Awareness According to C.G. Jung," in *The Book of the Self: Person, Pretext and Process*, edited by James A. Hall and Polly Young-Eisendrath, New York University Press, New York, © 1987; selections from *The Collected Works of C.G. Jung*, translated by R.F.C. Hull, Bollingen Series XX, Vol. 11: *Psychology and Religion: West and East*. Copyright © 1958, 1969 by Princeton University Press. Reprinted with permission of Princeton University Press; a reprint of "Tantric Buddhism and Jung—Connections, Similarities, Differences," in *Jung's Psychology and Tibetan Buddhism: Western and Eastern Paths to the Heart*, by Radmila Moacanin, Wisdom Publications, London, © 1986; a reprint of "Jung, Eastern Religion, and the Language of the Imagination," *Eastern Buddhist*, Spring 1984, Vol. XVII, No. 1.6; a reprint of "Zen Buddhism, Freud, and Jung," *Eastern Buddhist*, May 1977, Vol. X, No. 1; a reprint of "A Jungian Approach to the Jodoshinshu Concept of the Wicked," in *Essays on Jung and the Study of Religion*, Luther H. Martin and James Goss, eds., University Press of America, © 1985; a reprint of "Self Realization in the Ten Oxherding Pictures," in *Buddhism and Jungian Psychology*, Falcon Press, © 1985; a reprint of "The Psychodynamics of Buddhist Meditation: A Jungian Perspective," in *Buddhism and Jungian Psychology*, Falcon Press, © 1985; a reprint of "The Psychodynamics of Buddhist Meditation: A Jungian Perspective," in *Buddhism and Jungian Psychology*, by Mokusen Miyuki, Falcon Press, © 1985; a reprint of "Self-Realization in the The Ten Oxherding Pictures," *Quadrant*, Spring 1982; a reprint of "A Jungian Approach to the Jodoshinshu Concept of the 'Wicked,' " in *Essays on Jung and the Study of Religion*, Martin & Goss eds., University Press of America, © 1985; a reprint of "Jung, Eastern Religion and the Language of Imagination," by Peter Bishop, *Eastern Buddhist*, Spring 1984, Vol. XVII, No. 1; a reprint of "The Bodhisattva as Metaphor to Jung's Concept of the Self," by James D. Thomas, *Eastern Buddhist*, Autumn 1982, Vol. XV, No. 2; a reprint from *Psychologia* by C.G. Jung and S. Hisamatsu, 1968; a reprint from *Psychologia* by C.G. Jung on the conversation with Dr. Hisamatsu: Letter to the translator, 1960; a reprint from *Psychologia* by K. Sato, on the conversation of C.G. Jung and S. Hisamatsu, 1961; a reprint from "What is the true self? A Discussion," by K. Sato, H. Kataoka, R. Demartino, M. Abe, and H. Kawai, from *Psychologia*, 1961; a reprint of "The Self in Jung and Zen," by Masao Abe, *The Eastern Buddhist*, Vol. XVIII, No. 1, Spring 1985.

Introduction: The Dialogue Between Jungian Psychoanalysis and Buddhist Spirituality

We present this volume to you as part of a series intended to bring Jungian psychology and contemporary spiritual traditions into critical dialogue with one another. This is the first volume of the *Jung and Spirituality* series to treat the relationship of Jung's work to Eastern spirituality. Although his major works on religion directly concern the Jewish and Christian traditions, Jung played an important and undeniable role as an interpreter of the East. R.C. Zaehner, the great historian of religion, wrote that Jung "has done more to interpret Eastern religion to the West than any other man."[1] Indeed Jung's psychology of the collective unconscious facilitated the widespread interest in and popularization of Eastern thought by providing people in the West with a way of relating foreign ideas and images to the most intimate levels of personal experience. Some of the best known treatises and translations of Asian texts were first received by the American and European public with an accompanying commentary by Jung. They include the *I-Ching, The Secret of the Golden Flower, The Tibetan Book of the Dead,* and Suzuki's famous *Introduction to Zen Buddhism.* Jung wrote on "The Psychology of Eastern Meditation," "The Holy Man of India," and in general made reference to Eastern religion and philosophy throughout all of his works.

Since Jung's death, our knowledge of Eastern spirituality has increased greatly. Generally, we have a more discerning picture of the spiritual traditions of the East, their differences, histories, and the cultures in which they arose. Unfortunately, as Jungian psychology has continued to deepen its roots in the West, a critical sense of its value for understanding non-Western traditions has not kept pace. Most scholars of religion now recognize that if we are really to

1

understand another spiritual worldview, we must approach it on its own terms—i.e. by learning its language, history, and culture. In addition, we need always to be aware of how our own Western framework of experience and understanding might be influencing and perhaps distorting our perceptions of another. In the light of these concerns, most current study of religion and spiritual life which engages Jung's ideas in any way at all tends to fall prey to the Scylla or Charybdis of two imminent dangers.

The first is an uncritical, doctrinaire, and simplistic appropriation of Jungian thought—a kind of Jungian pietism. The Jungian community must cultivate a more serious level of scholarship and encourage an ongoing reevaluation of the foundations of Jungian thought. We feel that this is necessary if Jung's work is to continue to offer a profound paradigm for interpreting and responding to contemporary human experience.

Opposite to Jungian pietism, and perhaps partially in response to it, is a widespread, uninformed rejection of Jungian interpretive perspectives. In this case Jung is usually brought up in order to be knocked down for his alleged procrustean simplicity. This attitude is, however, equally doctrinaire, simplistic, and yet quite academically fashionable. It often stems from a justifiable disdain for the radical reductionism of much psychological analysis of religion—the "nothing-but-ism" which wipes away the difference, detail, and integrity of religious phenomena to reveal the psychological principles which underlie them. But this does not apply to Jung's own work to the degree that has been assumed. For his interpretive work on religion is perhaps the least reductive of any of the Western psychologists.

In all of Jung's essays on Eastern spirituality it is clear that his approach entails a hermeneutic of culture—an awareness that a text cannot be interpreted apart from a consideration of the context from which it came. In Jung's essays on Buddhism, the reader will note Jung's abiding awareness of fundamental differences in the "Eastern mind," and the Western-bred limitations we face in understanding it. To give one example, in his foreword to Suzuki's book on Zen, he writes of "the importance of the traditional spiritual atmosphere of Buddhism in Zen. Zen and its technique could only exist on the basis of Buddhist spiritual culture, and this is its premise."

In keeping with Jung's own hermeneutic of culture, we might

benefit most by approaching the relationship between Jungian thought and Buddhism via a middle path, if you will, which neither indulges the simple view that the wisdom of each is ultimately and essentially the same, nor austerely pronounces the two as unresolvable and essentially other. This way will perhaps allow us to tend to the universal aspects of the psyche, its structure and patterns as they are reflected in Buddhist spirituality, as well as the relative and richly cultural dimensions of myth and meaning.

This collection of essays is meant to be a resource for anyone interested in these two important sources of spiritual and psychological insight. It is for students of Buddhism and students of Jungian psychology alike, for spiritual seekers as well as those whose interests are primarily scholarly.

To quote Zaehner again on Jung and the East, he writes: "It would hardly be an exaggeration to say that Jungian psychology is a re-emergence of some aspects of Buddhism and Taoism in modern dress."[2] The similarities between Jung's work and many aspects of Eastern spirituality are clear. The nature and ultimate extent of these similarities are important questions which have yet to be fully explored.[3] Fruitful dialogue, however, need not rely on shared beliefs and practices, but on the shared human condition. In this same sense, John Cobb writes recently on the Buddhist-Christian dialogue. The fact that we participate in a common religiosity is not what makes the conversation possible, he says; "our common humanity, rather, is the necessary and sufficient basis for dialogue."[4]

Buddhism and Jungian thought have each provided a powerful, alternative response in the West to a pervasive sense of spiritual impoverishment. In contrast to modern, industrialized society, each places value on the imagination and the non-rational, and works toward a more spontaneous and less ego-bound way of being. At the very heart of each is a concern for the nature of the self and its relationship to human suffering and liberation. Most of the essays in this volume center around these issues.

We have been careful to present a balanced representation of the Jung-Buddhism dialogue. Accordingly, in addition to Jung's essays on Buddhism, the reader will discover a good deal of reflection on Jungian psychology on the part of Buddhists, as well as much comparative study of the two by scholars of religion and psychology.

The book is divided into three sections. Part One, *Jung on Bud-*

dhism, includes all four of Jung's major essays on this topic. Many aspects of these texts are treated in the various chapters which follow, including Coward's two commentaries. Reflecting the overall structure of the third part, Jung's essays treat Zen Buddhism (the Foreword to D.T. Suzuki's "Introduction to Zen Buddhism"), a Mahayana text from the Jodo Shinshu sect of Japanese Buddhism, the *Amitāyur Dhyāna Sūtra* ("The Psychology of Eastern Meditation"), and two Tibetan texts (*Psychological Commentary on "The Tibetan Book of the Dead,"* and *Psychological Commentary on "The Tibetan Book of the Great Liberation"*).

Part Two, *Jung and Hisamatsu*, contains a transcript of the conversation held between Jung and Zen Master Shin'ichi Hisamatsu in 1958 at Jung's home in Küsnacht. It should be noted that this is the first time that this text has been made available to a large audience.[5] The conversation focuses mainly on the nature of "self" as it is understood in both Zen and Jung's psychology, and their respective understandings of suffering and its treatment. Permission to publish the original English translation of this conversation (conducted in German and Japanese with a translator) was denied by Jung, who felt that he and Hisamatsu had failed to reach a mutual understanding. Jung's letter to this effect is included in this volume, along with Hisamatsu's commentary on the conversation. Shortly after their meeting, a symposium was held in Kyoto among five psychologists and philosophers of the Kyoto school of Buddhism to discuss the points of controversy and misunderstanding which arose in the conversation. The proceedings of this symposium are reprinted here ("What Is the True Self? A Discussion"), as well as a full-length essay on the Jung-Hisamatsu conversation by Professor Masao Abe ("The Self in Jung and Zen").

Part Three, *On Jungian Thought and Buddhism*, contains nine excellent essays on Jung's work in relation to several dimensions of Buddhism. The first two essays, and a later essay by Moacanin, will orient the reader to the Jung-Buddhism dialogue with a comparative overview. Thomas Kasulis' paper on Zen, Freud, and Jung compares Western psychoanalytic and Zen views of the person in light of three central aspects: Freud's notion of defense mechanisms, Freud's theory of transference, and Jung's theory of individuation. As compared to Freud, Kasulis suggests, Jung's psychology offers a more fruitful comparison with Zen. Jung's prospective notion of individuation involves an ongoing transcendence of one's limited perceptions and experience, and an increasing *mobility* among the psychological types of thinking, feeling, sensation, and intuition. The affinity which individuation has with Zen rests in the ambiguity between the determinacy and the indeterminacy of the person. "Both the individuated person and the Zen person is determinate only within a given situation, only at a given time: there is no abiding self or agent that filters or reconstructs the experience before it is made fully conscious."

Peter Bishop's chapter provides an introduction to Jung's writings on Eastern religion by identifying and exploring four recurring themes in these writings: the practical problems which the Westerner faces in using Eastern spiritual methods and philosophy; images of wholeness, especially the mandala and the Buddha; the meaning of meditational and active imagining experiences; and Jung's investigation of synchronicity, including the use of symbols and creative imagining in healing and spiritual transformation. Bishop argues that Jung's study of Eastern religion marks a fundamental turning point in the development of his ideas, corresponding to his decisive turn toward use of imaginative discourse. Jung's concern for meaning and insight over concrete and "objective" reality, and as facilitated by imaginative discourse, constitutes his most important contribution to the continuing conversation between East and West.

The following chapters focus on more specific aspects of Buddhist spirituality, beginning with Mokusen Miyuki's informed Jungian interpretation of the *Ten Oxherding Pictures* of Pu-ming and Kuo-an. These two series of pictures express the achievement of *satori*, or Zen enlightenment. Miyuki writes that because enlightenment is a psychological reality *par excellence*, the *Oxherding Pictures* can be viewed through Jung's interpretive system and understood as portraying the process of individuation. The pictures are interpreted alternatively in terms of the doctrine of *tathagatagarbha*—the realization of Buddha-nature—and Jung's theory of the unconscious and the fundamental urge to self realization. Through his analysis of the *Ten Oxherding Pictures*, Miyuki argues that the Zen experience of *satori* "does not consist in ego-transcendence or ego-negation, but

rather in a life-long process which demands that the ego make ceaseless efforts towards the integration of the unconscious contents."
Both series of pictures are reprinted here with Miyuki's essay.

James D. Thomas explores the image of the Bodhisattva as a
metaphor to Jung's notion of the self. Jung constantly sought figures,
analogues and metaphors for the paradoxical and often mysterious
nature of inner wholeness, which unfolds as the "self." Thomas
masterfully explores the Buddhist image of the Bodhisattva as a useful and stimulating model for the many dimensions of Jung's concept
of self. A brief history of the concept of Bodhisattva is given, along
with an extremely useful delineation of the aspects of the self, as Jung
defines it. They include self as: superordinate system; goal; center of
opposites; uniting symbol; agent; and archetypal expression. Thomas
summarizes the nature of each aspect and employs the metaphor of
the Bodhisattva to illuminate further Jung's picture of self.

Frederick Streng looks at the assumptions that underlie the shift
from self-deception to true awareness as that shift is understood in
Jung's writings and in the Indian Buddhist text *The Eight-Thousand
Line Perfection of Wisdom Sutra*. "The specific issue," Streng writes,
"in the shift from self-deception to true awareness can be formulated
as the awareness of the self as it lets go of the attachment to the
ego-image. That is, we are focusing on the experience of the nonego
as a process that frees one from attachment to the ego." The fundamental differences between Jung's thought and that of this early
Buddhist text are not only differences in the notion of self and non-
ego, but also in the modes or processes of "becoming aware."

Harold Coward's two chapters treat two of the four essays by
Jung included in this volume: Jung's commentary on the *Amitāyur
Dhyāna Sūtra* (forming the main body of his "The Psychology of
Eastern Meditation"), and his commentary on *The Tibetan Book of the
Dead*. Coward gives historical and conceptual background to both of
the Buddhist texts. He describes the nature of Jung's interest in
them, and evaluates Jung's readings of them, point by point. Beginning with Coward's essays, the remaining chapters are concerned
with Jung and Tantric Buddhism.

Radmila Moacanin looks at conceptual similarities between
Jung and Tantra in relation to consciousness and the unconscious,
spiritual transformation, the union of opposites, the notion of the

middle way as reformulated by Indian philosopher Nagarjuna, and the striking notion that God is redeemed and God's creation illuminated only through the expanding consciousness of humankind. Moacanin compares Jung's cautious view of Eastern traditions with parallel concerns in Tantric Buddhism for the risks inherent in the practice of their methods. She ends with a discussion of the role of ethics and concern for the world community in both Jung and Buddhism, concluding that Jung, like Buddhism, "has constantly reminded man—the only carrier of consciousness—of his responsibility and ethical obligation to transform himself, or shall I say, to transform God."

Nathan Katz' chapter on Tantric deities and Jungian archetypes is not, as he describes it, concerned largely with Jung's interpretations or hermeneutic, but rather "with comparing two more or less systematic images of what it means to be human, as taken from Jung's and Tibetan Buddhist writings." This Katz does by looking at Jung's specifically psychological writings and Tibetan hagiography, treating the two as "systems in their own right," and comparing them along the lines of their fundamental concerns. His focus is on Jung's notion of anima, and the *ḍākiṇī*—"demoness-like beings who magically inspire and initiate Vajrayāna adepts." Katz spells out these basic concepts and then considers three areas in which they overlap: their function of inspiration, their position in the subject/object dichotomy, and the symbolic concreteness "of which Jungians and Tibetans are fond." Katz states that Jung goes astray in claiming that the concepts of anima and persona are lacking in the Eastern view. "One might attribute such a claim," he writes, "to Jung's lack of familiarity with Buddhism and Buddhist texts. One might also attribute it to a pernicious 'Orientalism' in the sense of wanton overgeneralization." In spite of these problems, he argues that Jung and the Tantric authors are attending to a cross-cultural human phenomenon. "We would offer that this phenomenon, called anima or *ḍākiṇī*, could be treated as a paradigm for comparative religio-psychological study which neither reduces one perspective to another, nor sees the discourses of Buddhist and Jungian psychology as rigidly and artificially compartmentalized."

The range of possibilities for engaging Jungian and Buddhist concepts is immense. The very best available essays on this topic are gathered together here for the first time. We trust that the reader will find them illuminating, and we hope that this volume will fuel the ongoing conversation.

Daniel J. Meckel
Robert L. Moore
Chicago, 1991

Notes

1. R.C. Zaehner, "A New Buddha and a New Tao," in *The Concise Encyclopedia of Living Faiths*, R.C. Zaehner, ed., New York: Hawthorn Books, 1959, p. 403.
2. Ibid.
3. For an excellent and extended treatment of these questions, see Harold Coward's *Jung and Eastern Thought*, State University of New York Press, Albany, 1985.
4. John B. Cobb, Jr., *Beyond Dialogue: Toward a Mutual Transformation of Christianity and Buddhism*, Philadelphia: Fortress Press, 1982, p. 39.
5. A fuller history of this text is given in the "Editors' Comments" at the beginning of Part Two.

Part One
JUNG ON BUDDHISM

C.G. Jung

Foreword to Suzuki's "Introduction to Zen Buddhism"[1]

Daisetz Teitaro Suzuki's works on Zen Buddhism are among the best contributions to the knowledge of living Buddhism that recent decades have produced, and Zen itself is the most important fruit to have sprung from the tree whose roots are the collections of the Pali Canon.[2] We cannot be sufficiently grateful to the author, first for having brought Zen closer to Western understanding, and secondly for the manner in which he has performed this task. Oriental religious conceptions are usually so very different from our Western ones that even the bare translation of the words often presents the greatest difficulties, quite apart from the meaning of the terms used, which in certain circumstances are better left untranslated. I need only mention the Chinese "tao," which no European translation has yet got near. The original Buddhist writings contain views and ideas which are more or less unassimilable for ordinary Europeans. I do not know, for instance, just what kind of mental (or perhaps climatic?) background or preparation is necessary before one can form any completely clear idea of what is meant by the Buddhist "kamma." Judging by all we know of the nature of Zen, here too we are up against a central conception of unsurpassed singularity. This strange conception is called "satori," which may be translated as "enlightenment." "Satori is the *raison d'être* of Zen without which Zen is not Zen," says Suzuki.[3] It should not be too difficult for the Western mind to grasp what a mystic understands by "enlightenment," or what is known as such in religious parlance. Satori, however, designates a special kind and way of enlightenment which it is practically impossible for the European to appreciate. By way of illustration, I would refer the reader to the enlightenment of Hyakujo (Pai-chang Huai-hai, A.D. 724–814) and of the Confucian

11

poet and statesman Kozankoku (Huang Shan-ku),[4] as described by Suzuki.

The following may serve as a further example: A monk once went to Gensha, and wanted to learn where the entrance to the path of truth was. Gensha asked him, "Do you hear the murmuring of the brook?" "Yes, I hear it," answered the monk. "There is the entrance," the Master instructed him.

I will content myself with these few examples, which aptly illustrate the opacity of satori experiences. Even if we take example after example, it still remains exceedingly obscure how any enlightenment comes and of what it consists—in other words, by what or about what one is enlightened. Kaiten Nukariya, who was himself a professor at the So-to-shu Buddhist College in Tokyo, says, speaking of enlightenment:

> Having set ourselves free from the mistaken conception of self, next we must awaken our innermost wisdom, pure and divine, called the Mind of Buddha, or Bodhi, or Prajna by Zen masters. It is the divine light, the inner heaven, the key to all moral treasures, the centre of thought and consciousness, the source of all influence and power, the seat of kindness, justice, sympathy, impartial love, humanity, and mercy, the measure of all things. When this innermost wisdom is fully awakened, we are able to realize that each and every one of us is identical in spirit, in essence, in nature with the universal life or Buddha, that each ever lives face to face with Buddha, that each is beset by the abundant grace of the Blessed One, that He arouses his moral nature, that He opens his spiritual eyes, that He unfolds his new capacity, that He appoints his mission, and that life is not an ocean of birth, disease, old age, and death, nor the vale of tears, but the holy temple of Buddha, the Pure Land, where he can enjoy the bliss of Nirvana.[5]

That is how an Oriental, himself an adept in Zen, describes the essence of enlightenment. One must admit that this passage would need only a few trifling alterations in order to find its way into a Christian mystical book of devotion. Yet somehow it sends us away empty as regards understanding the satori experience described again and again in the literature. Presumably Nukariya is addressing himself to Western rationalism, of which he himself acquired a good dose, and that is why it all sounds so flatly edifying. The abstruse obscurity of the Zen anecdotes is distinctly preferable to this adaptation *ad usum Delphini:* it conveys a great deal more by saying less.

Zen is anything but a philosophy in the Western sense of the word.[6] This is also the opinion of Rudolf Otto, who says in his foreword to Ohazama's book on Zen that Nukariya has "imported the magical world of Oriental ideas into our Western philosophical categories" and confused it with these. "If psychophysical parallelism, that most wooden of all doctrines, is invoked in order to explain this mystical intuition of Non-duality and Oneness and the *coincidentia oppositorum,* then one is completely outside the sphere of the *koan,* the *kwatsu,* and *satori.*"[7] It is far better to allow oneself to become deeply imbued at the outset with the exotic obscurity of the Zen anecdotes, and to bear in mind the whole time that satori is a *mysterium ineffabile,* as indeed the Zen masters wish it to be. Between the anecdote and the mystical enlightenment there is, to our way of thinking, a gulf, and the possibility of bridging it can at best be hinted but never in practice achieved.[8] One has the feeling of touching upon a true secret, and not one that is merely imagined or pretended. It is not a question of mystification and mumbo-jumbo, but rather of an experience which strikes the experient dumb. Satori comes upon one unawares, as something utterly unexpected.

When, in the sphere of Christianity, visions of the Holy Trinity, the Madonna, the Crucified, or of the patron saint are vouchsafed after long spiritual preparation, one has the impression that this is all more or less as it should be. That Jakob Böhme should obtain a glimpse into the *centrum naturae* by means of a sunbeam reflected in a tin platter is also understandable. It is harder to digest Meister Eckhart's vision of the "little naked boy," not to speak of Swedenborg's "man in the purple coat," who wanted to dissuade him from overeating, and whom, in spite—or perhaps because—of this, he recognized as the Lord God.[9] Such things are difficult to swallow, bordering as they do on the grotesque. Many of the Zen anecdotes, however, not only border on the grotesque but are right there in the middle of it, and sound like the most crashing nonsense.

For anyone who has devoted himself, with love and sympathetic understanding, to studying the flowerlike mind of the Far East, many of these puzzling things, which drive the naïve European from one perplexity to another, simply disappear. Zen is indeed one of the most wonderful blossoms of the Chinese spirit[10]—a spirit fertilized by the immense world of Buddhist thought. Anyone who has really tried to understand Buddhist doctrine—even if only to the extent of giving up certain Western prejudices—will begin to suspect treacherous depths beneath the bizarre surface of individual satori experiences, or will sense disquieting difficulties which the religion and philosophy of the West have up to now thought fit to disregard. If he is a philosopher, he is exclusively concerned with the kind of understanding that has nothing to do with life. And if he is a Christian, he has of course no truck with heathens ("God, I thank thee that I am not as other men are"). There is no satori within these Western limits—that is a purely Oriental affair. But is this really so? Have we in fact no satori?

When one reads the Zen texts attentively, one cannot escape the impression that, however bizarre, satori is a *natural occurrence,* something so very simple,[11] even, that one fails to see the wood for the trees, and in attempting to explain it invariably says the very thing that throws others into the greatest confusion. Nukariya is therefore right when he says that any attempt to explain or analyse the content of Zen, or of the enlightenment, is futile. Nevertheless he does venture to assert that enlightenment "implies an insight into the nature of self,"[12] and that it is an "emancipation of mind from illusion concerning self."[13] The illusion concerning the nature of self is the common confusion of the self with the ego. Nukariya understands by "self" the All-Buddha, i.e., total consciousness of life. He quotes Pan Shan, who says: "The moon of mind comprehends all the universe in its light," adding: "It is Cosmic life and Cosmic spirit, and at the same time individual life and individual spirit."[14]

However one may define the self, it is always something other than the ego, and inasmuch as a higher insight of the ego leads over to the self, the self is a more comprehensive thing which includes the experience of the ego and therefore transcends it. Just as the ego is a certain experience I have of myself, so is the self an experience of my ego. It is, however, no longer experienced in the form of a broader or higher ego, but in the form of a non-ego.

Such thoughts were familiar to the anonymous author of the *Theologia Germanica:*

In whatsoever creature the Perfect shall be known, therein creature-nature, created state, I-hood, selfhood, and the like must all be given up and done away.[15]

Now that I arrogate anything good to myself, as if I were, or had done, or knew, or could perform any good thing, or that it were mine; that is all out of blindness and folly. For if the real truth were in me, I should understand that I am not that good thing, and that it is not mine nor of me.

Then the man says: "Behold! I, poor fool that I was, thought it was I, but behold! it is, and was, of a truth, God!"[16]

This tells us a good deal about the "content of enlightenment." The occurrence of satori is interpreted and formulated as a *break-through*, by a consciousness limited to the ego-form, into the non-ego-like self. This view is in accord not only with the essence of Zen, but also with the mysticism of Meister Eckhart:

When I flowed forth from God, all things declared: "He is a God!" Now this cannot make me blessed, for thereby I acknowledge myself a creature. But in the break-through,[17] when I shall stand empty in the will of God, and empty of this God's will, and of all his works, and of God himself—then I am more than all creatures, then I am neither God nor creature: I am what I was and what I shall remain, now and forevermore. Then I receive a thrust which raises me above all angels. In this thrust I become so rich that God cannot suffice me despite all that he is as God, despite all his godly works: for in this break-through I perceive that God and I are one. Then I am what I was,[18] I grow neither less nor more, for I am an unmoved Mover that moves all things. Here God can find no place in man, for man through his poverty has won back that which he was eternally and ever more shall remain.[19]

Here the Master may actually be describing a satori experience, a supersession of the ego by the self, which is endued with the "Buddha nature" or divine universality. Since, out of scientific modesty, I do not presume to make a metaphysical statement, but am referring only to a change of consciousness that can be experienced, I treat satori first of all as a psychological problem. For anyone who does not share or understand this point of view, the "explanation" will consist of nothing but words which have no tangible meaning. He is then incapable of throwing a bridge from these abstractions to the facts reported; that is to say, he cannot understand how the scent of the blossoming laurel or the tweaked nose[20] could bring about so formidable a change of consciousness. Naturally the simplest thing would be to relegate all these anecdotes to the realm of amusing fairytales, or, if one accepts the facts as they are, to write them off as instances of self-deception. (Another favourite explanation is "auto-suggestion," that pathetic white elephant from the arsenal of intellectual inadequacies!) But no serious and responsible investigation can pass over these facts unheedingly. Of course, we can never decide definitely whether a person is *really* "enlightened" or "released," or whether he merely imagines it. We have no criteria to go on. Moreover, we know well enough that an imaginary pain is often far more agonizing than a so-called real one, since it is accompanied by a subtle moral suffering caused by a dull feeling of secret self-accusation. In this sense, therefore, it is not a question of "actual fact" but of *psychic reality*, i.e., the psychic process known as satori.

Every psychic process is an image and an "imagining," otherwise no consciousness could exist and the occurrence would lack phenomenality. Imagination itself is a psychic process, for which reason it is completely irrelevant whether the enlightenment be called "real" or "imaginary." The person who has the enlightenment, or alleges that he has it, thinks at all events that he is enlightened. What others think about it decides nothing whatever for him in regard to his experience. Even if he were lying, his lie would still be a psychic fact. Indeed, even if all the reports of religious experiences were nothing but deliberate inventions and falsifications, a very interesting psychological treatise could still be written about the incidence of such lies, and with the same scientific objectivity with which one describes the psychopathology of delusional ideas. The fact that there is a religious movement upon which many brilliant minds have worked over a period of many centuries is sufficient reason for at least venturing a serious attempt to bring such processes within the realm of scientific understanding.

Earlier, I raised the question of whether we have anything like satori in the West. If we discount the sayings of our Western mystics, a superficial glance discloses nothing that could be likened to it in even the faintest degree. The possibility that there are stages in the development of consciousness plays no role in our thinking. The mere thought that there is a tremendous psychological difference between consciousness of the existence of an object and "consciousness of the consciousness" of an object borders on a quibble that hardly needs answering. For the same reason, one could hardly bring oneself to take such a problem seriously enough to consider the psychological conditions in which it arose. It is significant that questions of this kind do not, as a rule, arise from any intellectual need, but, where they exist, are nearly always rooted in an originally religious practice. In India it was yoga and in China Buddhism which supplied the driving force for these attempts to wrench oneself free from bondage to a state of consciousness that was felt to be incomplete. So far as Western mysticism is concerned, its texts are full of instructions as to how man can and must release himself from the "I-ness" of his consciousness, so that through knowledge of his own nature he may rise above it and attain the inner (godlike) man. John of Ruysbroeck makes use of an image which was also known to Indian philosophy, that of the tree whose roots are above and its branches below:[21] "And he must climb up into the tree of faith, which grows from above downwards, for its roots are in the Godhead."[22] He also says, like the yogi: "Man must be free and without ideas, released from all attachments and empty of all creatures."[23] "He must be untouched by joy and sorrow, profit and loss, rising and falling, concern for others, pleasure and fear, and not be attached to any creature."[24] It is in this that the "unity" of his being consists, and this means "being turned inwards." Being turned inwards means that "a man is turned within, into his own heart, that he may understand and feel the inner working and the inner words of God."[25] This new state of consciousness born of religious practice is distinguished by the fact that outward things no longer affect an ego-bound consciousness, thus giving rise to mutual attachment, but that an empty consciousness stands open to another influence. This "other" influence is no longer felt as one's own activity, but as that of a non-ego which has the conscious mind as its object.[26] It is as if the subject-character of the ego had been overrun, or taken over, by another subject which appears in place of the ego.[27] This is a well-known religious experience, already formulated by St. Paul.[28] Undoubtedly a new state of consciousness is described here, separated from the earlier state by an incisive process of religious transformation.

It could be objected that consciousness in itself has not changed, only the consciousness of something, just as though one had turned over the page of a book and now saw a different picture with the same eyes. I am afraid this is no more than an arbitrary interpretation, for it does not fit the facts. The fact is that in the texts it is not merely a different picture or object that is described, but rather an experience of transformation, often occurring amid the most violent psychic convulsions. The blotting out of one picture and its replacement by another is an everyday occurrence which has none of the attributes of a transformation experience. *It is not that something different is seen, but that one sees differently.* It is as though the spatial act of seeing were changed by a new dimension. When the Master asks: "Do you hear the murmuring of the brook?" he obviously means something quite different from ordinary "hearing."[29] Consciousness is something like perception, and like the latter is subject to conditions and limitations. You can, for instance, be conscious at various levels, within a narrower or wider field, more on the surface or deeper down. These differences in degree are often differences in kind as well, since they depend on the development of the personality as a whole; that is to say, on the nature of the perceiving subject.

The intellect has no interest in the nature of the perceiving subject so far as the latter only thinks logically. The intellect is essentially concerned with elaborating the contents of consciousness and with methods of elaboration. A rare philosophic passion is needed to compel the attempt to get beyond intellect and break through to a "knowledge of the knower." Such a passion is practically indistinguishable from the driving force of religion; consequently this whole problem belongs to the religious transformation process, which is incommensurable with intellect. Classical philosophy subserves this process on a wide scale, but this can be said less and less of the newer philosophy. Schopenhauer is still—with qualifications—classical, but Nietzsche's *Zarathustra* is no longer philosophy at all: it is a dramatic process of transformation which has completely swallowed up the intellect. It is no longer concerned with thought, but, in the highest sense, with the thinker of thought—and this on every page of the book. A new man, a completely transformed man, is to appear on the scene, one who has broken the shell of the old and who not only looks upon a new heaven and a new earth, but has created them. Angelus Silesius puts it rather more modestly than Zarathustra:

> My body is a shell in which a chick lies closed about;
> Brooded by the spirit of eternity, it waits its hatching out.[30]

Satori corresponds in the Christian sphere to an experience of religious transformation. As there are different degrees and kinds of such an experience, it may not be superfluous to define more accurately the category which corresponds most closely to the Zen experience. This is without doubt the mystic experience, which differs from other types in that its preliminary stages consist in "letting oneself go," in "emptying oneself of images and ideas," as opposed to those religious experiences which, like the exercises of Ignatius Loyola, are based on the practice of envisaging sacred images. In this latter class I would include transformation through faith and prayer and through collective experience in Protestantism, since a very definite assumption plays the decisive role here, and not by any means "emptiness" or "freeness." The characteristically Eckhartian assertion that "God is Nothingness" may well be incompatible in principle with the contemplation of the Passion, with faith and collective expectations.

Thus the correspondence between satori and Western experience is limited to those few Christian mystics whose paradoxical statements skirt the edge of heterodoxy or actually overstep it. As we know, it was this that drew down on Meister Eckhart's writings the condemnation of the Church. If Buddhism were a "Church" in our sense of the word, she would undoubtedly find Zen an insufferable nuisance. The reason for this is the extreme individualism of its methods, and also the iconoclastic attitude of many of the Masters.[31] To the extent that Zen is a movement, collective forms have arisen in the course of the centuries, as can be seen from Suzuki's *Training of the Zen Buddhist Monk* (Kyoto, 1934). But these concern externals only. Apart from the typical mode of life, the spiritual training or development seems to lie in the method of the *koan*. The koan is understood to be a paradoxical question, statement, or action of the Master. Judging by Suzuki's description, it seems to consist chiefly of master-questions handed down in the form of anecdotes. These are submitted by the teacher to the student for meditation. A classic example is the Wu anecdote. A monk once asked the Master: "Has a dog a Buddha nature too?" Whereupon the Master replied: "Wu!" As Suzuki remarks, this "Wu" means quite simply "bow-wow," obviously just what the dog himself would have said in answer to such a question.[32]

At first sight it seems as if the posing of such a question as an object of meditation would anticipate or prejudice the end-result, and that it would therefore determine the content of the experience, just as in the Jesuit exercises or in certain yoga meditations the content is determined by the task set by the teacher. The koans, however, are so various, so ambiguous, and above all so boundlessly paradoxical that even an expert must be completely in the dark as to what might be considered a suitable solution. In addition, the descriptions of the final result are so obscure that in no single case can one discover any rational connection between the koan and the experience of enlightenment. Since no logical sequence can be demonstrated, it remains to be supposed that the koan method puts not the smallest restraint upon the freedom of the psychic process and that the end-result therefore springs from nothing but the individual disposition of the pupil. The complete destruction of the rational intellect aimed at in the training creates an almost perfect lack of conscious assumptions. These are excluded as far as possible, but not unconscious assumptions—that is, the existing but unrecognized psychological disposition, which is anything but empty or unassuming. It is a nature-given factor, and when it answers—this being obviously the satori experience—it is an answer of Nature, who has succeeded in conveying her reaction direct to the conscious mind.[33] What the unconscious nature of the pupil opposes to the teacher or to the koan by way of an answer is, manifestly, satori. This seems, at least to me, to be the view which, to judge by the descriptions, formulates the nature of satori more or less correctly. It is also supported by the fact that the "glimpse into one's own nature," the "original man," and the depths of one's being are often a matter of supreme concern to the Zen master.[34]

Zen differs from all other exercises in meditation, whether philosophical or religious, in its principle of lack of supposition. Often Buddha himself is sternly rejected, indeed, almost blasphemously ignored, although—or perhaps just because—he could be the strongest spiritual presupposition of the whole exercise. But he too is an image and must therefore be set aside. Nothing must be present except what is actually there: that is, man with all his unconscious assumptions, of which, precisely because they are unconscious, he can never, never rid himself. The answer which appears to come from the void, the light which flares up from the blackest darkness, these have always been experienced as a wonderful and blessed illumination.

The world of consciousness is inevitably a world full of restrictions, of walls blocking the way. It is of necessity one-sided, because of the nature of consciousness itself. No consciousness can harbour more than a very small number of simultaneous perceptions. All else must lie in shadow, withdrawn from sight. Any increase in the simultaneous contents immediately produces a dimming of consciousness, if not confusion to the point of disorientation. Consciousness not only requires, but is of its very nature strictly limited to, the few and hence the distinct. We owe our general orientation simply and solely to the fact that through attention we are able to register a fairly rapid succession of images. But attention is an effort of which we are not capable all the time. We have to make do, so to speak, with a minimum of simultaneous perceptions and successions of images. Hence in wide areas possible perceptions are continuously excluded, and consciousness is always bound to the narrowest circle. What would happen if an individual consciousness were able to take in at a single glance a simultaneous picture of every possible perception is beyond imagining. If man has already succeeded in building up the structure of the world from the few distinct things that he can perceive at one and the same time, what godlike spectacle would present itself to his eyes if he were able to perceive a great deal more all at once and distinctly? This question applies only to perceptions that are *possible* to us. If we now add to these the unconscious contents—i.e., contents which are not yet, or no longer, capable of consciousness—and then try to imagine a total vision, why, this is beyond the most audacious fantasy. It is of course completely unimaginable in any conscious form, but in the unconscious it is a fact, since everything subliminal holds within it the ever-present possibility of being perceived and represented in consciousness. The unconscious is an ir-

representable totality of all subliminal psychic factors, a "total vision" *in potentia*. It constitutes the total disposition from which consciousness singles out tiny fragments from time to time.

Now if consciousness is emptied as far as possible of its contents, they will fall into a state of unconsciousness, at least for the
time being. In Zen, this displacement usually results from the energy
being withdrawn from conscious contents and transferred either to
the conception of emptiness or to the koan. As both of these must be
stable, the succession of images is abolished and with it the energy
which maintains the kinetics of consciousness. The energy thus
saved goes over to the unconscious and reinforces its natural charge
to bursting point. This increases the readiness of the unconscious
contents to break through into consciousness. But since the emptying and shutting down of consciousness is no easy matter, a special
training of indefinite duration[35] is needed in order to set up that
maximum tension which leads to the final break-through of unconscious contents.

The contents that break through are far from being random
ones. As psychiatric experience with insane patients shows, specific
relations exist between the conscious contents and the delusional
ideas that break through in delirium. They are the same relations as
exist between the dreams and the waking consciousness of normal
people. The connection is an essentially compensatory relationship:[36] the unconscious contents bring to the surface everything that
is necessary[37] in the broadest sense for the completion and wholeness
of conscious orientation. If the fragments offered by, or forced up
from, the unconscious are meaningfully built into conscious life, a
form of psychic existence results which corresponds better to the
whole of the individual's personality, and so abolishes the fruitless
conflicts between his conscious and unconscious self. Modern psychotherapy is based on this principle, in so far as it has been able to
free itself from the historical prejudice that the unconscious consists
only of infantile and morally inferior contents. There is certainly an
inferior corner in it, a lumber-room full of dirty secrets, though these
are not so much unconscious as hidden and only half forgotten. But
all this has about as much to do with the whole of the unconscious as
a decayed tooth has with the total personality. The unconscious is the
matrix of all metaphysical statements, of all mythology, of all philos-

ophy (so far as this is not merely critical), and of all expressions of life that are based on psychological premises.

Every invasion of the unconscious is an answer to a definite conscious situation, and this answer follows from the totality of possible ideas present, i.e., from the total disposition which, as explained above, is a simultaneous picture *in potentia* of psychic existence. The splitting up into single units, its one-sided and fragmentary character, is of the essence of consciousness. The reaction coming from the disposition always has a total character, as it reflects a nature which has not been divided up by any discriminating consciousness.[38] Hence its overpowering effect. It is the unexpected, all-embracing, completely illuminating answer, which works all the more as illumination and revelation since the conscious mind has got itself wedged into a hopeless blind alley.[39]

When, therefore, after many years of the hardest practice and the most strenuous demolition of rational understanding, the Zen devotee receives an answer—the only true answer—from Nature herself, everything that is said of satori can be understood. As one can see for oneself, it is the *naturalness* of the answer that strikes one most about the Zen anecdotes. Yes, one can accept with a sort of old-roguish satisfaction the story of the enlightened pupil who gave his Master a slap in the face as a reward.[40] And how much wisdom there is in the Master's "Wu," the answer to the question about the Buddha-nature of the dog! One must always bear in mind, however, that there are a great many people who cannot distinguish between a metaphysical joke and nonsense, and just as many who are so convinced of their own cleverness that they have never in their lives met any but fools.

Great as is the value of Zen Buddhism for understanding the religious transformation process, its use among Western people is very problematical. The mental education necessary for Zen is lacking in the West. Who among us would place such implicit trust in a superior Master and his incomprehensible ways? This respect for the greater human personality is found only in the East. Could any of us boast that he believes in the possibility of a boundlessly paradoxical transformation experience, to the extent, moreover, of sacrificing many years of his life to the wearisome pursuit of such a goal? And finally, who would dare to take upon himself the authority for such an unorthodox transformation experience—except a man who was little to be trusted, one who, maybe for pathological reasons, has too much to say for himself? Just such a person would have no cause to complain of any lack of following among us. But let a "Master" set us a hard task, which requires more than mere parrot-talk, and the European begins to have doubts, for the steep path of self-development is to him as mournful and gloomy as the path to hell.

I have no doubt that the satori experience does occur also in the West, for we too have men who glimpse ultimate goals and spare themselves no pains to draw near to them. But they will keep silent, not only out of shyness, but because they know that any attempt to convey their experience to others is hopeless. There is nothing in our civilization to foster these strivings, not even the Church, the custodian of religious values. Indeed, it is the function of the Church to oppose all original experience, because this can only be unorthodox. The only movement inside our civilization which has, or should have, some understanding of these endeavours is psychotherapy. It is therefore no accident that it is a psychotherapist who is writing this foreword.

Psychotherapy is at bottom a dialectical relationship between doctor and patient. It is an encounter, a discussion between two psychic wholes, in which knowledge is used only as a tool. The goal is transformation—not one that is predetermined, but rather an indeterminable change, the only criterion of which is the disappearance of egohood. No efforts on the part of the doctor can compel this experience. The most he can do is to smooth the path for the patient and help him to attain an attitude which offers the least resistance to the decisive experience. If knowledge plays no small part in our Western procedure, this is equivalent to the importance of the traditional spiritual atmosphere of Buddhism in Zen. Zen and its technique could only have arisen on the basis of Buddhist culture, which it presupposes at every turn. You cannot annihilate a rationalistic intellect that was never there—no Zen adept was ever the product of ignorance and lack of culture. Hence it frequently happens with us also that a conscious ego and a cultivated understanding must first be produced through analysis before one can even think about abolishing egohood or rationalism. What is more, psychotherapy does not deal with men who, like Zen monks, are ready to make any sacrifice for the sake of truth, but very often with the most stubborn of all

Europeans. Thus the tasks of psychotherapy are much more varied, and the individual phases of the long process much more contradictory, than is the case in Zen.

For these and many other reasons a direct transplantation of Zen to our Western conditions is neither commendable nor even possible. All the same, the psychotherapist who is seriously concerned with the question of the aim of his therapy cannot remain unmoved when he sees the end towards which this Eastern method of psychic "healing"—i.e., "making whole"—is striving. As we know, this question has occupied the most adventurous minds of the East for more than two thousand years, and in this respect methods and philosophical doctrines have been developed which simply put all Western attempts along these lines into the shade. Our attempts have, with few exceptions, all stopped short at either magic (mystery cults, amongst which we must include Christianity) or intellectualism (philosophy from Pythagoras to Schopenhauer). It is only the tragedies of Goethe's *Faust* and Nietzsche's *Zarathustra* which mark the first glimmerings of a break-through of total experience in our Western hemisphere.[41] And we do not know even today what these most promising of all products of the Western mind may at length signify, so overlaid are they with the materiality and concreteness of our thinking, as moulded by the Greeks.[42] Despite the fact that our intellect has developed almost to perfection the capacity of the bird of prey to espy the tiniest mouse from the greatest height, yet the pull of the earth drags it down, and the *samskaras* entangle it in a world of confusing images the moment it no longer seeks for booty but turns one eye inwards *to find him who seeks*. Then the individual falls into the throes of a daemonic rebirth, beset with unknown terrors and dangers and menaced by deluding mirages in a labyrinth of error. The worst of all fates threatens the venturer: mute, abysmal loneliness in the age he calls his own. What do we know of the hidden motives for Goethe's "main business," as he called his *Faust*, or of the shudders of the "Dionysus experience"? One has to read the *Bardo Thödol*, the Tibetan Book of the Dead, backwards, as I have suggested,[43] in order to find an Eastern parallel to the torments and catastrophes of the Western "way of release" to wholeness. This is the issue here—not good intentions, clever imitations, or intellectual acrobatics. And this, in shadowy hints or in greater or lesser fragments, is what the psychotherapist is faced with when he has freed himself from over-hasty and short-sighted doctrinal opinions. If he is a slave to his quasi-biological credo he will always try to reduce what he has glimpsed to the banal and the known, to a rationalistic denominator which satisfies only those who are content with illusions. But the foremost of all illusions is that anything can ever satisfy anybody. That illusion stands behind all that is unendurable in life and in front of all progress, and it is one of the most difficult things to overcome. If the psychotherapist can take time off from his helpful activities for a little reflection, or if by any chance he is forced into seeing through his own illusions, it may dawn on him how hollow and flat, how inimical to life, are all rationalistic reductions when they come upon something that is alive, that wants to grow. Should he follow this up he will soon get an idea of what it means to "open wide that gate/Past which man's steps have ever flinching trod."[44]

I would not under any circumstances like it to be understood that I am making any recommendations or offering any advice. But when one begins to talk about Zen in the West I consider it my duty to show the European where our entrance lies to that "longest road" which leads to satori, and what kind of difficulties bestrew the path which only a few of our great ones have trod—beacons, perhaps, on high mountains, shining out into the dim future. It would be a disastrous mistake to assume that satori or samādhi are to be met with anywhere below these heights. As an experience of totality it cannot be anything cheaper or smaller than the whole. What this means psychologically can be seen from the simple reflection that consciousness is always only a part of the psyche and therefore never capable of psychic wholeness: for that the indefinite extension of the unconscious is needed. But the unconscious can neither be caught with clever formulas nor exorcized by means of scientific dogmas, for something of destiny clings to it—indeed, it is sometimes destiny itself, as *Faust* and *Zarathustra* show all too clearly. The attainment of wholeness requires one to stake one's whole being. Nothing less will do; there can be no easier conditions, no substitutes, no compromises. Considering that both *Faust* and *Zarathustra*, despite the highest recognition, stand on the border-line of what is comprehensible to the European, one could hardly expect the educated public, which has only just begun to hear about the obscure world of the psyche, to form any adequate conception of the spiritual state of a man caught in the toils of the individuation process—which is my term for "becoming whole." People then drag out the vocabulary of pathology and console themselves with the terminology of neurosis and psychosis, or else they whisper about the "creative secret." But what can a man "create" if he doesn't happen to be a poet? This misunderstanding has caused not a few persons in recent times to call themselves—by their own grace—"artists," just as if art had nothing to do with ability. But if you have nothing at all to create, then perhaps you create yourself.

Zen shows how much "becoming whole" means to the East. Preoccupation with the riddles of Zen may perhaps stiffen the spine of the faint-hearted European or provide a pair of spectacles for his psychic myopia, so that from his "damned hole in the wall"[45] he may enjoy at least a glimpse of the world of psychic experience, which till now lay shrouded in fog. No harm can be done, for those who are too frightened will be effectively protected from further corruption, as also from everything of significance, by the helpful idea of "auto-suggestion."[46] I should like to warn the attentive and sympathetic reader, however, not to underestimate the spiritual depth of the East, or to assume that there is anything cheap and facile about Zen.[47] The assiduously cultivated credulity of the West in regard to Eastern thought is in this case a lesser danger, as in Zen there are fortunately none of those marvellously incomprehensible words that we find in Indian cults. Neither does Zen play about with complicated *hatha*-yoga techniques,[48] which delude the physiologically minded European into the false hope that the spirit can be obtained by just sitting and breathing. On the contrary, Zen demands intelligence and will power, as do all greater things that want to become realities.

Notes

1. [Originally published as a foreword to Suzuki, *Die grosse Befreiung: Einführung in den Zen-Buddhismus* (Leipzig, 1939). The Suzuki text had been translated into German by Heinrich Zimmer from the original edition of *An Introduction to Zen Buddhism*. The foreword by Jung was published in an earlier translation by Constance Rolfe in a new edition of the Suzuki work (London and New York, 1949).—EDITORS.]

2. The origin of Zen, as Oriental authors themselves admit, is to be found in Buddha's Flower Sermon. On this occasion he held up a flower to a gathering of disciples without uttering a word. Only Kasyapa understood him. Cf. Shuei Ohazama, *Zen: Der lebendige Buddhismus in Japan,* p. 3.

3. *Introduction to Zen Buddhism* (1949), p. 95.

4. Ibid., pp. 89 and 92f.

5. *The Religion of the Samurai,* p. 133.

6. "Zen is neither psychology nor philosophy."

7. In Ohazama, p. viii.

8. If in spite of this I attempt "explanations" in what follows, I am nevertheless fully aware that in the sense of satori I have said nothing valid. All the same, I had to make an attempt to manoeuvre our Western understanding into at least the proximity of an understanding—a task so difficult that in doing it one must take upon oneself certain crimes against the spirit of Zen.

9. Cf. Spamer, ed., *Texte aus der deutschen Mystik des 14. und 15. Jahrhunderts,* p. 143; Evans, *Meister Eckhart,* I, p. 438; William White, *Emanuel Swedenborg,* I, p. 243.

10. "There is no doubt that Zen is one of the most precious and in many respects the most remarkable [of the] spiritual possessions bequeathed to Eastern people." Suzuki, *Essays on Zen Buddhism,* I, p. 264.

11. "Before a man studies Zen, to him mountains are mountains and waters are waters; after he gets an insight into the truth of Zen, through the instruction of a good master, mountains to him are not mountains and waters are not waters; after this when he really attains to the abode of rest, mountains are once more mountains and waters are waters." Ibid., pp. 22f.

12. *Religion of the Samurai,* p. 123.

13. Ibid., p. 124.

14. Ibid., p. 132.

15. *Theologia Germanica,* ed. by Trask, p. 115.

16. Ibid., pp. 120–21.

17. There is a similar image in Zen: When a Master was asked what Buddhahood consisted in, he answered, "The bottom of a pail is broken through" (Suzuki, *Essays,* I, p. 229). Another analogy is the "bursting of the bag" (*Essays,* II, p. 117).

18. Cf. Suzuki, *Essays,* I, pp. 231, 255. Zen means catching a glimpse of the original nature of man, or the recognition of the original man (p. 157).

19. Cf. Evans, *Meister Eckhart,* p. 221; also *Meister Eckhart: A Modern Translation,* by Blakney, pp. 231f.

20. Suzuki, *Introduction,* pp. 93, 84.

21. "Its root is above, its branches below—this eternal fig-tree! . . . That is Brahma, that is called the Immortal." Katha Upanishad, 6, 1, trans. by Hume, *The Thirteen Principal Upanishads*, p. 358.
22. John of Ruysbroeck, *The Adornment of the Spiritual Marriage*, p. 47. One can hardly suppose that this Flemish mystic, who was born in 1273, borrowed this image from any Indian text.
23. Ibid., p. 51.
24. P. 57, modified.
25. Ibid., p. 62, modified.
26. "O Lord . . . instruct me in the doctrine of the non-ego, which is grounded in the self-nature of mind." Cited from the Lankavatāra Sutra, in Suzuki, *Essays*, I, p. 76.
27. A Zen Master says: "Buddha is none other than the mind, or rather, him who strives to see this mind."
28. Galatians 2:20: "It is no longer I who live, but Christ who lives in me."
29. Suzuki says of this change, "The old way of viewing things is abandoned and the world acquires a new signification . . . a new beauty which exists in the 'refreshing breeze' and in the 'shining jewel.'" *Essays*, I, p. 249. See also p. 138.
30. Trans. by Willard R. Trask (unpub.).
31. "*Satori* is the most intimate individual experience." *Essays*, I, p. 261.
    A Master says to his pupil: "I have really nothing to impart to you, and if I tried to do so you might have occasion to make me an object of ridicule. Besides, whatever I can tell you is my own and can never be yours." *Introduction*, p. 91.
    A monk says to the Master: "I have been seeking for the Buddha, but do not yet know how to go on with my research." Said the Master: "It is very much like looking for an ox when riding on one." *Essays*, II, p. 74.
    A Master says: "The mind that does not understand is the Buddha: there is no other." Ibid., p. 72.
32. *Essays*, II, pp. 84, 90.
33. "Zen consciousness is to be nursed to maturity. When it is fully matured, it is sure to break out as satori, which is an insight into the unconscious." *Essays*, II, p. 60.
34. The fourth maxim of Zen is "Seeing into one's nature and the attainment of Buddhahood" (I, p. 18). When a monk asked Hui-neng for instruction, the Master told him: "Show me your original face before you were born" (I, p. 224). A Japanese Zen book says: "If you wish to seek the Buddha, you ought to see into your own nature; for this nature is the Buddha himself" (I, p. 231). A satori experience shows a Master the "original man" (I, p. 255). Hui-neng said: "Think not of good,

think not of evil, but see what at the moment your own original features are, which you had even before coming into existence" (II, p. 42).

35. Bodhidarma, the founder of Zen in China, says: "The incomparable doctrine of the Buddha can only be understood after long and hard practice, by enduring what is most difficult to endure, by practising what is most difficult to practice. People of little strength and wisdom can understand nothing of it. All the labours of such ones will come to naught." Suzuki, *Essays*, I, p. 188.

36. This is more probable than one that is merely "complementary."

37. This "necessity" is a working hypothesis. People can, and do, hold very different views on this point. For instance, are religious ideas "necessary"? Only the course of the individual's life can decide this, i.e., his individual experience. There are no abstract criteria.

38. "When the mind discriminates, there is manifoldness of things; when it does not it looks into the true state of things." *Essays*, I, p. 99.

39. See the passage beginning "Have your mind like unto space. . . ." Suzuki, *Essays*, I, p. 223.

40. *Introduction to Zen Buddhism*, p. 94.

41. In this connection I must also mention the English mystic, William Blake. Cf. an excellent account in Percival, *William Blake's Circle of Destiny*.

42. The genius of the Greeks lay in the break-through of consciousness into the materiality of the world, thus robbing the world of its original dreamlike quality.

43. [Cf. above, par. 844.]

44. *Faust*, Part I, trans. by Wayne, p. 54.

45. Ibid., p. 44.

46. *Introduction*, p. 95.

47. "It is no pastime but the most serious task in life; no idlers will ever dare attempt it." Suzuki, *Essays*, I, p. 27; cf. also p. 92.

48. Says a Master: "If thou seekest Buddhahood by thus sitting cross-legged, thou murderest him. So long as thou freest thyself not from sitting so, thou never comest to the truth." *Essays*, I, p. 235. Cf. also II, p. 83f.

C.G. Jung

The Psychology of Eastern Meditation[1]

The profound relationship between yoga and the hieratic archi-
tecture of India has already been pointed out by my friend Heinrich
Zimmer, whose unfortunate early death is a great loss to Indology.
Anyone who has visited Borobudur or seen the stupas at Bharhut and
Sanchi can hardly avoid feeling that an attitude of mind and a vision
quite foreign to the European have been at work here—if he has not
already been brought to this realization by a thousand other impressions of Indian life. In the overflowing wealth of Indian spirituality
there is reflected a vision of the soul which at first appears strange
and inaccessible to the Greek-trained European mind. Our minds
perceive things, our eyes, as Gottfried Keller says, "drink what the
eyelids hold of the golden abundance of the world," and we draw
conclusions about the inner world from our wealth of outward impressions. We even derive its content from outside on the principle
that "nothing is in the mind which was not previously in the senses."
This principle seems to have no validity in India. Indian thought and
Indian art merely *appear* in the sense-world, but do not derive from
it. Although often expressed with startling sensuality, they are, in
their truest essence, unsensual, not to say suprasensual. It is not the
world of the senses, of the body, of colours and sounds, not human
passions that are born anew in transfigured form, or with realistic
pathos, through the creativity of the Indian soul, but rather an underworld or an overworld of a metaphysical nature, out of which strange
forms emerge into the familiar earthly scene. For instance, if one
carefully observes the tremendously impressive impersonations of
the gods performed by the Kathakali dancers of southern India, there
is not a single *natural* gesture to be seen. Everything is bizarre,
subhuman and superhuman at once. The dancers do not walk like
human beings—they glide; they do not think with their heads
but with their hands. Even their human faces vanish behind blue-

enamelled masks. The world we know offers nothing even remotely comparable to this grotesque splendour. Watching these spectacles one is transported to a world of dreams, for that is the only place where we might conceivably meet with anything similar. But the Kathakali dancers, as we see them in the flesh or in the temple sculptures, are no nocturnal phantoms; they are intensely dynamic figures, consistent in every detail, or as if they had grown organically. These are no shadows or ghosts of a bygone reality, they are more like realities which have *not yet been*, potential realities which might at any moment step over the threshold.

Anyone who wholeheartedly surrenders to these impressions will soon notice that these figures do not strike the Indians themselves as dreamlike but as real. And, indeed, they touch upon something in our own depths, too, with an almost terrifying intensity, though we have no words to express it. At the same time, one notices that the more deeply one is stirred the more our sense-world fades into a dream, and that we seem to wake up in a world of gods, so immediate is their reality.

What the European notices at first in India is the outward corporeality he sees everywhere. But that is not India as the Indian sees it; that is not *his* reality. Reality, as the German word "Wirklichkeit" implies, is that which *works*. For us the essence of that which works is the world of appearance; for the Indian it is the soul. The world for him is a mere show or façade, and his reality comes close to being what we would call a dream.

This strange antithesis between East and West is expressed most clearly in religious practice. We speak of religious uplift and exaltation; for us God is the Lord of the universe, we have a religion of brotherly love, and in our heaven-aspiring churches there is a *high altar*. The Indian, on the other hand, speaks of *dhyāna*, of self-immersion, and of *sinking* into meditation; God is within all things and especially within man, and one turns away from the outer world to the inner. In the old Indian temples the altar is sunk six to eight feet deep in the earth, and what we hide most shamefacedly is the holiest symbol to the Indian. We believe in *doing*, the Indian in impassive *being*. Our religious exercises consist of prayer, worship, and singing hymns. The Indian's most important exercise is yoga, an immersion in what we would call an unconscious state, but which he praises as the highest consciousness. Yoga is the most eloquent expression of the Indian mind and at the same time the instrument continually used to produce this peculiar attitude of mind.

What, then, is yoga? The word means literally "yoking," i.e., the disciplining of the instinctual forces of the psyche, which in Sanskrit are called *kleshas*. The yoking aims at controlling these forces that fetter human beings to the world. The *kleshas* would correspond, in the language of St. Augustine, to *superbia* and *concupiscentia*. There are many different forms of yoga, but all of them pursue the same goal. Here I will only mention that besides the purely physical exercises there is also a form called *hatha* yoga, a sort of gymnastics consisting chiefly of breathing exercises and special body postures. In this lecture I have undertaken to describe a yoga text which allows a deep insight into the psychic processes of yoga. It is a little-known Buddhist text, written in Chinese but translated from the original Sanskrit, and dating from A.D. 424. It is called the *Amitā-yur-dhyāna Sūtra*, the Sutra of Meditation on Amitāyus. This sutra, highly valued in Japan, belongs to the sphere of theistic Buddhism, in which is found the teaching that the Ādi-Buddha or Mahābuddha, the Primordial Buddha, brought forth the five Dhyāni-Buddhas or Dhyāni-Bodhisattvas. One of the five is Amitābha, "the Buddha of the *setting sun* of immeasurable light," the Lord of Sukhāvati, land of supreme bliss. He is the protector of our present world-period, just as Shākyamuni, the historical Buddha, is its teacher. In the cult of Amitābha there is, oddly enough, a kind of Eucharistic feast with consecrated bread. He is sometimes depicted holding in his hand the vessel of the life-giving food of immortality, or the vessel of holy water.

The text[2] begins with an introductory story that need not detain us here. A crown prince seeks to take the life of his parents, and in her extremity the Queen calls upon the Buddha for help, praying him to send her his two disciples Maudgalyāyana and Ānanda. The Buddha fulfils her wish, and the two appear at once. At the same time Shākyamuni, the Buddha himself, appears before her eyes. He shows her in a vision all the ten worlds, so that she can choose in which one she wishes to be reborn. She chooses the western realm of Amitābha.

He then teaches her the yoga which should enable her to retain rebirth in the Amitābha land, and after giving her various moral instructions he speaks to her as follows:

> You and all other beings besides ought to make it their only aim, with concentrated thought, to get a perception of the western quarter. You will ask how that perception is to be formed. I will explain it now. All beings, if not blind from birth, are uniformly possessed of sight, and they all see the setting sun. You should sit down properly, looking in the western direction, and prepare your thought for a close meditation on the sun: cause your mind to be firmly fixed on it so as to have an unwavering perception by the exclusive application of your thought, and gaze upon it more particularly when it is about to set and looks like a suspended drum. After you have thus seen the sun, let that image remain clear and fixed, whether your eyes be shut or open. Such is the perception of the sun, which is the First Meditation.

As we have already seen, the setting sun is an allegory of the immortality-dispensing Amitābha. The text continues:

> Next you should form the perception of water; gaze on the water clear and pure, and let this image also remain clear and fixed afterwards; never allow your thought to be scattered and lost.

As already mentioned, Amitābha is also the dispenser of the water of immortality.

> When you have thus seen the water you should form the perception of ice. As you see the ice shining and transparent, so you should imagine the appearance of lapis lazuli. After that has been done, you will see the ground consisting of lapis lazuli transparent and shining both within and without. Beneath this ground of lapis lazuli there will be seen a golden banner with the seven jewels, diamonds, and the rest, supporting the ground. It extends to the eight points of the compass, and thus the eight corners of the ground are perfectly filled up. Every side of the eight quarters consists of a hundred jewels, every jewel has a thousand rays, and every ray has eighty-four thousand colours which, when reflected in the ground of lapis lazuli, look like a thousand millions of suns, and it is difficult to see them all one by one. Over the

surface of that ground of lapis lazuli there are stretched golden ropes intertwined crosswise; divisions are made by means of [strings of] seven jewels with every part clear and distinct. . . .

When this perception has been formed, you should meditate on its constituents one by one and make the images as clear as possible, so that they may never be scattered and lost, whether your eyes be shut or open. Except only during the time of your sleep, you should always keep this in mind. One who has reached this stage of perception is said to have dimly seen the Land of Highest Happiness [Sukhāvati]. One who has obtained *samādhi* [the state of supernatural calm] is able to see the land of that Buddha country clearly and distinctly; this state is too much to be explained fully. Such is the perception of the land, and it is the Third Meditation.

Samādhi is 'withdrawnness,' i.e., a condition in which all connections with the world are absorbed into the inner world. Samādhi is the eighth phase of the Eightfold Path.

After the above comes a meditation on the Jewel Tree of the Amitābha land, and then follows the meditation on water:

In the Land of Highest Happiness there are waters in eight lakes; the water in every lake consists of seven jewels which are soft and yielding. Its source derives from the king of jewels that fulfils every wish [*cintāmani*, the wishing-pearl]. . . . In the midst of each lake there are sixty millions of lotus-flowers, made of seven jewels; all the flowers are perfectly round and exactly equal in circumference. . . . The water of jewels flows amidst the flowers and . . . the sound of the streaming water is melodious and pleasing. It proclaims all the perfect virtues [*pāramitās*], "suffering," "non-existence," "impermanence" and "non-self"; it proclaims also the praise of the signs of perfection, and minor marks of excellence, of all Buddhas. From the king of jewels that fulfils every wish stream forth the golden-coloured rays excessively beautiful, the radiance of which transforms itself into birds possessing the colours of a hundred jewels, which sing out harmonious notes, sweet and delicious, ever praising the remembrance of the Buddha, the remembrance of the Law, and the remembrance of the Church. Such is the perception of the water of eight good qualities, and it is the Fifth Meditation.

Concerning the meditation on Amitābha himself, the Buddha instructs the Queen in the following manner: "Form the perception of a lotus-flower on a ground of seven jewels." The flower has 84,000 petals, each petal 84,000 veins, and each vein possesses 84,000 rays, "of which each can clearly be seen."

When you have perceived this, you should next perceive the Buddha himself. Do you ask how? Every Buddha Tathāgata is one whose spiritual body is the principle of nature [*Dharmadhātu-kāya*], so that he may enter into the mind of all beings. Consequently, when you have perceived the Buddha, it is indeed that mind of yours that possesses those thirty-two signs of perfection and eighty minor marks of excellence which you see in the Buddha. In fine, it is your mind that becomes the Buddha, nay, it is your mind that is indeed the Buddha. The ocean of true and universal knowledge of all the Buddhas derives its source from one's own mind and thought. Therefore you should apply your thought with undivided attention to a careful meditation on that Buddha Tathāgata, the *Arhat,* the Holy and Fully Enlightened One. In forming the perception of that Buddha, you should first perceive the image of that Buddha; whether your eyes be open or shut, look at him as at an image like to Jambunada gold in colour, sitting on the flower.[3]

When you have seen the seated figure your mental vision will become clear, and you will be able to see clearly and distinctly the adornment of that Buddha-country, the jewelled ground, etc. In seeing these things let them be clear and fixed just as you see the palms of your hands. . . .

If you pass through this experience, you will at the same time see all the Buddhas of the ten quarters. . . . Those who have practised this meditation are said to have contemplated the bodies of all the Buddhas. Since they have meditated on the Buddha's body, they will also see the Buddha's mind. It is great compassion that is called the Buddha's mind. It is by his absolute compassion that he receives all beings. Those who have practised this meditation will, when they die, be born in the presence of the Buddhas in another life, and obtain a spirit of resignation wherewith to face all the consequences which shall hereafter arise. Therefore those who have wisdom should direct their thought to the careful meditation upon that Buddha Amitāyus.

Of those who practise this meditation it is said that they no longer live in an embryonic condition but will "obtain free access to the excellent and admirable countries of Buddhas."

After you have had this perception, you should imagine yourself to be born in the World of Highest Happiness in the western quarter, and to be seated, cross-legged, on a lotus-flower there. Then imagine that the flower has shut you in and has afterwards unfolded; when the flower has thus unfolded, five hundred coloured rays will shine over your body, your eyes will be opened so as to see the Buddhas and Bodhisattvas who fill the whole sky; you will hear the sounds of waters and trees, the notes of birds, and the voices of many Buddhas. . . .

The Buddha then says to Ānanda and Vaidehi (the Queen):

Those who wish, by means of their serene thoughts, to be born in the western land, should first meditate on an image of the Buddha, which is sixteen cubits high, seated on a lotus-flower in the water of the lake. As was stated before, the real body and its measurements are unlimited, incomprehensible to the ordinary mind. But by the efficacy of the ancient prayer of that Tathāgata, those who think of and remember him shall certainly be able to accomplish their aim. . . .

The Buddha's speech continues for many pages, then the text says:

When the Buddha had finished this speech, Vaidehi, together with her five hundred female attendants, guided by the Buddha's words, could see the scene of the far-stretching World of the Highest Happiness, and could also see the body of the Buddha and the bodies of the two Bodhisattvas. With her mind filled with joy she praised them, saying: "Never have I seen such a wonder!" Instantly she became wholly and fully enlightened, and attained a spirit of resignation, prepared to endure whatever consequences might yet arise. Her five hundred female attendants too cherished the thought of obtaining the highest perfect knowledge, and sought to be born in that Buddha-country. The World-Honoured One predicted that they would all be born in that Buddha-country, and be able to obtain samādhi of the presence of many Buddhas.

In a digression on the fate of the unenlightened, the Buddha sums up the yoga exercise as follows:

But, being harassed by pains, he will have no time to think of the
Buddha. Some good friend will then say to him: "Even if you
cannot exercise the remembrance of the Buddha, you may, at
least, utter the name, 'Buddha Amitāyus.'" Let him do so serenely with his voice uninterrupted; let him be continually thinking of the Buddha until he has completed ten times the thought,
repeating the formula, "Adoration to Buddha Amitāyus." On the
strength of his merit in uttering the Buddha's name he will, during every repetition, expiate the sins which involve him in births
and deaths during eighty millions of *kalpas*. He will, while dying,
see a golden lotus-flower like the disc of the sun appearing before
his eyes; in a moment he will be born in the World of Highest
Happiness.

The above quotations form the essential content of the yoga
exercise which interests us here. The text is divided into sixteen
meditations, from which I have chosen only certain parts, but they
will suffice to portray the intensification of the meditation, culminating in samādhi, the highest ecstasy and enlightenment.

The exercise begins with the concentration on the setting sun.
In southern latitudes the intensity of the rays of the setting sun is so
strong that a few moments of gazing at it are enough to create an
intense after-image. With closed eyes one continues to see the sun
for some time. As is well known, one method of hypnosis consists in
fixating a shining object, such as a diamond or a crystal. Presumably
the fixation of the sun is meant to produce a similar hypnotic effect.
On the other hand it should not have a soporific effect, because a
"meditation" of the sun must accompany the fixation. This meditation is a reflecting, a "making clear," in fact a *realization* of the sun,
its form, its qualities, and its meanings. Since the round form plays
such an important role in the subsequent meditations, we may suppose that the sun's disk serves as a model for the later fantasies of
circular structures, just as, by reason of its intense light, it prepares
the way for the resplendent visions that come afterwards. In this
manner, so the text says, "the perception is to be formed."

The next meditation, that of the water, is no longer based on any
sense-impression but creates through active imagination the image of
a reflecting expanse of water. This, as we know, throws back the full
light of the sun. It should now be imagined that the water changes
into ice, "shining and transparent." Through this procedure the im-

material light of the sun-image is transformed into the substance of water and this in turn into the solidity of ice. A concretization of the vision is evidently aimed at, and this results in a materialization of the fantasy-creation, which appears in the place of physical nature, of the world as we know it. A different reality is created, so to speak, out of soul-stuff. The ice, of a bluish colour by nature, changes into blue lapis lazuli, a solid, stony substance, which then becomes a "ground," "transparent and shining." With this "ground" an immutable, absolutely real foundation has been created. The blue translucent floor is like a lake of glass, and through its transparent layers one's gaze penetrates into the depths below.

The so-called "golden banner" then shines forth out of these depths. It should be noted that the Sanskrit word *dhvaja* also means 'sign' or 'symbol' in general. So we could speak just as well of the appearance of the "symbol." It is evident that the symbol "extending to the eight points of the compass" represents the ground plan of an eight-rayed system. As the text says, the "eight corners of the ground are perfectly filled up" by the banner. The system shines "like a thousand millions of suns," so that the shining after-image of the sun has enormously increased its radiant energy, and its illuminative power has now been intensified to an immeasurable degree. The strange idea of the "golden ropes" spread over the system like a net presumably means that the system is tied together and secured in this way, so that it can no longer fall apart. Unfortunately the text says nothing about a possible failure of the method, or about the phenomena of disintegration which might supervene as the result of a mistake. But disturbances of this kind in an imaginative process are nothing unexpected to an expert—on the contrary, they are a regular occurrence. So it is not surprising that a kind of inner reinforcement of the image is provided in the yoga vision by means of golden ropes.

Although not explicitly stated in the text, the eight-rayed system is already the Amitābha land. In it grow wonderful trees, as is meet and proper, for this is paradise. Especial importance attaches to the water of the Amitābha land. In accordance with the octagonal system it is arranged in the form of eight lakes, and the source of these waters is a central jewel, *cintāmani*, the wishing pearl, a symbol of the "treasure hard to attain,"[4] the highest value. In Chinese art it appears as a moonlike image, frequently associated with a dragon.[5] The wondrous sounds of the water consist of two pairs of opposites which proclaim the dogmatic ground truths of Buddhism: "suffering and non-existence, impermanence and non-self," signifying that all existence is full of suffering, and that everything that clings to the ego is impermanent. Non-existence and non-self deliver us from these errors. Thus the singing water is something like the teaching of the Buddha—a redeeming water of wisdom, an *aqua doctrinae*, to use an expression of Origen. The source of this water, the pearl without peer, is the Tathāgata, the Buddha himself. Hence the imaginative reconstruction of the Buddha-image follows immediately afterwards, and while this structure is being built up in the meditation it is realized that the Buddha is really nothing other than the activating psyche of the yogi—the meditator himself. It is not only that the image of the Buddha is produced out of "one's own mind and thought," but the psyche which produces these thought-forms *is the Buddha himself.*

The image of the Buddha sits in the round lotus in the centre of the octagonal Amitābha land. He is distinguished by the great compassion with which he "receives all beings," including the meditator. This means that the inmost being which is the Buddha is bodied forth in the vision and revealed as the true self of the meditator. He experiences himself as the only thing that exists, as the highest consciousness, even the Buddha. In order to attain this final goal it was necessary to pass through all the laborious exercises of mental reconstruction, to get free of the deluded ego-consciousness which is responsible for the sorrowful illusion of the world, and to reach that other pole of the psyche where the world as illusion is abolished.

Although it appears exceedingly obscure to the European, this yoga text is not a mere literary museum piece. It lives in the psyche of every Indian, in this form and in many others, so that his life and thinking are permeated by it down to the smallest details. It was not Buddhism that nurtured and educated this psyche, but yoga. Buddhism itself was born of the spirit of yoga, which is older and more universal than the historical reformation wrought by the Buddha. Anyone who seeks to understand Indian art, philosophy, and ethics from the inside must of necessity befriend this spirit. Our habitual understanding from the outside breaks down here, because it is hopelessly inadequate to the nature of Indian spirituality. And I wish particularly to warn against the oft-attempted imitation of Indian practices and sentiments. As a rule nothing comes of it except an artificial stultification of our Western intelligence. Of course, if anyone should succeed in giving up Europe from every point of view, and could actually *be* nothing but a yogi and sit in the lotus position with all the practical and ethical consequences that this entails, evaporating on a gazelle-skin under a dusty banyan tree and ending his days in nameless non-being, then I should have to admit that such a person understood yoga in the Indian manner. But anyone who cannot do this should not behave as if he did. He cannot and should not give up his Western understanding; on the contrary, he should apply it honestly, without imitation or sentimentality, to understanding as much of yoga as is possible for the Western mind. The secrets of yoga mean as much or even more to the Indian than our own Christian mysteries mean to us, and just as we would not allow any foreigner to make our *mysterium fidei* ludicrous, so we should not belittle these strange Indian ideas and practices or scorn them as absurd errors. By so doing we only block the way to a sensible understanding. Indeed, we in Europe have already gone so far in this direction that the spiritual content of our Christian dogma has disappeared in a rationalistic and "enlightened" fog of alarming density, and this makes it all too easy for us to undervalue those things which we do not know and do not understand.

If we wish to understand at all, we can do so only in the European way. One can, it is true, understand many things with the heart, but then the head often finds it difficult to follow up with an intellectual formulation that gives suitable expression to what has been understood. There is also an understanding with the head, particularly of the scientific kind, where there is sometimes too little room for the heart. We must therefore leave it to the good will and co-operation of the reader to use first one and then the other. So let us first attempt, with the head, to find or build that hidden bridge which may lead to a European understanding of yoga.

For this purpose we must again take up the series of symbols we have already discussed, but this time we shall consider their sense-content. The *sun*, with which the series begins, is the source of warmth and light, the indubitable central point of our visible world. As the giver of life it is always and everywhere either the divinity itself or an image of the same. Even in the world of Christian ideas, the sun is a favourite allegory of Christ. A second source of life, especially in southern countries, is *water*, which also plays an important role in Christian allegory, for instance as the four rivers of paradise and the waters which issued from the side of the temple (Ezekiel 47). The latter were compared to the blood that flowed from the wound in Christ's side. In this connection I would also mention Christ's talk with the woman of Samaria at the well, and the rivers of living water flowing from the body of Christ (John 7:38). A meditation on sun and water evokes these and similar associations without fail, so that the meditator will gradually be led from the foreground of visible appearances into the background, that is, to the spiritual meaning behind the object of meditation. He is transported to the psychic sphere, where sun and water, divested of their physical objectivity, become symbols of psychic contents, images of the source of life in the individual psyche. For indeed our consciousness does not create itself—it wells up from unknown depths. In childhood it awakens gradually, and all through life it wakes each morning out of the depths of sleep from an unconscious condition. It is like a child that is born daily out of the primordial womb of the unconscious. In fact, closer investigation reveals that it is not only influenced by the unconscious but continually emerges out of it in the form of numberless spontaneous ideas and sudden flashes of thought. Meditation on the meaning of sun and water is therefore something like a descent into the fountainhead of the psyche, into the unconscious itself.

Here, then, is a great difference between the Eastern and the Western mind. It is the same difference as the one we met before: the difference between the high and the low altar. The West is always seeking uplift, but the East seeks a sinking or deepening. Outer reality, with its bodiliness and weight, appears to make a much stronger and sharper impression on the European than it does on the Indian. The European seeks to raise himself above this world, while the Indian likes to turn back into the maternal depths of Nature.

Now just as Christian contemplation, for instance in the *Exercitia spiritualia* of Loyola, strives to comprehend the holy image as concretely as possible, with all the senses, so the yogi solidifies the water he contemplates first to ice and then to lapis lazuli, thereby creating a firm "ground," as he calls it. He makes, so to speak, a solid body for his vision. In this way he endows the figures of his psychic world with a concrete reality which takes the place of the outer world. At first he sees nothing but a reflecting blue surface, like that of a lake or ocean (also a favourite symbol of the unconscious in our Western dreams); but under the shining surface unknown depths lie hidden, dark and mysterious.

As the text says, the blue stone is *transparent*, which informs us that the gaze of the meditator can penetrate into the depths of the psyche's secrets. There he sees what could not be seen before, i.e., what was unconscious. Just as sun and water are the physical sources of life, so, as symbols, they express the essential secret of the life of the unconscious. In the *banner*, the symbol the yogi sees through the floor of lapis lazuli, he beholds, as it were, an image of the source of consciousness, which before was invisible and apparently without form. Through *dhyāna*, through the sinking and deepening of contemplation, the unconscious has evidently taken on form. It is as if the light of consciousness had ceased to illuminate the objects of the outer world of the senses and now illumines the darkness of the unconscious. If the world of the senses and all thought of it are completely extinguished, then the inner world springs into relief more distinctly.

Here the Eastern text skips over a psychic phenomenon that is a source of endless difficulties for the European. If a European tries to banish all thought of the outer world and to empty his mind of everything outside, he immediately becomes the prey of his own subjective fantasies, which have nothing whatever to do with the images mentioned in our text. Fantasies do not enjoy a good reputation; they are considered cheap and worthless and are therefore rejected as useless and meaningless. They are the *kleshas*, the disorderly and chaotic instinctual forces which yoga proposes to yoke. The *Exercitia spiritualia* pursue the same goal, in fact both methods seek to attain success by providing the meditator with an object to contemplate and showing him the image he has to concentrate on in order to shut out the allegedly worthless fantasies. Both methods, Eastern as well as Western, try to reach the goal by a direct path. I do not wish to question the possibilities of success when the meditation exercise is conducted in some kind of ecclesiastical setting. But, outside of some such setting, the thing does not as a rule work, or it may even lead to deplorable results. By throwing light on the unconscious one gets first of all into the chaotic sphere of the personal unconscious, which contains all that one would like to forget, and all that one does not wish to admit to oneself or to anybody else, and which one prefers to believe is not true anyhow. One therefore expects to come off best if one looks as little as possible into this dark corner. Naturally anyone who proceeds in that way will never get round this corner and will never obtain even a trace of what yoga promises. Only the man who goes through this darkness can hope to make any further progress. I am therefore in principle against the uncritical appropriation of yoga practices by Europeans, because I know only too well that they hope to avoid their own dark corners. Such a beginning is entirely meaningless and worthless.

This is also the deeper reason why we in the West have never developed anything comparable to yoga, aside from the very limited application of the Jesuit *Exercitia*. We have an abysmal fear of that lurking horror, our personal unconscious. Hence the European much prefers to tell others "how to do it." That the improvement of the whole begins with the individual, even with myself, never enters our heads. Besides, many people think it morbid to glance into their own interiors—it makes you melancholic, a theologian once assured me.

I have just said that we have developed nothing that could be compared with yoga. This is not entirely correct. True to our European bias, we have evolved a medical psychology dealing specifically with the kleshas. We call it the "psychology of the unconscious." The movement inaugurated by Freud recognized the importance of the human shadow-side and its influence on consciousness, and then got entangled in this problem. Freudian psychology is concerned with the very thing that our text passes over in silence and assumes is already dealt with. Yoga is perfectly well aware of the world of the kleshas, but the naturalness of its religion knows nothing of the *moral conflict* which the kleshas represent for us. An ethical dilemma divides us from our shadow. The spirit of India grows out of nature; with us spirit is opposed to nature.

The floor of lapis lazuli is not transparent for us because the question of the *evil in nature* must first be answered. This question *can* be answered, but surely not with shallow rationalistic arguments and intellectual patter. The ethical responsibility of the individual can give a valid answer, but there are no cheap recipes and no licences—one must pay to the last penny before the floor of lapis lazuli can become transparent. Our sutra presupposes that the shadow world of our personal fantasies—the personal unconscious—has been traversed, and goes on to describe a symbolical figure which at first strikes us as very strange. This is a geometrical structure raying out from a centre and divided into eight parts—an ogdoad. In the centre there is a lotus with the Buddha sitting in it, and the decisive experience is the final knowledge that the meditator himself is the Buddha, whereby the fateful knots woven in the opening story are apparently resolved. The concentrically constructed symbol evidently expresses the highest concentration, which can be achieved only when the previously described withdrawal and canalization of interest away from the impressions of the sense-world and from object-bound ideas is pushed to the limit and applied to the background of consciousness. The conscious world with its attachment to objects, and even the centre of consciousness, the ego, are extinguished, and in their place the splendour of the Amitābha land appears with ever-increasing intensity.

Psychologically this means that behind or beneath the world of personal fantasies and instincts a still deeper layer of the unconscious becomes visible, which in contrast to the chaotic disorder of the kleshas is pervaded by the highest order and harmony, and, in contrast to their multiplicity, symbolizes the all-embracing unity of the *bodhimandala*, the magic circle of enlightenment.

What has our psychology to say about this Indian assertion of a supra-personal, world-embracing unconscious that appears when the darkness of the personal unconscious grows transparent? Modern psychology knows that the personal unconscious is only the top layer, resting on a foundation of a wholly different nature which we call the collective unconscious. The reason for this designation is the circumstance that, unlike the personal unconscious and its purely personal contents, the images in the deeper unconscious have a distinctly mythological character. That is to say, in form and content they coincide with those widespread primordial ideas which underlie the myths. They are no longer of a personal but of a purely supra-personal nature and are therefore common to all men. For this reason they are to be found in the myths and legends of all peoples and all times, as well as in individuals who have not the slightest knowledge of mythology.

Our Western psychology has, in fact, got as far as yoga in that it is able to establish scientifically a deeper layer of unity in the unconscious. The mythological motifs whose presence has been demonstrated by the exploration of the unconscious form in themselves a multiplicity, but this culminates in a concentric or radial order which constitutes the true centre or essence of the collective unconscious. On account of the remarkable agreement between the insights of yoga and the results of psychological research, I have chosen the Sanskrit term *mandala* for this central symbol.

You will now surely ask: but how in the world does science come to such conclusions? There are two paths to this end. The first is the historical path. If we study, for instance, the introspective method of medieval natural philosophy, we find that it repeatedly used the circle, and in most cases the circle divided into four parts, to symbolize the central principle, obviously borrowing this idea from the ecclesiastical allegory of the quaternity as found in numerous representations of the *Rex gloriae* with the four evangelists, the four rivers of paradise, the four winds, and so on.

The second is the path of empirical psychology. At a certain stage in the psychological treatment patients sometimes paint or draw such mandalas spontaneously, either because they dream them or because they suddenly feel the need to compensate the confusion in their psyches through representations of an ordered unity. For instance, our Swiss national saint, the Blessed Brother Nicholas of Flüe, went through a process of this kind, and the result can still be seen in the picture of the Trinity in the parish church at Sachseln. With the help of circular drawings in a little book by a German mystic,[6] he succeeded in assimilating the great and terrifying vision that had shaken him to the depths.

But what has our empirical psychology to say about the Buddha sitting in the lotus? Logically one would expect Christ to be enthroned in the centre of our Western mandalas. This was once true, as we have already said, in the Middle Ages. But our modern mandalas, spontaneously produced by numerous individuals without any preconceived ideas or suggestions from outside, contain no Christ-figure, still less a Buddha in the lotus position. On the other hand, the equal-armed Greek cross, or even an unmistakable imitation of the swastika, is to be found fairly often. I cannot discuss this strange fact here, though in itself it is of the greatest interest.[7]

Between the Christian and the Buddhist mandala there is a subtle but enormous difference. The Christian during contemplation would never say "*I* am Christ," but will confess with Paul: "Not I, but Christ liveth in me" (Gal. 2:20). Our sutra, however, says: "Thou wilt know that *thou* art the Buddha." At bottom the two confessions are identical, in that the Buddhist only attains this knowledge when he is *anātman*, 'without self.' But there is an immeasurable difference in the formulation. The Christian attains his end *in Christ*, the Buddhist knows *he* is the Buddha. The Christian gets *out of* the transitory and ego-bound world of consciousness, but the Buddhist *still* reposes on the eternal ground of his inner nature, whose oneness with Deity, or with universal Being, is confirmed in other Indian testimonies.

Notes

1. [Delivered as a lecture to the Schweizerische Gesellschaft der Freunde ostasiatischer Kultur, in Zurich, Basel, and Bern, during March–May 1943, and published as "Zur Psychologie östlicher Meditation" in the Society's *Mitteilungen* (St. Gallen), V (1943), 33–53; repub. in *Symbolik des Geistes* (Zurich, 1948), pp. 447–72. Previously trans. by Carol Baumann in *Art and Thought*, a volume in honour of Ananda K. Coomaraswamy (London, 1948), pp. 169–79.]

   [The work of Heinrich Zimmer's which the author refers to in the opening sentence was his *Kunstform und Yoga im indischen Kultbild* (1926), the central argument of which has been restated in his posthumous English works, particularly *Myths and Symbols in Indian Art and Civilization* (1946) and *The Art of Indian Asia* (1955).—EDITORS.]

2. In *Buddhist Mahāyāna Sūtras*, Part II, pp. 159–201, trans. by J. Takakusu, slightly modified.

3. A river formed of the juice of the fruit of the Jambu-tree flows in a circle round Mount Meru and returns to the tree.

4. Cf. *Symbols of Transformation*, Part II, chs. 6 and 7, especially par. 510.

5. Cf. *Psychology and Alchemy*, fig. 61.

6. Cf. Stoeckli, *Die Visionen des Seligen Bruder Klaus*. Cf. also the sixth paper in *The Collected Works of Jung*, vol. II, pars. 474ff.

7. Cf. the first paper in *The Collected Works of Jung*, vol. II, pars. 136ff.

C.G. Jung

Psychological Commentary on
The Tibetan Book of the Great Liberation[1]

1. THE DIFFERENCE BETWEEN EASTERN AND WESTERN THINKING

Dr. Evans-Wentz has entrusted me with the task of commenting on a text which contains an important exposition of Eastern "psychology." The very fact that I have to use quotation marks shows the dubious applicability of this term. It is perhaps not superfluous to mention that the East has produced nothing equivalent to what we call psychology, but rather philosophy or metaphysics. Critical philosophy, the mother of modern psychology, is as foreign to the East as to medieval Europe. Thus the word "mind," as used in the East, has the connotation of something metaphysical. Our Western conception of mind has lost this connotation since the Middle Ages, and the word has now come to signify a "psychic function." Despite the fact that we neither know nor pretend to know what "psyche" is, we can deal with the phenomenon of "mind." We do not assume that the mind is a metaphysical entity or that there is any connection between an individual mind and a hypothetical Universal Mind. Our psychology is, therefore, a science of mere phenomena without any metaphysical implications. The development of Western philosophy during the last two centuries has succeeded in isolating the mind in its own sphere and in severing it from its primordial oneness with the universe. Man himself has ceased to be the microcosm and eidolon of the cosmos, and his "anima" is no longer the consubstantial *scintilla*, or spark of the *Anima Mundi*, the World Soul.

Psychology accordingly treats all metaphysical claims and assertions as mental phenomena, and regards them as statements about the mind and its structure that derive ultimately from certain unconscious dispositions. It does not consider them to be absolutely valid

48

or even capable of establishing a metaphysical truth. We have no intellectual means of ascertaining whether this attitude is right or wrong. We only know that there is no evidence for, and no possibility of proving, the validity of a metaphysical postulate such as "Universal Mind." If the mind asserts the existence of a Universal Mind, we hold that it is merely making an assertion. We do not assume that by such an assertion the existence of a Universal Mind has been established. There is no argument against this reasoning, but no evidence, either, that our conclusion is ultimately right. In other words, it is just as possible that our mind is nothing but a perceptible manifestation of a Universal Mind. Yet we do not know, and we cannot even see, how it would be possible to recognize whether this is so or not. Psychology therefore holds that the mind cannot establish or assert anything beyond itself.

If, then, we accept the restrictions imposed upon the capacity of our mind, we demonstrate our common sense. I admit it is something of a sacrifice, inasmuch as we bid farewell to that miraculous world in which mind-created things and beings move and live. This is the world of the primitive, where even inanimate objects are endowed with a living, healing, magic power, through which they participate in us and we in them. Sooner or later we had to understand that their potency was really ours, and that their significance was our projection. The theory of knowledge is only the last step out of humanity's childhood, out of a world where mind-created figures populated a metaphysical heaven and hell.

Despite this inevitable epistemological criticism, however, we have held fast to the religious belief that the organ of faith enables man to know God. The West thus developed a new disease: the conflict between science and religion. The critical philosophy of science became as it were negatively metaphysical—in other words, materialistic—on the basis of an error in judgment; matter was assumed to be a tangible and recognizable reality. Yet this is a thoroughly metaphysical concept hypostatized by uncritical minds. Matter is an hypothesis. When you say "matter," you are really creating a symbol for something unknown, which may just as well be "spirit" or anything else; it may even be God. Religious faith, on the other hand, refuses to give up its pre-critical *Weltanschauung*. In contradiction to the saying of Christ, the faithful try to *remain* children instead of becoming *as* children. They cling to the world of childhood. A famous modern theologian confesses in his autobiography that Jesus has been his good friend "from childhood on." Jesus is the perfect example of a man who preached something different from the religion of his forefathers. But the *imitatio Christi* does not appear to include the mental and spiritual sacrifice which he had to undergo at the beginning of his career and without which he would never have become a saviour.

The conflict between science and religion is in reality a misunderstanding of both. Scientific materialism has merely introduced a new hypostasis, and that is an intellectual sin. It has given another name to the supreme principle of reality and has assumed that this created a new thing and destroyed an old thing. Whether you call the principle of existence "God," "matter," "energy," or anything else you like, you have created nothing; you have simply changed a symbol. The materialist is a metaphysician *malgré lui*. Faith, on the other hand, tries to retain a primitive mental condition on merely sentimental grounds. It is unwilling to give up the primitive, childlike relationship to mind-created and hypostatized figures; it wants to go on enjoying the security and confidence of a world still presided over by powerful, responsible, and kindly parents. Faith may include a *sacrificium intellectus* (provided there is an intellect to sacrifice), but certainly not a sacrifice of feeling. In this way the faithful *remain* children instead of becoming *as* children, and they do not gain their life because they have not lost it. Furthermore, faith collides with science and thus gets its deserts, for it refuses to share in the spiritual adventure of our age.

Any honest thinker has to admit the insecurity of all metaphysical positions, and in particular of all creeds. He has also to admit the unwarrantable nature of all metaphysical assertions and face the fact that there is no evidence whatever for the ability of the human mind to pull itself up by its own bootstrings, that is, to establish anything transcendental.

Materialism is a metaphysical reaction against the sudden realization that cognition is a mental faculty and, if carried beyond the human plane, a projection. The reaction was "metaphysical" in so far as the man of average philosophical education failed to see through the implied hypostasis, not realizing that "matter" was just another name for the supreme principle. As against this, the attitude of faith shows how reluctant people were to accept philosophical criticism.

It also demonstrates how great is the fear of letting go one's hold on the securities of childhood and of dropping into a strange, unknown world ruled by forces unconcerned with man. Nothing really changes in either case; man and his surroundings remain the same. He has only to realize that he is shut up inside his mind and cannot step beyond it, even in insanity; and that the appearance of his world or of his gods very much depends upon his own mental condition.

In the first place, the structure of the mind is responsible for anything we may assert about metaphysical matters, as I have already pointed out. We have also begun to understand that the intellect is not an *ens per se,* or an independent mental faculty, but a psychic function dependent upon the conditions of the psyche as a whole. A philosophical statement is the product of a certain personality living at a certain time in a certain place, and not the outcome of a purely logical and impersonal procedure. To that extent it is chiefly subjective; whether it has an objective validity or not depends on whether there are few or many persons who argue in the same way. The isolation of man within his mind as a result of epistemological criticism has naturally led to psychological criticism. This kind of criticism is not popular with the philosophers, since they like to consider the philosophic intellect as the perfect and unconditioned instrument of philosophy. Yet this intellect of theirs is a function dependent upon an individual psyche and determined on all sides by subjective conditions, quite apart from environmental influences. Indeed, we have already become so accustomed to this point of view that "mind" has lost its universal character altogether. It has become a more or less individualized affair, with no trace of its former cosmic aspect as the *anima rationalis.* Mind is understood nowadays as a subjective, even an arbitrary, thing. Now that the formerly hypostatized "universal ideas" have turned out to be mental principles, it is dawning upon us to what an extent our whole experience of so-called reality is psychic; as a matter of fact, everything thought, felt, or perceived is a psychic image, and the world itself exists only so far as we are able to produce an image of it. We are so deeply impressed with the truth of our imprisonment in, and limitation by, the psyche that we are ready to admit the existence in it even of things we do *not* know: we call them "the unconscious."

The seemingly universal and metaphysical scope of the mind has thus been narrowed down to the small circle of individual consciousness, profoundly aware of its almost limitless subjectivity and of its infantile-archaic tendency to heedless projection and illusion. Many scientifically-minded persons have even sacrificed their religious and philosophical leanings for fear of uncontrolled subjectivism. By way of compensation for the loss of a world that pulsed with our blood and breathed with our breath, we have developed an enthusiasm for *facts*—mountains of facts, far beyond any single individual's power to survey. We have the pious hope that this incidental accumulation of facts will form a meaningful whole, but nobody is quite sure, because no human brain can possibly comprehend the gigantic sum total of this mass-produced knowledge. The facts bury us, but whoever dares to speculate must pay for it with a bad conscience—and rightly so, for he will instantly be tripped up by the facts.

Western psychology knows the mind as the mental functioning of a psyche. It is the "mentality" of an individual. An impersonal Universal Mind is still to be met with in the sphere of philosophy, where it seems to be a relic of the original human "soul." This picture of our Western outlook may seem a little drastic, but I do not think it is far from the truth. At all events, something of the kind presents itself as soon as we are confronted with the Eastern mentality. In the East, mind is a cosmic factor, the very essence of existence; while in the West we have just begun to understand that it is the essential condition of cognition, and hence of the cognitive existence of the world. There is no conflict between religion and science in the East, because no science is there based upon the passion for facts, and no religion upon mere faith; there is religious cognition and cognitive religion.[2] With us, man is incommensurably small and the grace of God is everything; but in the East, man is God and he redeems himself. The gods of Tibetan Buddhism belong to the sphere of illusory separateness and mind-created projections, and yet they exist; but so far as we are concerned an illusion remains an illusion, and thus is nothing at all. It is a paradox, yet nevertheless true, that with us a thought has no proper reality; we treat it as if it were a nothingness. Even though the thought be true in itself, we hold that it exists only by virtue of certain facts which it is said to formulate. We can produce a most devastating fact like the atom bomb with the help of this ever-changing phantasmagoria of virtually nonexistent thoughts, but it seems wholly absurd to us that one could ever establish the reality of thought itself.

"Psychic reality" is a controversial concept, like "psyche" or "mind." By the latter terms some understand consciousness and its contents, others allow the existence of "dark" or "subconscious" representations. Some include instincts in the psychic realm, others exclude them. The vast majority consider the psyche to be a result of biochemical processes in the brain cells. A few conjecture that it is the psyche that makes the cortical cells function. Some identify "life" with psyche. But only an insignificant minority regards the psychic phenomenon as a category of existence *per se* and draws the necessary conclusions. It is indeed paradoxical that *the* category of existence, the indispensable *sine qua non* of all existence, namely the psyche, should be treated as if it were only semi-existent. Psychic existence is the only category of existence of which we have *immediate* knowledge, since nothing can be known unless it first appears as a psychic image. Only psychic existence is immediately verifiable. To the extent that the world does not assume the form of a psychic image, it is virtually non-existent. This is a fact which, with few exceptions—as for instance in Schopenhauer's philosophy—the West has not yet fully realized. But Schopenhauer was influenced by Buddhism and by the Upanishads.

Even a superficial acquaintance with Eastern thought is sufficient to show that a fundamental difference divides East and West. The East bases itself upon psychic reality, that is, upon the psyche as the main and unique condition of existence. It seems as if this Eastern recognition were a psychological or temperamental fact rather than a result of philosophical reasoning. It is a typically introverted point of view, contrasted with the equally typical extraverted point of view of the West.[3] Introversion and extraversion are known to be temperamental or even constitutional attitudes which are never intentionally adopted in normal circumstances. In exceptional cases they may be produced at will, but only under very special conditions. Introversion is, if one may so express it, the "style" of the East, an habitual and collective attitude, just as extraversion is the "style" of the West. Introversion is felt here as something abnormal, morbid, or otherwise objectionable. Freud identifies it with an autoerotic, "narcissistic" attitude of mind. He shares his negative position with the National Socialist philosophy of modern Germany,[4] which accuses introversion of being an offence against community feeling. In the East, however, our cherished extraversion is depreciated as illusory

desirousness, as existence in the *samsāra*, the very essence of the
nidāna-chain which culminates in the sum of the world's sufferings.[5]
Anyone with practical knowledge of the mutual depreciation of values between introvert and extravert will understand the emotional
conflict between the Eastern and the Western standpoint. For those
who know something of the history of European philosophy the
bitter wrangling about "universals" which began with Plato will provide an instructive example. I do not wish to go into all the ramifica-
tions of this conflict between introversion and extraversion, but I
must mention the religious aspects of the problem. The Christian
West considers man to be wholly dependent upon the grace of God,
or at least upon the Church as the exclusive and divinely sanctioned
earthly instrument of man's redemption. The East, however, insists
that man is the sole cause of his higher development, for it believes in
"self-liberation."

The religious point of view always expresses and formulates the
essential psychological attitude and its specific prejudices, even in
the case of people who have forgotten, or who have never heard of,
their own religion. In spite of everything, the West is thoroughly
Christian as far as its psychology is concerned. Tertullian's *anima
naturaliter christiana* holds true throughout the West—not, as he
thought, in the religious sense, but in a psychological one. Grace
comes from elsewhere; at all events from outside. Every other point
of view is sheer heresy. Hence it is quite understandable why the
human psyche is suffering from undervaluation. Anyone who dares
to establish a connection between the psyche and the idea of God is
immediately accused of "psychologism" or suspected of morbid
"mysticism." The East, on the other hand, compassionately tolerates
those "lower" spiritual stages where man, in his blind ignorance of
karma, still bothers about sin and tortures his imagination with a
belief in absolute gods, who, if he only looked deeper, are nothing
but the veil of illusion woven by his own unenlightened mind. The
psyche is therefore all-important; it is the all-pervading Breath, the
Buddha-essence; it is the Buddha-Mind, the One, the *Dharmakāya*.
All existence emanates from it, and all separate forms dissolve back
into it. This is the basic psychological prejudice that permeates Eastern man in every fibre of his being, seeping into all his thoughts,
feelings, and deeds, no matter what creed he professes.

In the same way Western man is Christian, no matter to what

denomination his Christianity belongs. For him man is small inside, he is next to nothing; moreover, as Kierkegaard says, "before God man is always wrong." By fear, repentance, promises, submission, self-abasement, good deeds, and praise he propitiates the great power, which is not himself but *totaliter aliter*, the Wholly Other, altogether perfect and "outside," the only reality.[6] If you shift the formula a bit and substitute for God some other power, for instance the world or money, you get a complete picture of Western man—assiduous, fearful, devout, self-abasing, enterprising, greedy, and violent in his pursuit of the goods of this world: possessions, health, knowledge, technical mastery, public welfare, political power, conquest, and so on. What are the great popular movements of our time? Attempts to grab the money or property of others and to protect our own. The mind is chiefly employed in devising suitable "isms" to hide the real motives or to get more loot. I refrain from describing what would happen to Eastern man should he forget his ideal of Buddhahood, for I do not want to give such an unfair advantage to my Western prejudices. But I cannot help raising the question of whether it is possible, or indeed advisable, for either to imitate the other's standpoint. The difference between them is so vast that one can see no reasonable possibility of this, much less its advisability. You cannot mix fire and water. The Eastern attitude stultifies the Western, and vice versa. You cannot be a good Christian and redeem yourself, nor can you be a Buddha and worship God. It is much better to accept the conflict, for it admits only of an irrational solution, if any.

By an inevitable decree of fate the West is becoming acquainted with the peculiar facts of Eastern spirituality. It is useless either to belittle these facts, or to build false and treacherous bridges over yawning gaps. Instead of learning the spiritual techniques of the East by heart and imitating them in a thoroughly Christian way—*imitatio Christi!*—with a correspondingly forced attitude, it would be far more to the point to find out whether there exists in the unconscious an introverted tendency similar to that which has become the guiding spiritual principle of the East. We should then be in a position to build on our own ground with our own methods. If we snatch these things directly from the East, we have merely indulged our Western acquisitiveness, confirming yet again that "everything good is outside," whence it has to be fetched and pumped into our barren souls.[7]

It seems to me that we have really learned something from the East when we understand that the psyche contains riches enough without having to be primed from outside, and when we feel capable of evolving out of ourselves with or without divine grace. But we cannot embark upon this ambitious enterprise until we have learned how to deal with our spiritual pride and blasphemous self-assertiveness. The Eastern attitude violates the specifically Christian values, and it is no good blinking this fact. If our new attitude is to be genuine, i.e., grounded in our own history, it must be acquired with full consciousness of the Christian values and of the conflict between them and the introverted attitude of the East. We must get at the Eastern values from within and not from without, seeking them in ourselves, in the unconscious. We shall then discover how great is our fear of the unconscious and how formidable are our resistances. Because of these resistances we doubt the very thing that seems so obvious to the East, namely, the *self-liberating power of the introverted mind.*

This aspect of the mind is practically unknown to the West, though it forms the most important component of the unconscious. Many people flatly deny the existence of the unconscious, or else they say that it consists merely of instincts, or of repressed or forgotten contents that were once part of the conscious mind. It is safe to assume that what the East calls "mind" has more to do with our "unconscious" than with mind as we understand it, which is more or less identical with consciousness. To us, consciousness is inconceivable without an ego; it is equated with the relation of contents to an ego. If there is no ego there is nobody to be conscious of anything. The ego is therefore indispensable to the conscious process. The Eastern mind, however, has no difficulty in conceiving of a consciousness without an ego. Consciousness is deemed capable of transcending its ego condition; indeed, in its "higher" forms, the ego disappears altogether. Such an ego-less mental condition can only be unconscious to us, for the simple reason that there would be nobody to witness it. I do not doubt the existence of mental states transcending consciousness. But they lose their consciousness to exactly the same degree that they transcend consciousness. I cannot imagine a conscious mental state that does not relate to a subject, that is, to an ego. The ego may be depotentiated—divested, for instance, of its awareness of the body—but so long as there is awareness of something, there must be somebody who is aware. The unconscious, however, is a mental condition of which no ego is aware. It is only by indirect means that we eventually become conscious of the existence of an unconscious. We can observe the manifestation of unconscious fragments of the personality, detached from the patient's consciousness, in insanity. But there is no evidence that the unconscious contents are related to an unconscious centre analogous to the ego; in fact there are good reasons why such a centre is not even probable.

The fact that the East can dispose so easily of the ego seems to point to a mind that is not to be identified with our "mind." Certainly the ego does not play the same role in Eastern thought as it does with us. It seems as if the Eastern mind were less egocentric, as if its contents were more loosely connected with the subject, and as if greater stress were laid on mental states which include a depotentiated ego. It also seems as if *hatha* yoga were chiefly useful as a means for extinguishing the ego by fettering its unruly impulses. There is no doubt that the higher forms of yoga, in so far as they strive to reach samādhi, seek a mental condition in which the ego is practically dissolved. Consciousness in our sense of the word is rated a definitely inferior condition, the state of *avidyā* (ignorance), whereas what we call the "dark background of consciousness" is understood to be a "higher" consciousness.[8] Thus our concept of the "collective unconscious" would be the European equivalent of *buddhi*, the enlightened mind.

In view of all this, the Eastern form of "sublimation" amounts to a withdrawal of the centre of psychic gravity from ego-consciousness, which holds a middle position between the body and the ideational processes of the psyche. The lower, semi-physiological strata of the psyche are subdued by *askesis*, i.e., exercises, and kept under control. They are not exactly denied or suppressed by a supreme effort of the will, as is customary in Western sublimation. Rather, the lower psychic strata are adapted and shaped through the patient practice of *hatha* yoga until they no longer interfere with the development of "higher" consciousness. This peculiar process seems to be aided by the fact that the ego and its desires are checked by the greater importance which the East habitually attaches to the "subjective factor."[9] By this I mean the "dark background" of consciousness, the unconscious. The introverted attitude is characterized in general by an emphasis on the *a priori* data of apperception. As is well known, the act of apperception consists of two phases: first the perception of the object, second the assimilation of the perception to a preexisting pattern or concept by means of which the object is "comprehended." The psyche is not a nonentity devoid of all quality; it is a definite system made up of definite conditions and it reacts in a specific way. Every new representation, be it a perception or a spontaneous thought, arouses associations which derive from the storehouse of memory. These leap immediately into consciousness, producing the complex picture of an "impression," though this is already a sort of interpretation. The unconscious disposition upon which the quality of the impression depends is what I call the "subjective factor." It deserves the qualification "subjective" because objectivity is hardly ever conferred by a first impression. Usually a rather laborious process of verification, comparison, and analysis is needed to modify and adapt the immediate reactions of the subjective factor.

The prominence of the subjective factor does not imply a *personal subjectivism*, despite the readiness of the extraverted attitude to dismiss the subjective factor as "nothing but" subjective. The psyche and its structure are real enough. They even transform material objects into psychic images, as we have said. They do not perceive waves, but sound; not wave-lengths, but colours. Existence is as we see and understand it. There are innumerable things that can be seen, felt, and understood in a great variety of ways. Quite apart from merely personal prejudices, the psyche assimilates external facts in its own way, which is based ultimately upon the laws or patterns of apperception. These laws do not change, although different ages or different parts of the world call them by different names. On a primitive level people are afraid of witches; on the modern level we are apprehensively aware of microbes. There everybody believes in ghosts, here everybody believes in vitamins. Once upon a time men were possessed by devils, now they are not less obsessed by ideas, and so on.

The subjective factor is made up, in the last resort, of the external patterns of psychic functioning. Anyone who relies upon the subjective factor is therefore basing himself on the reality of psychic law. So he can hardly be said to be wrong. If by this means he succeeds in extending his consciousness downwards, to touch the basic laws of psychic life, he is in possession of that truth which the psyche will naturally evolve if not fatally interfered with by the non-psychic, i.e., the external, world. At any rate, his truth could be weighed against the sum of all knowledge acquired through the investigation of externals. We in the West believe that a truth is satisfactory only if it can be verified by external facts. We believe in the most exact observation and exploration of nature; our truth must coincide with the behaviour of the external world, otherwise it is merely "subjective." In the same way that the East turns its gaze from the dance of *prakriti* (physis) and from the multitudinous illusory forms of *māyā*, the West shuns the unconscious and its futile fantasies. Despite its introverted attitude, however, the East knows very well how to deal with the external world. And despite its extraversions the West, too, has a way of dealing with the psyche and its demands; it has an institution called the Church, which gives expression to the unknown psyche of man through its rites and dogmas. Nor are natural science and modern techniques by any means the invention of the West. Their Eastern equivalents are somewhat old-fashioned, or even primitive. But what we have to show in the way of spiritual insight and psychological technique must seem, when compared with yoga, just as backward as Eastern astrology and medicine when compared with Western science. I do not deny the efficacy of the Christian Church; but, if you compare the *Exercitia* of Ignatius Loyola with yoga, you will take my meaning. There is a difference, and a big one. To jump straight from that level into Eastern yoga is no more advisable than the sudden transformation of Asian peoples into half-baked Europeans. I have serious doubts as to the blessings of Western civilization, and I have similar misgivings as to the adoption of Eastern spirituality by the West. Yet the two contradictory worlds have met. The East is in full transformation; it is thoroughly and fatally disturbed. Even the most efficient methods of European warfare have been successfully imitated. The trouble with us seems to be far more psychological. Our blight is ideologies—they are the long-expected Antichrist! National Socialism comes as near to being a religious movement as any movement since A.D. 622. Communism claims to be paradise come to earth again. We are far better protected against failing crops, inundations, epidemics, and invasions from the Turk than we are against our own deplorable spiritual inferiority, which seems to have little resistance to psychic epidemics.

In its religious attitude, too, the West is extraverted. Nowadays it is gratuitously offensive to say that Christianity implies hostility, or even indifference, to the world and the flesh. On the contrary, the good Christian is a jovial citizen, an enterprising business man, an excellent soldier, the very best in every profession there is. Worldly goods are often interpreted as special rewards for Christian behaviour, and in the Lord's Prayer the adjective ἐπιούσιος, *supersubstantialis*,[10] referring to the bread, has long since been omitted, for the real bread obviously makes so very much more sense! It is only logical that extraversion, when carried to such lengths, cannot credit man with a psyche which contains anything not imported into it from outside, either by human teaching or divine grace. From this point of view it is downright blasphemy to assert that man has it in him to accomplish his own redemption. Nothing in our religion encourages the idea of the self-liberating power of the mind. Yet a very modern form of psychology—"analytical" or "complex" psychology—envisages the possibility of there being certain processes in the unconscious which, by virtue of their symbolism, compensate the defects and anfractuosities of the conscious attitude. When these unconscious compensations are made conscious through the analytical technique, they produce such a change in the conscious attitude that we are entitled to speak of a new level of consciousness. The method cannot, however, produce the actual process of unconscious compensation; for that we depend upon the unconscious psyche or the "grace of God"—names make no difference. But the unconscious process itself hardly ever reaches consciousness without technical aid. When brought to the surface, it reveals contents that offer a striking contrast to the general run of conscious thinking and feeling. If that were not so, they would not have a compensatory effect. The first effect, however, is usually a conflict, because the conscious attitude resists the intrusion of apparently incompatible and extraneous tendencies, thoughts, feelings, etc. Schizophrenia yields the most startling examples of such intrusions of utterly foreign and unacceptable contents. In schizophrenia it is, of course, a question of pathological distortions and exaggerations, but anybody with the slightest knowledge of the normal material will easily recognize the sameness of the underlying patterns. It is, as a matter of fact, the same imagery that one finds in mythology and other archaic thought-formations.

Under normal conditions, every conflict stimulates the mind to activity for the purpose of creating a satisfactory solution. Usually—

i.e., in the West—the conscious standpoint arbitrarily decides against the unconscious, since anything coming from inside suffers from the prejudice of being regarded as inferior or somehow wrong. But in the cases with which we are here concerned it is tacitly agreed that the apparently incompatible contents shall not be suppressed again, and that the conflict shall be accepted and suffered. At first no solution appears possible, and this fact, too, has to be borne with patience. The suspension thus created "constellates" the unconscious—in other words, the conscious suspense produces a new compensatory reaction in the unconscious. This reaction (usually manifested in dreams) is brought to conscious realization in its turn. The conscious mind is thus confronted with a new aspect of the psyche, which arouses a different problem or modifies an old one in an unexpected way. The procedure is continued until the original conflict is satisfactorily resolved. The whole process is called the "transcendent function."[11] It is a process and a method at the same time. The production of unconscious compensations is a spontaneous *process;* the conscious realization is a *method.* The function is called "transcendent" because it facilitates the transition from one psychic condition to another by means of the mutual confrontation of opposites.

This is a very sketchy description of the transcendent function, and for details I must refer the reader to the literature mentioned in the footnotes. But I had to call attention to these psychological observations and methods because they indicate the way by which we may find access to the sort of "mind" referred to in our text. This is the image-creating mind, the matrix of all those patterns that give apperception its peculiar character. These patterns are inherent in the unconscious "mind"; they are its structural elements, and they alone can explain why certain mythological motifs are more or less ubiquitous, even where migration as a means of transmission is exceedingly improbable. Dreams, fantasies, and psychoses produce images to all appearances identical with mythological motifs of which the individuals concerned had absolutely no knowledge, not even indirect knowledge acquired through popular figures of speech or through the symbolic language of the Bible.[12] The psychopathology of schizophrenia, as well as the psychology of the unconscious, demonstrate the production of archaic material beyond a doubt. Whatever the structure of the unconscious may be, one thing is certain: it contains an indefinite number of motifs or patterns of an archaic character, in principle identical with the root ideas of mythology and similar thought-forms.

Because the unconscious is the matrix mind, the quality of creativeness attaches to it. It is the birthplace of thought-forms such as our text considers the Universal Mind to be. Since we cannot attribute any particular form to the unconscious, the Eastern assertion that the Universal Mind is without form, the *arupaloka*, yet is the source of all forms, seems to be psychologically justified. In so far as the forms or patterns of the unconscious belong to no time in particular, being seemingly eternal, they convey a peculiar feeling of timelessness when consciously realized. We find similar statements in primitive psychology: for instance, the Australian word *aljira*[13] means 'dream' as well as 'ghostland' and the 'time' in which the ancestors lived and still live. It is, as they say, the 'time when there was no time.' This looks like an obvious concretization and projection of the unconscious with all its characteristic qualities—its dream manifestations, its ancestral world of thought-forms, and its timelessness.

An introverted attitude, therefore, which withdraws its emphasis from the external world (the world of consciousness) and localizes it in the subjective factor (the background of consciousness) necessarily calls forth the characteristic manifestations of the unconscious, namely, archaic thought-forms imbued with "ancestral" or "historic" feeling, and, beyond them, the sense of indefiniteness, timelessness, oneness. The extraordinary feeling of oneness is a common experience in all forms of "mysticism" and probably derives from the general contamination of contents, which increases as consciousness dims. The almost limitless contamination of images in dreams, and particularly in the products of insanity, testifies to their unconscious origin. In contrast to the clear distinction and differentiation of forms in consciousness, unconscious contents are incredibly vague and for this reason capable of any amount of contamination. If we tried to conceive of a state in which nothing is distinct, we should certainly feel the whole as one. Hence it is not unlikely that the peculiar experience of oneness derives from the subliminal awareness of all-contamination in the unconscious.

By means of the transcendent function we not only gain access to the "One Mind" but also come to understand why the East believes in the possibility of self-liberation. If, through introspection and the conscious realization of unconscious compensations, it is possible to transform one's mental condition and thus arrive at a solution of painful conflicts, one would seem entitled to speak of "self-liberation." But, as I have already hinted, there is a hitch in this proud claim to self-liberation, for a man cannot produce these unconscious compensations at will. He has to rely upon the possibility that they *may* be produced. Nor can he alter the peculiar character of the compensation: *est ut est aut non est*—'it is as it is or it isn't at all.' It is a curious thing that Eastern philosophy seems to be almost unaware of this highly important fact. And it is precisely this fact that provides the psychological justification for the Western point of view. It seems as if the Western mind had a most penetrating intuition of man's fateful dependence upon some dark power which must co-operate if all is to be well. Indeed, whenever and wherever the unconscious fails to co-operate, man is instantly at a loss, even in his most ordinary activities. There may be a failure of memory, of co-ordinated action, or of interest and concentration; and such failure may well be the cause of serious annoyance, or of a fatal accident, a professional disaster, or a moral collapse. Formerly, men called the gods unfavourable; now we prefer to call it a neurosis, and we seek the cause in lack of vitamins, in endocrine disturbances, overwork, or sex. The co-operation of the unconscious, which is something we never think of and always take for granted, is, when it suddenly fails, a very serious matter indeed.

In comparison with other races—the Chinese for instance—the white man's mental equilibrium, or, to put it bluntly, his brain, seems to be his tender spot. We naturally try to get as far away from our weaknesses as possible, a fact which may explain the sort of extraversion that is always seeking security by dominating its surroundings. Extraversion goes hand in hand with mistrust of the inner man, if indeed there is any consciousness of him at all. Moreover, we all tend to undervalue the things we are afraid of. There must be some such reason for our absolute conviction that *nihil est in intellectu quod non antea fuerit in sensu*, which is the motto of Western extraversion. But, as we have emphasized, this extraversion is psychologically justified by the vital fact that unconscious compensation lies beyond man's control. I know that yoga prides itself on being able to control even the unconscious processes, so that nothing can happen in the psyche as a whole that is not ruled by a supreme consciousness. I have not the slightest doubt that such a condition is more or less possible. But it is possible only at the price of becoming identical with the unconscious. Such an identity is the Eastern equivalent of our Western fetish of "complete objectivity," the machine-like subservience to one goal, to one idea or cause, at the cost of losing every trace of inner life. From the Eastern point of view this complete objectivity is appalling, for it amounts to complete identity with the samsāra; to the West, on the other hand, samādhi is nothing but a meaningless dream-state. In the East, the inner man has always had such a firm hold on the outer man that the world had no chance of tearing him away from his inner roots; in the West, the outer man gained the ascendancy to such an extent that he was alienated from his innermost being. The One Mind, Oneness, indefiniteness, and eternity remained the prerogative of the One God. Man became small, futile, and essentially in the wrong.

I think it is becoming clear from my argument that the two standpoints, however contradictory, each have their psychological justification. Both are one-sided in that they fail to see and take account of those factors which do not fit in with their typical attitude. The one underrates the world of consciousness, the other the world of the One Mind. The result is that, in their extremism, both lose one half of the universe; their life is shut off from total reality, and is apt to become artificial and inhuman. In the West, there is the mania for "objectivity," the asceticism of the scientist or of the stockbroker, who throw away the beauty and universality of life for the sake of the ideal, or not so ideal, goal. In the East, there is the wisdom, peace, detachment, and inertia of a psyche that has returned to its dim origins, having left behind all the sorrow and joy of existence as it is and, presumably, ought to be. No wonder that one-sidedness produces very similar forms of monasticism in both cases, guaranteeing to the hermit, the holy man, the monk or the scientist unswerving singleness of purpose. I have nothing against one-sidedness as such. Man, the great experiment of nature, or his own great experiment, is evidently entitled to all such undertakings—if he can endure them. Without one-sidedness the spirit of man could not unfold in all its diversity. But I do not think there is any harm in trying to understand both sides.

The extraverted tendency of the West and the introverted tendency of the East have one important purpose in common: both make desperate efforts to conquer the mere naturalness of life. It is the assertion of mind over matter, the *opus contra naturam*, a symptom of the youthfulness of man, still delighting in the use of the most powerful weapon ever devised by nature: the conscious mind. The afternoon of humanity, in a distant future, may yet evolve a different ideal. In time, even conquest will cease to be the dream.

2. COMMENTS ON THE TEXT

Before embarking upon the commentary proper, I must not omit to call the reader's attention to the very marked difference between the tenor of a psychological dissertation and that of a sacred text. A scientist forgets all too easily that the impartial handling of a subject may violate its emotional values, often to an unpardonable degree. The scientific intellect is inhuman and cannot afford to be anything else; it cannot avoid being ruthless in effect, though it may be well-intentioned in motive. In dealing with a sacred text, therefore, the psychologist ought at least to be aware that his subject represents an inestimable religious and philosophical value which should not be desecrated by profane hands. I confess that I myself venture to deal with such a text only because I know and appreciate its value. In commenting upon it I have no intention whatsoever of anatomizing it with heavy-handed criticism. On the contrary, my endeavour will be to amplify its symbolic language so that it may yield itself more easily to our understanding. To this end, it is necessary to bring down its lofty metaphysical concepts to a level where it is possible to see whether any of the psychological facts known to us have parallels in, or at least border upon, the sphere of Eastern thought. I hope this will not be misunderstood as an attempt to belittle or to banalize; my aim is simply to bring ideas which are alien to our way of thinking within reach of Western psychological experience.

What follows is a series of notes and comments which should be read together with the textual sections indicated by the titles.

The Obeisance

Eastern texts usually begin with a statement which in the West would come at the end, as the *conclusio finalis* to a long argument. We would begin with things generally known and accepted, and would end with the most important item of our investigation. Hence our dissertation would conclude with the sentence: "Therefore the *Trikāya* is the All-Enlightened Mind itself." In this respect, the Eastern mentality is not so very different from the medieval. As late as the eighteenth century our books on history or natural science began, as here, with God's decision to create a world. The idea of a Universal Mind is a commonplace in the East, since it aptly expresses the introverted Eastern temperament. Put into psychological language, the above sentence could be paraphrased thus: The unconscious is the root of all experience of oneness (*dharmakāya*), the matrix of all archetypes or structural patterns (*sambhogakāya*), and the *conditio sine qua non* of the phenomenal world (*nirmānakāya*).

The Foreword

The gods are archetypal thought-forms belonging to the *sambhogakāya*.[14] Their peaceful and wrathful aspects, which play a great role in the meditations of the Tibetan Book of the Dead, symbolize the opposites. In the *nirmānakāya* these opposites are no more than human conflicts, but in the *sambhogakāya* they are the positive and negative principles united in one and the same figure. This corresponds to the psychological experience, also formulated in Lao-tzu's *Tao Teh Ching*, that there is no position without its negation. Where there is faith, there is doubt; where there is doubt, there is credulity; where there is morality, there is temptation. Only saints have diabolical visions, and tyrants are the slaves of their *valets de chambre*. If we carefully scrutinize our own character we shall inevitably find that, as Lao-tzu says, "high stands on low," which means that the opposites condition one another, that they are really one and the same thing. This can easily be seen in persons with an inferiority complex: they foment a little megalomania somewhere. The fact that the opposites appear as gods comes from the simple recognition that they are exceedingly powerful. Chinese philosophy therefore declared them to be cosmic principles, and named them *yang* and *yin*. Their power increases the more one tries to separate them. "When a tree grows up to heaven its roots reach down to hell," says Nietzsche. Yet, above as below, it is the same tree. It is characteristic of our Western mentality that we should separate the two aspects into antagonistic personifications: God and the Devil. And it is equally characteristic of the worldly optimism of Protestantism that it should have hushed up the Devil in a tactful sort of way, at any rate in recent times. *Omne bonum a Deo, omne malum ab homine* is the uncomfortable consequence.

The "seeing of reality" clearly refers to Mind as the supreme reality. In the West, however, the unconscious is considered to be a fantastic irreality. The "seeing of the Mind" implies self-liberation. This means, psychologically, that the more weight we attach to unconscious processes the more we detach ourselves from the world of desires and of separated opposites, and the nearer we draw to the state of unconsciousness with its qualities of oneness, indefiniteness, and timelessness. This is truly a liberation of the self from its bondage to strife and suffering. "By this method, one's mind is understood." Mind in this context is obviously the individual's mind, that is, his psyche. Psychology can agree in so far as the understanding of the unconscious is one of its foremost tasks.

Salutation to the One Mind

This section shows very clearly that the One Mind is the unconscious, since it is characterized as "eternal, unknown, not visible, not recognized." But it also displays positive features which are in keeping with Eastern experience. These are the attributes "ever clear, ever existing, radiant and unobscured." It is an undeniable psychological fact that the more one concentrates on one's unconscious contents the more they become charged with energy; they become vitalized, as if illuminated from within. In fact they turn into something like a substitute reality. In analytical psychology we make methodical use of this phenomenon. I have called the method "active imagination." Ignatius Loyola also made use of active imagination in his *Exercitia.* There is evidence that something similar was used in the meditations of alchemical philosophy.[15]

The Result of Not Knowing the One Mind

"Knowledge of that which is vulgarly called mind is widespread." This clearly refers to the conscious mind of everybody, in contrast to the One Mind which is unknown, i.e., unconscious. These teachings "will also be sought after by ordinary individuals who, not knowing the One Mind, do not know themselves." Self-knowledge is here definitely identified with "knowing the One Mind," which means that knowledge of the unconscious is essential for any understanding of one's own psychology. The desire for such knowledge is a well-established fact in the West, as evidenced by the rise of psychology in our time and a growing interest in these matters. The public desire for more psychological knowledge is largely due to the suffering which results from the disuse of religion and from the lack of spiritual guidance. "They wander hither and thither in the Three Regions . . . suffering sorrow." As we know what a neurosis can mean in moral suffering, this statement needs no comment. This section formulates the reasons why we have such a thing as the psychology of the unconscious today.

Even if one wishes "to know the mind as it is, one fails." The text again stresses how hard it is to gain access to the basic mind, because it is unconscious.

The Results of Desires

Those "fettered by desires cannot perceive the Clear Light." The "Clear Light" again refers to the One Mind. Desires crave for external fulfilment. They forge the chain that fetters man to the world of consciousness. In that condition he naturally cannot become aware of his unconscious contents. And indeed there is a healing power in withdrawing from the conscious world—up to a point. Beyond that point, which varies with individuals, withdrawal amounts to neglect and repression.

Even the "Middle Path" finally becomes "obscured by desires." This is a very true statement, which cannot be dinned too insistently into European ears. Patients and normal individuals, on becoming acquainted with their unconscious material, hurl themselves upon it with the same heedless desirousness and greed that before had engulfed them in their extraversion. The problem is not so much a withdrawal from the objects of desire, as a more detached attitude to desire as such, no matter what its object. We cannot compel unconscious compensation through the impetuousness of uncontrolled desire. We have to wait patiently to see whether it will come of its own accord, and put up with whatever form it takes. Hence we are forced into a sort of contemplative attitude which, in itself, not rarely has a liberating and healing effect.

The Transcendent At-one-ment

"There being really no duality, pluralism is untrue." This is certainly one of the most fundamental truths of the East. There are no opposites—it is the same tree above and below. The *Tabula smaragdina* says: "Quod est inferius est sicut quod est superius. Et quod est superius est sicut quod est inferius, ad perpetranda miracula rei unius."[16] Pluralism is even more illusory, since all separate forms originate in the indistinguishable oneness of the psychic matrix, deep down in the unconscious. The statement made by our text refers psychologically to the subjective factor, to the material immediately constellated by a stimulus, i.e., the first impression which, as we have seen, interprets every new perception in terms of previous experience. "Previous experience" goes right back to the instincts, and thus to the inherited and inherent patterns of psychic functioning, the ancestral and "eternal" laws of the human mind. But the statement entirely ignores the possible transcendent reality of the physical world as such, a problem not unknown to Sankhya philosophy, where *prakriti* and *purusha*—so far as they are a polarization of Universal Being—form a cosmic dualism that can hardly be circumvented. One has to close one's eyes to dualism and pluralism alike, and forget all about the existence of a world, as soon as one tries to identify oneself with the monistic origin of life. The questions naturally arise: "Why should the One appear as the Many, when ultimate reality is All-One? What is the cause of pluralism, or of the illusion of pluralism? If the One is pleased with itself, why should it mirror itself in the Many? Which after all is the more real, the one that mirrors itself, or the mirror it uses?" Probably we should not ask such questions, seeing that there is no answer to them.

It is psychologically correct to say that "At-one-ment" is attained by withdrawal from the world of consciousness. In the stratosphere of the unconscious there are no more thunderstorms, because nothing is differentiated enough to produce tensions and conflicts. These belong to the surface of our reality.

The Mind in which the irreconcilables—samsāra and nirvāna—

are united is ultimately our mind. Does this statement spring from profound modesty or from overweening hybris? Does it mean that the Mind is "nothing but" our mind? Or that our mind is the Mind? Assuredly it means the latter, and from the Eastern point of view there is no hybris in this; on the contrary, it is a perfectly acceptable truth, whereas with us it would amount to saying "I am God." This is an incontestable "mystical" experience, though a highly objectionable one to the Westerner; but in the East, where it derives from a mind that has never lost touch with the instinctual matrix, it has a very different value. The collective introverted attitude of the East did not permit the world of the senses to sever the vital link with the unconscious; psychic reality was never seriously disputed, despite the existence of so-called materialistic speculations. The only known analogy to this fact is the mental condition of the primitive, who confuses dream and reality in the most bewildering way. Naturally we hesitate to call the Eastern mind primitive, for we are deeply impressed with its remarkable civilization and differentiation. Yet the primitive mind is its matrix, and this is particularly true of that aspect of it which stresses the validity of psychic phenomena, such as relate to ghosts and spirits. The West has simply cultivated the other aspect of primitivity, namely, the scrupulously accurate observation of nature at the expense of abstraction. Our natural science is the epitome of primitive man's astonishing powers of observation. We have added only a moderate amount of abstraction, for fear of being contradicted by the facts. The East, on the other hand, cultivates the psychic aspect of primitivity together with an inordinate amount of abstraction. Facts make excellent stories but not much more.

Thus, if the East speaks of the Mind as being inherent in everybody, no more hybris or modesty is involved than in the European's belief in facts, which are mostly derived from man's own observation and sometimes from rather less than his observation, to wit, his interpretation. He is, therefore, quite right to be afraid of too much abstraction.

The Great Self-Liberation

I have mentioned more than once that the shifting of the basic personality-feeling to the less conscious mental sphere has a liberating effect. I have also described, somewhat cursorily, the transcendent function which produces the transformation of personality, and

I have emphasized the importance of spontaneous unconscious compensation. Further, I have pointed out the neglect of this crucial fact in yoga. This section tends to confirm my observations. The grasping of "the whole essence of these teachings" seems also to be the whole essence of "self-liberation." The Westerner would take this to mean: "Learn your lesson and repeat it, and then you will be self-liberated." That, indeed, is precisely what happens with most Western practitioners of yoga. They are very apt to "do" it in an extraverted fashion, oblivious of the inturning of the mind which is the essence of such teachings. In the East, the "truths" are so much a part of the collective consciousness that they are at least intuitively grasped by the pupil. If the European could turn himself inside out and live as an Oriental, with all the social, moral, religious, intellectual, and aesthetic obligations which such a course would involve, he might be able to benefit by these teachings. But you cannot be a good Christian, either in your faith or in your morality or in your intellectual make-up, and practise genuine yoga at the same time. I have seen too many cases that have made me sceptical in the highest degree. The trouble is that Western man cannot get rid of his history as easily as his short-legged memory can. History, one might say, is written in the blood. I would not advise anyone to touch yoga without a careful analysis of his unconscious reactions. What is the use of imitating yoga if your dark side remains as good a medieval Christian as ever? If you can afford to seat yourself on a gazelle skin under a Bo-tree or in the cell of a *gompa* for the rest of your life without being troubled by politics or the collapse of your securities, I will look favourably upon your case. But yoga in Mayfair or Fifth Avenue, or in any other place which is on the telephone, is a spiritual fake.

Taking the mental equipment of Eastern man into account, we may suppose that the teaching is effective. But unless one is prepared to turn away from the world and to disappear into the unconscious for good, mere teaching has no effect, or at least not the desired one. For this the union of opposites is necessary, and in particular the difficult task of reconciling extraversion and introversion by means of the transcendent function.

The Nature of Mind

This section contains a valuable piece of psychological information. The text says: "The mind is of intuitive ("quick-knowing")

Wisdom." Here "mind" is understood to be identical with immediate awareness of the "first impression" which conveys the whole sum of previous experience based upon instinctual patterns. This bears out our remarks about the essentially introverted prejudice of the East. The formula also draws attention to the highly differentiated character of Eastern intuition. The intuitive mind is noted for its disregard of facts in favour of possibilities.[17]

The assertion that the Mind "has no existence" obviously refers to the peculiar "potentiality" of the unconscious. A thing seems to exist only to the degree that we are aware of it, which explains why so many people are disinclined to believe in the existence of an unconscious. When I tell a patient that he is chock full of fantasies, he is often astonished beyond all measure, having been completely unaware of the fantasy-life he was leading.

The Names Given to the Mind

The various terms employed to express a "difficult" or "obscure" idea are a valuable source of information about the ways in which that idea can be interpreted, and at the same time an indication of its doubtful or controversial nature even in the country, religion, or philosophy to which it is indigenous. If the idea were perfectly straightforward and enjoyed general acceptance, there would be no reason to call it by a number of different names. But when something is little known, or ambiguous, it can be envisaged from different angles, and then a multiplicity of names is needed to express its peculiar nature. A classical example of this is the philosophers' stone; many of the old alchemical treatises give long lists of its names.

The statement that "the various names given to it [the Mind] are innumerable" proves that the Mind must be something as vague and indefinite as the philosophers' stone. A substance that can be described in "innumerable" ways must be expected to display as many qualities or facets. If these are really "innumerable," they cannot be counted, and it follows that the substance is well-nigh indescribable and unknowable. It can never be realized completely. This is certainly true of the unconscious, and a further proof that the Mind is the Eastern equivalent of our concept of the unconscious, more particularly of the collective unconscious.

In keeping with this hypothesis, the text goes on to say that the Mind is also called the "Mental Self." The "self" is an important concept in analytical psychology, where much has been said that I need not repeat here. I would refer the interested reader to the literature given below.[18] Although the symbols of the "self" are produced by unconscious activity and are mostly manifested in dreams,[19] the facts which the idea covers are not merely mental; they include aspects of physical existence as well. In this and other Eastern texts the "Self" represents a purely spiritual idea, but in Western psychology the "self" stands for a totality which comprises instincts, physiological and semi-physiological phenomena. To us a purely spiritual totality is inconceivable for the reasons mentioned above.[20]

It is interesting to note that in the East, too, there are "heretics" who identify the Self with the ego.[21] With us this heresy is pretty widespread and is subscribed to by all those who firmly believe that ego-consciousness is the only form of psychic life.

The Mind as "the means of attaining the Other Shore" points to a connection between the transcendent function and the idea of the Mind or Self. Since the unknowable substance of the Mind, i.e., of the unconscious, always represents itself to consciousness in the form of symbols—the self being one such symbol—the symbol functions as a "means of attaining the Other Shore," in other words, as a means of transformation. In my essay on psychic energy I said that the symbol acts as a transformer of energy.[22]

My interpretation of the Mind or Self as a symbol is not arbitrary; the text itself calls it "The Great Symbol."

It is also remarkable that our text recognizes the "potentiality" of the unconscious, as formulated above, by calling the Mind the "Sole Seed" and the "Potentiality of Truth."

The matrix-character of the unconscious comes out in the term "All-Foundation."

The Timelessness of Mind

I have already explained this "timelessness" as a quality inherent in the experience of the collective unconscious. The application of the "yoga of self-liberation" is said to reintegrate all forgotten knowledge of the past with consciousness. The motif of $\dot{\alpha}\pi о\kappa\alpha\tau\dot{\alpha}\sigma\tau\alpha\sigma\iota\varsigma$ (restoration, restitution) occurs in many redemption myths and is also an important aspect of the psychology of the unconscious, which reveals an extraordinary amount of archaic material in the dreams and spontaneous fantasies of normal and insane people. In the systematic analysis of an individual the spontaneous reawakening of ancestral patterns (as a compensation) has the effect of a restoration. It is also a fact that premonitory dreams are relatively frequent, and this substantiates what the text calls "knowledge of the future."

The Mind's "own time" is very difficult to interpret. From the psychological point of view we must agree with Dr. Evans-Wentz's comment here.[23] The unconscious certainly has its "own time" inasmuch as past, present, and future are blended together in it. Dreams of the type experienced by J. W. Dunne,[24] where he dreamed the night before what he ought logically to have dreamed the night after, are not infrequent.

Mind in Its True State

This section describes the state of detached consciousness[25] which corresponds to a psychic experience very common throughout the East. Similar descriptions are to be found in Chinese literature, as, for instance, in the *Hui Ming Ch'ing:*

> A luminosity surrounds the world of spirit.
> We forget one another when, still and pure, we draw strength from
> the Void.
> The Void is filled with the light of the Heart of Heaven . . .
> Consciousness dissolves in vision.[26]

The statement "Nor is one's own mind separable from other minds" is another way of expressing the fact of "all-contamination." Since all distinctions vanish in the unconscious condition, it is only logical that the distinction between separate minds should disappear too. Wherever there is a lowering of the conscious level we come across instances of unconscious identity,[27] or what Lévy-Bruhl calls "participation mystique."[28] The realization of the One Mind is, as our text says, the "at-one-ment of the *Trikāya*"; in fact it creates the at-one-ment. But we are unable to imagine how such a realization could ever be complete in any human individual. There must always be somebody or something left over to experience the realization, to say "I know at-one-ment, I know there is no distinction." The very fact of the realization proves its inevitable incompleteness. One cannot know something that is not distinct from oneself. Even when I say "I know myself," an infinitesimal ego—the knowing "I"—is still distinct from "myself." In this as it were atomic ego, which is completely ignored by the essentially non-dualist standpoint of the East, there nevertheless lies hidden the whole unabolished pluralistic universe and its unconquered reality.

The experience of "at-one-ment" is one example of those "quick-knowing" realizations of the East, an intuition of what it would be like if one could exist and not exist at the same time. If I were a Moslem, I should maintain that the power of the All-Compassionate is infinite, and that He alone can make a man to be and not to be at the same time. But for my part I cannot conceive of such a possibility. I therefore assume that, in this point, Eastern intuition has overreached itself.

Mind Is Non-Created

This section emphasizes that as the Mind is without characteristics, one cannot assert that it is created. But then, it would be illogical to assert that it is non-created, for such a qualification would amount to a "characteristic." As a matter of fact you can make no assertion whatever about a thing that is indistinct, void of characteristics and, moreover, "unknowable." For precisely this reason Western psychology does not speak of the One Mind, but of the unconscious, regarding it as a thing-in-itself, a noumenon, "a merely negative borderline concept," to quote Kant.[29] We have often been reproached for using such a negative term, but unfortunately intellectual honesty does not allow a positive one.

The Yoga of Introspection

Should there be any doubt left concerning the identity of the One Mind and the unconscious, this section certainly ought to dispel it. "The One Mind being verily of the Voidness and without any foundation, one's mind is, likewise, as vacuous as the sky." The One Mind and the individual mind are equally void and vacuous. Only the collective and the personal unconscious can be meant by this statement, for the conscious mind is in no circumstances "vacuous."

As I have said earlier, the Eastern mind insists first and foremost upon the subjective factor, and in particular upon the intuitive "first impression," or the psychic disposition. This is borne out by the statement that "All appearances are verily one's own concepts, self-conceived in the mind."

The Dharma Within

Dharma, law, truth, guidance, is said to be "nowhere save in the mind." Thus the unconscious is credited with all those faculties which the West attributes to God. The transcendent function, however, shows how right the East is in assuming that the complex experience of *dharma* comes from "within," i.e., from the unconscious. It also shows that the phenomenon of spontaneous compensation, being beyond the control of man, is quite in accord with the formula "grace" or the "will of God."

This and the preceding section insist again and again that introspection is the only source of spiritual information and guidance. If introspection were something morbid, as certain people in the West opine, we should have to send practically the whole East, or such parts of it as are not yet infected with the blessings of the West, to the lunatic asylum.

The Wondrousness of These Teachings

This section calls the mind "Natural Wisdom," which is very much the same expression that I used in order to designate the symbols produced by the unconscious. I called them "natural symbols."[30] I chose the term before I had any knowledge of this text. I mention this fact simply because it illustrates the close parallelism between the findings of Eastern and Western psychology.

The text also confirms what we said earlier about the impossibility of a "knowing" ego. "Although it is Total Reality, there is no perceiver of it. Wondrous is this." Wondrous indeed, and incomprehensible; for how could such a thing ever be *realized* in the true sense of the word? "It remains undefiled by evil" and "it remains unallied to good." One is reminded of Nietzsche's "six thousand feet beyond good and evil." But the consequences of such a statement are usually ignored by the emulators of Eastern wisdom. While one is safely ensconced in one's cosy flat, secure in the favour of the Oriental gods, one is free to admire this lofty moral indifference. But does it agree with our temperament, or with our history, which is not thereby conquered but merely forgotten? I think not. Anyone who affects the higher yoga will be called upon to prove his professions of moral indifference, not only as the doer of evil but, even more, as its victim. As psychologists well know, the moral conflict is not to be settled merely by a declaration of superiority bordering on inhumanity. We are witnessing today some terrifying examples of the Superman's aloofness from moral principles.

I do not doubt that the Eastern liberation from vices, as well as from virtues, is coupled with detachment in every respect, so that the yogi is translated beyond this world, and quite inoffensive. But I suspect every European attempt at detachment of being mere liberation from moral considerations. Anybody who tries his hand at yoga ought therefore to be conscious of its far-reaching consequences, or else his so-called quest will remain a futile pastime.

The Fourfold Great Path

The text says: "This meditation [is] devoid of mental concentration." The usual assumption about yoga is that it chiefly consists in intense concentration. We think we know what concentration means, but it is very difficult to arrive at a real understanding of Eastern concentration. Our sort may well be just the opposite of the Eastern, as a study of Zen Buddhism will show.[31] However, if we take "devoid of mental concentration" literally, it can only mean that the meditation does not centre upon anything. Not being centred, it would be rather like a dissolution of consciousness and hence a direct approach to the unconscious condition. Consciousness always implies a certain degree of concentration, without which there would be no clarity of mental content and no consciousness of anything. Meditation without concentration would be a waking but empty condition, on the verge of falling asleep. Since our text calls this "the most excellent of meditations" we must suppose the existence of less excellent meditations which, we infer, would be characterized by more concentration. The meditation our text has in mind seems to be a sort of Royal Road to the unconscious.

The Great Light

The central mystical experience of enlightenment is aptly symbolized by Light in most of the numerous forms of mysticism. It is a curious paradox that the approach to a region which seems to us the way into utter darkness should yield the light of illumination as its fruit. This is, however, the usual *enantiodromia per tenebras ad lucem.* Many initiation ceremonies[32] stage a κατάβασις εἰς ἄντρον (descent into the cave), a diving down into the depths of the baptismal water, or a return to the womb of rebirth. Rebirth symbolism simply describes the union of opposites—conscious and unconscious—by means of concretistic analogies. Underlying all rebirth symbolism is the transcendent function. Since this function results in an increase of consciousness (the previous condition augmented by the addition of formerly unconscious contents), the new condition carries more insight, which is symbolized by more light.[33] It is therefore a more enlightened state compared with the relative darkness of the previous state. In many cases the Light even appears in the form of a vision.

The Yoga of the Nirvanic Path

This section gives one of the best formulations of the complete dissolution of consciousness, which appears to be the goal of this yoga: "There being no two such things as action and performer of action, if one seeks the performer of action and no performer of action be found anywhere, thereupon the goal of all fruit-obtaining is reached and also the final consummation itself."

With this very complete formulation of the method and its aim, I reach the end of my commentary. The text that follows, in Book II, is of great beauty and wisdom, and contains nothing that requires further comment. It can be translated into psychological language and interpreted with the help of the principles I have here set forth in Part I and illustrated in Part II.

Notes

1. [Written in English in 1939 and first published in *The Tibetan Book of the Great Liberation,* the texts of which were translated from Tibetan by various hands and edited by W. Y. Evans-Wentz (London and New York, 1954), pp. xxix–lxiv. The commentary is republished here with only minor alterations.—EDITORS.]
2. I am purposely leaving out of account the modernized East.
3. *Psychological Types,* Defs. 19 and 34.
4. Written in the year 1939.
5. *Samyutta-nikāya* 12, *Nidāna-samyutta.*

6. [Cf. Otto, *The Idea of the Holy*, pp. 26ff.—EDITORS.]
7. "Whereas who holdeth not God as such an inner possession, but with every means must fetch Him from without . . . verily such a man hath Him not, and easily something cometh to trouble him." Meister Eckhart (Büttner, II, p. 185). Cf. *Meister Eckhart*, trans. by Evans, II, p. 8.
8. In so far as "higher" and "lower" are categorical judgments of consciousness, Western psychology does not differentiate unconscious contents in this way. It appears that the East recognizes subhuman psychic conditions, a real "subconsciousness" comprising the instincts and semi-physiological psychisms, but classed as a "higher consciousness."
9. *Psychological Types* (1923 edn., pp. 472ff.).
10. This is not the unacceptable translation of ἐπιούσιος by Jerome but the ancient spiritual interpretation by Tertullian, Origen, and others.
11. *Psychological Types*, Def. 51.
12. Some people find such statements incredible. But either they have no knowledge of primitive psychology, or they are ignorant of the results of psychopathological research. Specific observations occur in my *Symbols of Transformation* and *Psychology and Alchemy*, Part II; Nelken, "Analytische Beobachtungen über Phantasien eines Schizophrenen," pp. 504ff.; Spielrein, "Über den psychologischen Inhalt eines Falls von Schizophrenie," pp. 329ff.; and C. A. Meier, "Spontanmanifestationen des kollektiven Unbewussten."
13. Lévy-Bruhl, *La Mythologie primitive*, pp. xxiii ff.
14. Cf. the *Shrī-Chakra-Sambhara Tantra*, in Avalon, ed., *Tantric Texts*, VII.
15. My *Psychology and Alchemy*, Part III.
16. "What is below is like what is above. And what is above is like what is below, so that the miracle of the One may be accomplished." Cf. Ruska, *Tabula Smaragdina*, p. 2.
17. Cf. *Psychological Types*, Def. 36.
18. My *Two Essays on Analytical Psychology*, index, s.v. "Self"; *Psychological Types*, Def. 16; *Psychology and Alchemy*, Part II; *Aion*.
19. One such case is described in Part II of *Psychology and Alchemy*.
20. This is no criticism of the Eastern point of view *in toto;* for, according to the *Amitāyur-dhyāna Sūtra*, the Buddha's body is included in the meditation.
21. Cf. for instance, *Chhāndogya Upanishad*, viii. 8.
22. "On Psychic Energy" (1928 edn., p. 54).
23. Cf. his *Tibetan Book of the Great Liberation*, p. 210, n. 3.
24. *An Experiment with Time*. [Cf. Jung's "Synchronicity" (1955 edn., p. 38).—EDITORS.]

25. I have explained this in my commentary on *The Secret of the Golden Flower* (1931 edn., pp. 21ff.).
26. From the [German] trans. of L. C. Lo, I, p. 114.
27. *Psychological Types*, Def. 25.
28. Cf. Lévy-Bruhl, *How Natives Think*. Recently this concept as well as that of the *état prélogique* have been severely criticized by ethnologists, and moreover Lévy-Bruhl himself began to doubt their validity in the last years of his life. First he cancelled the adjective "mystique," growing afraid of the term's bad reputation in intellectual circles. It is rather to be regretted that he made such a concession to rationalistic superstition, since "mystique" is just the right word to characterize the peculiar quality of "unconscious identity." There is always something numinous about it. Unconscious identity is a well-known psychological and psychopathological phenomenon (identity with persons, things, functions, roles, positions, creeds, etc.), which is only a shade more characteristic of the primitive than of the civilized mind. Lévy-Bruhl, unfortunately having no psychological knowledge, was not aware of this fact, and his opponents ignore it.
29. Cf. *The Critique of Pure Reason*, sec. i, Part I, 2, 3 (cf. trans. by Meiklejohn, p. 188).
30. Cf. the first paper in this volume, chs. 2 and 3.
31. Cf. Suzuki, *Essays in Zen Buddhism*.
32. As in the Eleusinian mysteries and the Mithras and Attis cults.
33. In alchemy the philosophers' stone was called, among other things, *lux moderna, lux lucis, lumen luminum*, etc.

C.G. Jung

Psychological Commentary on
The Tibetan Book of the Dead[1]

Before embarking upon the psychological commentary, I should like to say a few words about the text itself. The Tibetan Book of the Dead, or the *Bardo Thödol*, is a book of instructions for the dead and dying. Like the Egyptian Book of the Dead, it is meant to be a guide for the dead man during the period of his *Bardo* existence, symbolically described as an intermediate state of forty-nine days' duration between death and rebirth. The text falls into three parts. The first part, called *Chikhai Bardo*, describes the psychic happenings at the moment of death. The second part, or *Chönyid Bardo*, deals with the dream-state which supervenes immediately after death, and with what are called "karmic illusions." The third part, or *Sidpa Bardo*, concerns the onset of the birth-instinct and of prenatal events. It is characteristic that supreme insight and illumination, and hence the greatest possibility of attaining liberation, are vouchsafed during the actual process of dying. Soon afterward, the "illusions" begin which lead eventually to reincarnation, the illuminative lights growing ever fainter and more multifarious, and the visions more and more terrifying. This descent illustrates the estrangement of consciousness from the liberating truth as it approaches nearer and nearer to physical rebirth. The purpose of the instruction is to fix the attention of the dead man, at each successive stage of delusion and entanglement, on the ever-present possibility of liberation, and to explain to him the nature of his visions. The text of the *Bardo Thödol* is recited by the lama in the presence of the corpse.

I do not think I could better discharge my debt of thanks to the two previous translators of the *Bardo Thödol*, the late Lama Kazi Dawa-Samdup and Dr. Evans-Wentz, than by attempting, with the aid of a psychological commentary, to make the magnificent world of ideas and the problems contained in this treatise a little more intelligible to the Western mind. I am sure that all who read this book with open eyes, and who allow it to impress itself upon them without prejudice, will reap a rich reward.

The *Bardo Thödol*, fitly named by its editor, Dr. W. Y. Evans-Wentz, "The Tibetan Book of the Dead," caused a considerable stir in English-speaking countries at the time of its first appearance in 1927. It belongs to that class of writings which are not only of interest to specialists in Mahayana Buddhism, but which also, because of their deep humanity and their still deeper insight into the secrets of the human psyche, make an especial appeal to the layman who is seeking to broaden his knowledge of life. For years, ever since it was first published, the *Bardo Thödol* has been my constant companion, and to it I owe not only many stimulating ideas and discoveries, but also many fundamental insights. Unlike the Egyptian Book of the Dead, which always prompts one to say too much or too little, the *Bardo Thödol* offers one an intelligible philosophy addressed to human beings rather than to gods or primitive savages. Its philosophy contains the quintessence of Buddhist psychological criticism; and, as such, one can truly say that it is of an unexampled superiority. Not only the "wrathful" but also the "peaceful" deities are conceived as samsaric projections of the human psyche, an idea that seems all too obvious to the enlightened European, because it reminds him of his own banal simplifications. But though the European can easily explain away these deities as projections, he would be quite incapable of positing them at the same time as real. The *Bardo Thödol* can do that, because, in certain of its most essential metaphysical premises, it has the enlightened as well as the unenlightened European at a disadvantage. The ever-present, unspoken assumption of the *Bardo Thödol* is the antinominal character of all metaphysical assertions, and also the idea of the qualitative difference of the various levels of consciousness and of the metaphysical realities conditioned by them. The background of this unusual book is not the niggardly European "either-or," but a magnificently affirmative "both-and." This statement may appear objectionable to the Western philosopher, for the West loves clarity and unambiguity; consequently, one philosopher clings to the position, "God is," while another clings equally fervently to the negation, "God is not." What would these hostile brethren make of an assertion like the following:

> Recognizing the voidness of thine own intellect to be Buddha-
> hood, and knowing it at the same time to be thine own conscious-
> ness, thou shalt abide in the state of the divine mind of the
> Buddha.

Such an assertion is, I fear, as unwelcome to our Western philosophy as it is to our theology. The *Bardo Thödol* is in the highest
degree psychological in its outlook; but, with us, philosophy and
theology are still in the medieval, pre-psychological stage where only
the assertions are listened to, explained, defended, criticized and
disputed, while the authority that makes them has, by general consent, been deposed as outside the scope of discussion.

Metaphysical assertions, however, are *statements of the psyche,*
and are therefore psychological. To the Western mind, which com-
pensates its well-known feelings of resentment by a slavish regard
for "rational" explanations, this obvious truth seems all too obvious,
or else it is seen as an inadmissible negation of metaphysical "truth."
Whenever the Westerner hears the word "psychological," it always
sounds to him like "*only* psychological." For him the "soul" is something pitifully small, unworthy, personal, subjective, and a lot more
besides. He therefore prefers to use the word "mind" instead,
though he likes to pretend at the same time that a statement which
may in fact be very subjective indeed is made by the "mind," naturally by the "Universal Mind," or even—at a pinch—by the "Absolute" itself. This rather ridiculous presumption is probably a compensation for the regrettable smallness of the soul. It almost seems as
if Anatole France had uttered a truth which were valid for the whole
Western world when, in his *Penguin Island,* Cathérine d'Alexandrie
offers this advice to God: "Donnez-leur une âme, mais une petite!"

It is the psyche which, by the divine creative power inherent in
it, makes the metaphysical assertion; it posits the distinctions between metaphysical entities. Not only is it the condition of all metaphysical reality, it *is* that reality.

With this great psychological truth the *Bardo Thödol* opens. The
book is not a ceremonial of burial, but a set of instructions for the
dead, a guide through the changing phenomena of the *Bardo* realm,
that state of existence which continues for forty-nine days after
death until the next incarnation. If we disregard for the moment the
supratemporality of the soul—which the East accepts as a self-

evident fact—we, as readers of the *Bardo Thödol*, shall be able to put ourselves without difficulty in the position of the dead man, and shall consider attentively the teaching set forth in the opening section, which is outlined in the quotation above. At this point, the following words are spoken, not presumptuously, but in a courteous manner:

> O nobly born (so and so), listen. Now thou are experiencing the Radiance of the Clear Light of Pure Reality. Recognize it. O nobly-born, thy present intellect, in real nature void, not formed into anything as regards characteristics or colour, naturally void, is the very Reality, the All-Good.
>
> Thine own intellect, which is now voidness, yet not to be regarded as of the voidness of nothingness, but as being the intellect itself, unobstructed, shining, thrilling, and blissful, is the very consciousness, the All-good Buddha.

This realization is the *Dharmakāya* state of perfect enlightenment; or, as we should express it in our own language, the creative ground of all metaphysical assertion is consciousness, as the invisible, intangible manifestation of the soul. The "Voidness" is the state transcendent over all assertion and all predication. The fulness of its discriminative manifestations still lies latent in the soul.

The text continues:

> Thine own consciousness, shining, void, and inseparable from the Great Body of Radiance, hath no birth, nor death, and is the Immutable Light—Buddha Amitābha.

The soul is assuredly not small, but the radiant Godhead itself. The West finds this statement either very dangerous, if not downright blasphemous, or else accepts it unthinkingly and then suffers from a theosophical inflation. Somehow we always have a wrong attitude to these things. But if we can master ourselves far enough to refrain from our chief error of always wanting to *do* something with things and put them to practical use, we may perhaps succeed in learning an important lesson from these teachings, or at least in appreciating the greatness of the *Bardo Thödol*, which vouchsafes to the dead man the ultimate and highest truth, that even the gods are the radiance and reflection of our own souls. No sun is thereby eclipsed for the Oriental as it would be for the Christian, who would feel robbed of his God; on the contrary, his soul is the light of the God-head, and the Godhead is the soul. The East can sustain this paradox better than the unfortunate Angelus Silesius, who even today would be psychologically far in advance of his time.

It is highly sensible of the *Bardo Thödol* to make clear to the dead man the primacy of the psyche, for that is the one thing which life does not make clear to us. We are so hemmed in by things which jostle and oppress that we never get a chance, in the midst of all these "given" things, to wonder by whom they are "given." It is from this world of "given" things that the dead man liberates himself; and the purpose of the instruction is to help him towards this liberation. We, if we put ourselves in his place, shall derive no lesser reward from it, since we learn from the very first paragraphs that the "giver" of all "given" things dwells within us. This is a truth which in the face of all evidence, in the greatest things as in the smallest, is never known, although it is often so very necessary, indeed vital, for us to know it. Such knowledge, to be sure, is suitable only for contemplatives who are minded to understand the purpose of existence, for those who are Gnostics by temperament and therefore believe in a saviour who, like the saviour of the Mandaeans, is called "knowledge of life" (Manda d'Hayye). Perhaps it is not granted to many of us to see the world as something "given." A great reversal of standpoint, calling for much sacrifice, is needed before we can see the world as "given" by the very nature of the psyche. It is so much more straightforward, more dramatic, impressive, and therefore more convincing, to see all the things that happen to me than to observe how I make them hap-pen. Indeed, the animal nature of man makes him resist seeing him-self as the maker of his circumstances. That is why attempts of this kind were always the object of secret initiations, culminating as a rule in a figurative death which symbolized the total character of this reversal. And, in point of fact, the instruction given in the *Bardo Thödol* serves to recall to the dead man the experiences of his initia-tion and the teachings of his guru, for the instruction is, at bottom, nothing less than an initiation of the dead into the *Bardo* life, just as the initiation of the living was a preparation for the Beyond. Such was the case, at least, with all the mystery cults in ancient civiliza-tions from the time of the Egyptian and Eleusinian mysteries. In the initiation of the living, however, this "Beyond" is not a world beyond death, but a reversal of the mind's intentions and outlook, a psychological "Beyond" or, in Christian terms, a "redemption" from the trammels of the world and of sin. Redemption is a separation and deliverance from an earlier condition of darkness and unconsciousness, and leads to a condition of illumination and releasedness, to victory and transcendence over everything "given."

Thus far the *Bardo Thödol* is, as Dr. Evans-Wentz also feels, an initiation process whose purpose it is to restore to the soul the divinity it lost at birth. Now it is a characteristic of Oriental religious literature that the teaching invariably begins with the most important item, with the ultimate and highest principles which, with us, would come last—as for instance in Apuleius, where Lucius is worshipped as Helios only right at the end. Accordingly, in the *Bardo Thödol*, the initiation is a series of diminishing climaxes ending with rebirth in the womb. The only "initiation process" that is still alive and practised today in the West is the analysis of the unconscious as used by doctors for therapeutic purposes. This penetration into the ground-layers of consciousness is a kind of rational maieutics in the Socratic sense, a bringing forth of psychic contents that are still germinal, subliminal, and as yet unborn. Originally, this therapy took the form of Freudian psychoanalysis and was mainly concerned with sexual fantasies. This is the realm that corresponds to the last and lowest region of the *Bardo*, known as the *Sidpa Bardo*, where the dead man, unable to profit by the teachings of the *Chikhai* and *Chönyid Bardo*, begins to fall a prey to sexual fantasies and is attracted by the vision of mating couples. Eventually he is caught by a womb and born into the earthly world again. Meanwhile, as one might expect, the Oedipus complex starts functioning. If his karma destines him to be reborn as a man, he will fall in love with his mother-to-be and will find his father hateful and disgusting. Conversely, the future daughter will be highly attracted by her father-to-be and repelled by her mother. The European passes through this specifically Freudian domain when his unconscious contents are brought to light under analysis, but he goes in the reverse direction. He journeys back through the world of infantile-sexual fantasy to the womb. It has even been suggested in psychoanalytical circles that the trauma par excellence is the birth-experience itself—nay more, psychoanalysts even claim to have probed back to memories of intra-uterine origin. Here Western reason reaches its limit, unfortunately. I say "unfortunately," because one rather wishes that Freudian psychoanalysis could have happily pursued these so-called intra-uterine experiences still further back. Had it succeeded in this bold undertaking, it would surely have come out beyond the *Sidpa Bardo* and penetrated from behind into the lower reaches of the *Chönyid Bardo*. It is true that, with the equipment of our existing biological ideas, such a venture would not have been crowned with success; it would have needed a wholly different kind of philosophical preparation from that based on current scientific assumptions. But, had the journey back been consistently pursued, it would undoubtedly have led to the postulate of a pre-uterine existence, a true *Bardo* life, if only it had been possible to find at least some trace of an experiencing subject. As it was, the psychoanalysts never got beyond purely conjectural traces of intra-uterine experiences, and even the famous "birth trauma" has remained such an obvious truism that it can no longer explain anything, any more than can the hypothesis that life is a disease with a bad prognosis because its outcome is always fatal.

Freudian psychoanalysis, in all essential aspects, never went beyond the experiences of the *Sidpa Bardo;* that is, it was unable to extricate itself from sexual fantasies and similar "incompatible" tendencies which cause anxiety and other affective states. Nevertheless, Freud's theory is the first attempt made by the West to investigate, as if from below, from the animal sphere of instinct, the psychic territory that corresponds in Tantric Lamaism to the *Sidpa Bardo*. A very justifiable fear of metaphysics prevented Freud from penetrating into the sphere of the "occult." In addition to this, the *Sidpa* state, if we are to accept the psychology of the *Sidpa Bardo*, is characterized by the fierce wind of karma, which whirls the dead man along until he comes to the "womb-door." In other words, the *Sidpa* state permits of no going back, because it is sealed off against the *Chönyid* state by an intense striving downwards, towards the animal sphere of instinct and physical rebirth. That is to say, anyone who penetrates into the unconscious with purely biological assumptions will become stuck in the instinctual sphere and be unable to advance beyond it, for he will be pulled back again and again into physical existence. It is therefore not possible for Freudian theory to reach anything except an essentially negative valuation of the unconscious. It is a "nothing but." At the same time, it must be admitted that this view of the psyche is typically Western, only it is expressed more blatantly, more plainly, and more ruthlessly than others would have dared to express it, though at bottom they think no differently. As to what "mind" means in this connection, we can only cherish the hope that it will carry conviction. But, as even Max Scheler[2] noted with regret, the power of this "mind" is, to say the least of it, doubtful.

I think, then, we can state it as a fact that with the aid of psychoanalysis the rationalizing mind of the West has pushed forward into what one might call the neuroticism of the *Sidpa* state, and has there been brought to an inevitable standstill by the uncritical assumption that everything psychological is subjective and personal. Even so, this advance has been a great gain, inasmuch as it has enabled us to take one more step behind our conscious lives. This knowledge also gives us a hint of how we ought to read the *Bardo Thödol*—that is, backwards. If, with the help of our Western science, we have to some extent succeeded in understanding the psychological character of the *Sidpa Bardo*, our next task is to see if we can make anything of the preceding *Chönyid Bardo*.

The *Chönyid* state is one of karmic illusion—that is to say, illusions which result from the psychic residua of previous existences. According to the Eastern view, karma implies a sort of psychic theory of heredity based on the hypothesis of reincarnation, which in the last resort is an hypothesis of the supratemporality of the soul. Neither our scientific knowledge nor our reason can keep in step with this idea. There are too many if's and but's. Above all, we know desperately little about the possibilities of continued existence of the individual soul after death, so little that we cannot even conceive how anyone could prove anything at all in this respect. Moreover, we know only too well, on epistemological grounds, that such a proof would be just as impossible as the proof of God. Hence we may cautiously accept the idea of karma only if we understand it as *psychic heredity* in the very widest sense of the word. Psychic heredity does exist—that is to say, there is inheritance of psychic characteristics such as predisposition to disease, traits of character, special gifts, and so forth. It does no violence to the psychic nature of these complex facts if natural science reduces them to what appear to be physical aspects (nuclear structures in cells, and so on). They are essential phenomena of life which express themselves, in the main, psychically, just as there are other inherited characteristics which express themselves, in the main, physiologically, on the physical level.

Among these inherited psychic factors there is a special class which is not confined either to family or to race. These are the universal dispositions of the mind, and they are to be understood as analogous to Plato's forms (*eidola*), in accordance with which the mind organizes its contents. One could also describe these forms as *categories* analogous to the logical categories which are always and everywhere present as the basic postulates of reason. Only, in the case of our "forms," we are not dealing with categories of reason but with categories of the *imagination*. As the products of imagination are always in essence visual, their forms must, from the outset, have the character of images and moreover of *typical* images, which is why, following St. Augustine, I call them "archetypes." Comparative religion and mythology are rich mines of archetypes, and so is the psychology of dreams and psychoses. The astonishing parallelism between these images and the ideas they serve to express has frequently given rise to the wildest migration theories, although it would have been far more natural to think of the remarkable similarity of the human psyche at all times and in all places. Archetypal fantasy-forms are, in fact, reproduced spontaneously anytime and anywhere, without there being any conceivable trace of direct transmission. The original structural components of the psyche are of no less surprising a uniformity than are those of the visible body. The archetypes are, so to speak, organs of the pre-rational psyche. They are eternally inherited forms and ideas which have at first no specific content. Their specific content only appears in the course of the individual's life, when personal experience is taken up in precisely these forms. If the archetypes were not pre-existent in identical form everywhere, how could one explain the fact, postulated at almost every turn by the *Bardo Thödol*, that the dead do not know that they are dead, and that this assertion is to be met with just as often in the dreary, half-baked literature of European and American Spiritualism? Although we find the same assertion in Swedenborg, knowledge of his writings can hardly be sufficiently widespread for this little bit of information to have been picked up by every small-town medium. And a connection between Swedenborg and the *Bardo Thödol* is completely unthinkable. It is a primordial, universal idea that the dead simply continue their earthly existence and do not know that they are disembodied spirits—an archetypal idea which enters into immediate, visible manifestation whenever anyone sees a ghost. It is significant, too, that ghosts all over the world have certain features in common. I am naturally aware of the unverifiable spiritualistic hypothesis, though I have no wish to make it my own. I must content myself with the hypothesis of an omnipresent, but differentiated, psychic structure which is inherited and which necessarily gives a certain form and direction to all experience. For, just as the organs of the body are not mere lumps of indifferent, passive matter, but are dynamic, functional complexes which assert themselves with imperious urgency, so also the archetypes, as organs of the psyche, are dynamic, instinctual complexes which determine psychic life to an extraordinary degree. That is why I also call them *dominants* of the unconscious. The layer of unconscious psyche which is made up of these universal dynamic forms I have termed the *collective unconscious*.

So far as I know, there is no inheritance of individual prenatal, or pre-uterine, memories, but there are undoubtedly inherited archetypes which are, however, devoid of content, because, to begin with, they contain no personal experiences. They only emerge into consciousness when personal experiences have rendered them visible. As we have seen, *Sidpa* psychology consists in wanting to live and to be born. (The *Sidpa Bardo* is the "*Bardo* of Seeking Rebirth.") Such a state, therefore, precludes any experience of transubjective psychic realities, unless the individual refuses categorically to be born back again into the world of consciousness. According to the teachings of the *Bardo Thödol*, it is still possible for him, in each of the *Bardo* states, to reach the *Dharmakāya* by transcending the four-faced Mount Meru, provided that he does not yield to his desire to follow the "dim lights." This is as much as to say that the dead man must desperately resist the dictates of reason, as we understand it, and give up the supremacy of egohood, regarded by reason as sacrosanct. What this means in practice is complete capitulation to the objective powers of the psyche, with all that this entails; a kind of symbolical death, corresponding to the Judgment of the Dead in the *Sidpa Bardo*. It means the end of all conscious, rational, morally responsible conduct of life, and a voluntary surrender to what the *Bardo Thödol* calls "karmic illusion." Karmic illusion springs from belief in a visionary world of an extremely irrational nature, which neither accords with nor derives from our rational judgments but is the exclusive product of uninhibited imagination. It is sheer dream or "fantasy," and every well-meaning person will instantly caution us against it; nor indeed can one see at first sight what is the difference between fantasies of this kind and the phantasmagoria of a lunatic. Very often only a slight *abaissement du niveau mental* is needed to unleash this world of illusion. The terror and darkness of this moment has its equivalent in the experiences described in the opening sections of the *Sidpa Bardo*. But the contents of this *Bardo* also reveal the archetypes, the karmic images which appear first in their terrifying form. The *Chönyid* state is equivalent to a deliberately induced psychosis.

One often hears and reads about the dangers of yoga, particularly of the ill-reputed *kundalini* yoga. The deliberately induced psychotic state, which in certain unstable individuals might easily lead to a real psychosis, is a danger that needs to be taken very seriously indeed. These things really are dangerous and ought not to be meddled with in our typically Western way. It is a meddling with fate, which strikes at the very roots of human existence and can let loose a flood of sufferings of which no sane person ever dreamed. These sufferings correspond to the hellish torments of the *Chönyid* state, described in the text as follows:

> Then the Lord of Death will place round thy neck a rope and drag thee along; he will cut off thy head, tear out thy heart, pull out thy intestines, lick up thy brain, drink thy blood, eat thy flesh, and gnaw thy bones; but thou wilt be incapable of dying. Even when thy body is hacked to pieces, it will revive again. The repeated hacking will cause intense pain and torture.

These tortures aptly describe the real nature of the danger: it is a disintegration of the wholeness of the *Bardo* body, which is a kind of "subtle body" constituting the visible envelope of the psychic self in the after-death state. The psychological equivalent of this dismemberment is psychic dissociation. In its deleterious form it would be schizophrenia (split mind). This most common of all mental illnesses consists essentially in a marked *abaissement du niveau mental* which abolishes the normal checks imposed by the conscious mind and thus gives unlimited scope to the play of the unconscious "dominants."

The transition, then, from the *Sidpa* state to the *Chönyid* state is a dangerous reversal of the aims and intentions of the conscious mind. It is a sacrifice of the ego's stability and a surrender to the extreme uncertainty of what must seem like a chaotic riot of phantasmal forms. When Freud coined the phrase that the ego was "the true seat of anxiety," he was giving voice to a very true and profound intuition. Fear of self-sacrifice lurks deep in every ego, and this fear is often only the precariously controlled demand of the unconscious forces to burst out in full strength. No one who strives for selfhood (individuation) is spared this dangerous passage, for that which is feared also belongs to the wholeness of the self—the sub-human, or supra-human, world of psychic "dominants" from which the ego originally emancipated itself with enormous effort, and then only partially, for the sake of a more or less illusory freedom. This liberation is certainly a very necessary and very heroic undertaking, but it represents nothing final: it is merely the creation of a *subject*, who, in order to find fulfilment, has still to be confronted by an *object*. This, at first sight, would appear to be the world, which is swelled out with projections for that very purpose. Here we seek and find our difficulties, here we seek and find our enemy, here we seek and find what is dear and precious to us; and it is comforting to know that all evil and all good is to be found out there, in the visible object, where it can be conquered, punished, destroyed, or enjoyed. But nature herself does not allow this paradisal state of innocence to continue for ever. There are, and always have been, those who cannot help but see that the world and its experiences are in the nature of a symbol, and that it really reflects something that lies hidden in the subject himself, in his own transubjective reality. It is from this profound intuition, according to lamaist doctrine, that the *Chönyid* state derives its true meaning, which is why the *Chönyid Bardo* is entitled "The *Bardo* of the Experiencing of Reality."

The reality experienced in the *Chönyid* state is, as the last section of the corresponding *Bardo* teaches, the reality of thought. The "thought-forms" appear as realities, fantasy takes on real form, and the terrifying dream evoked by karma and played out by the unconscious "dominants" begins. The first to appear (if we read the text backwards) is the all-destroying God of Death, the epitome of all terrors; he is followed by the twenty-eight "power-holding" and sinister goddesses and the fifty-eight "blood-drinking" goddesses. In spite of their demonic aspect, which appears as a confusing chaos of terrifying attributes and monstrosities, a certain order is already discernible. We find that there are companies of gods and goddesses who are arranged according to the four directions and are distinguished by typical mystic colours. It gradually becomes clearer that all these deities are organized into mandalas, or circles, containing a cross of the four colours. The colours are coordinated with the four aspects of wisdom:

(1) White = the light-path of the mirror-like wisdom;
(2) Yellow = the light-path of the wisdom of equality;
(3) Red = the light-path of the discriminative wisdom;
(4) Green = the light-path of the all-performing wisdom.

On a higher level of insight, the dead man knows that the real thought-forms all emanate from himself, and that the four light-paths of wisdom which appear before him are the radiations of his own psychic faculties. This takes us straight to the psychology of the lamaistic mandala, which I have already discussed in the book I brought out with the late Richard Wilhelm, *The Secret of the Golden Flower*.

Continuing our ascent backwards through the region of the *Chönyid Bardo*, we come finally to the vision of the Four Great Ones: the green Amogha-Siddhi, the red Amitābha, the yellow Ratna-Sambhava, and the white Vajra-Sattva. The ascent ends with the effulgent blue light of the *Dharmadhātu*, the Buddha-body, which glows in the midst of the mandala from the heart of Vairochana.

With this final vision the karmic illusions cease; consciousness, weaned away from all form and from all attachment to objects, returns to the timeless, inchoate state of the *Dharmakāya*. Thus (reading backwards) the *Chikhai* state, which appeared at the moment of death, is reached.

I think these few hints will suffice to give the attentive reader some idea of the psychology of the *Bardo Thödol*. The book describes a way of initiation in reverse, which, unlike the eschatological expectations of Christianity, prepares the soul for a descent into physical being. The thoroughly intellectualistic and rationalistic worldly-mindedness of the European makes it advisable for us to reverse the sequence of the *Bardo Thödol* and to regard it as an account of Eastern initiation experiences, though one is perfectly free, if one chooses, to substitute Christian symbols for the gods of the *Chönyid Bardo*. At any rate, the sequence of events as I have described it offers a close parallel to the phenomenology of the European unconscious when it is undergoing an "initiation process," that is to say, when it is being analysed. The transformation of the unconscious that occurs under

analysis makes it the natural analogue of the religious initiation ceremonies, which do, however, differ in principle from the natural process in that they forestall the natural course of development and
substitute for the spontaneous production of symbols a deliberately
selected set of symbols prescribed by tradition. We can see this in the
Exercitia of Ignatius Loyola, or in the yoga meditations of the Buddhists and Tantrists.

The reversal of the order of the chapters, which I have suggested here as an aid to understanding, in no way accords with the
original intention of the *Bardo Thödol.* Nor is the psychological use
we make of it anything but a secondary intention, though one that is
possibly sanctioned by lamaist custom. The real purpose of this singular book is the attempt, which must seem very strange to the educated
European of the twentieth century, to enlighten the dead on their
journey through the regions of the *Bardo.* The Catholic Church is the
only place in the world of the white man where any provision is made
for the souls of the departed. Inside the Protestant camp, with its
world-affirming optimism, we only find a few mediumistic "rescue
circles," whose main concern is to make the dead aware of the fact
that they *are* dead. But, generally speaking, we have nothing in the
West that is in any way comparable to the *Bardo Thödol,* except for
certain secret writings which are inaccessible to the wider public and
to the ordinary scientist. According to tradition, the *Bardo Thödol,*
too, seems to have been included among the "hidden" books, as Dr.
Evans-Wentz makes clear in his Introduction. As such, it forms a
special chapter in the magical "cure of the soul" which extends even
beyond death. This cult of the dead is rationally based on the belief in
the supra-temporality of the soul, but its irrational basis is to be found
in the psychological need of the living to do something for the departed. This is an elementary need which forces itself upon even the
most "enlightened" individuals when faced by the death of relatives
and friends. That is why, enlightenment or no enlightenment, we
still have all manner of ceremonies for the dead. If Lenin had to
submit to being embalmed and put on show in a sumptuous mauso-
leum like an Egyptian pharaoh, we may be quite sure it was not
because his followers believed in the resurrection of the body. Apart,
however, from the Masses said for the soul in the Catholic Church,
the provisions we make for the dead are rudimentary and on the
lowest level, not because we cannot convince ourselves of the soul's

immortality, but because we have rationalized the above-mentioned psychological need out of existence. We behave as if we did not have this need, and because we cannot believe in a life after death we prefer to do nothing about it. Simpler-minded people follow their own feelings, and, as in Italy, build themselves funeral monuments of gruesome beauty. The Catholic Masses for the soul are on a level considerably above this, because they are expressly intended for the psychic welfare of the deceased and are not a mere gratification of lachrymose sentiments. But the highest application of spiritual effort on behalf of the departed is surely to be found in the instructions of the *Bardo Thödol*. They are so detailed and thoroughly adapted to the apparent changes in the dead man's condition that every serious-minded reader must ask himself whether these wise old lamas might not, after all, have caught a glimpse of the fourth dimension and twitched the veil from the greatest of life's secrets.

Even if the truth should prove to be a disappointment, one almost feels tempted to concede at least some measure of reality to the vision of life in the *Bardo*. At any rate, it is unexpectedly original, if nothing else, to find the after-death state, of which our religious imagination has formed the most grandiose conceptions, painted in lurid colours as a terrifying dream-state of a progressively degenerative character. The supreme vision comes not at the end of the *Bardo*, but right at the beginning, at the moment of death; what happens afterward is an ever-deepening descent into illusion and obscuration, down to the ultimate degradation of new physical birth. The spiritual climax is reached at the moment when life ends. Human life, therefore, is the vehicle of the highest perfection it is possible to attain; it alone generates the karma that makes it possible for the dead man to abide in the perpetual light of the Voidness without clinging to any object, and thus to rest on the hub of the wheel of rebirth, freed from all illusion of genesis and decay. Life in the *Bardo* brings no eternal rewards or punishments, but merely a descent into a new life which shall bear the individual nearer to his final goal. But this eschatological goal is what he himself brings to birth as the last and highest fruit of the labours and aspirations of earthly existence. This view is not only lofty, it is manly and heroic.

The degenerative character of *Bardo* life is corroborated by the spiritualistic literature of the West, which again and again gives one a sickening impression of the utter inanity and banality of communications from the "spirit world." The scientific mind does not hesitate to explain these reports as emanations from the unconscious of the mediums and of those taking part in the séance, and even to extend this explanation to the description of the Hereafter given in the Tibetan Book of the Dead. And it is an undeniable fact that the whole book is created out of the archetypal contents of the unconscious. Behind these there lie—and in this our Western reason is quite right —no physical or metaphysical realities, but "merely" the reality of psychic facts, the data of psychic experience. Now whether a thing is "given" subjectively or objectively, the fact remains that it *is*. The *Bardo Thödol* says no more than this, for its five Dhyāni-Buddhas are themselves no more than psychic data. That is just what the dead man has to recognize, if it has not already become clear to him during life that his own psychic self and the giver of all data are one and the same. The world of gods and spirits is truly "nothing but" the collective unconscious inside me. To turn this sentence round so that it reads "The collective unconscious is the world of gods and spirits outside me," no intellectual acrobatics are needed, but a whole human lifetime, perhaps even many lifetimes of increasing completeness. Notice that I do not say "of increasing perfection," because those who are "perfect" make another kind of discovery altogether.

The *Bardo Thödol* began by being a "closed" book, and so it has remained, no matter what kind of commentaries may be written upon it. For it is a book that will only open itself to spiritual understanding, and this is a capacity which no man is born with, but which he can only acquire through special training and special experience. It is good that such to all intents and purposes "useless" books exist. They are meant for those "queer folk" who no longer set much store by the uses, aims, and meaning of present-day "civilization."

Notes

1. [Originally published as "Psychologischer Kommentar zum Bardo Thödol" (preceded by an "Einführung," partially translated in the first two pars. here), in *Das Tibetanische Totenbuch*, translated into German by Louise Göpfert-March (Zurich, 1935). As ultimately revised for the 5th (revised and expanded) Swiss edition (1953), the commentary was translated by R. F. C. Hull for publication in the 3rd (revised and expanded) English edition (the original) of *The Tibetan Book of the Dead, or*

The After-Death Experience on the "Bardo" Plane, according to Lama Kazi Dawa-Samdup's English rendering, edited by W. Y. Evans-Wentz, with foreword by Sir John Woodroffe (London and New York, 1957). With only minor alterations, it is the translation presented here.—EDITORS.]

2. [German philosopher and sociologist (1874–1928) working mainly in the field of values.—EDITORS.]

Part Two
JUNG AND HISAMATSU

Shin'ichi Hisamatsu (1889–1980)

A leading disciple of Kitaro Nishida, Hisamatsu became the foremost Zen philosopher of contemporary Japan. He was Professor of Buddhism at Kyoto University. More than a scholar of Buddhism, however, Hisamatsu had a profound *satori* experience. Hisamatsu was thus a living embodiment of Zen spirit, and yet also a reformer of traditional Zen in Japan. He was an excellent calligrapher, a tea master, and a poet. Hisamatsu's publications include *Zen and the Fine Arts*, Kodansha International, 1975, "Memories of My Academic Life," *The Eastern Buddhist*, Vol. XVIII, No. 1, 1985. See also Masao Abe, "Hisamatsu's Philosophy of Awakening," *The Eastern Buddhist*, Vol. XIV, No. 1, 1981, pp. 26–28.

EDITORS' COMMENTS

On May 16, 1958, Shin'ichi Hisamatsu, Zen scholar and Professor of Buddhism at Kyoto University, visited C.G. Jung at his home in Küsnacht, Switzerland.[1] With the help of an interpreter, Kōichi Tsujimura, they discussed the relationship of Jung's psychology to Zen. Specifically, their conversation centered on Jung's notion of Self and the Zen notion of "No Mind," as well as their respective views on human suffering and its alleviation. The content of this conversation is reprinted here in a new English translation done by Professor Isshi Yamada, in cooperation with Daniel J. Meckel. The reader will find the text both intriguing and frustrating, as both Jung and Hisamatsu clearly struggled to reach some degree of mutual understanding, an understanding which was hindered by enormous differences of language and culture.

The history of this text itself is an interesting one. Transcriptions of the conversation were compiled by Tsujimura (in Japanese) and by Jung's secretary, Frau Aniela Jaffé (in German). The Japanese text was subsequently published in *Fushin*, a magazine of Hisamatsu's Zen group, with an additional commentary by Hisamatsu (also reprinted here in new translation). In 1960, Koji Sato, the editor of *Psychologia*, a Japanese journal (published in English), asked Jung to revise an English translation of the Japanese text for publication. Jung refused. In a letter to the translator, he wrote: "I am sorry to say that your plan of publishing Dr. Hisamatsu's interview with me in the form of a protocol is a most delicate and correspondingly dangerous procedure, with which I can hardly consent." Jung explained that a satisfactory mutual understanding had not been reached in the course of their brief encounter. Based on the limitations both of his own knowledge of Zen and of Hisamatsu's knowledge of Western psychology, Jung argued that a good deal more groundwork needed to be done before a thorough understanding could occur. Jung's letter is reprinted in this volume.

After Jung's death, Frau Jaffé sent a copy of the German manuscript to Hisamatsu. It was translated into Japanese by Tsujimura, an expert in German philosophy, and published in the first volume of a collection of Hisamatsu's work. A second English translation was also published in *Psychologia*.[2] The Japanese translation was clearly the best and most reliable. From it was done the new English translation which appears in this volume. This translation was checked and revised by Masao Abe and Richard DeMartino.

A number of articles by Zen scholars followed the first publication of the Jung-Hisamatsu conversation. Among them were a brief commentary by Hisamatsu, a symposium held between several philosophers and psychologists of the Kyoto school, and an essay by Professor Masao Abe. All of these texts are presented here in revised form.

Notes

1. For more information about Hisamatsu see p. 100.
2. The conversation appeared under the title "On the Unconscious, the Self, and the Therapy: A Dialogue," in *Psychologia*, Vol. 11, 1968, pp. 25–32.

Self and Liberation:

A Dialogue Between
Carl G. Jung and Shin'ichi Hisamatsu

Hisamatsu: I have been in the United States, where psychoanalysis has become so popular, and I have spoken with many psychoanalysts. It is a great pleasure for me to have this opportunity to meet and speak with you, the one who has so uniquely developed that science. Now I wish to hear the views of Professor Jung on the current status of psychoanalysis.

Jung: Will you please first give me your own views on psychoanalysis, so that I know exactly what to talk about in response to your question? The Oriental language is greatly different from our Occidental language of thought. In India, I spoke with many Indian philosophers and found it necessary to first explore their thinking before answering their questions. If I failed to do this and simply surmised the nature of their questions, proceeding according to my own conjecture, I often missed the point of their thoughts.

Hisamatsu: I am not a specialist in psychoanalysis. So first I wish to know the ultimate and final point of psychoanalysis and then compare it with Zen.

Jung: That's fine. But as you know, Zen is a philosophy and I am a psychologist. Please take that into consideration.

Hisamatsu: Zen can be said to be a philosophy in a sense. But it is quite different from ordinary philosophy which depends upon human intellectual activity. Therefore we can also say that Zen is not a philosophy. Zen is a philosophy and a religion at the same time. Yet it is not an ordinary religion, it is a "religion-and-philosophy."

103

Jung: I must ask you the following questions so that I may clearly understand your thought and respond to it appropriately. Does Professor Hisamatsu want to know how I respond, from the standpoint of a psychologist, to the goals and challenges which Zen presents to us? The central issue in both Zen and psychology is the same. In Zen, is it not the question of the way in which the human being is related to "No Mind"?

Hisamatsu: There have been many different interpretations of "No Mind." Therefore it is necessary to have a genuine and strictly Zen definition of "No Mind." This is very important. How does Professor Jung understand "No Mind"?

Jung: It is the "unknown." But it is the unknown which excites and disturbs me psychically; it is the unknown which influences me positively or negatively. I am aware *that* it is, but I don't know *what* it is.

Hisamatsu: Is this "unknown" the same as the "unconscious"— I mean the collective unconscious—or does it differ from the unconscious?

Jung: The "unknown" disturbs me or influences me in certain specific ways, otherwise I would not be able to talk about it. For example, many times I have felt that a personal memory is disturbing or influencing me, yet I also have dreams, images, and fantasies which are not derived from the subjective, but have a universal character. For instance, the image which I have of my father is a personal image. But if this image has a religious character, then it is no longer connected only with the personal.

Hisamatsu: Is the non-personal unconscious a fundamental and original unconscious? In other words, is this non-personal unconscious that which you call the "collective unconscious"? And is this the most fundamental, or is there anything which is more fundamental?

Jung: The "personal unconscious" comes into existence in the course of our life through experiences, the memories of which I usually expel and suppress. Another unconscious—namely the collective unconscious—is inherent and universal to all humans. My collective unconscious is the same as yours, even though you were born in Japan and I here in Europe.

Hisamatsu: Is the collective unconscious, then, universal and suprapersonal.

Jung: All one can say about the collective unconscious is that it is common to all instinctive psychic reactions. This commonality can be found everywhere. For instance, the very possibility of our speaking to each other intellectually is based on this common ground. Otherwise, you would be so different from me that we could not understand each other.

Hisamatsu: In fairy tales there is a variety of joys and sorrows. Do they all emerge from within the collective unconscious?

Jung: I will give you an example: when you study a child or a very primitive man, each, of course, has a certain degree of consciousness. Yet, the child who cannot yet say "I," for instance, remains in a universal psychic state, common to all children. This is the universal state common to all human beings prior to attaining consciousness. Consciousness emerges in the process of individual development and [collective] history. It is experience. The development of psyche in history is recapitulated in the development of the individual. In the case of the child, consciousness develops out of a collective unconscious state. An instinctive life of worries, joys, pains, hate, and love exists before consciousness in the proper sense develops. These are already recognized in animals and are connected with the essence of the unconscious. They are instinctive activities which can be observed in animals. Probably one can say that the issues surrounding the so-called *kleśa* concern the various aspects and symptoms of the unconscious.

Hisamatsu: From our point of view, the *kleśa* belong, rather, to the sphere of consciousness.

Jung: Of course, consciousness is necessary. Without it, we

could not even be sure that such things exist at all. The question, for us, is whether or not it is consciousness that produces *kleśa*. The answer is no; consciousness is rather the victim of *kleśa*. Passions are already there, before the presence of consciousness. One cannot ask an angry animal if it is angry; the animal is the victim of its anger. It is the anger that has seized the animal, not the animal who has seized the anger.

Hisamatsu: From an ordinary point of view, *kleśa* are thought to belong to consciousness, but in what way is this area of consciousness related to the unconscious?

Jung: I understand your question to be: how is the unconscious related to consciousness? Is that what you want to know? I cannot give you a definite answer for this. Based on our experience, we acknowledge that consciousness emerges from the unconscious. This can be observed in children, primitive people and other cases. I recognize this as a physician when I have to treat a patient who is seized by the unconscious. The unconscious is like a terrain where there are mountains, lakes and forests, but it is night and nothing can be seen. Suppose a fire is kindled in a certain spot, then suddenly you can see what is there: mountains, lakes, forests, and so on. That fire is consciousness.

Hisamatsu: Now then, which is our True Self, the unconscious or consciousness? Which one is called "True Self" or "Self"?

Jung: Consciousness calls itself "I" (*ich*), while the Self (*Selbst*) is not "I" at all. The Self is the whole, because personality—you as the whole—consists of consciousness and the unconscious. It is the whole or, in other words, the "Self." But I know only consciousness; the unconscious remains unknown to me.

Hisamatsu: According to your view, the "Self" is the whole. From this the question follows: Is "I-consciousness" different from "Self-consciousness" or not?

Jung: In ordinary usage, people say "self-consciousness," but psychologically this is only "I-consciousness." The Self is unknown, for it indicates the whole, that is, consciousness and the unconscious. The conscious part of a person is none other than you, and moreover it is the person you know. The unconscious part of the person, that is to say, the person as unconscious, is also none other than you. And moreover, it is the person whom you do not know. The Self of a man is indescribable because only one-third or perhaps two-thirds of it enters into experience, and because that which does enter into experience belongs to the "I." What is known is not the entirety of the Self. In essence, "self-consciousness," in ordinary usage, psychologically means consciousness as *ego*. The Self is more than the *ego*.

Hisamatsu: What? The self cannot be known?

Jung: Perhaps only one half of it is known, and that is the *ego*. The *ego* is half of the Self.

Hisamatsu: Is the way in which one does not know this "unknown" [Self] the same as the way in which one does not know the "unconscious"?

Jung: It is practically the same. I don't know what is in it. I am quite unconscious of it.

Hisamatsu: Is that which we call "I," in everyday life, really the *ego*, which has many and various emotions? The ordinary "I" belongs to the sphere of consciousness. How is this ordinary "I" related to the fundamental and unknown self? What place does the *ego* have in the personality as a whole?

Jung: The *ego* is like a light in the darkness of night.

Hisamatsu: In the case of mental illness, the patient cannot escape deep suffering. To relieve the patient of his suffering is probably considered to be the therapy. By such therapy, the patient is brought to a state in which there is no suffering. If this release is the essence of therapy, then how is therapy related to the fundamental unconscious?

Jung: When the sickness is caused by things of which we are not conscious, there exists the possibility of cure through making the causes conscious. The cause, however, does not always exist within the unconscious. Rather, there are also a fair number of cases in which the various symptoms indicate the existence of conscious causes. I will give you an example: there was a man who had lost his ordinary consciousness, so to speak. He became only dimly conscious or, one may say, half-conscious, and it was as though he had lost his capacity for judgment. The cause was that his wife had given birth to a child who was not his own. But he was not conscious of this fact. As a result, his consciousness was confused and he became abnormal. Eventually he began chasing after an elderly woman. This happened because he had lost discretion. But this lack of discretion was not the fundamental cause of his suffering. He was not conscious of the fact which generated his suffering. In his case, the treatment was to reveal to him that his wife had been unfaithful.

Hisamatsu: What will happen to him when he comes to know clearly that his child is not his own? Is it not quite possible that once he knows this fact, he will suffer in another way? Does the treatment lie in exposing the various causes of suffering?

Jung: In this case, yes, but not in all cases. For example, sometimes the causes of the suffering are already known to the patient, such as a relationship [of discord] between himself and his mother or father. Both he and those around him are aware of the causes. What they do not know are the kinds of influences which the discord has on the patient's personality, which attitude the patient should have toward these things, and how he should respond. Most patients complain either that the father or the mother is responsible for the illness. But as a physician, the question is how to treat the patient to enable him to determine his own attitude. The parents' responsibility relates to the origin of the illness. The most important problem in treatment relates to its aim. And this problem leads ultimately to the question: "What is the meaning of my life?"

Hisamatsu: There are many worries in our ordinary existence. The essence of cure is liberation from worries. Now then, what sorts of changes in the sphere of the unconscious correspond to this liberation?

Jung: It has to do with one's conscious attitude. What matters most of all is the attitude that I hold toward such worries and the measures I take in response to them. Suppose that, for such and such a reason, I feel distressed and sad. If I feel that "this is all too much to bear and I really can't stand it," then my worries increase all the more. But if one can say, "Well, there is good and bad in this world, and every day has its mishaps; the sun cannot always shine; there also are rainy days and snowy days," then his worries will diminish. If one can assume an objective attitude, namely, if he can accept his worries, then he has discovered the attitude by which he can liberate himself from neurotic, pathological worries. If one can accept one's worries, they are no longer so painful.

Hisamatsu: Fear of death is a universal suffering which is common to everyone. How can this fear be treated with psychotherapy?

Jung: There is no universal rule or method. Each case is different. People fear death for a variety of reasons, and the particular treatment will be determined by those reasons. For example, if I experience anxiety about death, the cause may be quite different from that of a young, healthy man's anxiety. Why is the latter afraid of death? He has no reason at all. Nevertheless, he is afraid. As such, the situation varies from case to case. There is no universal method of cure. We must consider each case individually. The old man's anxiety about death and the young man's anxiety must be treated in entirely different ways.

Hisamatsu: I have taken the fear of death only as an example, because death is unavoidable for everyone. There are so many different worries and we must live most of the time in suffering. Now what I would like to ask is this: Is it possible or not for a human being to discard all of his suffering at a stroke, and can this be achieved by psychotherapy?

Jung: How can such a method be possible? A method which enables us to free ourselves from suffering itself?

Hisamatsu: Is there no universally applicable treatment for suffering?

Jung: Is there really such a method by which we can free ourselves from suffering itself?

Hisamatsu: Doesn't psychotherapy emancipate us from suffering all at once?

Jung: Liberate man from suffering itself? What we are trying to do is to reduce human suffering. Still some suffering remains. If the beautiful and wonderful do not appear in contrast to the ugly and troublesome, then they will disappear. Schopenhauer, the German philosopher, once said, "Happiness is the cessation of suffering." We need suffering. Without it, life is no longer interesting. Therefore, even psychotherapy has no right to meddle in the [philosophical] question of the ultimate meaning of human suffering. Should this be done, people would be dissatisfied.

Hisamatsu: Suffering is, in a way, necessary to human life. This is true. Nevertheless, within man is a genuine wish to be liberated from suffering itself.

Jung: Of course, when there is an excess of suffering, it is the physician's duty to reduce it. But it is not the physician's duty to completely eradicate suffering.

Hisamatsu: But in the case of physical illness, the doctor attempts to release the patient from sickness and to eradicate sickness from the human world. Is this not the same in the case of mental illness?

Jung: Of course, it is the same.

Hisamatsu: The great messengers of religious truth, such as Christ or Buddha, all say that we human beings share equally in universal suffering—suffering related to death, or suffering related to sin, for example. The intention of these religious founders was to liberate human beings from fundamental suffering. Is it really possible that such great freedom can be achieved by psychotherapy?

Jung: It is not inconceivable, if you treat suffering not as an individual sickness, but as an impersonal occurrence, such as a disaster or an evil. Psychotherapy, for example, is concerned with making the patient understand that his sufferings have non-personal aspects, and helping him become conscious of the causal sequence. In many cases, psychotherapy's concern is to release him from unnecessary suffering caused by the passions, or *kleśa*. He is entangled in the *kleśa*, and can be liberated from them through inner wisdom. The aim of psychotherapy is exactly the same as that of Buddhism.

Hisamatsu: The essential point of this liberation is how we can be awakened to our Original Self. The Original Self is the self which is no longer bound by a myriad of things. To attain this self is the essential point of freedom. It is necessary, therefore, to release oneself even from the collective unconscious and the bondage which derives from it.

Jung: If one is caught in a myriad of things and thus bound within it, this is because he is caught within the collective unconscious at the same time. He can be freed only when he is liberated from both of them. One person may be dragged along more by the unconscious, another by things. In short, through liberation, man must be brought to a point where he is free from the compulsion to chase after a myriad of things or from being controlled by the collective unconscious. Both are fundamentally the same: *Nirvāṇa*.

Hisamatsu: In what you have just said about the unconscious, Professor Jung, do you mean that the collective unconscious is something from which, in its nature, we can free ourselves?

Jung: Yes it is.

Hisamatsu: What we generally call "self" is the same as the self [*Selbst*] characterized by you, Professor Jung. But it is only after the emancipation of this self that the "Original Self" of Zen emerges. It is the True Self described in Zen as the Self which is realized in absolute emancipation and is without dependence on anything. [*dokudatsu mue*]

Jung: Your "self" means something like *kleśa* in the *Yoga Sūtra*.

On the contrary, my "Self" corresponds to *Ātman* or *Puruṣa*. The personal *Ātman* corresponds to the Self. The individual *Ātman* is, at the same time, a super-individual *Ātman*. In other words, my "self" is at the same time "Self itself" [non-individual Self]. According to my terminology, "Self" is the counterpart who works against "ego." What you call "self" is for me "ego." And what I call "Self" is the whole, and *Ātman*.

Hisamatsu: Etymologically, "Original Self" corresponds to *Ātman*. But what we call *Ātman* in its ordinary usage implies some substantial essence and is not what I call True Self. The True Self has no substance. The True Self has no form or substance, whatsoever.

Jung: Even though I identify the Self with *Ātman,* this is simply a rough comparison. Because the Oriental way of thinking is different from my way of thinking, the two are not commensurable. I can say that the Self exists and yet does not exist, for I cannot say anything decisively about it. I can only say that the Self seems to me to be bigger than "I." If someone should tell me that *Ātman* has substance or that it has no substance, I can only respond as follows: "You say so, but in fact I do not know what the true *Ātman* is. I only know what people say about the *Ātman*." I can only say that it *is* such and such, and at the same time, that it *is not* such and such.

Hisamatsu: There is neither form nor substance in the True Self of Zen. It is quite different from the ordinary *Ātman*. Zen's True Self has neither spiritual form nor physical shape.

Jung: Even if you say so, I cannot in fact know what I do not know. I cannot know if the Self has various states or not, because I am quite unconscious in these regards. The whole of the human being consists of consciousness and the unconscious. I know no more than that it is possible that this whole can exist in such and such a state. It is possible. But I do not know. Naturally, I can make certain assertions and strenuously maintain various positions regarding metaphysical problems. However, the very act of doing so would reveal that ultimately I do not know.

Hisamatsu: The True Self has no form and no substance. Therefore the True Self can never be bound by a myriad of things. Liberation, the essence of religious freedom, rests on this point. The religious character of Zen lies in this. Ultimately, to become "The Formless Self" [*musō no jiko*] is the essence of Zen. My earlier statement, that Zen is a philosophy and religion at the same time, derives from this.

===

Jung's Commentary on the Conversation:
A Letter to the Original Translator

I am sorry to say that your plan of publishing Dr. Hisamatsu's interview with me in the form of a protocol is a most delicate and correspondingly dangerous procedure, with which I can hardly consent.

Our interview, first of all, suffered intensely from the fact that I am ignorant of the Japanese language. Thus the elucidation of terms was a difficult task. Moreover there is a very considerable difference in the definition of philosophical, i.e. psychological terms between Eastern and Western mentality. I feel a deep uncertainty about terms like "conscious," "unconscious," "collective," "individual," etc., when I am talking to an Eastern mind. I am never certain that we exactly mean the same thing, as our *point de départ* is so very different. I had no chance whatever in my conversation with Dr. Hisamatsu to discuss all these differences.

If one could hope to reach a common understanding which does not only consist in words, but in facts, one would need at least several weeks of careful comparative work, since the question of the different mentalities is far from being thoroughly dealt with up to now. I have only a limited experience of Hindu, Chinese and Japanese mentality. But the little I have experienced in reality has shown me that there is a terrific gap between the Western and Eastern mind, when it comes to the problem of rational understanding. Every word is uncertain. Thus I consider my interview with Dr. Hisamatsu as a mutual sign of good will and as an honest attempt to create a mutual basis of understanding, but I would under no conditions go so far as to assume it to be a sufficient foundation for a valid representation of the Eastern, as well as of the Western views. The indispensable groundwork has not yet been done, in order to reach real understanding. I should go to Japan and study Zen philosophy for at least

114

one year, or Dr. Hisamatsu should go to Switzerland and study my work equally thoroughly. Only under these conditions could we hope for the beginning of a proper understanding.

I am absolutely against increasing the limitless flood of words which already obscures the world. The more there are words, the less there is understanding, and even a million words don't constitute a single fact or form a satisfactory equivalent of one.

I for my part would not dream of claiming a competent view about Zen from the mere exchange of tentative words with Dr. Hisamatsu. I appreciated his visit very highly indeed and am very grateful to him for the trouble he took to enlighten my ignorance. In exchange I tried to give him some very roundabout glimpses of our *point de vue*, without the slightest expectation of transmitting to him a real knowledge of European psychology.

I refrain therefore from correcting your typescript, as there are too many more or less subtle divergences from accuracy. They demand almost a treatise by itself. You would be astonished at how little our knowledge and understanding of Zen is, which I gathered from my talk with Dr. Hisamatsu. That is not his fault, but my incompetence. Yet this is equally true as regards our European psychology of the Unconscious in Dr. Hisamatsu's case. If we really want a satisfactory understanding we are compelled to omit all assumptions and above all the fallacy of the illusion that we can understand each other by mere words. We must be particularly careful to avoid all prejudicial statements based on ignorance, as the world is already full of bias and misapprehension.

Hisamatsu's Commentary
on the Conversation

We in Japan can hardly imagine how many psychoanalysts there are in the United States. They have their own fixed posts in public institutions such as hospitals, schools, and companies. Not only are they very active in the treatment of mental illness, they also enjoy large practices in their own offices, which are found throughout the United States, though patients have to pay rather expensive fees.

In Japan, when we talk about the department of mental illness, we usually think of a place where they treat the abnormal, the insane. In the United States, however, the department of psychoanalysis is a place where they treat the mental and emotional sicknesses of normal men. Recently, owing to the works of D.T. Suzuki, many psychoanalysts have taken a great interest in Zen. During my stay in the United States, I had many talks with these psychoanalysts and also attended their meetings. Having thus come into contact with them, I was compelled to consider the many problems regarding the relationship between psychoanalysis and Zen. Among these issues, the following three are the most important:

(1) The identity and difference between the "unconscious" in psychoanalysis and "No Mind" in Zen.

(2) The identity and difference between the "Self" of psychoanalysis and the "Self" in Zen.

(3) The identity and difference between treatment in psychoanalysis and treatment in Zen.

During my stay in America, I was able to arrive at some tentative positions regarding these issues, but I wished to confirm them by talking with some outstanding authority in the field. This was my purpose in visiting Professor Jung [in Switzerland]. Through the courteous responses of Professor Jung, I was able to reach the following conclusions:

(1) The *unconscious* of psychoanalysis is entirely different from "No Mind" of Zen. In the *unconscious* of psychoanalysis is the *personal unconscious*, deriving from experience, and the non-personal unconscious, namely the *collective unconscious*, which exists prior to individual experience. They are both unknown to the "I." "No Mind" of Zen is, on the contrary, not only known, but most clearly known, as it is called "*Kaku*" (awakening) or "*ryōryō jōchi*" (always clearly comprehending). But this is not a state in which something is merely known. Rather, it is a clear "self awakening in and to itself" that is without a separation between knower and known. "No Mind" is a state in which self is most clearly awakened to itself, such as when we are utterly absorbed in our work.

(2) What is usually called "self" corresponds to ego (*ich*) in psychoanalysis. But *self (Selbst)* is both the ego and the *unconscious*, which excites and disturbs the *ego*, while it is unknown in the depth of the ego. Therefore the self is not identical with the ego. The *self* is made up of the ego plus the *unconscious*. But the "Self" of Zen is not concerned with anything internal or external, as it is called "*dokudatsu mue*" (perfect liberation and non-dependence) or "*muge jizai*" (freedom without obstruction). Rather, it is unbounded self-awakening. Therefore, the "Self" of Zen is neither the *ego* of psychoanalysis, which is excited and disturbed by the *unconscious*, nor is it the self, which is composed of *ego* and unconscious.

(3) In psychoanalysis, treatment entails finding the causes of the individual mental sicknesses within the *unconscious*, and removing them. Therefore, psychoanalysis treats individual disorders separately. But in Zen, as is indicated in the expressions "*do issaikuyaku*" (to deliver from all suffering) and "*kukyō gedatsu*" (ultimate freedom), it is to be awakened to the Self not bound by anything, and to be liberated from all diseases at once. If each disease is treated individually, then when one disease is gone, another disease will come along. Hence, we shall never be delivered from sickness forever. This in itself may be said to be a disease in a very profound sense. It is what I have pointed out as the vicious circle of psychoanalytic therapy. It is the fatal shortcoming of psychoanalytic treatment. The final cure must be achieved by severing the root of all sickness. When I said to Professor Jung that in order to achieve this, it is necessary to deliver oneself from the *collective unconscious* and from the bondage which is derived from the *collective unconscious*, he replied that to the

extent that one is released from the compulsion to chase after things
or from being helplessly dominated by the *unconscious*, the deliverance must be achieved. This is Nirvāṇa. Further, I posed this question: "Can it be said that the *collective unconscious* is such that we can
free ourselves from it?" To this Professor Jung replied very positively, "Yes."

From the standpoint of Zen, this was the appropriate and necessary answer; yet from the psychoanalytic standpoint it was unexpected. During this dialogue, when I asked Professor Jung whether
or not it was possible for the human being to be released from all
suffering at once, twice he exclaimed: "How could that be?" In spite
of this, he later acknowledged *nirvāṇa* as ultimate liberation (*kukyō
gedatsu*) and declared that we can be liberated even from the *collective
unconscious*. One must say that this is an important statement, coming
from a psychoanalyst. If Professor Jung's statement is accurate, it
seems that there is an open passage from psychoanalysis to Zen, and
that the vicious circle of psychoanalysis can be overcome and psychoanalysis itself can advance a step forward. As a result, various new
problems may arise.

*Koji Sato, Hitoshi Kataoka, Richard DeMartino,
Masao Abe, and Hayao Kawai*[1]

What Is the True Self?
A Discussion

Sato: We wish to discuss today the problem, "What is the true self?" Professor Hisamatsu has emphasized the importance of being awakened to the True Self, and he repeated it also during his conversation with Professor Jung.

DeMartino: I read the Japanese translation of Dr. Jung's conversation with Dr. Hisamatsu. Frankly speaking my impression is that, for whatever reasons, Dr. Jung did not really gain an adequate understanding of what Dr. Hisamatsu meant.

Sato: In order to understand each other, they should study each other's point of view for one year at least, as Professor Jung suggested in his letter to Sachi Toyomura, the English translator of the Jung-Hisamatsu dialogue.[2] Or someone who has a good understanding of both sides should work as a bridge.

DeMartino: Since Dr. Hisamatsu is ill and cannot himself attend this discussion today, I think it would be well for us to examine his article "The Characteristics of Oriental Nothingness."[3]

Kataoka: That was originally published in Dr. Hisamatsu's book *Zettai-Shutai Do* (*The Way of the Absolute Subject*), wasn't it?

Abe: Yes. This is one of his best systematic presentations of the Buddhist notion of "Nothingness." After a negative delineation, he turns to a positive delineation and discusses the characteristics of Oriental Nothingness: (a) The "not-a-single-thing" nature, (b) the

119

"like-empty-space" nature, (c) the "mind-in-itself" nature, (d) the "self" nature, (e) the "freedom" nature, and (f) the "creative" nature. These characteristics overlap each other, and one should read through the whole paper if one wishes to grasp it adequately. But the section on "the 'self' nature" will help to develop our discussion.

Sato: Please read some important paragraphs for us, Mr. DeMartino.

DeMartino: "Oriental Nothingness can be said to be Mind in the sense described in the previous section. Even though we say mind, however, it is not such a mind as can be viewed objectively outside of ourselves. That is, it must be such that that Mind is Myself and that I am that Mind. This Mind is not the Mind which is seen, but is, on the contrary, the Mind which sees."

Kataoka: The True Self is this Mind.

DeMartino: "As indicated before, the Mind of which I am speaking is not merely that which is ordinarily called mind, but is the Mind which is itself Buddha." And further, "The Buddha of which I am speaking, however, is not a subject in the sense of transcending and controlling me, but is a subject in the sense that Buddha is I, Myself. While the transcending, controlling Buddha is to be called an objective-subject, it cannot be spoken of as being a pure subject. In contrast to this, the Buddha which is I, Myself, is to be called a subjective-subject, and is a pure, absolute subject." "It is for this reason that, although in Zen it is said that Buddha cannot be known by man and that man should die the Great Death, Zen especially emphasizes the 'Self' nature of Buddha, saying that Buddha is Self, is Self-Mind, is Self-Nature, and the like."

Sato: Then the True Self is at the same time the Mind and the Buddha. I wish to turn the subject of the discussion to the relationship of the Self to consciousness. In the dialogue, Dr. Jung explained the concept of Self in his analytical psychology and Dr. Hisamatsu was surprised to hear that the Self was half-conscious and half-unconscious. Professor Hisamatsu says that the Self is always clearly aware. But I wish to call attention to the sayings of Master Dogen:

"To learn Buddhism is to learn the Self; to learn the Self is to forget the Self." We know that when one is very conscious of oneself, one's behavior becomes rather awkward, and when one is absorbed in one's activities, these activities go smoothly and nicely. How do you think of the relationship of Dogen's forgetting of oneself and the unconscious of Dr. Jung, Mr. Kawai?

Kawai: One of the merits of Dr. Jung consists in the recognition of the positive meaning of the unconscious, I believe. That is, he puts importance on the way of living relying upon the wisdom of the unconscious rather than merely living under the conscious control of the ego. One who lives by the control of the ego looks like a good person, but lacks something important. The evaluation of the unconscious in Jung and Freud is different. Later Freudians said "regression in service of the ego." Jungian psychologists say "ego-function in the service of self-realization." Such a way of thinking is to be compared with the Zen saying that "the bottom of the bucket is fallen off." Merely relying upon the ego-control or ego-consciousness is problematic. The Self in Jungian psychology is rather near to that of Zen. But they do not say "True Self." Zen or philosophy may distinguish true and false; psychology does not.

Sato: Jung's Self is not inborn, but it is an achievement attained by a few people after arduous endeavor. Jung was rather concerned with the middle and later years of life, and the Self also was explained as a problem coming up in these years.

Abe: Jung's idea of the collective unconscious is interesting from the Zen point of view, but there is an essential difference between the Self in Jungian psychology and that of Zen. The Self in Jungian psychology, I understand, consists of the conscious which is called "I" and the unconscious. Now, when Western psychologists, including Jung, discuss the unconscious, they do so from the standpoint of consciousness, namely standing on the side of the conscious and looking at the unconscious. However deep and basic the unconscious may be taken, it is understood as relative to consciousness from the side of consciousness. Jung's so-called "Self" is the whole of such unconsciousness and consciousness which seems to me to have a kind of framework. It is quite different in Zen. Zen does not discuss the unconscious or so-called "No Mind" from the side of consciousness; nor does it stay in the unconscious in Jung's sense. It is the way of Zen to go deep into the unconscious and break through its bottom through *zazen*, seated meditation and struggling with *koan*. Zen asks us to break through the framework of self. True Self in Zen, which Dr. Hisamatsu calls "Formless Self," is none other than the self-awakening which is realized through such breaking-through of the framework of self.

Sato: We will return to the starting point. How will the True Self be conscious, when the bottom is fallen off? Jung, Rogers, and other self-psychologists have taken a phenomenological approach, but in my view, they have not yet gone through.

Abe: Professor Kataoka, will you tell us your view as an expert of Zen?

Kataoka: The way of Zen and the ways of these psychologists are very much different. From the philosophical or logical point of view, the True Self, the true subject cannot be grasped consciously. Kant also affirmed this.

Sato: Not Kant, but Zen!

Kataoka: It cannot be grasped consciously also in Zen. It cannot appear on the usual plane of consciousness. It sees, but is never seen. It thinks, but does not become the object of thought. Such a true subject, however, should be recognized. Master Dogen said: "Think the unthinkable." Zen requires one to think the unthinkable. If one does not accept this, one cannot enter into Zen.

Sato: Dr. Hisamatsu, who emphasizes the clear awareness of the True Self, then, cannot enter into Zen?

Kataoka: *Ryōryō-jōchi* (thoroughly clear ever-present awareness) comes after that. The True Self cannot be grasped by usual consciousness. It needs quite a different way of approach. That is to grasp by becoming one with the undifferentiated whole of the phenomena and the act of consciousness.

Sato: Here again comes Dogen's "To learn the Self is to forget the Self."

Kataoka: To become one is to forget it. To become one with hotness is to forget the hotness. If one becomes sorrow itself, the sorrow fades away. If one becomes consciousness itself, the contents of the consciousness will become *ku* (empty, void).

DeMartino: The term "forget" is not good. Its real meaning is that the ordinary structure of consciousness is broken through. What is meant to become "thoroughly clear ever-present awareness" itself? Here we may again read from Dr. Hisamatsu's article: "But even further, 'No Mind' or 'No Consciousness' is penetratingly clear to a degree which is absolutely impossible in any other state. It does not permit the slightest obscurity of turbidity. It has the absolute clarity of a polished mirror or an autumn moon. Whatever other condition one may speak of, there is no condition in which one is so clearly aware as in that of 'No Mind' or 'No Consciousness,' and there is no time when life is so alive and so ready to burst as in the 'Great Death Itself.' "

Sato: Here we return to our original problem: the True Self, the conscious and the unconscious.

DeMartino: Before the paragraph cited above, Dr. Hisamatsu distinguishes ordinary unconsciousness from what is called in Zen "No Mind": "Whether we speak of Oriental Nothingness as 'No Mind,' 'No Consciousness,' the 'Great Death Itself,' or 'Nirvāna,' it is not the unconsciousness of sleep, fainting, or ordinary death." On the contrary, in his positive delineation Dr. Hisamatsu writes: "Oriental Nothingness is perfectly lucid and clear, is thoroughly clear ever-present awareness, that is, is that of which we are most clearly aware. Although we say 'are clearly aware,' this is not an awareness in which Nothingness is external or objective, different from the one who is aware. This is rather awareness in which subject and object are one. That is, Oriental Nothingness is that awareness of Oneself in which the subject and object of awareness are one and not two."

Kataoka: This thoroughly clear ever-present awareness is awareness which ensues from the No Mind. It is so-called empty wisdom in Buddhism, awareness of the No Mind, Formless Self. Formless Self has no Self. It is, so to speak, No Mind grasped intuitively. The term "forget" is often misunderstood. Soto Zen easily lapses into "silently illuminating Zen," but Dogen's Zen has enlightenment.

Sato: Next, we wish to consider how to represent the True Self in a Schema. We are familiar with such representations in Freud and Jung. How do you think of it, Mr. Abe?

Abe: To forget self in Dogen's saying means body and mind falling off. If we refer to Jung, it is to get rid of the whole Self, conscious and unconscious. Self is always restricted by body and mind, and, through them, by the outer world. When self is active in controlling body and mind, and, through them, controlling the outer world, self is, just in doing so, restricted by them. Self is contradictory in its nature. This contradictory nature of self is the root of human suffering. Body and mind falling off means that self turns into an entirely free and true Self getting rid of its contradiction. We usually as subject look at and act on something as an object. There everything appears to us not as it is, but as it is objectified by us: by our intellect and by our desire. However, for True Self, which is no more restricted nor disturbed by body and mind, everything appears most clearly and lucidly, that is, appears as it is. But this True Self is not apart from our daily life. As Master Rinzai said, "The True person goes in and out from your facial gates [i.e. sense organs]." It is active at every moment of our daily behavior. We used to try, however, to grasp it as something objective from the standpoint of the so-called self as subject; then we lose the original feature. When we get rid of the contradictory nature of self, namely, when we break through the framework of self, the world manifests itself where all appears clear and lucid, mountains as mountains, rivers as rivers, I as I, you as you.

Sato: Then does *ryōryō-jōchi* refer to the object? And is the self forgotten?

Abe: *Ryōryō-jōchi* refers to the awareness of the True Self which goes beyond the subject-object duality, or self-world dichotomy. In the True Self everything appears not as object to us, but as it is. On the basis of the True Self we can see and act on everything in its reality.

DeMartino: But "appear" is not just "appear." It should imply "arising, yet not arising," "appearing, yet not appearing."

Abe: It is precisely this point. My favorite statement of Master Ishin of Seigen is this: "When I had not yet practiced Zen, to me a mountain was a mountain, and water was water; after I got an insight into the truth of Zen through the instruction of a good master, I thought that a mountain was not a mountain, and water was not water; but now that I have really attained to the abode of rest, as before a mountain is just a mountain, and water is just water." An individual thing manifests itself in its total reality in the field of "Nothingness," through the absolute negation, if we follow a philosophical way of thinking. Only in the field of Absolute Nothingness or Non-being, every individual thing manifests itself without harming any reality of each other. The framework of the human self must once be broken through completely. It is characterized as the Great Death. This Great Death is not a state of trance, not a sinking into the unconscious, but turns self into a new self, namely the True Self which has a formless form and is real Self-Awareness.

Kataoka: There are many aspects in Zen which cannot be expressed in concepts.

DeMartino: I may be mistaken, but it seems to me that for Dr. Jung the unconscious is still a kind of "being." Whether the collective unconscious or the personal unconscious, the unconscious is an aspect or dimension of "being" with its own specific contents. With Dr. Erich Fromm, following Freud, the aim of psychoanalysis is, specifically, to make the unconscious conscious. "Where there was Id there shall be ego." For Freud and Fromm as well, therefore, the unconscious—or for Fromm, unconsciousness—is a quality of "being," whether as one part of the personality (Freud) or as a state of unawareness (Fromm). Carl Rogers' concept of the "fully functioning person" is, again, that of an organism with form, that is, with being. Further, for Rogers, every organism has within it its own directional force, of which, I venture to interpolate, it may or may not, in the case of man, be conscious. But whether the human organism is conscious of it or is not conscious of it, the directional force is "there," that is, is in some state of "being," actual or potential, and is positive. The unconscious for Jung is also primarily positive, whereas for Freud it is primarily negative. For Zen, however, the main point is that the entire structure of being, including its unconscious aspect, must radically be broken through. The aim of Zen is not for the unconscious aspect of being—whether personal or collective—to come to consciousness. The aim of Zen is, rather, the breaking-up of the very dualistic structure of consciousness-and-unconsciousness, and of being-and-non-being.

Kawai: The opposition of the unconscious and the conscious belongs to psychological thinking. Only philosophy can go beyond it.

DeMartino: But Jung and Freud, and Fromm also, may be said to have a philosophical aspect to them. Rogers may be a little different, but even he, it seems to me, has a great deal of Dewey's philosophy behind him, consciously or unconsciously. In dealing with the matter of the True Self, that is, of the ultimate nature or reality of Man, the issue, I feel, is not that of psychology versus philosophy. The issue is, rather, can man's True Self—or, if you will, True Being—be actualized or realized within the framework of ordinary, dualistic ego-consciousness, of relative form and formlessness, of relative being and non-being? Zen says it cannot. Satori, or, more precisely, the Great Awakening, in Zen, is the break-up of just this relative, dualistic structure of ego-consciousness-and-being. It is exactly with this dying of the ego to itself (the Great Death), exactly with this falling through of the bottom of the bucket or, in Dogen's phrase, "the falling off of ordinary body-and-mind," that Man awakens to his True Self.

Notes

1. This discussion was originally conducted in Japanese in August 1961, and was translated into English (the present translation) by Koji Sato and

Sachi Toyomura with the cooperation of Richard DeMartino and Masao Abe.

2. Toyomura was the first to translate the transcription of the conversation into English. His translation appeared in *Psychologia*.

3. Shin'ichi Hisamatsu, "The Characteristics of Oriental Nothingness," *Philosophical Studies of Japan*, R. DeMartino (trans.), 1960, Vol. 2, Tokyo: Maruzen.

The Self in Jung and Zen

The most conspicuous difference between Buddhism and Western psychology is perhaps found in their respective treatments of the concept of "self." In Western psychology, the existence of a "self" is generally affirmed; Buddhism denies the existence of an enduring "self" and substitutes instead the concept of *anātman*, "no-self."

In Western spiritual traditions one of the classical examples of the affirmation of an enduring self is Plato's notion of the immortal soul. The basis of the modern Western conception of the self was established by Descartes' *cogito ergo sum*, which led to a dualistic interpretation of mind as thinking substance and matter as extended substance. Christianity, which is not based on human reason but divine revelation, emphasizes self-denial or self-sacrifice in devotion to one's God and fellow human beings. Even so, as a responsible agent in an I-Thou relationship, the human self is affirmed as something essential. Although it is a relatively new scientific discipline, modern Western psychology shares with older Western spiritual traditions the affirmation of the existence of a self.

In ancient India, the Brahmanical tradition propounded the idea of atman or the eternal, unchanging self which is fundamentally identical with Brahman, the ultimate Reality of the universe. The Buddha did not accept this age-old notion of atman and discoursed instead about anātman, no-self. As Walpola Rahula states:

> Buddhism stands unique in the history of human thought in denying the existence of such a Soul, Self, or Atman. According to the teaching of the Buddha, the idea of self is an imaginary, false belief which has no corresponding reality, and it produces harmful thoughts of 'me' and 'mine', selfish desire, craving, attachment, hatred, ill-will, conceit, pride, egoism, and other defilements, impurities and problems. It is the source of all the troubles

in the world from personal conflicts to wars between nations. In short, to this false view can be traced all the evil in the world.[1]

Throughout his life, the Buddha taught the means to remove and destroy such a false view and thereby enlighten human beings.

To those who desire self-preservation after death, the Buddhist notion of no-self may sound not only strange but frightening. This was true even for the ancient Indians who lived in the time of the Buddha. A bhikkhu once asked the Buddha: "Sir, is there a case where one is tormented when something permanent within oneself is not found?" Not unaware of such fear, the Buddha answered, "Yes, bhikkhu, there is." Elsewhere the Buddha says: "O bhikkhus, this idea that I may not be, I may not have, is frightening to the uninstructed worldling."[2] Nevertheless, the Buddha preached the notion of no-self tirelessly until his death, simply because the doctrine is so essential to his teaching: to emancipate human beings from suffering and to awaken them to the fundamental reality of human existence.

To properly understand the Buddhist notion of no-self, it would be helpful to consider the following five points:

First, the doctrine of no-self is the natural result of, or the corollary to, the analysis of the five skandhas or five aggregates, that is, matter, sensation, perception, mental formations, and consciousness. According to Buddhism, human beings are composed of these five aggregates and nothing more.[3]

Second, the notion of no-self, that is, the notion of no substantial unchanging own-being, is applied not only to human beings, but also to all beings. This is why one of the three essentials peculiar to Buddhism is that "all dharmas [i.e., all entities] are without self." Thus, not only conditioned, relative things, but also unconditioned, absolute things are understood to be without self, without their own-being. Accordingly, not only samsara, but also nirvana, not only delusion, but also enlightenment, are without own-being. Neither relative nor absolute things are self-existing and independent.

Third, the notion of no-self entails, therefore, the denial of one absolute God who is self-existing, and instead forwards the doctrine of dependent origination. That is, in Buddhism, nothing whatever is independent or self-existing; everything is dependent on everything else. Thus, all unconditioned, absolute, and eternal entities such as

Buddha or the state of nirvana co-arise and co-cease with all conditioned, relative, and temporal entities, such as living beings or the state of samsara.

Fourth, in accordance with these teachings, the ultimate in Buddhism is neither conditioned nor unconditioned, neither relative nor absolute, neither temporal nor eternal. Therefore, the Buddhist ultimate is called *śūnyatā,* that is, "Emptiness." It is also called the "Middle Way," because it is neither an eternalist view which insists on the existence of an unchanging eternal entity as the ultimate, nor an annihilationist view which maintains that everything is null and void.

Fifth, if one clearly understands that the Buddhist notion of no-self is essentially connected with its doctrine of dependent origination and *śūnyatā* or Emptiness, one may also naturally understand that the Buddhist notion of no-self does not signify the mere lack or absence of self, as an annihilationist may suggest, but rather constitutes a standpoint which is beyond both the eternalist view of self and the nihilistic view of no-self. This is forcefully illustrated by the Buddha himself when he answered with silence both the questions "Is there a self?" and "Is there no-self?" Keeping silence to both the affirmative and negative forms of the question concerning the "self," the Buddha profoundly expressed the ultimate Reality of humanity. His silence itself does not indicate an agnostic position, but is a striking presence of the true nature of human being which is beyond affirmation and negation.

In the light of these five points, I hope it is now clear that the Buddhist notion of no-self does not signify a mere negation of the existence of the self, but rather signifies a realization of human existence which is neither self nor no-self. Since the original human nature cannot be characterized as self or no-self, it is called No-self. Therefore, No-self represents nothing but the true nature or true Self of humanity which cannot be conceptualized at all and is beyond self and no-self.

In the Buddhist tradition, Zen most clearly and vividly emphasizes that the Buddhist notion of No-self is nothing but true Self. Rinzai's phrase, the "true person of no rank" serves as an example. "No rank" implies freedom from any conceptualized definition of human being. Thus the "true person of no rank" signifies the "true person" who cannot be characterized either by self or no-self. "True person of no rank" is identical with the true nature of human being presenting itself in the silence of the Buddha. Unlike the Buddha who emphasizes meditation, however, Rinzai is an active and dynamic Zen master, directly displaying his own "true Self" while demanding his disciples to actively demonstrate this "true Self" in themselves. The following exchange vividly illustrates this dynamic character:

> One day Rinzai gave this sermon: "There is the true person of no rank in the mass of naked flesh, who goes in and out from your facial gates [i.e., sense organs]. Those who have not testified [to the fact], look! look!"
> A monk came forward and asked, "Who is this true person of no rank?"
> Rinzai came down from his chair and, taking hold of the monk by the throat, said, "Speak! Speak!"
> The monk hesitated.
> Rinzai let go his hold and said, "What a worthless dirt-stick this is!"[4]

In this exchange, "true person of no rank" represents a living reality functioning through our physical body. Furthermore, Rinzai is asking his audience to notice the living reality functioning in himself by saying "Look! Look!" and demanding from the monk a demonstration of his own true nature, taking him by the throat and saying "Speak! Speak!" Zen does not intend to provide an explanation or interpretation of the nature of true Self, but rather to precipitate a direct and immediate testimony or demonstration of it through a dynamic encounter between master and disciple.

II

In seeking to point out the similarities and dissimilarities between modern Western psychology and Buddhism, especially Zen, with regard to their understanding of the concept of the "self," let us examine a dialogue between Shin'ichi Hisamatsu (1889–1980) and Carl Gustav Jung (1875–1961).

Shin'ichi Hisamatsu was a professor of Buddhism at Kyoto University. He is regarded as one of the outstanding Zen thinkers of contemporary Japan. But Hisamatsu was also a Zen layman who had attained a very profound, clear-cut Zen awakening, and his subsequent thinking and way of life were deeply rooted in this awakening. He was an excellent calligrapher, tea master, and poet as well. In all, he was a real embodiment of the Zen spirit, outstanding even among contemporary Zen masters in Japan.[5] This dialogue with Carl Jung took place at Jung's home at Küsnacht, on the outskirts of Zurich, on May 16, 1958. While there were many stimulating exchanges and many interesting points raised in the course of the dialogue, I would like to focus here on the issue of self as understood by Jung and Hisamatsu.

After a discussion about the relation between consciousness and the unconscious, Hisamatsu asked, "Which is our true Self, the 'unconscious' or 'conscious'?" Jung replied,

> Consciousness calls itself 'I', while the 'Self' is not 'I' at all. The Self is the whole, because personality—you as the whole—consists of consciousness and the unconscious. It is the whole, or in other words, the 'Self'. But 'I' know only the consciousness. The 'unconscious' remains unknown to me. (p. 106)[6]

This is Jung's well known distinction between I or ego, and self. To Jung, "ego" is the center of the field of consciousness and the complex entity to which all conscious contents are related, whereas "self" is the total personality which, though always present, cannot fully be known.[7]

Later in the dialogue, the following exchange occurs:

> *Hisamatsu:* "Is 'I-consciousness' (ego-consciousness) different from 'Self-consciousness' or not?"
> *Jung:* "In ordinary usage, people say 'self-consciousness', but psychologically this is only 'I-consciousness'. The Self is unknown, for it indicates the whole, that is, consciousness and the unconscious . . ."
> *Hisamatsu:* "What? The self can not be known?"
> *Jung:* "Perhaps only one half of it is known, and it is the *ego*. The *ego* is the half of the 'self'."

Hisamatsu's surprise is understandable, because in Zen practice the self is to be clearly known. Satori is "self-awakening," that is, the self awakening to itself. The awakened self is characterized as *ryōryōjōchi* 了々常知 , that is, "always clearly aware."

Here we can see an essential difference between Jung and Zen. In Jung, self as the total personality consists of the consciousness as "I" or "ego," which is known to itself, and the unconscious, which remains unknown. Furthermore, the unconscious includes the personal unconscious which owes its existence to personal experience, and the collective unconscious, the content of which has never been conscious and which owes its existence exclusively to heredity. Whereas the personal unconscious can sooner or later present itself to consciousness, the collective unconscious, being universal and impersonal, consists of pre-existent forms, or archetypes, which give definite form to certain psychic contents, but which can only become conscious secondarily.[8] It would therefore be appropriate to say that in Jung, the collective unconscious, as the depth of the self, is seen from the side of the conscious ego as something beyond, or as something "over there," though not externally but inwardly. It is in this sense that the unconscious is unknown. In contrast to this, according to Zen, the self is not the unknown, but rather the clearly known. More strictly speaking, the knower and the known are one, not two. The knower itself is the known, and vice versa. Self is not regarded as something existing "over there," somewhere beyond, but rather is fully realized right here and now.

We must therefore recognize clearly that although both Jung and Zen discuss the concept of the self, the entity of the self is understood by them in fundamentally different ways. According to Zen, in order to awaken to the true Self, it is necessary to realize No-self. Only through the clear realization of No-self can one awaken to the true Self. And the realization of No-self in Zen would reflect the realization of the non-substantiality of the unconscious self as well as the conscious ego, to use Jungian terminology. In Jung, self is the total personality which cannot be fully known. It consists of the conscious and the unconscious. But in Zen the true Self is awakened to only through overcoming or breaking through the self in the Jungian sense. I will try to clarify later how this process can occur, but at this point I would merely like to observe that there is no suggestion of the realization of the No-self in Jung. Since the No-self, that is the nonsubstantiality of self, is not clearly realized in Jung, it therefore remains as something unknown to the ego.

III

The dialogue now turns to the case of a patient's mental suffering and the method of curing the infirmity. Hisamatsu asked, "How is therapy related to the fundamental unconscious?" Jung replied, "When a sickness is caused by things of which we are not conscious, there exists the possibility of cure through making the causes conscious. The cause, however, does not always exist within the unconscious. Rather there are also a fair number of cases in which the various symptoms indicate the existence of conscious causes." Emphasizing the existence of the worries and difficulties in our daily life, Hisamatsu then raises several other questions. "[If] the essence of cure is liberation from worries . . . what sort of changes in the sphere of the unconscious correspond to this liberation?" "Is it possible or not for a human being to discard all of his suffering at a stroke, and can this be achieved by psychotherapy?"

> *Jung:* "How can such a method be possible? A method which enables us to free ourselves from suffering itself?"
> *Hisamatsu:* "Doesn't psychotherapy emancipate us from suffering all at once?"
> *Jung:* "Liberate man from suffering itself? What we are trying to do is to reduce human suffering. Still some suffering remains."

At this point in the conversation, Jung's reaction to the possibility of sudden emancipations from suffering itself was quite negative. Referring to Jesus Christ and Gautama Buddha, Hisamatsu says, "The intention of these religious founders was to liberate human beings from fundamental suffering. Is it really possible that such great freedom can be achieved by psychotherapy?" Jung's response to this question is not simply negative.

> *Jung:* "It is not inconceivable, if you treat suffering not as an individual sickness, but as an impersonal occurrence, such as a

disaster or an evil . . . [The patient] is entangled in the *kleśa,* and can be liberated from them through inner wisdom. The aim of psychotherapy is exactly the same as that of Buddhism."

This leads to a crucial point in the dialogue:

Hisamatsu: "The essential point of this liberation is how we can be awakened to our Original Self. The Original Self is the self which is no longer bound by a myriad of things. To attain this self is the essential point of freedom. It is necessary, therefore, to release oneself even from the collective unconscious and the bondage which derives from it."

Jung: "If someone is caught in a myriad of things and thus bound within it, this is because he is caught within the collective unconscious at the same time. He can be freed only when he is liberated from both of them. One person may be dragged along more by the unconscious, another by things. In short, through liberation, man must be brought to a point where he is free from the compulsion to chase after a myriad of things or from being controlled by the collective unconscious. Both are fundamentally the same: *Nirvāṇa.*"

Hisamatsu: "In what you have just said about the unconscious, Professor Jung, do you mean that the collective unconscious is something from which, in its nature, we can free ourselves?"

Jung: "Yes it is."

Hisamatsu: "What we generally call "self" is the same as the self [*Selbst*] characterized by you, Professor Jung. But it is only after the emancipation of this self that the "Original Self" of Zen emerges. It is the True Self described in Zen as the Self which is realized in absolute emancipation and is without dependence on anything [*dokudatsu mue*].

At this point, Jung answered affirmatively Hisamatsu's question as to whether the collective unconscious is something from which one must be emancipated for real freedom. Earlier in the dialogue, he answered negatively a question concerning the possibility of gaining freedom from suffering all at once. Towards the end of the conversation, however, Jung clearly agreed with Hisamatsu on the need of overcoming even the collective unconscious for a complete cure of the patient. According to Tsujimura Kōichi, who acted as interpreter for the dialogue, Jung's affirmative response surprised people in the room, for if the collective unconscious can be overcome, then Jung's analytical psychology must be fundamentally reexamined.

IV

Looking back over the dialogue, I would like to make three remarks:

First, the psychotherapeutic method of relieving a patient's suffering and the Zen method of dissolving a student's suffering are different. In Jungian psychotherapy, to cure a patient's suffering, the analyst tries to help the patient become aware of the causes of his suffering, which previously had been unconscious, or he tries to help the patient realize the aim or meaning of his life, or he tries to help change the patient's attitude towards psychic worry and make him more accepting and positive. But as Jung says in the conversation, there is no universal rule or method for the cure. There are only individual cases, and in psychotherapy the analyst must cure the patient's worries as fully as possible in each individual case. As Hisamatsu points out in his additional note, however, "If each disease is treated individually, then when one disease is gone, another disease will come along. Hence, we shall never be delivered from sickness forever. This in itself may be said to be a disease in a very profound sense." (p. 117)

Hisamatsu calls this "the vicious circle" of psychoanalytic therapy. Unless the root of all possible diseases is dug out and cut away, the vicious circle of psychoanalytic therapy will not be overcome. What, then, is the root of all possible psychic diseases? According to Jung it is the collective unconscious or the unknown self which is responsible for hindering us psychically. Instead of analyzing psychic diseases one by one, Zen tries to dig out and cut away the very root of the human consciousness beyond consciousness, including the Jungian or any other hypothesized realm of an unconscious. Zen insists that only then can complete emancipation from human suffering be achieved and the true Self be awakened. The realization of No-self, which is indispensable for the awakening to true Self, is simply another way of describing "cutting away" the root of human consciousness.

Second, in Jung, the collective unconscious is something un-known which must be intensively analyzed to discover the cause of a patient's suffering, but it is at the same time a realm that can never be completely known. By definition, the collective unconscious re-mains an unknown "x" for both analyst and analysand. In Zen, through zazen and koan practice with a Zen master, the Zen student not only digs out the root of the unknown "x" but also becomes one with it. For the Zen student the unknown "x" is not something "over there." It comes to be realized as "here and now." In other words, it is totally, completely and experientially realized by the student *as the unknown* "x." In this total, experiential realization, it ceases to be an *object* to the student, and instead the two become one with each other. Now, the student *is* the unknown "x" and the unknown "x" *is* the student. Only in this way can the student overcome the unknown "x," "cut off" its root, and awaken to his true Self.

This event can be illustrated by a *mondō* (a question and answer exchange) between Bodhidharma, the first patriarch in the Zen tradi-tion, and Hui-ko, who later became the second patriarch. In deep anguish and mental perplexity after many years of inner struggle, Hui-ko approached Bodhidharma and asked him:

> "My mind is not yet pacified. Pray, Master, pacify it."
> "Bring your mind here and I will pacify it." said Bodhi-dharma. "I have sought it for many years," Hui-ko replied, "I am still unable to take hold of it. My mind is really unattainable."
> "There! Your mind is pacified once and for all," Bodhi-dharma confirmed.[9]

Instead of analyzing the causes of Hui-ko's suffering, Bodhi-dharma asked Hui-ko to bring forth his mind. Confronted with this straight-away command, Hui-ko, who had sought after his mind for many years, clearly realized that the mind is unattainable. Suddenly, he totally and experientially realized the mind to be the unattainable and the unattainable to be the mind; there was no longer even the slightest gap between himself and the unattainable. His internal per-plexity was resolved in this existentially complete realization of the mind as the unattainable. Recognizing this, Bodhidharma immedi-ately said, "There! Your mind is pacified once and for all."

In Jung, the depth of mind is *objectively* regarded from the side of the conscious "I" as the unknown collective unconscious. In contrast, by overcoming such an objective approach, Zen straightforwardly enters into the depth of mind and breaks through it by becoming completely identical with it. In Zen, this breaking through is called the Great Death—because it signifies the complete denial of human consciousness, including any such Jungian notion of the collective unconscious. And yet the Great Death in Zen is at one and the same time a resurrection in the Great Life—because in this breaking through of mind, not only is the realization that mind is unattainable or unknowable included, but also the realization that the unattainable or the unknowable is precisely the true Mind or true Self. This is why 'No mind' in Zen is not a negative but a positive entity. That is to say, unlike the Jungian unconscious, No-mind in Zen is not an extra-conscious psyche, but rather is the true Mind or Original Mind which is realized beyond Jung's framework of the mind.

A significant aspect of Zen in this connection is perhaps the emphasis in koan practice on the Great Doubt. Most koans, such as Joshu's *Mu* and Hakuin's "Listen to the sound of the single hand," are designed to drive a Zen student into a mental corner, to break through the wall of the human psyche, and to open up an entirely new spiritual dimension beyond analytic or dualistic thinking. For example, the koan, "Show your Original Face before your parents were born," does not refer to one's pre-existence in a temporal sense, but rather asks of a student to demonstrate his or her original nature which can be *immediately* realized at the depth of existence. Only when the student demonstrates it can he or she break through the framework of a self-centered psyche. The phrase, "Original Face *before your parents were born*" can be understood to refer to that which lies beyond even the hypothesized collective unconscious and which is impersonal, universal, and yet is the root-source of your own being and which is unknown to the "I" which is limited by time and space.

Zen emphasizes the importance for a Zen student to become a "Great Doubting Mass": "At the base of Great Doubt lies Great Awakening." This emphasis on Great Doubt implies that a Zen student must dig up and grapple with the unknown "x" so thoroughly that he turns into the unknown "x" itself. To become a Great Doubting Mass is to turn into the unknown "x." To turn into the unknown "x" is to come to know existentially that the unknown "x"

is nothing but the true Self. And that knowing is the Great Awakening to the true Self, characterized as *ryōryōjōchi*, "always clearly aware." Koan practice has proved an effective way to lead a student to the Great Awakening through Great Doubt.

Third, despite the essential differences between Zen and Jungian psychology in their understandings of self and their respective methods of curing human suffering, I believe there are also points at which these two disciplines can profitably learn from each other, although the scope and depth of their mutual learning may perhaps not be equal. Since Zen is so overwhelmingly concerned with cutting off the root of the human consciousness in order to attain No-self as true Self, or to attain No-mind as true Mind, it tends on the whole to neglect psychological problems that occur sometimes in the process of Zen practice, in particular the delusory apparitions known as *makyō*.[10] But if Zen learns from Jungian psychology about the theory of the archetype as an unconscious organizer of human ideas, and the process of individuation, it might help the Zen practicer to better understand such mental fabrication.

Modern Western psychology, and particularly Freudian and Jungian psychology, have claimed to discover the existence of a psyche outside consciousness. With this discovery the position of the ego, until then absolute as the center of human consciousness and the active source of man's spiritual act, was relativized.[11] In Jung, the ego is no longer identical with the whole of the individual but is a limited substance serving as the center of non-unconscious phenomena. If this relativization of the ego is strengthened, that is, the substance of the ego is understood to be even more limited, it could help open the way to the realization of No-self. But in Jung, instead of a relativization of the position of ego, the position of the self as the total personality based on the collective unconscious is strongly maintained. If the collective unconscious is something ultimate in which human suffering is rooted, then, as Hisamatsu suggests in his dialogue with Jung, Jungian psychotherapy may not be free from an inevitable "vicious circle," because even though it can relieve a particular disease separately and individually, other forms of psychic disease may recur endlessly. Only when the true source is reached beyond such possible psychological realms as the collective unconscious, can human beings go beyond the root of suffering itself and be released from the "vicious circle" of particular manifestations of suffering. Zen offers a way to break through even the collective unconscious and similar theories about the structure of the mind.

In this respect, it is extremely significant that in his dialogue with Hisamatsu, Jung seemed eventually to agree with the possibility and necessity of freedom from the collective unconscious. Ultimately, Jung and Zen seem to agree that there is hope for human beings to be emancipated from suffering itself, rather than their being destined to remain in a samsaric cycle, finding relief from one suffering only to be faced with another.

Notes

1. Walpola Rahula, *What The Buddha Taught* (New York: Grove Press, 1959), p. 51.
2. Rahula, p. 56.
3. Rahula, pp. 52 and 57.
4. D. T. Suzuki, Erich Fromm, and Richard DeMartino, *Zen Buddhism and Psychoanalysis* (London: George Allen & Unwin, 1960), p. 32. (with a slight adaptation)
5. On Hisamatsu's life and thought, see my articles, "A Buddhism of Self-Awakening, Not a Buddhism of Faith" in *Añjali: A Felicitation Volume Presented to Oliver Hector de Alwis Wijesekera on his Sixtieth Birthday* (Peradeniya, Ceylon, 1970), pp. 33–39; and "Hisamatsu's Philosophy of Awakening" in *The Eastern Buddhist* Vol. XIV, No. 1 (Spring 1981), pp. 26–42; for his obituary, see pp. 142–147 of the latter.
6. Page numbers from the dialogue as it appears in this volume are given in parentheses.
7. C. G. Jung, *Aion: Contributions to the Symbolism of the Self,* Collected Works, Volume 9.2 (New York: Pantheon Books, 1959), pp. 3, 5.
8. C. G. Jung, *Archetypes and the Collective Unconscious,* Collected Works, Vol. 9.1 (New York: Pantheon Books, 1959), p. 43.
9. D. T. Suzuki, *Essays in Zen Buddhism,* First Series (London, Rider, 1949; reprinted 1973), p. 190; adapted.
10. The 18th century Zen master Hakuin was an exception; his disciple Tōrei discusses some of the psychological problems that may occur in the process of Zen practice in his *Shūmon mujintō ron* (The Inexhaustible Lamp of Zen), Taishō 81: 581a–605b.
11. Jung, *Aion,* p. 6.

Part Three
ON JUNGIAN THOUGHT
AND BUDDHISM

Part Three
CONFUCIAN THOUGHT
AND BUDDHISM

Thomas P. Kasulis

Zen Buddhism, Freud, and Jung

In this paper we will compare the Zen view of the person with three central aspects of the psychoanalytic theories of Freud and Jung. The Western psychoanalytic understanding of the person has been chosen as a basis for comparison with Zen Buddhism for four reasons. First, unlike the Christian view, for example, that of psychoanalysis is a product of the twentieth century and it therefore reflects a distinctively modern Western approach to the issue. Secondly, unlike many other contemporary perspectives such as that of the personalists or existentialists, psychoanalysis has developed an extensive system of therapeutic techniques based on its understanding of the nature of the person. The affinity between technique and theory is also central to Zen Buddhism and the dyadic relationships of analyst/analysand and of Zen Master/disciple, for example, provide ready points of comparison. Thirdly, although there have been previous comparisons between Zen and Western psychoanalysis,[1] these projects have often been quite general in scope and few detailed comparisons on specific points have been attempted. It is hoped that the three specific comparisons outlined here will shed further light on the distinctive way in which the person is understood within the Zen Buddhist framework. Lastly, in the case of Jung, we have a Western psychoanalyst who, in fact, was quite cognizant of many basic Zen Buddhist ideas[2] and a comparison between Zen and Jung, therefore, assumes a particular appropriateness.

I. ZEN AND FREUD'S MECHANISMS OF DEFENSE

It is not difficult to note obvious ways in which Freud's psychoanalytic theories are not in accord with the basic viewpoint of Zen Buddhism. Most important of all, the primary distinction in

143

psychoanalysis—the split between the conscious and unconscious mind—has no correlate in Zen.[3] At those rare points when Zen Buddhists do make distinctions concerning the nature of mind, it is usually more along the lines of the "thinking/not-thinking/non-thinking" characterization used by Dōgen, a characterization that he in fact inherited from Yüeh-shan.[4] The distinctions among these three modes of consciousness constitute a complex issue in Dōgen's thought, but even a brief set of definitions will reveal the contrast with psychoanalytic categories. "Thinking" is basically any category-affirming attitude within consciousness while "not-thinking" is the negation of that attitude. That is to say, "not-thinking" is the name for the outright rejection of all conceptualization. "Non-thinking," on the other hand, takes neither an affirming nor a negating attitude for its intentionality. Since it does not objectify ideas, there is no object for it to either affirm or deny. For Dōgen, this pre-reflective or pre-conceptual state of mind is more fundamental than the other two and it is the proper attitude to assume in seated meditation. Although we will make some further references to Dōgen's triadic distinction later in this paper, for now we only wish to point out that in the Zen Buddhist distinction we find no equivalent to the Freudian or Jungian conception of the unconscious. A similar point could be made about Zen Buddhism's attitude toward the remainder of Freud's system, e.g., his analyses of ego, id, and superego. These notions would not be so much rejected as neglected by Zen. Considered to be reflective, reconstructive conceptualizations of experience, these ideas would have no place within Zen's practical emphasis on pre-reflective experience. Furthermore, even in terms of therapeutic theory, the situation of the monastery and that of the analyst's office are so strikingly different that there would seem to be little ground for fruitful comparison. In particular, Zen's path of personal development goes beyond returning neurotic and psychotic patients to functional normality. Indeed, it is meant to be the basis of a whole way of living quite separate from that of "normal" people.

Despite the ease with which we can list such evident incompatibilities between Zen and Freud's psychoanalysis, if we look below the surface, we can see certain significant affinities. We can, of course, find several general themes held in common by the two such as the belief that personal freedom is essentially based on overcoming dominance by the passions, or the conviction that "liberation" follows from self-knowledge rather than from devotion to something transcendent.[5] In this brief discussion, however, I have in mind a much more specific point of comparison, viz., their common realization that conceptualization or rationality may actually function as a *hindrance* to one's liberation from unconscious compulsions. In Freud, this realization is expressed in his concern for removing the negative effects of particular "mechanisms of defense" in the ego; in Zen, it is visible in the Master's insistence that the disciple overcome dependence on concepts.

In order to understand the importance of Freud's conception of mechanisms of defense, a few remarks about his overall project will give this theory a framework. In his later writings, Freud recognizes three interrelated agencies that must be given due consideration: the id, the superego, and the ego. In most general terms, the id is the repository of the instinctual, libidinal drives. As such, the id forms the foundation of the pleasure principle, the tendency toward direct, immediate self-gratification. On the other hand, there is an opposing reality principle that checks this first tendency. Not only is direct gratification often impossible because of physical conditions, but also, it is often forbidden by various rules imposed by culture and society. These rules of acceptable behavior are considered to be embodied in the dictates of the superego, one of its major enterprises being the development of conscience. Because of the potential conflict between the pleasure and reality principles, there is the need for a third, negotiating agency that can mediate the demands of these other two. This third agency is, of course, the ego. Besides being the center of differentiating consciousness (thought), it also establishes (conscious and unconscious) structural mechanisms through which individuals adapt their behavior to the external world. To function adequately, the conscious part of the ego obviously must have access to the material from the id and superego *in an undistorted form.* Unfortunately, this is not always the case. For example, material that has been repressed (painful memories of specific traumatic events, libidinal desires that the superego considers sinful or improper, etc.) can often make itself available to consciousness only in an altered fashion. Undoing this distortion is a primary aim of Freud's therapeutic analysis: the more patients understand the nature of their conflicting needs and the more they understand how the distorted manifestations of repressed psychic data have affected their behavior, the more freely the ego can develop adequate courses of action. In other words, Freud's basic project is to bring repressed, unconscious material to the level of consciousness.

Let us consider now the role of mechanisms of defense within this general framework.

> For the ego has to try from the very outset to fulfil its task of mediating between its id and the external world in the service of the pleasure principle, and to protect the id from the dangers of the external world. If, in the course of these efforts, the ego learns to adopt a defensive attitude towards its own id as well and to treat the latter's instinctual demands as external dangers, this happens, at any rate in part, because it understands that a satisfaction of instinct would lead to conflicts with the external world. Thereafter, under the influence of education, the ego grows accustomed to removing the scene of the fight from outside to within and to mastering the *internal* danger before it has become an *external* one; and probably it is most often right in doing so. During this fight on two fronts—later there will be a third front as well [with the superego]—the ego makes use of various procedures for fulfilling the task, which, to put it in general terms, is to avoid danger, anxiety and unpleasure. We call these procedures 'mechanisms of defense.'[6]

In other words, Freud discovered that the ego consciously and unconsciously utilizes various procedures for preventing direct confrontation with psychic material that might prove threatening or disturbing. Threatening to what? *To the maintenance of the status quo of the ego itself.*[7] Through the organizing structures of the ego, a state of equilibrium is achieved, a state that allows some of the instinctual drives of the id to be expressed (either directly or indirectly) within the limitations posed by the prohibitions of the superego and the demands of external reality. Through the utilization of the mechanisms of defense, the ego fends off psychic contents that pose a threat to this equilibrium. Some of these mechanisms include repression, regression, projection, sublimation and "undoing."[8] Although Freud felt that some of this defensive apparatus is probably necessary in order to keep at bay the overwhelming urges of the id, the mechanisms of defense can nonetheless become "fixated" in such a way that they may do more harm than good.[9] In such instances, they become automatic, stylized responses to certain types of situations, responses that might have been appropriate at an earlier stage of psychic development, but which are no longer suitable. In effect, such fixated defenses become blinders that limit the person's perception of the actual situation and they may "bring about ever more extensive alienation from the external world."[10] Because these mechanisms are utilized both by and for the ego, Freud notes that the analyst's effort in therapy is "constantly swinging backwards and forward like a pendulum between a piece of id-analysis and a piece of ego-analysis."[11]

The implications of this Freudian discovery are relevant to our particular discussion of Zen in two ways. First, we can see that even for Freud, the ego is by no means infallible or fully objective in its structuring processes and, in fact, the ego is always designing compromising constructions that reflect only as much of "reality" as can be handled at any given time. Yet, this is the *ideal* functioning of the ego and, in most cases, it blocks out even more of reality than is appropriate. For this very reason, the analyst must set out to disassemble many of the ego's mechanisms of defense. As in Zen, mere thinking or mental structuring is itself no guarantee of objectivity. In fact, dependence on defense mechanisms is an example of being so determined by past conditioning that one is unable to respond freely in the present—precisely one of the situations Zen endeavors to avoid. Zen disagrees with Freud only as to the *extensiveness* of defensive mechanisms in that it considers *all* intellectual constructions to be defense mechanisms insofar as they become patterns of response whose appropriateness is not evaluated in each new situation. In other words, any conceptual framework, even Freud's id/superego/ego, can become the basis for automatic, stylized modes of response and Zen consequently regards them all with suspicion.

Another comparative point about Freud's view of the ego's mechanisms of defense is that it endeavors to explain why they develop whereas Zen is indefinite on precisely this point: it attacks complete dependence on thinking/not-thinking, but it gives no detailed etiology of the dependence. Extending the Freudian thesis (beyond Freud's own intent), we may ask if Zen would also assert that rationalistic thinking is essentially a defense mechanism that arises out of the need to exclude unpleasant aspects of reality. The answer is that it would, but the nature of what is excluded is different from Freud's conception (as we might expect, insofar as Freud is primarily concerned only with the psychoanalytic dimensions relevant to psychotherapy). Within the traditional Zen viewpoint, the repressed object is neither the id's forbidden impulses nor painfully traumatic memories, but rather, the *experience of impermanence*. As a withdrawal from this perception of change, conceptual frameworks reify experience into substantial entities that may undergo change, but remain self-identical. The epitome of this process, according to Zen, is the objectification of the self. Freud, too, recognizes that the ego becomes an object for itself, though for him, this is an inevitable and often very positive development in the personality. For Zen, though, this is a flight from the reality of pre-reflective experience into the stasis of intellectually restructured memories.

In summary, we have seen that both Freud and Zen endeavor to prevent our behavior from being strictly determined by defensive reactions inherited from past experience; both seek an opening up of our options so that we can realize our capacity to understand and act freely within present situations. Beyond this basic similarity, however, we have also noted a distinctive divergence between the two systems. Specifically, although both Freud and Zen maintain that conceptualizations may become restrictions on human freedom, Freud maintains that dependence on at least *some* mechanisms of defense is inevitable. Because of its emphasis on pre-reflective experience, Zen maintains that all such dependence must be overcome. In other words, Freud seeks to replace inadequate, fixated ego structures with ones that better correspond to the patient's present situation, but Zen seeks to open the present to the disciple by helping one become independent of all such structures. As we shall now see, this same distinction also underlies the difference between the analyst/analysand relationship in Freud and that of the Master/student in Zen.

II. FREUD AND ZEN ON "TRANSFERENCE"

The interaction between Zen Master and disciple is an integral part of Zen training and we will here investigate this association further by comparing it to a contemporary Western one, namely, that between the Freudian analyst and patient. In both cases the dyadic nature of the relationship is essential: although one may have more than one teacher or even more than one confessor at a time, a client has only one analyst, a disciple only one Zen Master. One consequence of the gradual disappearance of apprenticeship in our modern Western society is that the dyadic relationship of learning has become quite rare. The psychoanalytic situation is a significant exception to this general rule and it serves as an illuminating point of comparison with the interpersonal dynamics between Zen Master and disciple. We will begin our discussion with an explication of Freud's conception of transference.

Whatever his original ideal of the analyst's objective distance might have been, Freud came to realize early in his career that "any analysis without transference is an impossibility."[12] Although the term "transference" has become a general one referring to the entire relationship between analyst and patient, in Freud's own usage it is more specific.[13] At first, transference was considered to be a type of "displacement," i.e., the process of raising to consciousness the affect from a repressed (unconscious) memory by means of changing the affect's original object.[14] For example, having repressed the memory of a traumatic incident concerning his father, a patient can release some of the suppressed emotion by "transferring" it onto someone else with whom he has direct contact. In this manner the emotion has an outlet even though the repressed memory itself has not become conscious. What Freud gradually discovered is that the new object of the transferred affect is most often the analyst. In this more specialized sense then, "transference" indicates that the patient, without apparent justification, projects various emotions onto the analyst and the analyst inevitably becomes involved in the patient's emotional life.[15] Depending on the circumstances, the analyst may be the object (by transference) of the patient's love or hostility (or both).

Although the appearance of a "transference-neurosis" may seem to present an inescapable obstacle to the further progress of analysis, Freud discovered that it could also present the opportunity for the patient to have a significant insight into the unconscious. By raising the repressed affect to consciousness, even though it may be in a seriously transferred or displaced form, the very act of repression becomes manifest to the patient. Through the analyst's careful guidance, the analysand may be brought to the point of recognizing that there is no rational justification for his or her emotional projections and this insight may itself constitute a crucial turning point in the patient's self-understanding. The implication is that the transference-neurosis may itself become a concrete phenomenon by which both the analyst and the analysand can gain entry into the material within the latter's unconscious. Freud summarizes the centrality of transference very clearly in the following passage:

> Thus our therapeutic work falls into two phases. In the first, all the libido is forced from the symptoms into the transference and concentrated there; in the second, the struggle is waged around this new object and the libido is liberated from it. The change which is decisive for a favorable outcome is the elimination of repression in the renewed conflict, so that the libido cannot withdraw once more from the ego by flight into the unconscious. This is made possible by the alteration of the doctor's suggestion. By means of the work of interpretation, which transforms what is unconscious into what is conscious, the ego is enlarged at the cost of this unconscious.[16]

The centrality of this phenomenon within the psychoanalytic setting leads us to wonder if a similar occurrence takes place in the relationship between Zen Master and disciple.

Certainly, something at least resembling transference does occur in this relationship and in fact, in certain respects, the transference is even more intense within the Zen framework than it is in the psychoanalytic situation. For instance, the Zen disciple regards the Master as an example of what one wishes to become. This identification is stronger than that achieved in psychoanalysis in at least two ways. First, the analysands do not typically consider the training to be completed only if they themselves become analysts, but the Zen disciples ultimately seek the Master's certification that allows them to become Masters themselves. Secondly, both the Zen Master and the student believe that the Master has achieved something ("realization" or "enlightenment") that the student also desires to achieve. This underscores the basis of the Master's authority. The analyst, on the other hand, is primarily distinguishable from the analysand in his or her command of a special methodology for uncovering repressed material and mitigating its effects.[17] Although the patient may lack the ability to cope with certain situations, that ability is not solely possessed by psychoanalysts; in fact, it is precisely something that all "normal" people are expected to have. In other words, the analyst is a person who has *special knowledge* of certain techniques, but the Zen Master is considered a *special person*, one who has achieved a special state of spiritual insight and self-realization. Again, this difference would seem to imply that the transference-neurosis is probably more likely to arise in Zen than in psychoanalysis.

Even in the actual interaction between Master and disciple the possibility of transference is clearly present. For example, in the *sanzen* interview, the disciple makes an effort to respond in the same mode (non-thinking) as the Master. In trying to imitate the Master, it is easy for the student to fall into filial affection and dependence. On the other hand, since the Master's demands on the student can often be the cause of great frustration, hostility may also arise. To experience the Great Doubt is by no means a pleasant experience and the student may hold the Master responsible for one's own suffering. In this regard, the Zen Master may encounter "resistance" on the part of the student in much the same way as an analyst might encounter it within the analysand. Even though the cause of the resistance is somewhat different in the two cases (in the former, it is a resistance to giving up dependence on conceptualization; in the latter a resistance to unearthing repressed memories and desires), to the extent the process of self-understanding is painful, it is natural that the person undergoing that process will sometimes doubt its ultimate value.

Despite these similarities with the psychoanalytic phenomena of transference and resistance, the Zen situation is also very different in some fundamental ways. First, and most importantly, the Zen student's reactions to the Master *are* justifiable within the terms of their actual interrelationship. No affect need be transferred from a previously repressed traumatic experience: the Master indeed behaves in a manner deserving of both affection and hostility. That the Master is sometimes a kindly, caring, supportive figure and at other times a stern, unfeeling task master is not a mere matter of projection, but is quite objectively the case.[18] Secondly, although it is very likely that *some* genuine Freudian transference will arise, Zen differs from psychoanalysis in its treatment of this phenomenon. In particular, the Zen Master does not try to convince the student that such feelings are ungrounded, i.e., the Master does not use the transference phenomenon as an entry into the analysis of repressed, traumatic memories. In comparison with Freud, Zen is markedly unconcerned with the student's past; abreaction[19] has no formal place within the monastery. The student is constantly challenged to be a full participant in the present, rather than to return to the past in order to free the present. Thirdly, within the Zen situation, there is ideally no possibility of counter-transference. While it is assumed that the psychoanalysts can never be completely free of the affects of their repressed unconscious, the Zen Masters are judged to be no longer determined by the past. Not bound to any particular set of conceptualizations, the Master is free of unconscious compulsions. Because of the far more active role taken by the Zen Master in comparison with the analyst, the purity of the Master's own self-understanding is proportionally more significant. In accord with the enormous influence that a Master exerts over students, the credentials to be a Master are cautiously guarded and only given to selected students after many years of careful supervision. Even though the training of an analyst also requires several years of specialization, the final authorization is not as comprehensive as that of a Zen Master: in conferring authorization upon a student, the Master must testify to the fact that the student's realization is *as deep as one's own*, a declaration not likely to be taken lightly.

Therefore, although we might wish to speak of a transference relationship within Zen training, the nature of this transference and the way in which it is treated are quite distinct from those of the psychoanalytic situation. To further elaborate on this difference, we can now briefly consider one aspect of technique shared by Zen Masters and psychoanalysts, viz., the emphasis on spontaneity. By examining how this common emphasis has a distinctively different rationale in the two systems, we will better see in what way Freudian psychotherapy and Zen training are fundamentally divergent in their goals.

Much of the development of psychoanalytic technique has been concerned with ways of gaining access to unconscious material by circumventing the censoring processes of the ego. The theory is that if the patient is required to respond spontaneously, the mechanisms of defense will be caught off guard and important data from the unconscious will become available (even though it may still appear in somewhat distorted form). Some of the better known techniques developed by psychoanalysts include Freud's free association and dream interpretation, Jung's word association test and active imagination, and Rorschach's inkblot test. As an example of one of Freud's earliest techniques, we can consider the following practice described in *Studies in Hysteria:*

> I inform the patient that, a moment later, I shall apply pressure to his forehead, and I assure him that, all the time the pressure lasts, he will see before him a recollection in the form of a picture or will have it in his thoughts in the form of an idea occurring to him, and I pledge him to communicate this picture or idea to me, whatever it may be.[20]

Here we see Freud calling upon the patient to react *without thinking about the significance of what is happening.* This is strikingly like the Zen Master's provoking his student into making an immediate, unpremeditated response to a koan, a gesture or a challenge. In such cases the Zen Master will not accept even a moment's hesitation. Freud, too, realized that hesitancy is a sign of conscious (or "preconscious") restructuring of the experience.

> The longer the pause between my hand pressure and the patient's beginning to speak, the more suspicious I become and the more it is to be feared that the patient is re-arranging what has occurred to him and is mutilating it in his reproduction of it.[21]

Despite the similarities, however, the Freudian emphasis on spontaneity has a distinctively different emphasis from that of Zen. In particular, Freud is looking for a link with a repressed memory of a traumatic experience. Therefore, the psychoanalyst is primarily concerned with following up the response with a series of questions that will enable the analysand to recall the original experience and to express the affect verbally.[22] On the other hand, the Zen Master seeks to encourage spontaneity on the part of the student so that the student can show *independence* of past conditioning, rather than dependence on concepts or words. Hence, the spontaneous reaction of the analysand fits into a larger pattern of determinism; the spontaneous response of the Zen disciple reveals the freedom from being determined by such a pattern. From the other side of the relationship, the Zen student accepts the Master's action and responds to it directly, but the psychoanalytic patient ultimately responds not to the pressure of the hand but to something else entirely, viz., the repressed memory and its accompanying affect. Therefore, although both the Zen Master and the analyst try to provoke spontaneous responses in their subjects, the nature of the spontaneity and the direction of the response are distinctively different in the two situations.

To sum up these points about the comparison between Freudian analysis and Zen, we can say that while many aspects of the general structure have much in common, there is nonetheless a basic difference in perspective. Freudian analysis is primarily aimed at revealing aspects of the unconscious to the conscious; Zen is concerned with the different modes of consciousness, viz., thinking, not-thinking, and non-thinking. Equally significant is the fact that Freudian analysis is primarily directed to the patient's *past* experience since therein lie the roots of the patient's problems in the present, but when Zen endeavors to break down the disciple's dependence on previous conditioning, it does so by concentrating its attention on the *directly experienced present*. Stated differently, Freud frees the patient's present by disassembling unfortunate patterns of conditioning acquired in the past, helping the patient to reexperience and verbalize the past traumatic incident as-it-*was*. In contrast, Zen maintains that prereflective non-thinking is a form of experience that has not yet been restructured either by conscious or unconscious forces: if the Zen disciple manages to ground oneself in that mode of relating, there is no need to be concerned with the specific nature of past experiences in that one already grasps present experience as-it-*is*. Both Freud's psychoanalysis and Zen endeavor to relieve people of their being compelled by unknowingly contrived and unspontaneous modes of behavior, but the processes by which they seek to achieve results and the rationales behind those processes are radically different.

A further contrast is that the relationship between analyst and analysand is primarily one between doctor and patient, but in Zen, the tie between Master and disciple is much stronger than this. In psychoanalysis, patients go to analysts because they have special knowledge which will help cure the patients' disease and return them to "normalcy"; in Zen, the disciples ultimately want to become like the Master—the disciples want to be more than "normal" and indeed, to a certain extent, to be extraordinary. To concentrate our attention on this goal of going beyond mere normalcy, we will turn now to another major figure in psychoanalysis, C. G. Jung. In particular, we will investigate his model of "individuation" to see if it can shed further light on the Zen ideal of the person.

III. ZEN AND JUNG'S INDIVIDUATION

As we have seen, although Freud and Zen share several points in their interpretations of the person, Zen also differs radically from Freud in that (1) it denies the ultimate value of replacing unsatisfactory mechanisms of defense with new ego structures and (2) it rejects Freud's basic project of freeing the present by resolving the repressed problems of the past. For those familiar with other traditions of psychoanalysis, the question might arise of whether Jung's system would offer a more fruitful comparison especially insofar as he emphasizes (1) the cooperation of the conscious and the unconscious (with no tension between ego and id) and (2) a prospective rather than retrospective therapy. In this brief section we will focus our comments by considering in particular Jung's theory of individuation or self-realization as it compares with the developmental image of the person in Zen.

In order to frame the remarks to follow, we will first consider Jung's general outlook, particularly insofar as it deviates from the tradition established by Freud. Freud primarily saw himself as formulating a new science which would harken a new era for mankind —an era in which what he called the "dictator of reason" would push back the forces of the unconscious and reclaim fresh territory for the forces of the ego. In accord with this sense of giving humankind a fresh start, Freud postdated his *Interpretation of Dreams* from 1899 to 1900 so that this work would usher in the new century. As we saw in the two previous sections of this chapter, Freud tends toward a mechanistic view of the psyche and his therapeutic process is primarily one of repair: he seeks to release the repressed cathexes that misdirect psychic energies and trap them within the unconscious. To remove the impediments to the ego's control of the individual, the person must return to the memory of the original trauma and release its cathexis through abreaction or catharsis.

Jung, on the other hand, does not see himself as a technologist assisting the imperial forces of the ego, but rather, as a rediscoverer, an archeologist of the psyche who digs into the unconscious, unearthing the psychical roots that link the individual with the rest of humanity, even with cultures and times other than our own. Consequently, rather than opposing one aspect of the psyche to another, Jung sets his goal as the integrating of the various forces into a whole, a process he labels "individuation." In line with this difference in emphasis from Freud, Jung's image of the psychological functions is organic rather than mechanical: unlike a machine, the psyche has no purpose that we can empirically determine and, like other organisms, the psyche possesses the potential to cure itself through its inherent compensating forces of self-adjustment. Therefore, rather than trying to repair a machine by removing obstructions in its energy flow, Jung merely seeks to act in harmony with the psyche's own process of healing. Rather than correcting the malfunctions inherited from the past, Jung tries to let the present develop of its own accord toward the equilibrium and integration of the self—the process he calls "individuation."

What is this process and how does it arise of its own accord? Although clearly a central idea in Jung's system, individuation lacks a single classic definition. While Freud strives for the definitional clarity of a science, Jung implies that clearcut definitions deprive psychoanalytic concepts of their web-like interconnections and disguise the underlying ambiguity characteristic of living processes. Unfortunately, this often leads to disorganization and obscurity, and in our considerations here we will outline a description of individuation that is more implicit than explicit in Jung's own writings. It is only one of several possible accounts that we might present, but for our comparative purposes, it is particularly useful. We shall attempt to develop our interpretation with the help of two basic features in Jung's thought: his theory of types and his conception of the transcendent function.

As is well known, Jung developed a comprehensive system for determining and classifying each individual's "psychological type."[23] Indeed, his classification of the two "attitude types" of extravert and introvert has found its way into our everyday language. Our concern here, however, is primarily with the other types, the "function types" of thinking, feeling, sensation, and intuition. Jung's theory is that just as each individual has a natural propensity to be either an extravert or an introvert (depending on whether one primarily directs psychical energy outward or inward), individuals also develop a typical pattern of apprehension that is operative in primarily one of two ways: either through sensation or through intuition. Furthermore, Jung discovered that each individual also typically favors one of two ways of structuring experience: either by thinking or by feeling. We should bear in mind that these categories are only to be considered as *general* tendencies within a given individual. Also, although Jung himself describes the types and their combinations in great detail, for the purposes of our present project, such a venture into the intricate distinctions and interrelations is unnecessary; our goal here is merely to have a general understanding of the rationale behind the typologies.

Given these basic typologies, we can theoretically locate a person's psychological type on a three-dimensional graph with the parameters being extraversion—introversion, thinking—feeling, sensation—intuition. However, since the attitude types are generally considered to be innate rather than developed, our primary interest is in the four function types and we can represent the graph two-dimensionally as follows:

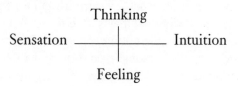

Thinking

Sensation —————|————— Intuition

Feeling

If we look at this graph and think of where we might locate the personalities of various people we know, it should be clear that although individuals tend to be more of one type than another, very few persons indeed can be considered to be totally limited to one point or even one quadrant. This realization was critical in the development of Jung's theory in that it implied that the four quadrants represent types of functioning *potentially open to all of us*. Yet, we typically do not realize this potential and the personality tends to adopt one particular quadrant as its "own" to the neglect of the others. In this sense, we have a Jungian parallel to Freud's fixation of the mechanisms of defense: the personality becomes fixed within certain modes of responding and the potential openness to a variety of experiences and possible responses is not realized. For Jung, however, this situation does not call for the abreaction of a repressed memory. Rather, he claims that within the personality itself a compensating function will arise of its own accord. This compensating process is called the "transcendent function."[24] Let us consider an example of its operation.

For instance, in a person who is overly limited to the thinking-sensation quadrant, Jung would claim that a compensating urge toward feeling-intuition will necessarily emerge and problems arise only to the extent the individual resists this compensatory tendency. Just as we cannot persist in ignoring *physiological* compensatory signals (warnings about needs for sleep, proper nutrition, relaxation), we cannot successfully resist these *psychological* signals either. If we persist in our refusal to see that "other side of ourselves" which yearns for more attention, that unknown aspect (the "shadow") becomes detached from the self, achieving its own independent functioning. In mild cases this alter ego may make persistent appearances in dreams (as the archetype of the Shadow or perhaps of the Anima, the symbol of intuition and feeling). In more severe cases of conscious resistance, the compensatory aspect of the personality will unexpectedly intrude into everyday activities, i.e., for no patently explicable reason, the individual may suddenly act "not like oneself." In even more severe cases, the counter image will begin to dominate large parts of the person's personality and there is a danger of schizophrenia. The Jungian analyst's task, therefore, is to help the patient to understand what is being expressed by these images or archetypes.

Although Freud considers symbols to be the distorted residues of repressed memories, Jung understands them to be warnings about what must be accomplished if psychic equilibrium is to be re-established. Freud's analysis is fundamentally retrospective; Jung's is prospective.

Within this framework, individuation is the continuous responding to this compensatory tendency called the "transcendent function." This function is "transcendent" because it urges the person to transcend one's present limited standpoint and to open oneself to other ways of perceiving and structuring experience. Consequently, the more the person is able to respond to the transcendent function, the more mobile one becomes among the various typological quadrants and the more the psyche becomes centered and balanced. No longer a caricature of one's full potential to experience in a variety of ways, the individuated person responds to phenomena as is appropriate in each situation, not blocking out possibilities of responding merely because they are antipodal to the former self-image. Bound neither by conceptual thinking nor by sheer feeling, neither by the piecework objectivity of sensation nor by the integrative monism of intuition, the ideally individuated person is of no *fixed* psychological type—one changes the mode of functioning to suit the circumstances. Without conscious direction, one responds to the balancing forces in the psyche that bring equilibrium. Although Jung understands individuation to be a limiting ideal that can only be very crudely approximated, there is much in this conception that has an affinity with the Zen view of the person and we will now consider four of the most significant of these points.

First, there is in this model of individuation, as in Zen, the ambiguity between the determinancy and indeterminancy of the person. The less the person is characterizable as a fixed psychological type, the more open one is to the possibility of experiencing the newness of each situation. Within Zen this idea is expressed in terms of there being no objectified "self" or "agent." Both the individuated person and the Zen person is determinate only within a given situation, only at a given time: there is no abiding self or agent that filters or reconstructs the experience before it is made fully conscious. Secondly, the Zen ideal and the individuated person are both free from being totally directed by the unconscious forces of compulsion.

This point is a corollary of the first in that the transcendence of a fixed sense of self eliminates the resistance that gives rise to compulsive outbreaks (when the person is suddenly "not oneself"). Thirdly, both the individuated and Zen persons deal with the present *in* the present: there is no Freudian project of recapturing the past in order to free new possibilities of responding in the present. Lastly, in both Jung's and Zen's ideal, the personality functions as a psychic whole without conflict between conscious and unconscious or ego and id. In Freud, on the other hand, these subdivisions of the personality are always antagonistic to each other's aims.

Once again, though, we must not let the similarities between Zen and Jung on this single point collapse into the position that their projects are equivalent. First of all, Jung's psychoanalytic enterprise is still primarily *interpretive*. In other words, the analyst's main duty is to help the analysand to interpret the messages from the unconscious as they are communicated through archetypal images. Although Jung believes that the full interpretation of these images requires imagination and intuition as well as scientific objectivity, the Zen Master would still consider them counter-productive in that they reify experience. For Zen, to be attached to interpretations of archetypes is as dangerous as to be dependent on interpretations of words: both are flights from the pre-reflective character of non-thinking. Second, Zen would find Jung's theory to be too self-oriented. The very term "individuation" seems egotistical and it appears to refer to the process of self-knowledge that does not recognize Dōgen's admonition that "to know the self is to forget the self." Stated differently, within Jung's system each person is pursuing "one's own" path to self-discovery and this assumes a self-consciousness quite foreign to Zen. There is no place in Jung's theory for the emptiness of Zen's "original face," or "the Person of his original part," i.e., there is no sense of a return to something more basic than the differentiated self. Lastly, in Zen there is a strong sense of there being something specific to be "realized"—in both senses of the term—something to be recognized and something to be accomplished. Each Master's realization is handed down to the disciples and a tradition is thereby established, whereas Jung himself offers little practical guidance—each person must find one's own way. There is no "tradition" of individuation and there never can be—for Jung, each person's process is unique.

Now let us generalize the points we have made concerning Zen and psychoanalysis.

IV. CONCLUSION: ZEN AND PSYCHOANALYSIS

In Japan I heard a story about a discussion between a Zen Master and an American who was formerly a psychotherapist but who had been practicing Zen in a monastery for six months. During their conversation, the American noted that he had sensed a continuity between his two experiences in that both Zen and psychotherapy were directed at helping people—what we have been calling here the common goal of freeing the person to respond more creatively to his present situation. Speaking slowly, the Master replied, "Yes, but Zen and psychotherapy are not really the same. In psychotherapy the doctor is still a patient." Then, with a smile beginning to sweep across his face, he added, "Furthermore, although psychotherapy might be able to help somewhat, can it help a rock? Can it set a pair of shoes in order?"

Using these statements as a point of departure, we can generalize the major conclusions reached in the three comparisons discussed in this paper.

"In psychotherapy the doctor is still a patient."

For better or worse, the analyst lacks the authority of the Zen Master. Being a psychoanalyst is an occupation; being a Zen Master is a way of life. The analysand improves his or her situation by working through the techniques and interpretations suggested by the analyst, but the Zen disciple becomes more aware of himself or herself simply through the direct interaction with the Master's personal authenticity. Fromm makes a similar point:

Accordingly, the [Zen] teacher is not a teacher in the Western sense. He is a master, inasmuch as he has mastered his own mind, and hence is capable of conveying to the student the only thing that can be conveyed: his existence.[25]

The corollary of this idea is that the Master's authority does not go unchallenged. In the *sanzen* interview the Master as well as the student are under pressure to display the "original face." The authenticity of the Master's state of non-thinking is not merely assumed: it must be *manifest*. Unlike the analyst who seeks a doctor's objectivity toward the patient's condition (a doctor with a heart condition, for example, may treat a patient with a similar condition), the Zen Master teaches solely by *exemplifying* that which the disciple seeks. The Chinese Zen Master Rinzai (Ch: Lin-chi) was known to his followers as the "crouching lion" because of the dynamic spontaneity he displayed in *sanzen*. Through his non-thinking responsiveness, he was capable of almost any action: he might strike, roar, pounce or sit back and purr. Again, the Zen Master is not a person with special knowledge or special techniques; the Master is a special person.

> Furthermore, although psychotherapy might be able to help people somewhat, can it help a rock? Can it set a pair of shoes in order?

This koan-like comment was perhaps directed specifically to the state of mind of the American Zen student and its full implications are undoubtedly closed to us. Nevertheless, it will be discussed here insofar as it is suggestive of two observations we have already made in this paper:

(1) Zen would maintain that one of the problems in psychoanalysis is that people are often confused with their parts: the conscious/unconscious, ego/id/superego, conscious psychological type/unconscious shadow, etc. For the Zen Master, the person is what is manifested here at this very moment. No conceptual mediation or questions about past experiences are necessary; the Master responds to students just-as-they-are. When placing a rock in a rock garden, the Master does not characterize the parts of the rock nor inquire into its past. Given the rock and the garden, the Master intuitively responds to the appropriateness of the situation, putting the rock where it "should be." This ideal applies to the Master's treatment of disciples. The Zen system of training is based on the assumption that if the teacher establishes a responsive, non-thinking relationship with the student, there is no need for explicit concern about technique or about the problem of transference. To have a previously

planned strategy of teaching only limits the teacher's capacity to fully respond to the student's existence as presented.

(2) The other point, an extension of the first, is the *everyday nature* of the Zen Master's non-thinking relationship. Non-thinking is not a mode of consciousness reserved for *sanzen* interviews. In psychoanalysis, as we have seen, there is much consideration given to the special relationship between analyst and analysand. For the Zen Master, his relationship to the student is only one example of non-thinking. The Master is also in a relationship of non-thinking when drinking tea or sweeping the garden. Of course, the response to the student is different from that to a teacup or a broom, because the student manifests himself or herself in a different way. The Master merely goes through the day setting shoes in order, sweeping leaves in the garden, moving bowels, helping students. Unaware of individuation, the Master feels no need to interpret dreams nor to distinguish the conscious from the unconscious. Since non-thinking is a *mode of relating* and not a technique nor a special understanding, it continues throughout the day in whatever the Master does. It is in this respect that the Zen Buddhist view of the person goes beyond the more restricted psychoanalytic categories of Freud and Jung.

Notes

1. See, for example, Fromm, Suzuki and DeMartino, *Zen Buddhism and Psychoanalysis* (New York: Harper and Row, 1960). On p. 78 of that volume, Fromm notes some previous writings in the area.
2. See, for example, Jung's Foreword to D. T. Suzuki's *Introduction to Zen Buddhism* (New York: Grove Press, 1964).
3. In deference to an audience of psychoanalysts, D. T. Suzuki once lectured on the nature of the "unconscious" in Zen Buddhism, but his usage of the term is patently not Freudian. Not only does Suzuki call this unconscious "ante-scientific" and "Cosmic," but it is also clearly a state of awareness rather than unawareness. See Fromm, *ZB and Psychoanalysis*, pp. 10–24.
4. The translation of *shiryō* (思量), *fushiryō* (不思量) and *hishiryō* (非思量) as "thinking," "not-thinking" and "non-thinking" follows the rendering of Waddell and Abe in their translation of Dōgen's *Fukanzazengi* (*The Eastern Buddhist*, VI: 2, October 1973, p. 123). In some contexts, it might be helpful to translate the third term, *hishiryō*, as "without thinking." An English discussion of Dōgen's distinction can be found in Hee-Jin Kim's excellent book, *Dōgen Kigen: Mystical Real-*

ist (Tucson: University of Arizona Press, 1975), pp. 76–78. The only serious criticism I have of Kim's account is that he tends to introduce too many metaphysical and mystical nuances by translating the second term, *fushiryō,* as "the unthinkable." An excellent, dialectically oriented discussion of the three terms can be found in Akiyama Hanji's Japanese work, *Dōgen no kenkyū [A Study of Dōgen]* (Tokyo: Iwanami shoten, 1935; republished by Reimei shobō in 1965), pp. 258–66. See also my *Zen Action/Zen Person* (Honolulu: University of Hawaii Press, 1981), pp. 71–77.

5. For a consideration of some of the humanistic ideals shared by Freud and Zen, see Fromm's essay, "Psychoanalysis and Zen Buddhism," in Fromm, *ZB and Psychoanalysis,* pp. 77–141.

6. Sigmund Freud, "Analysis Terminable and Interminable" (1937) in *The Standard Edition of the Complete Psychological Works of Sigmund Freud,* ed. and trans. James Strachey (London: The Hogarth Press and the Institute of Psycho-Analysis, 1958), XXIII: 235. Henceforth, *Standard Edition* is abbreviated *SE* with volume and page numbers.

7. *Ibid.,* p. 238.

8. For a comprehensive examination of the varieties of defense mechanisms, see Anna Freud, *The Ego and the Mechanisms of Defense,* trans. Cecil Baines (New York: International Universities Press, 1946).

9. "It sometimes turns out that the ego has paid too high a price for the services they [the mechanisms of defense] render it. The dynamic expenditure necessary for maintaining them, and the restrictions of the ego which they almost invariably entail, prove a heavy burden on the psychical economy. . . . They become regular modes of reaction in his character, which are repeated throughout his life whenever a situation occurs that is similar to the original one." Freud, "Terminable," *SE,* XXIII: 237.

10. *Ibid.,* p. 238.

11. *Ibid.*

12. Freud, *An Autobiographical Study* (1925), in *SE,* XX: 42.

13. For an excellent summary of Freud's use of the term "transference" throughout his career, see J. Laplanche and J. B. Pontalis, *The Language of Psychoanalysis,* trans. Donald Nicholson-Smith (New York: W. W. Norton, 1973), pp. 455–64.

14. Freud, *Interpretation of Dreams* (1900), in *SE,* V: 562–63.

15. Of course, the interrelationship between patient and analyst is also functional in the opposite direction as well. Although Freud himself only touched on this topic, later analysts have taken up the study of "countertransference." That is to say, repressed material may also arise from the *analyst's* unconscious causing irrational attachment or hostil-

ity to a particular patient. For a comprehensive treatment, see Heinrich Racker's *Transference and Counter-transference* (London: Hogarth Press and the Institute of Psycho-Analysis, 1968).

16. Freud, "Analytic Therapy," in *Introductory Lectures on Psycho-Analysis* in *SE*, XVI: 455.

17. "Analysts are people who have learned to practice a particular art; alongside of this, they may be allowed to be human beings like everyone else." Freud, "Terminable," *SE*, XXIII: 247.

18. The same ambivalence is formalized in the roles of the five officers of the monastery. For example, the *jikijitsu* is the stern disciplinarian and the *shoji* is the supportive guardian of the monks' welfare. Importantly, the five officers periodically rotate their roles so that the stern *jikijitsu*, for example, may suddenly become the kindly *shoji*. For further details about the roles of the officers, see Joshu Sasaki, *Buddha is the Center of Gravity* (San Cristobal, New Mexico: The Lama Foundation, 1974), pp. 64–65.

19. abreaction—the psychic re-enactment of a previously repressed traumatic experience so as to relieve the psychic tension accrued from the original incident and the repression of its memory.

20. Freud, *Studies in Hysteria* (1895), in *SE*, II: 270.

21. *Ibid.*, p. 279.

22. For Freud's emphasis on the importance of putting the affect into words, see *Studies in Hysteria, SE*, II: 255.

23. See Carl G. Jung, *Psychological Types* (1921), in *The Collected Works of Carl G. Jung*, trans. R. F. C. Hull (Princeton: Princeton University Press, 1971), VI.

24. See Jung, "The Transcendent Function" (written in 1916; rev. and pub. 1958), in *Collected Works*, VIII: 67–91.

25. Fromm, *ZB and Psychoanalysis*, p. 120.

Jung, Eastern Religion, and the Language of the Imagination

All of Jung's major writing on Buddhism and on Eastern religion generally, were undertaken between 1936–1944, with the exception of 'The Secret of the Golden Flower' which appeared in 1929. He produced the work on mandala symbolism in 1950 and subsequently reconsidered his commentaries and two Tibetan texts in 1953. His visit to India took place between 1938 and 1939. It is important to situate these works in the development of Jung's opus. The earlier phase which led to his cooperation with Freud ended in 1912, with the publication of *Symbols of Transformation*. This work with its rich use of symbolism, the hero myth and the idea of matriarchy, not only sealed his split from Freud, it also plunged Jung into a period of isolation and introspection which ended in 1921 with the publication of *Psychological Types*. From 1921 to 1936 Jung was attempting to find objective parallels to the process he had discovered both in his own inner explorations, and in those of his patients and colleagues. Gnosticism and then *The Secret of the Golden Flower* (an alchemical and Taoist text), provided him with such models. In 1936, when his first works on Buddhism appeared, Jung was already sixty-one years old. His ideas had been maturing over the past twenty-four years but had not yet found their way to the alchemical framework which dominated his work in the last twenty-five years of his life. Jung's studies in Eastern religion mark a fundamental turning point in the development of his ideas. In this period Jung took a decisive step into the use of imaginative discourse as an analytical tool.

When looking at Jung's references to Eastern religion, four recurring themes stand out:

1. He was concerned with the practical problems for a Westerner using Eastern spiritual methods and philosophy.

2. The image of wholeness, of a goal, or of an organizing principle of healing became central to this thinking. The mandala and the Buddha were images which drew his attention.
3. Practical insights into *the meaning* of meditational and active imagining experiences occur in Jung's work of this period.
4. Under the name synchronicity, Jung began to investigate a-causal reality. This included imaginative discourse and the use of symbols in healing and spiritual transformation.

THE WESTERN USE OF EASTERN RELIGION

According to Jung we have to read Eastern texts in the light of their context. He insisted upon a psycho-cultural analysis of the context from which any spiritual practice or philosophy is drawn. He saw four major problems with the indiscriminate mimicry of Buddhism, and Eastern religion generally.

1. The Descent into Interior Reality

Reading Eastern texts from cover to cover, Jung puzzled over the extensive psychological systems of Indian and Tibetan religious thought, and their concomitant lack of the systematic study of external reality. He saw this as being in marked contrast to the West's extensive scientific and technological studies and the relative absence of psychological work. He realized that these concerns reflected the valuation of inner and outer reality in the two cultural matrices. Jung considered that the West was over-concerned with an extroverted attitude and the East with an introverted one. He viewed both attitudes as being one-sided:

> In the East the inner man has always had such a firm hold on the outer man that the world had no chance of tearing him away from his inner roots; in the West, the outer man gained the ascendancy to such an extent that he was alienated from his innermost being.[1]

Jung was not reducing these two great cultures to 'nothing but' extroversion or introversion. He was simply trying to identify the dominant psychological attitude from which knowledge arose. Jung was one of the first students of East-West studies to direct attention to the *way* in which the East has been read by the West and what the East *means* to the West. This approach asks such questions as: under what conditions were the various Eastern cultures encountered by the West, and what was the mythic or imaginative substructure which supported the East-West interchange and upon which concepts and ideas were moved around? Such a perspective views the cross-cultural interchange as resting upon an ocean of symbols.[2]

Jung maintained that when a Westerner (with a dominant extroverted tone) approaches an Eastern psychological/spiritual text (with its dominant introverted tone) he or she should entirely *reverse* the instructions. So in the case of *The Tibetan Book of the Dead* and *The Tibetan Book of the Great Liberation*, Jung suggested that it traditionally represented the initiation process moving from the highest, and most exalted state of pure mind, to the lowest, which is rebirth in the womb and the movement into the world. However, in the West, psychology as an initiation system works in the reverse order. It begins with incarnate life in the world, and "regresses" back to the memories of earliest childhood and the birth trauma and thence to intra-womb and intrauterine experience. Such psychological experiences prior to the moment of conception are beginning to be tentatively explored in transpersonal psychology, as the introverted undercurrent begins to reassert itself in the West.[3]

Jung also turned his attention towards Kundalini Yoga, which could apply equally to certain forms of Tibetan Yoga. The traditional path of awakening is from the lowest to the highest. In Kundalini this is expressed as moving upwards from the lowest chakra, the *mūlādhāra*, which is located near the genitals. This chakra indicates the state from where we begin, our taken-for-granted world. But, as Jung pointed out, in the West 'we do not go up into the unconscious we go down'.[4] He continued:

> In adapting the system to ourselves, we must realize where we stand before we can assimilate such a thing. In the East the unconscious is above . . . so we can reverse the whole thing.

In the West we begin in the external world and have to undertake a *nekyia*, a descent into interior reality. Jung claimed that with the East it is an opposite movement.

2. The Question of Fantasy Content

In his commentary on *The Secret of the Golden Flower*, Jung drew attention to the injunction in this work to reject all fantasy contents. This, he wrote, appeals to the pragmatic scientific Western mind. But the Eastern dictum is not addressed to this rational extroverted mind with its relative poverty and ignorance of fantasy. Jung insisted that in the East there is so much awareness of mythic reality that,

> protection is required against the excess of fantasy. We, on the other hand, look upon fantasy as valueless, subjective daydreaming.[5]

He continued:

> The East can reject these fantasies because long ago it extracted their essence and condensed it in profound teachings. But we have never even experienced these fantasies. . . . The East came to its knowledge of inner things in relative ignorance of the external world. We, on the other hand, will investigate the psyche and its depths supported by a tremendously extensive historical and scientific knowledge.

Jung warned that any Western 'reading' of other knowledge systems must take cognizance of the conditioned onesidedness from which we view the world. Failure to do this could lead either to non-comprehension and a feeling of cultural superiority, or to a naive and unreflective acceptance.

3. Avoidance of the Shadow

As early as 1929, Jung wrote,

> I am in principle against the uncritical appropriation of yoga practices by Europeans because I know only too well that they hope to avoid their own dark corners.[6]

I think this is why certain Buddhist teachers, such as Chogyam Trungpa, radically changed their style to a far more rugged one, when they came to the West; hence the title of one of his books:

Cutting Through Spiritual Materialism (Berkeley: Shambhala, 1976). This book is aimed at precisely the same misuse of spiritual techniques that Jung was warning about over fifty years ago. James Hillman has recently continued this critique:

> In the East the spirit is rooted in the thick yellow loam of richly pathologized imagery—demons, monsters, grotesque goddesses, tortures and obscenities. . . . But once uprooted and imported to the West it arrives debrided of its imaginal ground, dirt-free and smelling of sandalwood![7]

This could be called "export quality" mysticism.

My experiences with Tibetan Buddhism in the West have certainly borne out Jung's concerns. I have consistently encountered a bewilderment and sometimes an hostility whenever Tibetan Buddhism is mentioned in tones which are less than sacrosanct. In numerous conversations I have found that many cannot accept the fact that Tibetan monastic Buddhism has evolved alongside political power struggles and violence. Even if these are grudgingly conceded, then it is quickly pointed out that this is not the 'real' Buddhism. However, Christianity does not receive the same laissez-faire treatment. Christianity and its shadow side are generally associated together, even if lip service is given to the equality of all religions. This may seem to be a harsh generalization but I have encountered it so often, from Europe to Australia, that it does seem consistent. A veneer of spiritual tolerance can easily become established. Ironically the image of Tibetan Buddhism as being *tolerant* can become incorporated into the belief in its superiority.

The problem from the imaginative point of view is that the avoidance of the shadow removes paradox. Imaginative cognition can become paralysed beneath Eastern religion's pure persona in the West.

4. The Thin Veneer

Jung considered that the cultural soul of the West has been largely untouched by Christianity. He wrote of the

> unconscious and undeveloped psyche which is as pagan and archaic as ever, . . . a psychic condition that has remained archaic and has not been even remotely touched by Christianity.[8]

In Jung's imaginative reconstruction of history, the West is fundamentally a half-savage culture covered by a thin layer of Oriental
religious civilization:

> Only a little more than a thousand years ago we stumbled out of
> the crudest beginnings of polytheism into a highly developed
> Oriental religion which lifted the imaginative minds of half-
> savages to a height that in no way corresponded to their spiritual
> development.[9]

In other words the 'primitive' culture of the West was transformed
from outside and not by an organic evolution from within. Christianity, that one time 'Oriental' religion, attempted to lift the psyche
of our ancestors and utilized methods that were often brutal. In actuality the depths remained largely untouched. However, instead of
recognizing this untouched primitivity, Westerners ignored and repressed it.[10] Jung had in mind the religious persecutions, witch burn-
ings, religious wars, world wars, together with the iniquities of colo-
nialism and imperialism. We could also add to this list the disregard
for ecology and human rights.

This concern of Jung's was not so much one of the shadow or
the repressed, as it was of the untouched cultural soul. He wrote,
'how thin is the wall that separates us from pagan times'.[11] These
unrecognized elements of the psyche, untouched by Oriental Christianity, 'naturally did not develop, but went on vegetating in their
original barbarism.'[12]

In a sense, Jung was pointing to an *earlier* importation of Eastern, or Oriental religion and to its consequences. The West has
always been vulnerable to Eastern religion. In addition to Christianity, Jung cited the earlier Roman adoption of Mithraic religion,
which also was initially an Eastern cult. Once again,

> while we are turning the material world of the East upside down
> with our technical proficiency, the East with its superior psychic
> proficiency is throwing our spiritual world into confusion.[13]

For Jung, the lesson was quite clear. Westerners have repeatedly
adopted or copied Eastern religion. We have been attracted to its

sublime and lofty conclusion. 'We would like to scale the heights of a philosophical religion, but in fact are incapable of it'.[14]

The danger is that the depths of the psyche remain untouched. Jung stressed that unless the instinctual, or unconscious mind is given equal respect to that given to the conscious mind, then that which is repressed will return with a vengeance. This explains why depth psychology moves towards the instinctual and the pathological in human experience. Jung saw the psychopathological symptoms—hysteria, schizophrenia, depression and so on—as the psyche crying out and trying to articulate its demands. The attraction to the religions of the East, of paganism, of shamanism, of theosophy, are also viewed by Jung as calls from the psyche. But according to him they should be seen as a first stumbling step towards illumination, and to be 'read' psychologically, to be insighted mythologically and not adopted philosophically nor in terms of technique. They are signs pointing to deeper rumblings in the psyche and do not constitute imported answers: 'Christianity must indeed begin again from the very beginning if it is to meet its high educative task'.[15]

THE IMAGE OF WHOLENESS

Jung drew upon two images of wholeness from Eastern religion. These were the Buddha and the Mandala.[16]

Jung considered the Buddha to be a more complete image of wholeness than Christ.[17] The Christ figure for Jung was too bright, and too good. Hence any shadow had to be carried by the Devil. Any image of wholeness must, according to Jung, be a complex balance of all possible opposites. Darkness and paradox must have their place. This would clearly be the case for example in Vajrayāna or Shingon Buddhism, as well as in the I Ching, or in Taoism.

In his later work, Jung wrote that the so-called unity of consciousness is an illusion. Wholeness and authenticity is a multi-dimensional psychic process, which is in constant change. Personality is less a unity, than the result of many contending inner figures. It was called a *complexio oppositorum* in Jung's alchemical language. But in Jung's work this process orientation sometimes became a bit static and fixed, as the Judeo-Christian view reasserted itself. But Jung stressed that the mandala represented not just a process of integration, but also one of *differentiation*.[18]

PRACTICAL INSIGHTS INTO THE DEVELOPMENT OF MEDITATION AND ACTIVE IMAGINING

It is clear that Jung did not fully appreciate Buddhist meditation. He tended to see meditative concentration and absorption (*samādhi*) as an unconscious state. For Jung if there was not an object of consciousness, there could be no consciousness.[19] Jung made sweeping statements about meditation without recognizing their variety. For example, he saw Buddhist meditation as wholly dependent on the individual—this is the 'self-power' of Zen. But Jung ignores the idea of 'other-power', found in Japanese Shin Buddhism. Jung also gives the unconscious a rather negative tone when he discusses meditation. He saw meditation as primarily a one-sided attempt to withdraw from the world.[20] He saw it as a surrender to the collective unconscious, an introverted journey into self absorption. In part, this suspicion stems from the first two points discussed above. Jung was continually concerned about the avoidance of the shadow and of the *content* of psyche.

Jung's studies in Eastern religion also raised the issue of the use of collectively structured images as opposed to individually spontaneous ones. There is much debate, for example, in humanistic and depth psychology, over the difference between guided imagining using prestructured imagery to initiate inner revelation and individual, spontaneous, unprepared imaginings.[21] There seems to be a continual struggle in spiritual practices to discipline the imagination and to harness it for its purposes. In such attempts, it is important to ascertain both the social and individual implications. To what extent, for example, is the individual's symbol forming capacity being appropriated, paralyzed, blocked or denied, let alone channelled into a particular direction, by stereotyped religious imagery? Jung wrote that 'every closed system of religion has an undoubted tendency to suppress the unconscious in the individual as much as possible, thus paralyzing his fantasy activity. Instead, religion offers stereotyped symbolic concepts that are meant to take the place of his unconscious once and for all.'[22]

In his analysis of Pure Land Buddhist meditation, *The Tibetan Book of the Dead*, *The Tibetan Book of the Great Liberation*, and *The Secret of the Golden Flower*, Jung was mainly concerned with them as *statements* of psychological processes. He was not praising them as *methods* to be adopted. When asked by a psychologist how dreams fitted into his system, Jung replied mischievously, 'What system?' He also wrote that 'there are ways which bring us nearer to living experience, yet we should beware of calling these ways "methods." The very word has a deadening effect'.[23]

There have been numerous studies relating Jung's ideas to Zen meditation, but few on Jung and Tibetan Vajrayāna practices.[24] This is a strange omission when it is realized that a considerable proportion of Jung's writings on Eastern religion was directed towards commentaries on two extremely esoteric Tibetan texts.

Whatever the reason for this omission, the studies on Jung and Zen fail to bring out the issue of pre-structured meditational imagery.[25] This is unfortunate for it also tends to avoid the problem of the way in which Eastern ideas have been randomly used as *techniques* in the West. The Tibetan Vajrayāna is particularly vulnerable to being reduced to a series of techniques.[26] If Jung was averse to his own ideas being reduced to methods and techniques, one can imagine he would be equally opposed to the same thing happening to Eastern traditions.

In Tibet, for example, the practice of Vajrayāna may well be considered as including many techniques, but this is within a complex traditional cultural setting of devotion and faith. The image of 'technique' rests on an entirely different ocean of symbols to what it does in the West. Also, there is no reason to believe that a 'tool' taken from one culture will produce exactly the same results in another. To describe Vajrayāna as a series of very advanced techniques, can lead to a stress on psychic powers, magical masters, spiritual technocrats, mystical astronauts and religious athletes. Athletics can replace devotion or investigation and turn the religions of the world into a kind of spiritual Olympics. The myth of inner progress can easily be substituted for the myth of outer progress.

The use of science and technology as a metaphor has been a rich and rewarding one in the field of comparative knowledges, but it must always be remembered that science itself is a metaphor and a symbol. It is not literally true or false. To literalize Eastern religion as a science is as great an error as dismissing it as a true childish fantasy.

A-CAUSAL OR MYTHIC CONSCIOUSNESS

The period of his Eastern studies occupies a crucial place in Jung's movement towards a consistent mythical style. Jung attempted to reconstruct the language which was specific to the psyche and the imagination. He wrote in 1935:

> For the human psyche is not a psychiatric nor a physiological problem; it is not a biological one. It is a field of its own with its own peculiar laws. Its nature cannot be deduced from the principles of other sciences without doing violence to the idiosyncrasies of the psyche. It cannot be identified with the brain, or the hormones or any known instinct, for better or worse it must be accepted as a phenomenon unique in its kind.[27]

He insisted that the depth imagination resists being known except in its own terms. It was Jung's attempt to articulate this idiosyncratic language of the imagination, which caused him to be the focus of scorn.

Jung's language, style and method of investigation are far from being the peripheral issue they are usually taken to be. They have received the excesses of both praise and scorn. Heisig, in his study of Jung's psychology of religion, documents some of these comments. One theorist claimed:

> Jung isn't a thinker in the proper sense. He's a dreamer who carried himself with the sureness of a sleepwalker.

and Aldous Huxley wrote:

> Jungian Literature is like a vast quaking bog. At every painful step the reader sinks to the hip in jargon and generalizations, with never a patch of firm intellectual ground to rest on, and only rarely, in that endless expanse of jelly, the blessed relief of a hard concrete fact.[28]

It was the dedication to this neglected form of cognition that caused a certain misunderstanding on the part of some commentators concerned with Jung's supposedly antirational stance. For example, Piaget wrote:

> Jung has an amazing capacity for construction, but a certain contempt for logic and rational activity; ... this has made him inclined to be content with too little in the way of proof.[29]

Nothing could be further from the truth. For Jung, reason and its description of reality were not wrong, but one-sided and insufficient. Jung wrote in 1946,

> Intellectual or supposedly scientific theories are not adequate to the nature of the unconscious, because they make use of a terminology which has not the slightest affinity with its pregnant symbolism. ... (The approach) must therefore be plastic and symbolical and itself the outcome of personal experience with unconscious contents. It should not stray too far in the direction of abstract intellectualism; hence we are best advised to remain within the framework of traditional mythology.[30]

Jung gave many names to both systems of cognition and thought. On the one hand there is 'thinking in words', 'thinking with directed attention', 'logical or directed thinking'.[31] On the other hand there is fantasy thinking, which occurs once we do not think in a directed fashion. At this point, thinking in 'verbal form ceases, image piles on image, feeling on feeling.'
Jung asked:

> How are fantasies made and what is their nature? From the poets we learn much, from the scientists little.[32]

He was insistent upon this cognitive dichotomy, because the object of investigation in both cases is entirely different. Imaginative discourse and perception is concerned with the region of depth experience and of meaning.
It has been the task of esoteric (religious, occult, hermetic) language through the ages to transform and re-educate cognition. The

symbol calls for a response and a commitment. It cannot be ignored. The use of riddles, koans, and other forms of paradox, to block the rational mind, and hence to force the intuitive, the imaginative leap, are common. There is also the use of the *via negativa* as in the Buddhist *Heart Sutra*, which exhausts the assumptions and speculations of the rational mind.

Another example of the special power and place of imaginative description can be seen when we compare the more mythic accounts of altered states of consciousness, with much of the recent rational psychological work in that area. The rational-scientific descriptions of altered states of consciousness abound in abbreviations—there are "ASC's," and "BPM 1, 2, 3, 4."[33] This style of nomenclature can also be found in ancient religious traditions such as Buddhism, where meditative absorption levels are known as 1st Jhana, 2nd Jhana, etc. However, the mythic or imaginative perspective personifies these realms so that they become deities and heroes. Instead of abstract levels and categories, we find kinship systems, disputes, marriages, wars, a long involved history of struggles, dominance, subjugation and harmony. These altered states of consciousness and altered worlds of consciousness, such as the Buddhist Pure Lands, suggest a certain grandeur and autonomy. They are not neatly categorized, nor can they be reviewed in an aloof and detached manner. They are ancient lands which seem to exert a compulsion over us.

Another place in Buddhism where imaginative discourse is to be found, is in the use of the dohās, or tantric poetry. The siddha Saraha is the most well-known composer of dohās. In a story of Saraha's life it is recounted how this Indian Siddha was sent to find an arrowsmith woman. When he found this woman, she told him, 'My dear young man, the Buddha's meaning can be known through symbols and actions, not through words and books'.[34] In the use of tantric symbols —mantra, mudra, mandala—there is an attempt to 'awaken', to 'tune', to 'massage' and to 'educate' the depth imagination.

Guenther makes some important comments on the use of language in the dohās.[35] He writes that Buddhism is a practical discipline which attempts not only to change outlook and experiences but that these 'are felt to be valuable in their own right'. In other words, they must be meaningful to the subject. Guenther goes on to write that the poem or song is not only 'the realization in its medium of language (or music) of the experience', it becomes equally 'the point of departure into fancy and reflection on the part of the audience'. The image exists in its own right; it is 'felt' immediately, 'it invites us to explore the depth', it does not represent anything else.

Whilst commenting on Saraha's poetry, Guenther writes that 'another kind of language is needed . . . to avoid the *concretizing* of inner processes into permanent externalized facts'.[36] The key word here is 'concretizing'. The Dalai Lama in talks given in 1982 in Melbourne, Australia, said that the purpose of mantra work and its associated practices is to overcome the sense that ourselves and the world are 'ordinary'. In other words, the purpose is to de-literalize the World. It is a process of an *opus contra naturam,* an alchemical work against the taken-for-grantedness of things. It is the attempt to see the world and ourselves as 'extra-ordinary', as fantasies in the fullest sense, as parts in the play of illusion. Rather than concretizing awareness, it is the depth imagination which is to be awakened and, most importantly, educated and made symbolically literate.

Jung was not interested in studying meditation from either a psychophysical perspective (e.g., bio-feedback or stress reduction), nor from a philosophical one. He was concerned with the *meaning* that such activity had for the meditator. To this extent archetypal psychology attempts to understand not consciousness in general but the internal dynamics of that elusive phenomenon, insight (*vipassanā, mahāmudrā, satori*). This approach is best revealed in Hillman's study of parapsychology, and Jung's study of U.F.O.'s.[37] Neither was concerned with the 'objective' reality of these phenomena and whether or not flying saucers or telepathy exist objectively. They wanted to know what the belief in these things meant to those who experienced them. Jung wanted to allow the images to tell their own story and to plot the process by which meaning and insight arise. Hence the value of alchemy, of *The Secret of the Golden Flower* and of the esoteric Buddhist texts with their dramatic imagistic records.

Jung by no means adequately conveyed the totality of Buddhism nor of any Eastern religious tradition. He was very selective and drew upon a limited number of esoteric texts. However, he did make a hesitant first step towards understanding the psycho-social matrix which supports the East-West interchange of ideas. These studies also allowed him to consolidate his commitment to imaginative discourse in his search to understand meaning and insight. This is undoubtedly the most important conclusion from Jung's Eastern studies and the one which is perhaps the most fruitful in any continuing interchange between East and West.

Notes

1. C. G. Jung, *Collected Works*, vol. 11 (London: Routledge & Kegan Paul, 1978), para. 785 (referred to hereafter as *C.W.*).
2. E.g. J. Campbell attempted an identification of specific mythological 'signatures' of the East and the West, in *Masks of God*, vols. 2 and 3 (London: Souvenir Press, 1974); Henri Baudet in his study *Paradise on Earth* (New Haven: Yale University Press, 1965) sketched the history of European images of non-European peoples and countries. Most recently, E. Said's *Orientalism* (New York: Vintage Books, 1979) has used the ideas of M. Foucault to analyse the fantasy of 'Orientalism' in the West.
3. *C.W.* 11, para. 842–855; e.g. S. Grof, *Realms of the Human Unconscious* (New York: E. P. Dutton, 1976).
4. 'Psychological Commentary on Kundalini Yoga', *Spring 1975* (New York, Spring Publications), p. 12; see also *C.W.* 11, para. 875.
5. *C.W.* 13, para. 63.
6. *C.W.* 11, para. 939.
7. J. Hillman, *Re-visioning Psychology* (New York: Harper and Row, 1977), p. 67.
8. *C.W.* 12, para. 12–13.
9. *C.W.* 13, para. 70–71.
10. *C.W.* 12, para. 12–13.
11. *C.W.* 9ii, para. 270–272.
12. *C.W.* 13, para. 70–71.
13. *C.W.* 10, para. 179–194.
14. *C.W.* 13, para. 70–71.
15. *C.W.* 12, para. 12–13.
16. See J. Thomas, 'The Bodhisattva as Metaphor to Jung's Concept of Self' in this volume, for a full discussion of Eastern religion and Jung's development of the concept of Self.
17. *C.W.* 12, para. 22.
18. J. Hillman, in his book *Re-visioning Psychology* (p. 67) writes that the first task is to 'fall apart', not to 'get things together'. Again, his insights come, in part, from Buddhism with its radical view of change, impermanence, and non-self. R. Avens, another contemporary archetypal theorist, refers to the *Avatamsaka Sutra* with its description of wholeness in terms of interpenetrating worlds of mutual concealment, and of relevation (*Imagination is Reality*, Irving: Spring Publications, 1980, p. 99).

19. See R. Jones, 'Jung and Eastern Religious Traditions', *Religion* 9, 2: Autumn 1979, p. 147, for a critique of Jung's reading of Eastern religions.
20. E.g. *C.W.* 11, para. 774.
21. See M. Watkins, *Waking Dreams* (New York: Harper and Row, 1977) for a detailed discussion of the use of visual imagery in Western therapy.
22. *C.W.* 5, para. 80.
23. *C.W.* 11, para. 501; see also *C.W.* 11, para. 868–871.
24. See D. Lauf, *Secret Doctrines of the Tibetan Book of the Dead* (Boulder: Shambhala, 1977) as an example of a Jungian approach to Vajrayāna Buddhism; see also P. Bishop, 'The Karma-Kargyudpa Lineage Tree' in *Spring 1981* (Dallas: Spring Publications, 1981). P. Beyer in his study *The Cult of Tara* (Berkeley: University of California Press, 1973) also draws substantially upon an archetypal perspective.
25. Recent studies of the relationship between Jung and Zen Buddhism include M. Miyuki, 'The Psychodynamics of Buddhist Meditation: A Jungian Perspective', *Eastern Buddhist* X, 2: 1977, and T. Kasulis, 'Zen Buddhism, Freud and Jung', *Eastern Buddhist* X, 1: 1977.
26. See for example, W. Anderson's introduction to Tibetan Buddhism, *Open Secrets* (Harmondsworth: Penguin, 1980), pp. 5, 14–15, 21.
27. *C.W.* 16, para. 22.
28. J. Heisig, *Imago Dei: A Study of C. G. Jung's Psychology of Religion* (Lewisburg: Bucknell University Press, 1979), p. 107.
29. J. Piaget, *Play, Dreams and Imitation in Childhood* (New York: W. W. Norton and Co., 1962), p. 196.
30. *C.W.* 16, para. 478.
31. *C.W.* 5, para. 11–32.
32. *C.W.* 5, para. 33.
33. E.g. C. Tart, *Altered States of Consciousness* (New York: Doubleday, 1972); and Grof, *Realms of the Human Unconscious*.
34. H. Guenther, *The Royal Song of Saraha* (Seattle: University of Washington Press, 1969), p. 5; see also J. Ardussi, 'Brewing and Drinking the Beer of Enlightenment in Tibetan Buddhism: The Dohā Tradition in Tibet', *Journal of the American Oriental Society* 97, 2: 1977.
35. Guenther, *ibid.* pp. 23–24; see also H. Guenther, 'Tantra & Revelation', *History of Religions* 7, 4: May 1968, and G. Elder, 'Problems of Language in Buddhist Tantra', *History of Religions* 15, 3: February 1976.
36. Guenther, pp. 5–26.
37. J. Hillman, *Loose Ends* (Irving: Spring Publications, 1978); *C.W.* 10.

Mokusen Miyuki

Self-Realization in the Ten Oxherding Pictures

In my paper entitled, "A Jungian Approach to the Pure Land Practice of *Nien-fo*," I challenged the prevailing psychological view of Eastern religions as aiming at the "dissolution," or at the least the "depotentiation," of the ego.[1] I argued that the Pure Land Buddhist practice of *nien-fo* (the mental and/or verbal recitation of Amitabha's name), for example, aids the individual to strengthen, rather than dissolve, the ego through the integration of unconscious contents. In this paper, I would like to further support this point by examining the Zen tradition's *Oxherding Pictures*.[2] These pictures are products of the Zen "mind" and express in an art form the experience of *satori* or Zen enlightenment. Since enlightenment is a psychological reality *par excellence*, these pictures can be analyzed by employing Jungian methodology and his conceptual framework, and by viewing them as portraying what C. G. Jung calls "the individuation process."

Although only a few sets of the *Oxherding Pictures* exist today, in the past there must have been several sets of pictures—and those of various numbers. The variety of sets can be inferred from the fact that there are records of differing "verses" which accompany such pictures.[3] The Zen scholar D. T. Suzuki has made two sets of the *Ten Oxherding Pictures* which are well known in the West: namely, the set whose accompanying ten *Prefaces* and *Verses* were written by the twelfth century Zen master Kuo-an (Kaku-an in Japanese) and another earlier version to which the Zen master Pu-ming wrote the ten accompanying *Verses*.[4] The version by Kuo-an has enjoyed wide acceptance in Japan while the one by Pu-ming was popular in China.[5]

Pu-ming's *Ten Oxherding Pictures* portray a wild, black ox that becomes increasingly white as the pictures proceed. These pictures are entitled: (1) Undisciplined, (2) Discipline Begun, (3) In Harness, (4) Faced Round, (5) Tamed, (6) Unimpeded, (7) *Laissez Faire*, (8)

All Forgotten, (9) The Solitary Moon, and (10) Both Vanished. Evidently, the emphasis in these pictures is placed upon the gradual achievement of *satori* (Zen enlightenment), which is shown by the progressive whitening of the black ox. The concept of whitening that which is black is based on the Buddhist doctrine of *tathagata-garbha*, the realization of the Buddha-nature, or the genuine self, which is obscured by the dark side of the personality.

According to Ts'u-yuan, who wrote the *Preface* to Kuo-an's version, Kuo-an was not satisfied with the idea of a gradual whitening of the ox, nor with the gradual, progressive liberation of the Buddha-nature; thus, he presented his experience of *satori* in a different manner. His pictures are entitled: (1) Searching for the Ox, (2) Seeing the Traces, (3) Seeing the Ox, (4) Catching the Ox, (5) Herding the Ox, (6) Coming Home on the Ox's Back, (7) The Ox Forgotten, (8) The Ox and the Man Both Forgotten, (9) Returning to the Origin, Back to the Source, and (10) Entering the City with Bliss-bestowing Hands. The notion expressed in these pictures is the sudden gain or loss of one's genuine self, as symbolized by the ox.[6]

The Oxherding Pictures have also been referred to as the *Mind-ox Pictures*, thus indicating that the ox, or the genuine self, in the picture represents the Zen concept of "mind."[7] In Chinese Buddhism, the term "*hsin*," "mind," which also refers to the "heart" or essence, has been used interchangeably with the term "*hsing*," which means nature or essence. Accordingly, in Zen the psychic reality connected with the word "mind" is that of *satori* in the sense of "seeing one's own nature" (*chien-hsing*). A famous Zen tenet illustrates this connection:

A special transmission outside the scriptures,
Not depending upon letters,
Pointing directly to the Mind (literally "human mind")
See into Nature itself and attain Buddhahood.[8]

In this tenet the words "mind," "nature," and "Buddhahood" are all used to express different aspects of one and the same reality; namely, *satori*.

The view of *satori* implied in the pictures of both Pu-ming and Kuo-an is to be understood in terms of the doctrine of *tathagata-garbha*, or realization of the Buddha-nature. This doctrine assures the possibility of universal enlightenment and has become basic to the so-called "sinified Buddhism," such as Hua-yen, T'ien-tai, Ch'an (Zen in Japanese), or Ch'ing-t'u (Pure Land). For instance, Chih-yen (602–668 A.D.), the third patriarch of Hua-yen Buddhism, viewed the Buddha-nature as having a tripartite character: (1) the Buddha-nature itself, the genuine essence which is universally ever-present in all beings, although it is in a state of dark ignorance and passion, obscured and defiled; (2) the Buddha-nature as the driving force, (*yin-chu*) or the fundamental urge to realize itself through the practice of *prajna* (wisdom) and *samadhi* (concentration); and (3) the Buddha-nature as perfectly realized through practice.[9] In Zen, as mentioned above, both terms, "mind" and "nature" are used interchangeably in designating the Buddha-nature. Hence, the Zen concept of "mind" refers to something quite different from the Western concept of the word.

Jung was well aware of the fact that the Eastern concept of "mind" is radically different from that in the West. He states: "In the West, 'mind' is more or less equated with consciousness, whereas in the East the word 'mind' is closer to what the West refers to as the unconscious."[10] Jung seems to imply here that in the East the word "mind" designates what he means by the "psyche," or the psychological process which includes both conscious and unconscious. Were this so, the Zen concept of mind could be taken as equivalent to Jung's concept of the total psyche, or the Self.

Jung explains the relationship of consciousness to the unconscious as follows:

> Consciousness, no matter how extensive it may be, must always remain the smaller circle within the greater circle of the unconscious, an island surrounded by the sea; and like the sea itself, the unconscious yields an endless and self-replenishing abundance of living creatures, a wealth beyond our fathoming.[11]

From this viewpoint, then, the *Oxherding Pictures* can be understood as depicting the attempt of the oxherd, or the ego, to creatively relate itself to the inexhaustible treasure of the "mind-ox," or the unconscious. In Kuo-an's version, however, this confrontation of the ego with the unconscious ceases with the seventh picture wherein an "individuated man" is portrayed. Accordingly, the last three pictures by Kuo-an can be taken as describing the life of the genuine man, or the individuated ego, working in the service of the Self in and through common, daily activities.

In writing about individuation, Jung states: "Individuation means becoming a single, homogeneous being, and, in so far as 'individuality' embraces our innermost, last, and incomparable uniqueness, it also implies becoming one's own self. We could therefore translate individuation as 'coming to selfhood' or 'Self-realization.' "[12] The German term *Selbstverwirklichung,* which is translated here as "self-realization" in English, indicates the psychological urge of the Self to realize itself—the Self being the center and the whole circumference embracing both conscious and unconscious psyche. This point is clarified by Edward F. Edinger when he states: "Individuation seems to be the innate urge of life to realize itself consciously. The transpersonal life energy in the process of self-unfolding uses human consciousness, a product of itself, as an instrument for its own self realization."[13]

According to Jung, therefore, individuation begins with the innate urge of the Self for realization, regardless of the conscious will or external situation. To become "a single, homogenous being" is not something the ego can create at will. Being driven by the Self's urge, it becomes possible for the ego, the center of the conscious personality, to evolve. Jung states:

> "The ego stands to the self as the moved to the mover, or as object to subject, because the determining factors which radiate out from the self surround the ego on all sides and are therefore supraordinate to it. The self, like the unconscious, is an *a priori* existent out of which the ego evolves. It is, so to speak, an unconscious prefiguration of the ego. It is not I who create myself, rather I happen to myself."[14]

This fundamental urge of self-realization is basic to the creative life of the individual as well exemplified in Jung's *Memories, Dreams, Reflections* which begins with the following statement:

> "My life is a story of the self-realization of the unconscious. Everything in the unconscious seeks outward manifestation, and the personality too desires to evolve out of its unconscious condition and to experience itself as a whole."[15]

The innate urge for self-realization has been designated in Buddhism as that aspect of the Buddha-nature which, to use Chih-yen's conception, is manifested as the driving force to realize itself. The Buddha-nature is always present as Kuo-an states in his *Preface* to the first picture: "The beast has never gone away, and what is the use of searching for him" (p. 129). In Kuo-an's version, the eternal presence of the Buddha-nature as the Self's urge to realize itself is symbolized by the circle in which each of the ten pictures are depicted. For, the circle, which conveys the idea of the non-beginning and non-ending quality of eternity, represents the ever-presence of the Buddha-nature in which Zen practice takes place.

Once the innate urge of the Self to realize itself is activated, the Self relentlessly imposes on the ego the task of integrating the dark side of the psyche, or the unconscious. For as "the smaller circle within the greater circle of the unconscious,"[16] the ego is constantly conditioned by the Self as the determining factor for its existence and development. Since the Self is the paradoxical totality in which the opposites such as conscious and unconscious, light and darkness, good and evil, are united, there is no conscious realization of totality without integration of the opposites. Jung states: "Whenever the archetype of the self predominates, the inevitable psychological consequence is a state of conflict ... and man must suffer from the opposite of his intention for the sake of completeness."[17] The ego, thus endangered by the demand of the Self's urge to realize itself, is depicted in Pu-ming's version of the *Oxherding Pictures* by the gradual process of whitening, that is, the depotentiating and integrating the wild black ox as the symbol of the overwhelming energy of the unconscious.

Self-realization, or the ego's encounter of the archetype of the Self, is not a neutral experience. As a numinous experience, it exercises a powerful influence on the shaping or reshaping of conscious contents. Jung states:

> ... the archetypes have, when they appear, a distinctly numinous character which can only be described as "spiritual," if "magical" is too strong a word. Consequently this phenomenon is of the utmost significance for the psychology of religion. In its effects it is anything but unambiguous. It can be healing or destructive, but never indifferent, provided of course that it has attained a certain degree of clarity.[18]

The Ten Oxherding Pictures of Pu-ming

1. Undisciplined

2. Discipline Begun

3. In Harness

4. Faced Round

5. Tamed

6. Unimpeded

7. Laissez Faire

8. All Forgotten

9. The Solitary Moon

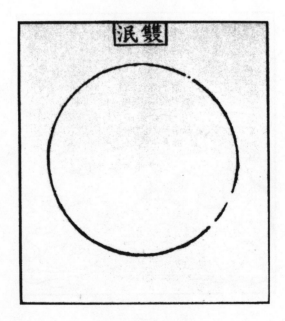

10. Both Vanished

The Ten Oxherding Pictures of Kuo-an

1. Searching for the Ox

2. Seeing the Traces

3. Seeing the Ox

4. Catching the Ox

5. Herding the Ox

6. Coming Home on the Ox's Back

7. The Ox Forgotten

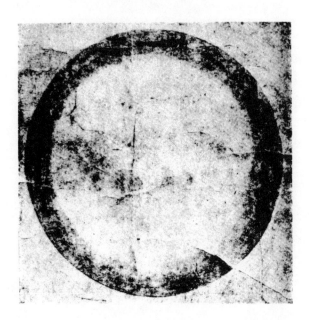

8. The Ox and the Man Both Gone Out of Sight

9. Returning to the Origin

10. Entering the City

Edward F. Edinger characterized the development of the ego in its confrontation with the Self as a circular process of alternating ego-Self separation and ego-Self union. He states: "Indeed, this cyclic (or better, spiral) formula seems to express the basic process of psychological development from birth to death."[19] In this manner, the progressive differentiation of the conscious life takes place continually throughout life as the result of conscious assimilation of the unconscious contents, or the enrichment of consciousness by the integration of the unconscious. The idea of the progressive enrichment of the conscious life is evidently depicted by Pu-ming, as mentioned above, by the gradual process of whitening, or integrating, the wild black ox, or the unconscious. It is also indicated by Kuo-an in the tenth picture of his version of the *Oxherding Pictures*. In this picture "Entering the City with Bliss-bestowing Hands," the scene of an old man meeting a young boy in the market place is portrayed, showing thus that enrichment of conscious life in and through common activities, such as meeting or greeting people on the street. With this last picture, the development of the ego reverts to ordinary life depicted in the first picture but on a richer level of consciousness.

Psychologically speaking, the circle symbolizes the *temenos*, the magic circle, or the protective function of the Self. The ego consciousness, as mentioned above, constantly faces the danger of being assimilated by the menacing energy of the unconscious. If it is to resist assimilation and be protected from the danger of fragmentation or disintegration, it is of prime importance for the ego to be strengthened by integrating the unconscious contents. In self-realization, the Self, which is the paradoxical totality, provides the ego with the strength and stability for its development while it simultaneously imposes on the ego the task of integrating the dark side of the personality. The protective function of the Self is indicated, in Kuo-an's version of the *Oxherding Pictures*, by the circle in which each of the ten pictures is depicted, representing thus the ever-presence of the Buddha-nature, or the Self, which provides the practitioner with strength and stability. The square in which Pu-ming portrayed each of the ten pictures in his version can also be taken as showing the utmost importance of the integration of the unconscious into consciousness, being supported by the Self's protective function.

In Zen practice, the archetype of the Self is projected onto the master as the ideal self-image; hence, the encounter of the ego with the Self takes place, as projected on the master-disciple relationship. Accordingly, Zen emphasizes the importance of meeting the "right" master for the disciple in seeking for a genuine realization of *satori*. The encouragement as well as the admonition of the master provides the disciple with the *temenos* within which the latter's psychological security is gained. Being thus protected from an unconscious outburst and disintegration, the disciple can attempt to creatively relate himself to the treasure house of the Buddha-nature or the unconscious.

Jung has observed that in the numinous experience, or the confrontation with the Self, mandala symbolism often emerges in the manifested unconscious materials, such as dreams, fantasies, psychic episodes, myths, fairytales, and such religious depictions as the *Oxherding Pictures*.

According to Jung, a mandala is a symmetrical structure consisting of ternary or quaternary combinations which are concentrically arranged. The ternary combinations symbolize the dynamic process of development or growth, whereas the quaternary configurations represent a static structural wholeness, or completion.[20] Jung's observation about the combination of the numbers three and four can be seen in the first seven pictures in Kuo-an's *Ten Oxherding Pictures*. Were it possible for us to understand the third picture, "Seeing the Ox," as representing the Zen "goal" of "seeing into Nature itself,"[21] then, the fourth picture, "Catching the Ox," can be taken as representing attained wholeness or completion. Since self-realization is cyclic or spiral, as symbolized by the empty circle, the achieved totality is both the end and the beginning. Thus, as soon as the fourth state is realized, a new struggle begins on a higher level of consciousness. The new process thus initiated in the fourth picture reaches its culmination in the sixth picture, with the seventh picture, as the fourth of this second series, depicting the completion of the second ternary process. Therefore, in the first seven pictures, we can observe two sets of processes: the process from the first to the third picture with the fourth as the completion, and the process from the fourth to the sixth picture with the seventh as a second completion. Since the number seven comprises the union and totality of the ternary process and the quaternary completion, the seventh picture can be taken as portraying a final accomplishment.

The view that the seventh picture of Kuo-an's version is symbolic of the completion of the process is supported by the title, "The Ox Forgotten, Leaving the Man Alone." In the preceding pictures, individuation or self-realization—in terms of the dialectical confrontation of the ego (the oxherd) and the Self (the ox)—has led the individual to experience a transformation of personality symbolized as "the Man." Kuo-an states in his *Verse:* "Where Lo! the ox is no more [in Sanskrit, literally "emptied"]; the man alone sits serenely" (p. 132). Thus, the ox, the Self, has "emptied" itself to become the "man." With this seventh picture, the oxherding scenes cease and the "man" is depicted instead of the ox. In Pu-ming's version, this individuated man is portrayed in the ninth picture, entitled "The Solitary Moon."

In Kuo-an's *Ten Oxherding Pictures,* therefore, *satori* as the ongoing process is depicted as three sets of processes; namely, the initial process from the first to the third picture with the fourth as the completion; the continuing process from the fourth to the sixth picture with the seventh as a second completion, which is followed by the life of the "individuated ego," or the "Self-centered ego," the ego which functions in the service of the Self, portrayed from the eighth to the tenth pictures. This third process reverts to the first picture as a third completion, returning thus to the "beginning" on a different level of consciousness.

The genuine "man" in the seventh stage must face, and struggle with another serious problem, or *duhkha* ("dis-ease"), precisely because this is the final state of achievement for the ego that has attempted conscious assimilation of unconscious contents. At this stage, individuation as the confrontation of the ego with the Self ceases as such; for, as far as the ego is concerned, there are no resources to draw upon in order to affect any change regarding the realization of the next stage. This stage can manifest as the perilous state of psychic stagnation against which it is said that the ego has no means to cope. This danger of psychic stagnation has been recognized in Buddhism and designated as "the danger of the Bodhisattva, or [of] the seeker for the ultimate enlightenment sinking into *sunyata*, or "emptiness."

According to the *Dasabhumi-sutra*, the "*Sutra* of the Ten 'Stages,' " which describes the ten stages of the Bodhisattva's spiritual progress, the Bodhisattva faces the danger of "sinking into *sunyata*," especially when he arrives at the seventh stage called the "Far-going" which follows the realization of the truth of "Interdependent Origination" at the sixth stage.[22] Since no means is available for the ego to overcome this psychic danger, the leap from this state to the next is no longer felt as an activity of the ego. Thus the *Dasabhumi-sutra* metaphorically speaks of the transition from the seventh stage, "Far-going," to the eighth, "Immovable," as follows: A sleeping man sees himself in a dream trying desperately to cross a raging torrent and to reach the yonder shore. His hopeless attempt awakens him. Once awakened, he finds himself free from all dis-ease (*duhkhas*) of worry, despair, frustration, or agony. The *sutra* describes this experience of *satori*, or awakening as "without merits" (*anabhogatas*).[23] The phrase "without merits" refers to the psychological condition wherein self-realization takes place so as the ego comes to function in an "ex-centric" manner in the service of the Self. Jung refers to this psychological state as "an ego-less mental condition," "consciousness without an ego," or the like, which is also expressed by St. Paul as the state in which "It is no longer I who live, but Christ who lives in me" (*Galatians* 2:20).[24] The *Dasabhumi-sutra* maintains, therefore, that the practice of the ten *paramitas*, or "perfections," in this eighth stage—as well as the last two stages—is carried out in and through the realization of the Buddha's wisdom and compassion. In other words, in these three last stages, the Bodhisattva is in the service of, and in perfect unison with, the spontaneous manifestation of the activity of the Buddha's wisdom and compassion. The expression "without merits" designates this "Self-centric" functioning of the psyche in self-realization.[25]

In the eighth picture, the "Self-centric" functioning of the psyche is symbolized by the empty circle. As mentioned above, the circle in which each of the ten pictures is portrayed represents the

ever-present activity of the Buddha-nature, or the Self in which Zen
practice is pursued. Therefore, the "empty circle" of the eighth picture can be taken as depicting the fully manifested activity of the
Buddha-nature, or the Self, in the conscious life of the practitioner
whose ego functions in the service of the Self. This is to say, in this
"Self-centric" condition of the psyche, the individual experiences
the paradoxical state-process of simultaneous occurrence of empty-
ing-fulfilling, or negating-affirming, in regard to the psychological
life. The ego is emptied by the very act of the Self realizing, or
fulfilling, its urge. To put it differently, in facing the emptying activity of the Self's urge, the ego is forced endlessly and relentlessly to
sacrifice whatever it has achieved. Yet this sacrifice of the ego is, at
the same time, the fulfillment of the urge of the Self, or the genuine man.

Accordingly, this ego-sacrifice in the sense of Self-fulfillment
must not be confused with ego-dissolution or ego-depotentiation.
On the contrary, the integrated ego is strong and flexible enough to
develop the attitude of listening in order to function harmoniously
with the Self. The ego thus strengthened can function in unison
with, and in the service of the Self. Therefore, the word "forgotten"
used in Kuo-an's title, "The Ox and the Man both Forgotten," designates the emptying activity of the Buddha-nature, or the Self, which
is supraordinate to the function of the ego. Hence, once the "Self-
centric" functioning of the psyche takes place, the "ego-centric"
functioning of the psyche is "forgotten" or has disappeared. What is
overcome is not the ego itself but the function of the ego which is to
be characterized as "ego-centric." In Buddhism the term "ego-centric" is used to describe the ego's appropriating orientation which is
conditioned by the darkness or ignorance and the egoistic passion of
defilement and which, accordingly, obscures the genuine activity of
the Buddha-nature. In the Taoist tradition, the word "forgotten"
(wang) has been used synonymously with wu-wei, "non-doing" or
"letting something be," or tsu-jan, "naturalness" or "being through
itself." Therefore, the word "forgotten" indicates the psychological
condition of "being emptied" (kung, sunyata) wherein the ego is
opened to the service of the activity of the Self, the matrix of life.

The last two pictures of Kuo-an's version continue to describe the "Self-centric" functioning of the psyche. For the individuated ego, or the ego functioning in the service of the Self, neither the human world nor the natural world are experienced as alien to itself. Both nature and human activity become authentic to the genuine man. He experiences both as the Buddha-nature realizing itself in different modalities. Psychologically viewed, the experience of the Buddha-nature, or the Self, in nature and human relationships can be understood as paralleling the archetype of the Self which is sometimes associated with synchronistic or parapsychological events. In the *Preface* to the ninth picture, "Returning to the Origin, Back to the Source," Kuo-an states: "From the very beginning, pure and immaculate, the man has never been affected by defilement" (p. 133). This "original so-ness" refers to the universal presence of the activity of the Buddha-nature, or the Self, which realizes itself in and through the receptive, flexible ego. The same idea of "naturalness" is also referred to in the last line of Kuo-an's *Verse:* "Behold the streams flowing whither nobody knows; and the flowers vividly red—for whom are they?" (p. 134). This verse can be translated literally as follows: "The stream flows on its own accord, and the flower is red on its own accord." The Chinese term *tsu*, "of its own accord," is used as a compound, *tsu-jan*, in Taoist thought, meaning "naturalness," occurring as the creative spontaneity of nature, within and without. In other words, *tsu-jan* can be taken psychologically as the living reality of self-realization, or the creative urge of the Self manifesting itself in nature.

The living reality of the Self is also experienced in human affairs as interpersonal relationships. This is the theme of the last picture, in Kuo-an's version entitled "Entering the City with Bliss-bestowing Hands." A common, everyday occurrence is portrayed in which a young man is meeting an old man in the market place. In his *Preface*, Kuo-an states: "Carrying a gourd he [the old man] goes into the market, leaning against a staff he comes home. He is found in company with wine-bibbers and butchers, he and they are all converted into Buddhas" (p. 134).

It should be noted here that the old man depicted in the picture has a belly protruding like that of the so-called laughing Buddha. D.T. Suzuki interprets this emphasis on the belly as showing the significance of "diaphragmatic thinking," or "a sort of 'thinking' which is done with the whole body or the whole 'person.' "[26] This man embodies what Lin-chi (d. 866) calls "the total action of total being."[27] A man who "thinks" thus goes anywhere he likes and makes all sorts of friends as a manifested activity of *sunyata*, which is symbolized by the gourd he carries. In other words, this man is the genuine man in and through whom self-realization or emptying/fulfilling activity of the Buddha-nature, takes place. Tsu-te, the author of the *Six Oxherding Pictures*, depicts in the last, sixth, picture the life of the genuine man, or the Self, as a person who can function as a total being, or the Self, by playfully assuming any *samsaric* form of existence, depending on the circumstances in which he finds himself.[28] This playfulness is, psychologically understood, "an ego-less" or the "Self-centric" condition of the psyche wherein self-realization takes place. In Buddhism, it is the play of the Bodhisattva who, out of selfless compassion, mingles with sentient beings in suffering in order to liberate them. In this manner, this last picture merges with the first picture on a different level of consciousness.

Psychologically, the *Oxherding Pictures* can be taken as portraying in an art form what Jung calls individuation. Our study, employing Jung's concepts and methodology, has afforded us a psychological understanding of Zen *satori* (enlightenment) in terms of self-realization, or the urge of the Self to realize itself. The essential feature of *satori* does not consist in ego-transcendence or ego-negation, but rather in a life-long process which demands that the ego make ceaseless efforts towards the integration of the unconscious contents. The ego thus enriched and strengthened through the assimilation of the unconscious is freed from "egocentric" ways of functioning, which are conditioned by the darkness of ignorance and passion. Consequently, the ego can attain an attitude which allows it to function in an "ex-centric" manner in perfect unison with, and in the service of, the Self. This state can be designated as "Self-centric." Lin chi calls it "the total action of the total being," or the Self realizing itself in its totality.

Notes

1. J. Jacobi, *The Way of Individuation*, trans. R.F.C. Hull (New York: Harcourt, Brace & World, Inc., 1967), p. 72. J. Henderson, "The Jungian Orientation to Eastern Religion" (taped lecture. Los Angeles:

C.G. Jung Institute, 1975). See M. Miyuki, "A Jungian Approach to the Pure Land Practice of *Nien-fo*," *The Journal of Analytical Psychology* (London: The Society of Analytical Psychology), Vol. 24, no. 3 (July 1980), pp. 265–274.

2. This article is a further elaboration of the paper entitled "*Selbstverwirklichung* in the Ten Oxherding Pictures," presented at the Eighth International Congress of International Association for Analytical Psychology. San Francisco. September, 1980.

3. Various numbers of the *Verses* which accompany *The Oxherding Pictures* are found in the *Zoku zokyo* as follows: Kuo-an's *Prefaces and Verses to The Ten Oxherding Pictures* (1. 2. 113, pp. 459a–460b and 1. 2. 116, pp. 489a–b); Pu-ming's *Verses to The Ten Oxherding Pictures* (1. 2. 113, pp. 461a–462a), which are followed by those of many other masters who also wrote their *Verses* to accompany the pictures used by Pu-ming. Hence, the popularity of Pu-ming's version is undeniable. The last of these masters is Chu-che, who also wrote the ten verses to *The White Ox Pictures* (1. 2. 113, pp. 470b–471a). There are also two other masters' *Verses to The Oxherding Pictures;* namely, the *Verses for The Six Oxherding Pictures,* composed by Tsu-te Hui-hui of the twelfth century (1. 2. 116, pp. 489b–490a) and the *Verses for The Four Oxherding Pictures* (1. 2. 137, pp. 210a–b) by Hsueh-ting, a contemporary of Kuo-an. These different *Verses,* composed by the five Zen Masters, to *The Oxherding Pictures* of various numbers are translated into English by Zenkei Shibayama. See *The Zen Oxherding Pictures.* Commentaries by Zenkei Shibayama and Paintings by Gyokusei Jikihara (Osaka: Sogensha, 1975). For an English translation and exposition of *The Six Oxherding Pictures,* see Z. Shibayama, *The Six Oxherding Pictures,* trans. Sumiko Kudo (Kyoto?): The Nissha Printing Co., Ltd. No Date).

4. For the English translation of Kuo-an's and Pu-ming's texts, I have used D.T. Suzuki's translation in his *Manual of Zen Buddhism* (London: Rider and Company, 1950), pp. 127–144. Suzuki's translation of Kuo-an's text with his discussion is also found in his article, "The Awakening of a New Consciousness in Zen," in *Man and Transformation.* Bollingen Series XXX 5 (New York: Pantheon Books, 1964), pp. 179–202. For another translation and discussion of Kuo-an's version, see M.H. Treavor, tr. *The Ox and His Herdsman: A Chinese Zen Text* (Tokyo: Hoduseido Press, 1969).

5. Yanagida Seizan, "Ni-hon zen no toku-shoku" (Characteristics of Japanese Zen), in Ogisu Jundo, ed., *Zen to ni-hon buk-ka no sho mon-dai* (Problems of Zen and Japanese Culture) (Kyoto, Heirakuji shoten, 1969), pp. 79–84.

6. *Zoku zokyo* 1. 2. 113, p. 459a.

7. Z. Shibayama, *The Six Oxherding Pictures*, pp. 3–4.

8. See D.T. Suzuki, *Studies in Zen* (London: Rider and Company, 1955), p. 48.

9. Chih-yen, *Hua-yen ching K'ung-mu chang* (The Essentials of the *Hua-yen Sutra*), Taisho 45, p. 549b–c.

10. C.G. Jung, "On 'The Tibetan Book of the Great Liberation'," *Psychology and Religion: West and East. The Collected Works of C.G. Jung* (hereafter abridged as CW) 11 (New York: Pantheon Books, Inc., 1958), par. 774.

11. C.G. Jung, *The Practice of Psychotherapy*, CW 16, par. 366.

12. C.G. Jung, *Two Essays on Analytical Psychology*, CW 7, par. 266.

13. E.F. Edinger, *Ego and Archetype* (Baltimore, Maryland: Penguin Books, Inc., 1973), p. 104.

14. C.G. Jung, "Transformation Symbolism in the Mass," CW 11, par. 391.

15. C.G. Jung, *Memories, Dreams, Reflections*, recorded and edited by Aniela Jaffe: Trans. Richard and Clara Winston (New York: Pantheon Books, 1961), p. 3.

16. See footnote 11 above.

17. C.G. Jung, *Aion*, CW 9, ii, par. 123.

18. C.G. Jung, "On the Nature of the Psyche," *The Structure and Dynamics of the Psyche*, CW 8, par. 405.

19. Edward F. Edinger, *Ego and Archetype*, p. 5.

20. Ibid., p. 188. For a discussion on the mandala symbolism of the ternary process and quaternary completion in the major teachings of Buddhism, see M. Miyuki, "The Ideational Content of the Buddha's Enlightenment as *Selbstverwirklichung*" (see present volume).

21. See D.T. Suzuki, *Studies in Zen*, p. 48.

22. *The Dasabhumisvaro nama mahayanasutram*, Edited Pyuko Kindo (Tokyo: The Daijyo Bukkyo Kenkyu-kai, 1936), p. 119. The first seven stages are the stages in which the Bodhisattva is said not to be completely free from *klesa* or defilement. The finality of the Bodhisattva's realization in the eighth stage is also suggested by its name, i.e., "Immovable (*acala*), which indicates that the Bodhisattva firmly establishes himself in Buddha's wisdom and compassion.

23. Ibid., p. 135.

24. See C.G. Jung, "On 'The Tibetan Book of the Great Liberation'," CW 11, par 744. Also see C.G. Jung's "Foreword to 'Introduction to Zen Buddhism'." CW, par. 890.

25. The ninth stage is called "Excellent Wisdom" (*sadhumati*). At this stage the Bodhisattva attains the four wisdoms of non-hinderances by which he can preach the profound *dharma* of the Buddha. The tenth

stage is called "*Dharma*-Cloud" (*dharma-magha*). At this stage of the final realization, the Bodhisattva bestows Buddha's wisdom and compassion, or an abundance of *dharma* like rain on all sentient beings in order to liberate them from the *samsaric* existence of suffering and sorrow.

26. D.T. Suzuki, "The Awakening of a New Consciousness in Zen," in *Man and Transformation*, p. 201.
27. Lin-chi, *Chen-chou Lin-chi Hui-chao ch'an-shih y-lu* (The Dialogues of the Zen Master Lin-chi Hui-chao), Taisho 47, p. 501b.
28. See Z. Shibayama, *The Six Oxherding Pictures*, p. 44.

James D. Thomas

The Bodhisattva as Metaphor to Jung's Concept of Self

When alone I proceed through myself, I meet him wherever I go.
He is the same as me, yet I am not he!

LIANG-CHIEH[1]

This "something" is strange to us and yet so near, wholly ourselves and yet unknowable. . . .

C. G. JUNG[2]

It was in 1929, while in collaboration with Richard Wilhelm on
The Secret of the Golden Flower, that Carl Jung wrote: "I reached the
central point in my thinking and in my researches, namely, the concept of the self. . . ."[3] Despite the wide range of subjects for his
curiosity and prodigious research, there is little doubt that Jung's
consummate interest was in unfolding the mysteries of the self.

In searching for a term that expressed the center of his explorations, Jung was extremely cautious. He settled on

> . . . the psychological name of the 'self' . . . a term on the one
> hand definite enough to express the indescribable and indeter-
> minable nature of this wholeness. The paradoxical qualities of
> the term are in keeping with the fact that wholeness consists
> partly of the conscious man and partly of the unconscious man.[4]

Jung's caution at this point reveals his attraction to and fear of philosophic abstractions. Jung saw himself as an empiricist and pointed
with mock pride to "an unimpeachable source," the *British Medical
Journal,* proclaiming him "an empiricist first and last."[5] The problem
is that neither Jung's eclecticism nor his subject matter will allow for
strict empirical description. With both philosophical and psychologi-

206

cal consistency one can point to the ego as the conscious aspect of self, but what can be reasonably stated about the self's involvement in the unconscious?

Jung declares that "the self is absolutely paradoxical in that it represents in every respect thesis, antithesis and at the same time synthesis."[6] Given the style of Jung and the nature of his subject, ambiguities are unavoidable. Jung struggles with definitions empirical through paradoxical to enigmatic when he describes the self as ". . . not only the center but the whole circumference."[7] At every stage, it is as though he is warning that a figure can only carry the idea of self so far before it tends to obscure and/or limit it. After his travels in India, Jung wrote:

> Though very well acquainted with the self's peculiar and paradoxical phenomenology, we remain conscious of the fact that we are discerning, with the limited means at our disposal, something essentially unknown and expressing it in terms of psychic structures which may not be adequate to the nature of what is to be known.[8]

Jung constantly sought figures, analogues and metaphors that were dynamic and specific enough without making pretensions to conceptual closure. Clearly, Jung was caught up in the tension between philosophy and symbolic expression. It was for Jung a creative tension, for he alternately used the one to extend and illuminate the other. Jung points up this creative impasse by writing that

> . . . a psychology that satisfies the intellect alone can never be practical, for the totality of the psyche can never be grasped by intellect alone. Whether we will or no, philosophy keeps breaking through, because the psyche seeks an expression that will embrace its total nature.[9]

Philosophy keeps breaking through as the necessary result of meaning; and meaning is the necessary result of observation of phenomena. The trouble is, that philosophy, poorly engaged, can reduce a living subject matter to a sterile "nothing but" formula. Properly used, philosophy can illuminate without unduly restricting its subject. One of the most useful of philosophic tools in this regard is metaphor. The genius of the metaphor is its broader perspective beyond the restrictive confines of the literal. Its special hazard is its style of being purposefully nonspecific and suggestive of not only the unknown but the unknowable. The latter suggestion is, of course, a great threat to rationalism and scientific method, which explains in part the understandable suspicion that surrounds the use of metaphor.

James Onley explores metaphor in larger context as he suggests that those Socratic and Einsteinian world pictures, models, hypotheses, myths and cosmologies are better called metaphors.

Metaphor in this sense is a classical and essential way of knowing. We can say "this is like that" forever but it is the metaphor that gives an overall pattern of meaning to the connections. It acts as a human-made bridge between subjective consciousness and the objective world.

> A metaphor, then, through which we stamp our own image on the face of nature, allows us to connect the known of ourselves to the unknown of the world, and, making available new rational patterns, it simultaneously organizes the self into a new and richer entity; so that the old known self is joined to and transformed into the new, the heretofore unknown, self. Metaphor says very little about what the world is, or is like, but a great deal about what I am, or am like, and about what I am becoming; and in the end it connects me more nearly with the deep reaches of myself than with any objective universe.[10]

Metaphor has none of the features of an austere and parsimonious system that addresses itself to facts and objective reality. Metaphor is often rather flamboyant and even reckless in its expression. Donald Rhoades writes:

> We say that tables have 'legs', needles and hurricanes have 'eyes', machines have 'arms' and 'fingers', and all sorts of things have 'mouths'. . . . The religious man, the philosopher, and the scientist—and the man on the street—differ only in that their morphisms are different; no one is without them.[11]

Metaphor is a highly personal and suggestive way of knowing. Its peculiar advantage, where honestly used, is to encourage introspection of the person using it. For metaphor seems irretrievably intertwined with the projection and the acceptance of projection of self. This is so no matter what the object of metaphor might be.

When it comes to the self as the conceptual object of attention, Onley believes that it is only adequately carried by metaphor since the self is already at work seeking to express itself through metaphor. It is far wiser to identify this function and ally with it in extension of understanding.

> The self expresses itself by the metaphors it creates and projects, and we know it by those metaphors; but it did not exist as it now does and as it now is before creating its metaphors. We do not see or touch the self, but we do see and touch its metaphors; and thus we 'know' the self, activity as agent, represented in the metaphor and the metaphorizing.[12]

Even more necessary is the use of metaphor when attempting to express one's own sense of self:

> One cannot . . . hope to capture with a straight on look, or expect to transmit directly to another, one's own sense of self; at most one may be able to discover a similitude, a metaphor, for the feeling of selfhood.[13]

The concept of self as well as the personal sense of self has the quality of myth about it. It resists being either something concrete or a hypothetical reference. Any attempt to define or explain the self in terms that exclude the function of myth and metaphor tends to reify it.

Certainly Jung was no stranger to metaphor. Seeking means to develop a theory of self, he used the mandala as a metaphor. The mandala, a magic circle encompassing a square, suggests that the self is at once a center, a goal, a totality, an inner tension and a union of opposites. The mandala as metaphor has several advantages. It is sufficiently removed from our Western scientific attitude to give fresh perspective; it is also visually crisp and geometrically pleasing, however it is cold and impersonal.

Further, Jung struggled to portray the self in its uniquely human and yet godlike potential. He writes of the Original Man, the

Anthropos, the androgynous Adam, "... of that more universal, truer, more eternal man dwelling in the darkness of the primordial night. There he is still the whole, and the whole is in him, indistinguishable from nature and bare of all egohood."[14] What figure is adequate to this task? Explaining the difficulty in writing an autobiography, Jung writes:

> Man cannot compare himself with any other creature; he is not a monkey, not a cow, not a tree. I am a man. But what is it to be that? Like every other being, I am a splinter of the infinite deity, but I cannot contrast myself with any animal, any plant, any stone. Only a mythical being has any range greater than man's. How then can a man have any definite opinion about himself.[15]

Jung, still seeking a fuller model to carry his insights into self, drew upon the figure of Christ. The self expresses itself through the conscious ego in just such a way as God seeks to become flesh through Christ. The figure is almost too powerful. For the implications for theology are considerable. Even while Jung insisted that he was not writing theology, he was calling for people to be responsible by withdrawing their projections from the historical Jesus and looking to their own Christ/self within. This may well be metaphor working overtime. To say that the intrapsychic self is like an extrapsychic phenomenon is valid, but to use that metaphor as persuasion concerning the outer reality is questionable. There is no evidence that this was Jung's intention. But the hazard is there even though one can understand why the metaphor was so attractive. Jung was reared in a Christian atmosphere and many of his family were theologians. The figure was just too close. It was bound to be as confusing to some as it was revealing to others.

Since the concept of self has peculiar emotive connotations and powerful subjective implications, there is advantage in choosing a model that is culturally and/or historically removed. One could argue that Christ would be a better model of self for the Westerner. However, it seems to me that this threatens more conflict than it promises benefit as a heuristic device. Jung, in speaking of the Christian's relation to Christ and the Buddhist's identification with Buddha, writes this:

> Fundamentally these confessions are identical, inasmuch as the Buddhist only attains this knowledge when he is without self,

"anatman." But there exists an immense difference between the two formulations. The Christian attains his end in Christ, the Buddhist recognizes that he is Buddha. The Christian, starting from the transitory and egocentric world of his consciousness, dissolves in Christ, but the Buddhist still rests on the eternal foundations of inner nature, whose at-one-ness with the divinity as with the universal Being, we meet in the other Indian confessions as well.[16]

For the Westerner, there seems to be an unavoidable conflict here. Does one partake of (take part in) the object of identification or does one aim at becoming that object? To the extent that the object (Christ) is also God, grave theological problems arise for the orthodox Christian. Buddhist doctrine presents no such problem. If it cannot be said that the Buddha was deified, it must be recognized that his image has tended to be elevated to a superhuman level.

To the extent that this is so, the bodhisattva figure presents itself as a more accessible model. To be sure, the bodhisattva was deified. But the bodhisattva has stubborn roots in the merely human and is as much a process as a condition. The very name denotes an exalted state in the making. It combines the very human with a spiritual potentiality. Every human being is a potential bodhisattva. But since the bodhisattva figure itself is controversial, let us speak more precisely to the concept.

The conception of the bodhisattva emerged concurrent with the development of Mahāyāna Buddhism. In the fourth century BC an ideological split began to appear in Buddhism that was to widen into two distinct forms known as Theravāda (Way of the Elders) and Mahāyāna (Great Vehicle, Great Ferryboat). By the first century AD the doctrinal differences were clearly drawn and visible in the sutras (scriptures). In the early Mahāyāna sutras the term "bodhisattva" (bodhi: enlightenment and sattva: being) came to mean a "Buddha-designate." Although definitions vary, the central distinction to be made is between a Buddha-being (having arrived in nirvana) and a Buddha-designate (being on the way but short of nirvana). The bodhisattva is distinguished by conscious postponement of nirvana because of identification with and compassion for all living things.

One of the central conditions that gave rise to the bodhisattva figure was the growing elitism of the Buddhist priesthood. It was charged that the priests, called Arahats and Paccekabuddhas (private

Buddhas), were interested only in their own complete nirvana. They were interested neither in teaching nor service and neglected to emulate the compassionate feature of the Buddha. Early Buddhist doctrine did emphasize that each life was a separate entity and completely responsible for its own spiritual condition. This concept was implemented by Jain doctrine to severe and austere extremes. As such, it had less and less appeal to the masses.

The figure of the Buddha had undergone idealization and spiritualization to such an extent as to make it inaccessible to the common person. Hinduism in the second century BC underwent a great revival which must have posed a threat to Buddhism. There was a great upheaval of Bhakti (devotion, worship, love) as the religious means of expression. Buddhism had developed in such a way as to appeal very little to the masses. It had become a metaphysical doctrine or an esoteric psychology with nothing that could appeal as an object of devotion.

Mahāyāna Buddhism emerged as an answer to these conditions. Indigenous in Buddhist doctrine and alongside the principle of individual accountability is the concept of the interdependence of all things. This tenet gave Mahāyānists their answer to extreme individualism and became a logical basis for the doctrine of "vicarious merit." It follows that if all beings are interdependent then the dharma (merit) of one may be devoted to the good of others.

Complementing this doctrine in its appeal to the imagination of the common person was Mahāyāna's re-emphasis that the Buddha-being resides potentially in every person and thing. These two principles tended to bring Buddhism closer to the people. Not only do good intention and acts of devotion make a difference but the benefits of grace are accessible to everyone.

The central carrier of these Mahāyāna doctrines is the bodhisattva, who is designated for Buddhahood but remains human and in the factual here-and-now. In fact, because of wisdom and compassion it identifies with all ignorant and struggling creatures so completely that its own nirvana is postponed. The Bodhisattva is the worthy object of adoration, for its endless compassion overflows with grace on all who come near. At the same time it embodies the gospel that the Buddha-being potential resides in everyone.

Bodhisattvas appear in the literature expressing themselves in a wide range of characteristics—from deified saviors to "household" bodhisattvas. Richard Robinson, in dealing with the term "house-holder" bodhisattva observes that ". . . no sūtra preaches devotion to a celestial bodhisattva until the third century AD, a full three centuries after these beings entered the literature."[17]

Mahāyāna Buddhism taught that every man and woman—every creature—can and must eventually become a bodhisattva. This being so, at what point does a mere human being become a bodhisattva? There seem to be both conservative and liberal answers to this question.

The Mahāyāna sūtras address themselves to monastics and laity alike and although they are written by monks alone some are quite liberal in their inclusion of the laity. Robinson draws from the Vima-lakīrti Sūtra a view of

> . . . the householder bodhisattva encouraging a crowd of young patricians to leave the household life. When they protest that they cannot do so without their parents' permission, Vimalakīrti tells them to arouse the thought of enlightenment and practice diligently, since that is the equivalent to 'going forth.'. . . The householder bodhisattva was welcome to study meditation and philosophy, and probably was allowed to spend protracted pe-riods of retreat in the monasteries. He could teach the doctrine and was encouraged to propagate it.[18]

These household bodhisattvas are too numerous to mention. Only the exceptional ones will have been lionized. The bodhisattva image is then both a goal to be attained and a way of achieving it. Even the celestial bodhisattvas are pictured constantly working at the same menial tasks that engage ordinary human beings. Lord Avalo-kita, who is portrayed as a god, has a double meaning in his name.

Evans-Wentz translates Avalokiteśvara as both "The Lord look-ing down in pity" and "The Lord seen within."[19] No matter how engrandized the bodhisattva figure becomes, the subjective implica-tions are still there. "We are all reflections of the image of the bodhi-sattva. The sufferer within us is that divine being. We and that pro-tecting father are one."[20]

The bodhisattva image originally emerged as an answer to the elitism of monastics and the inaccessibility of religious expression for the common people. The bodhisattva was a living model for the doctrine of inner potential and perfectability of all creatures—at once a superdemocratic and an aristocratic ideal. The bodhisattva was also carrier/model for yet another and complementary doctrine —that of the ideal being in the here and now. The bodhisattva in Mahāyāna Buddhism points toward nirvana that is not annihilation or the loss of this world but rather is attainment of full potentiality. To suppose that nirvana requires the end of discrimination and the loss of this world is completely in error. This teaching as a philosophic principle goes all the way back to Nāgārjuna (c. AD 200) who takes the Buddha's doctrines of anattā (not-self) and anicca (impermanence) to a radical extreme. Not only is there no substantial self and no permanence in reality, there is no Buddhahood and no nirvana. Reality for Nāgārjuna is emptiness.

> To apprehend this emptiness, or void, one must have the correct viewpoint. One may see things either (1) under the aspect of eternity (*paramārtha satya*) or (2) from the viewpoint of human finitude (*saṃvṛiti satya*). From the viewpoint of finite, mortal apprehension, the delusion of substantive existence to concede apparent or empirical existence of the world around him, and at the same time maintain that from the viewpoint of eternity all this was delusory and unreal. . . . Nāgārjuna's argument might be paraphrased as the assertion of a kind of universal relativity. All things possess only relative being; nothing really or ultimately exists.[21]

The immediate implication of this position is that the world of relativity and that of nirvana are one and only seem to differ by virtue of being seen from different points of view. D. T. Suzuki, in his study of the Laṅkāvatāra Sūtra, insists that identity between nirvana and samsara is fundamental to Mahāyāna Buddhism.

> So long as dualism is adhered to, there is no Nirvana, no self-realization. Light and shadow, long and short, black and white— they are mutually related; when they stand alone each by itself, they have no meaning. So with Nirvana. When it is sought after in relation to Samsara, we have a sort of Nirvana. But this kind vanishes when separated from the condition of mutuality in which it exists. True Nirvana is that which is realized in the oneness of Nirvana and Samsara, absolute or sūnya in its nature

and above the relativity of eternalism and nihilism. Mahāyāna followers strive to realize this kind of Nirvana.[22]

The aim of this doctrine is to countermand the other-worldly tendencies of Buddhism. The message is that reality is one; that it is now; and that it is universally common property for those who are willing to accept it.

> This world is the Buddha-world
> Within which enlightenment may be sought.
> To seek enlightenment by separating from this world
> Is as foolish as to search for a rabbit's horn.[23]

The bodhisattva, then, in this branch of Buddhism, becomes a very human hero. The Chinese Buddhist Master Fen-yang (947–1024) is speaking about Mañjuśrī, a bodhisattva who is often grandly deified:

> There are some Buddhist learners who have already made the mistake of seeking for Mañjuśrī at Mount Wu-t'ai. There is no Mañjuśrī at Wu-t'ai. Do you want to know Mañjuśrī? It is something at this moment working within you, something which remains unshakable and allows no room for doubt. This is called the living Mañjuśrī.[24]

In this view, the bodhisattva is not a god with superhuman compassion as its only motivation. Compassion is there, of course, but it does not solely explain his reason for not crossing over. The Bodhisattva feels deeply for all suffering beings. Its heart is "full of karuna (love) for all beings who are unable to step out of the dualistic whirlpools of sat and asat. . . . His own heart is free from such attachments as are ordinarily cherished by the unemancipated, but that which feels persists."[25] "That which feels" is that aspect of the Bodhisattva that continues to belong to that which is human. It identifies itself with all other creatures and sees itself as inseparably interinvolved.

Lin Yutang writes: "The word bodhisattva, the most important doctrine of Mahāyāna religion, is such a common Chinese word that we use it in speaking of sweet child (like the word 'cherub') and of clay doll."[26] This common applicability of the term seems to me to be further evidence of its egalitarian application and of its movement from metaphor to model for ideal self.

What is the nature of this stopping or pausing just short of the goal? It is not a position of absolute detachment and is in no way monastic. The bodhisattva is fully in the world, and may have a wife, husband or children and possessions. The Bodhisattva may even be in a position of power and authority. What is the explanation for this double position of both in and out of the world? It can be understood as the act of a superhero whose compassion for all creatures is almost beyond belief. Or, as Suzuki understands it, the bodhisattva is not acting altogether altruistically.[27] In fact, it is something of a hedonist, in the best sense, motivated by a special understanding of the way things are. Simply put, its pleasure depends on the pleasure of all: its attainment of nirvana depends on its attainment by all.

To what extent can this "stopping short" be compared to the prayer of young Augustine: "Lord, give me chastity, but not yet?" Certainly the theology of his time required that an either/or choice and sacrifice must be made. The prayer seems to be motivated by carnal or egocentric need. He wanted to put off a higher goal and task that was for the moment too difficult. There is no indication in Augustine of an attempt to accommodate both spheres—the spiritual and the carnal. He was simply putting off a difficult calling.

The reverse is true of the bodhisattva. Early Buddhism was clear in its teachings of samsara (cycle of rebirth, repeating an experience of life and death) as painful. One should seek to get out of it as soon as possible. For an early Buddhist, nirvana is the ultimate cessation of this misery and to postpone it is the ultimate folly. But the bodhisattva does postpone it, not for a while, but virtually forever—until all creatures are in nirvana. If one considers nirvana as a place to be in the future, then this act of putting off by the bodhisattva can only be understood as that of a martyr-savior.

If, however, nirvana is understood as a "state of mind," "an understanding," "a special attitude," then the picture is quite different.

But as for the Bodhisattva he never enters into Nirvana as he has a deep insight into the nature of things which are already in Nirvana even as they are. . . . They (Bodhisattvas) are already in Nirvana because their views are not at all beclouded by discrimination. To them no discrimination takes place as to things seized and seizing.[28]

In one sense the bodhisattva's position must be considered as "stopping short" but to the degree that enlightenment is attained, there comes the realization that there is nothing short of which one is stopped.

In our attempt to understand the motivation of the bodhisattva, the pivotal issue is the relationship between prajna (special knowledge) and karuna (compassion). Is it pure compassion that makes him "pause" and wait forever for all suffering creatures? Or is this "pausing" a reasonable response to a special insight concerning the nature of all things? Most scholars insist that it is both principles operating in unison.

> Mahāyāna stands firmly on two legs, Prajna and Karuna, transcendental idealism and all-embracing affection for all kinds of beings, animate as well as inanimate. The former sees into the unity of things and the latter appreciates their diversity. The Bodhisattva weeps with suffering beings and at the same time realizes that there is one that never weeps, being above sufferings, tribulations and contaminations. Buddhist life finds its perfect realization in a harmonious blending of the two conceptions: philosophically, the one and the many, sat and asat; religiously, the pure and the defiled.[29]

Jung was attracted to the human aspect of Buddhism. He wrote that the "Buddha is the more complete human being. He is a historical personality, and therefore easier for men to understand. Christ is at once a historical man and God and therefore more difficult to comprehend."[30] The model for self that Jung sought was not of a purely idealistic nature. In his writing, "The Holy Men of India," he expresses his disdain for and suspicion of the purely wise and holy man.

> The man who is only wise and only holy interests me about as much as a skeleton of a rare saurian, which would not move me to tears. The insane contradiction, on the other hand, between existence beyond Maya in the cosmic Self, and that amiable human

weakness which fruitfully sinks many roots into the black earth, repeating for all eternity the weaving and rending of the veil as the ageless melody of India—this contradiction fascinates me; for how else can one perceive the light without the shadow, hear the silence without the noise; attain wisdom without foolishness.[31]

The man that fascinated Jung ". . . has found meaning in the rushing phantasmagoria of Being, freedom in bondage, victory in defeat."[32]

It seems to me that the figure that Jung seeks is the bodhisattva —that miraculous figure whose only miracle is the full realization of his human potential. D. T. Suzuki writes of that full potential.

> Thou art it. . . . All the Bodhisattvas including the Buddha are ourselves and their doings are our doings. They looked so full of mystery, they were miracles, as long as they were observed from this earthly end, where we imagined that there was really something at the other end; but as soon as the dividing-wall constructed by our imagination is removed, Samantabhadra's arms raised to save sentient beings become our own, which are now engaged in passing the salt to a friend at the table, and Maitreya's opening to the Vairocana Tower for Sudhana is our ushering a caller into the parlour for a friendly chat. . . . This again reminds us of P'ang's reputed verse—

> How wondrously supernatural!
> And how miraculous this!
> I draw water, I carry fuel![33]

Jung writes in Suzuki's *Introduction to Zen Buddhism*, "Like the Ego is a certain experience of Myself, so is the self an experience of my ego which however is no longer experienced in the form of a wider or higher ego, but in the shape of a Non-Ego."[34] This is exactly the point of "no-mind" or "the man of no title" and the goal of the bodhisattva.

The bodhisattva stands clearly for self as that borderline entity; borderline in the sense of being both of this world and out of it—possessing consciousness but also somehow being in alliance with the unconscious domain. Jung thoroughly studied Nietzsche's Zarathustra figure. One aspect of Zarathustra pictures the stance of the bodhisattva.

> Zarathustra looked at the people and wondered. Then he said: "Man is a rope, stretched between beast and *Ubermensche*—a rope across an abyss. A dangerous crossing over, a dangerous on-the-way, a dangerous looking back, a dangerous shuddering and stopping.[35]

This is the particular moment I wish to examine: the bodhisattva/self in its reflexive position—pausing, looking back, just prior to crossing over. It is dangerous to the self/bodhisattva because so much is invested here; because looking back runs the risk of losing the goal; because of the delicate distinction between self and loss of self; or because of the distinction between self and ego. Zarathustra is certainly a dangerous projection of this figure. The bodhisattva and the self seem forever to be on the edge of the much promised and sought after wholeness (nirvana). Looking back is a risk. Paradoxically, looking back is necessary to wholeness. Kwan-yin (a Chinese female bodhisattva) is often pictured as suspended between heaven and earth; between Kwan-yin and earth is a zygote—an unborn baby in embryo. The self seems forever so suspended.

In myth and legend, the hero/heroine is often found in a borderline situation—on a frontier. It is in this position that he/she acts, and strangely enough, acts not only in response to individual condition but suggests that this action is a model for everyone. Erik Erikson considers this aspect of the hero in one of the last crisis stages in development toward maturation.

In his epilogue to *Young Man Luther*, he suggests that the hero internalizes the problems of his age and deals with them intimately as though they were private life or death issues. Surprisingly, this private struggle can become the model of behavior or answer to the problems of an age. He writes of this period as an

> ... integrity crisis which again leads men to the portals of nothingness ... and that for him all human integrity stands or falls with the one style of integrity of which he partakes. ... He acts as if mankind were starting all over again with his own beginning

as an individual, conscious of his singularity as well as his humanity.... To him history ends as well as starts with him.[36]

This is exactly the stance of the bodhisattva and is exactly that stance
to which the self is drawn.

It was surely by design that Jung left the great bulk and the heart
of his work virtually inaccessible to conceptual systematization. If
anything he took the term 'self' out beyond the reach of conceptualization and its tendency to reduction and reification. But at the same
time, he was energetically involved in enlarging the working edges of
the self as concept. I believe that certain specific generalizations
which characterize the self emerge in Jung's writings. These characteristics can be best portrayed as operating as an open system. I
propose that the self, as Jung defines it can be regarded as:

1. Superordinate system   4. Uniting symbol
2. Goal   5. Agent
3. Center of opposites   6. Archetypal expression

The self is simultaneously all of these aspects. Each aspect is
dependent on the others within the superordinate system and there is
overlap between the various features or aspects of the self. I am
dealing with self in the context of health and the self as definitive of
health. Jung was a psychiatrist and he dealt with the pathology of self.
He also fashioned a psychological theory that gives perspective into
the creative function of self. The latter is my concern. The self can
be viewed as either process or structure. It is a matter of perspective
and surely one implies the other. For the moment, however, I am
emphasizing the structural features but I insist (with the model of
open system) that it is impossible to think of this as structure without
process. I am suggesting that Jung's concept of self can be viewed as
an open system and can be regarded as having these six discernible
aspects.

Further, I propose that the bodhisattva is an adequate and stimulating metaphor to this conceptual model. This metaphor is admit-
tedly a bridge built from the Western conceptual end. Even so, it
must be recognized that the foundations of the bodhisattva are ideally
rooted in ideology and history at the other end. This is as much as we
could hope for in a bridge between the cognitive and intuitive ap-

proaches. Without going into extensive detail, I will summarize the nature of these six aspects and then employ the bodhisattva figure as metaphor to illuminate Jung's picture of self.

SELF AS GOAL

Jung points out that the self is not a given condition along with the state of consciousness. Rather, it is latent in the unconsciousness and must be sought after and worked at as a goal. The discipline of this task is called "individuation" and requires of an individual that one disown all that is not natural. One must resist being collectivized by the coercive dictates of the primordial unconscious and being deracinated by the arrogance of the conscious ego. This prize of self is not a singular end product. Rather, it involves a never ending series of maturational stages. For Jung, self is an ideal potential, characterized by the quality of wholeness, toward which one aspires forever.

The language of both Jung and Buddhism is a study in elaborate avoidance of metaphysics. The language of both strives to be purely empirical. They are making an effort simply to report certain psychological features they have explored and developed. The central purpose of this great effort in both sources is to avoid the philosophic and experiential hazards around the issue of the substantiality of the self.

Eliot Deutsch suggests that the theory of nonreality of the "substantial" self, so prominent in Buddhist teaching must be understood in both historic and psychological context. "The assertion that the empirical self is an ever changing, unstable pattern of feeling, thought, etc., does not contradict the Upanishadic view; it represents only a different emphasis."[37]

Both Jung and Buddhism insist that, as an object, self is a hazard, and that selfhood is a heuristic abstraction. The self, in this sense, is not something that is owned as an exclusive entity. The Buddhist sūtras continually deny the existence of self in this sense. But the goal of Buddhism, nirvana, is seriously misunderstood in the West as simply the peaceful loss of all identity.

The bodhisattva figure, as an ideal expression of maturation, is a direct contradiction of this misinterpretation. The vows made and disciplines entered into represent a regimen of heroic effort to achieve some goal. The career of the bodhisattva is divided into stages or epochs, called bhūmi.[38] The word denotes 'earth', 'place' or 'region' and has a connotation of 'stage', 'level' or 'state of consciousness'. The bhūmi can be considered stages of sequential maturation and are descriptive of the levels of achievement. Bodhisattvahood itself is described as the ideal goal of wholeness, completion of potentiality, at-one-ment. Nothing is lost in the tragic sense—all is gained. This is exactly Jung's description of self as goal.

SELF AS CENTER OF OPPOSITES

Jung pictured the self as a borderline condition. Self, in this sense, can only be considered in its functional role. He speaks of it as that "... desired midpoint of the personality, that ineffable something betwixt the opposites."[39]

The self as a center of opposites takes on a spatial feature which expresses itself as a bridge, borderline, condition-in-between or midwife. The solitary "I" of the self finds itself alone and in between all conscious distinctions. The "I" becomes conscious of its interstitial posture with the recognition of inside/outside, self/not-self, male/female, yin/yang, etc.

The creative role of self in this position is arbitration. The intransigent ego and the overwhelming unconscious domain struggle for dominant expression. The self, at its creative best, acts as midwife. This condition of in-between is captured in the image of the bodhisattva—both in task and position. "A Bodhisattva is a being compounded of the two contradictory forces of wisdom and compassion. In his wisdom, he sees no persons; in his compassion, he is resolved to save them."[40]

That the Bodhisattva maintains in this position and acts out of it is the very mark of creativity, remaining at the point of tension with respect to motivation. Is this act out of compassion or out of hedonism? Such questions are not solved once and for all but are suffered or confronted experientially at each volitional juncture. This very position just short of nirvana is one of ambiguous tension. Such is the abode of self as experienced. Its place is in the midst of an eternal becoming; in transit between the unconscious sphere and consciousness; in tension between the "I" and "not-I." This is the condition of both self and bodhisattva.

SELF AS UNITING SYMBOL

From an altogether different perspective and in a different expression of itself, the self is not only that point of tension between opposites but it is also the symbol for the resolution of those opposites. Jung speaks of that position of creative tension as the "transcendent function."

> The shuttling to and fro of arguments and affects represents the transcendent function of opposites. The confrontation of the two positions generates a tension charged with energy and creates a living third thing . . . a movement out of the suspension between opposites, a living birth that leads to a new level of being, a new situation.[41]

This living third thing is the self as it presents itself in myth and dreams as the symbol for wholeness. Jung reports from his analytic inquiry that the self seems to "present" itself in dream content as a 'goal-seeking' figure. It appears in forms, ranging from obvious hero figures to obscure mandalas. The central characteristic of this presentation is that it points toward wholeness in the form of a totality symbol. Empirically, the self seems to consistently present itself as a union of opposites, ". . . it can also appear as a united duality, in the form, for instance, of *tao* as the interplay of yang and yin."[42]

Jung found that when the conscious ego treated the self as a Thou (in Buber's sense—a uniting symbol), it (the ego) is caught up in the symbol, transformed and enhanced by it. The bodhisattva is a uniting symbol par excellence, standing between all opposites, bridging the union of those opposites. The Bodhisattva does not avoid death or rebirth—but exemplifies the continuing resolution of both. So it is with nirvana/samsara, truth/illusoriness, enlightenment/compassion, maleness/femaleness, the jewel/the lotus, yang/yin, the bodhisattva stands as the *mysterium coniunctionis*.

Speaking of monks who seek the bodhisattva Mañjuśrī in exalted places, Suzuki writes:

Do you wish to know where he is? There is something this very moment at work in you, showing no tendency to waver, betraying no disposition to doubt—this is your living Mañjuśrī. The light of non-discrimination which flashes through every thought of yours—this is your Samantabhadra who remains true all the time.[43]

SELF AS AGENT

The self as agent is a crucial issue of our picture. The self must be something more than object (that which is acted upon); it must also be subject. The problem is to find its place between the hazards of servility and hubris. If the ego is the sole agent, the result is ego inflation and disaster. It is necessary for the ego to take its rightful place in intensive, localized consciousness. In this position, it is capable of sensing the world and ordering its perceptions into conceptions. It is capable of choosing, intending and making concrete the object of its attention. The ego can more fully function in this domain, if it realizes its proper relationship to the self that consists also of the unconscious. Here the self as agent must shift its weight in between ego and self into a position that Erich Neumann calls the ego-self axis. From this position, the self is truly agential but not ego-maniacal.

On the crucial issue of the agential role of the self, Jung took great pains to differentiate between the ego and the self. The doctrines of Buddhism and the disciplines of the bodhisattva likewise put great emphasis on the false claims of the ego. The insight of both Jung and Buddhism is that the self is not the ego but is rooted in the totality of the universe and yet somehow expressed in its particularity as "suchness."

Jung sees the universal aspect of self as rooted in the unconscious; for the Buddhist, it is rooted in the Buddha-being. For the individual to ignore rootedness in the universal principle is the ultimate in folly. The individual must find a sense of self both in the conscious and the unconscious domains—in sat (existence) and asat (nonexistence). It is also the task of the individual to accept the responsibility of consciousness.

Jung points out that the self must accept its full responsibility in the domain of consciousness, volition and sensation. Certainly, this is not the totality of self but it is an important feature. The bodhisattva takes a first step by "arousing the thought." The bodhicitta is a truth that can be known and he/she sets out to know and act upon it. "The Bodhisattva would be a man who does not only set himself free but who is skillful in devising means for bringing out and maturing the latent seeds of enlightenment in others."[44]

Because the supreme test of the bodhisattva is eternal readiness to serve, discipline is required in the nonexperience of ego. This task is assisted by his contemplation of the principles of the interpenetration of all things, or the principle of "form is emptiness and emptiness, form." The final goal is knowledge or wisdom but the means indicated is action. Ego-clogged acts tend to enslave.

> . . . but the candidate for the Wisdom of the Other Shore behaves consistently as though he had already left behind the delusion of the world display. In every act of his daily living he makes a decision in favor of the self-transcending alternative, until at last, as a consequence of infinitely numerous deed-experiences of this kind, he does actually transcend the delusions of his phenomenal psychology: thenceforward he behaves instinctively as though his ego, with its false impressions, did not exist.[45]

As a discipline, this could well be adapted to Jung's prescriptions for individuation. The hazards of ego-possession or inflation are vividly illustrated in case studies. However, it must be noted that the Buddhist doctrine goes a step beyond that of Jung. Whereas Buddhism would completely dissolve the ego, Jung would shift the sense of self apart from, but inclusive of the ego. To the extent that the bodhisattva remains forever in existence with the accompanying implications of involvement with ego, to that extent there is only a difference of degree. To the degree that Buddhism posits the elimination of the ego as an idea, there is a distinct difference of opinion. Obviously this is one of the central ideological impasses between East and West.

Nevertheless the parallel still holds. The self and the bodhisattva exist in a world in which their freedom, choice and action are crucial. Zimmer speaks of action in his chapter on "The Way of the Bodhisattva."

Practice precedes insight; knowledge is the reward of action: therefore try! That is the thought. For it is by doing things that one becomes transformed. . . . Knowledge is to be attained . . . not through inaction (as in the Jaina and the classic Yoga disciplines) but through a bold and advertent living of life.[46]

THE SELF AS ARCHETYPE

The self as archetype is too simply worded. Rather, the self seems to operate from an archetypal base and present itself as an image which seeks fulfillment in consciousness and action. Just as the physical body seems to operate out of a genetic design that is discernible by its pattern, the psyche possesses general and typical modes of functioning. These are based in archetypes. They are inherited possibilities which reflect backwards to collective experience and point forward to specific potential.

Across the threshold of consciousness come images of saoshyant (the recurring one), the hero, the god/man, etc., which bid to be recognized and integrated in order to fulfill a potentiality. The conscious ego that can entertain such archetypal images of self will tend to be transformed by the images. It is as though the unconscious is fecund with the image of a potential self. Its prolific expression seeks to be fertilized.

Basic to Buddhism is the concept that Buddha-being lies inherent in all things waiting to be fulfilled. In discussing the bodhisattva, Suzuki writes: "Owing to its self-expanding and self-creating power, a great loving heart transforms this earthly world into one of splendor and mutual fusion, and this is where the Buddha is always abiding."[47] And again, describing the

> . . . way that the Bodhisattva comes: he comes where an all-embracing love abides, because he desires to discipline all beings; he comes where there is a great compassionate heart, because he desires to protect all beings against sufferings; he comes out of the skilful means born of transcendental knowledge because he is ever in conformity with the mentalities of all beings.[48]

Only the word "archetype" is missing from the many descriptions of the bodhisattva's appearance and function. It appears when the occasion is right for it to fulfill itself. It also appears in the form and functions in the manner that will fulfill its own nature. Jung speaks of the self as an archetype and more specifically as the organizing archetype or the archetype of order. In his most comprehensive work on the self, he states it is "the real organizing principle of the unconscious."⁴⁹

At this point, Jung presents his case in as strongly empirical a way as is possible for this subject matter. Out of the thousands of dream studies appeared a factor that demanded attention. There appeared in these dreams an insistent theme which not only bid for psychic wholeness but prescribed the nature of that wholeness. It was as though the self itself (with the aid of its unconscious domain) symbolically presents its own prescription for wholeness. Jung called this aspect of self the self-archetype and it seems forever to be working as an organizing principle toward its own wholeness. The bodhisattva, in training, is taught that to seek is to be sought after. Chang Chung-yuan writes:

> Master Po-chang asked a student to poke in a fire pot in search of a burning coal. When the student reported that there was none, Po-chang poked deep in the fire pot and extracted a small glowing piece of charcoal which he showed to the student saying, "Is this not a burning piece? . . . The Sutra says, 'To behold the Buddha-nature one must wait for the right moment and the right conditions.' When the time comes, one is awakened as from a dream. It is as if one's memory recalls something long forgotten. One realizes that what is obtained is one's own and not from outside one's self."⁵⁰

SELF AS A SUPERORDINATE SYSTEM

The self as a superordinate system is an abstract construct which is not experienced, but posited—much like the structure of the atom. It is at once a hypothetical center (and unity) and a total content of personality. It is not identified with or circumscribed by the conscious ego. In an ideal sense the self and the conscious ego hold one another in mutual regard. This superordinate system acts like an abstract universal within which operates the particular, the concrete and the unique aspects of self. Intellectually, it may be considered a transparent unity—or as a "hypothetical summation of an indescribable totality."[51]

We are saying that the self expresses itself in five distinct ways. These aspects overlap in an interdependent complexity that is confusing without context. This context is the referential self, which I have designated as the superordinate system.

The figure of the bodhisattva also presents itself in Buddhist literature as a multidimensional expression. The seeming duplicity of the bodhisattva in all of its expressions is not duplicity at all when viewed from a certain vantage point. It is altruistic from one point of view and self-fulfilling from another. What is the general frame of reference within which the bodhisattva makes sense? One can say that this context is historical. At one time, it expresses itself one way, whereas at another time, it expresses itself differently.

However, D. T. Suzuki is not content with this explanation. Suzuki, of all the scholars who write on the bodhisattva, presents the most esoteric picture. He would be the last to consider the condition of the bodhisattva to be a state of being that is once and for all achieved. This is so because there is nothing to achieve—there is only the way or process. Yet he uses the term "bodhisattvahood" to describe the condition within which the bodhisattva takes his various expressions. The term serves the same function as superordinate system.

The term "superordinate system" has the quality of a formal abstraction. It is the opposite of a personal framework. It serves as a neutral carrier. It is in this sense "empty." It is that abstract form out of which rises the drama of self experienced as selves. In this context Edward Whitmont writes: "The Self as a predisposition which is 'empty' in itself actualizes as representational images and as patterns of emotion and behavior."[52]

Suzuki writes of the self as "comparable to a circle which has no circumference, it is thus Sunyata, emptiness."[53] Here again is that aspect of self that is describable only as an extreme abstraction. Suzuki discusses Rinzai's term for self: "the true man of no rank," which is sometimes called the "Way-man." He describes self as ". . . a kind of metaphysical self in opposition to the psychological or ethical self which belongs in a finite world of relativity.

Rinzai's man is defined as 'of no rank' or 'independent of' or 'with no clothes on'."[54]

Later, in Suzuki's description of the bodhisattva, he again calls upon Rinzai's figure of the

> man of no title: he is the one who is in the house and yet does not stay away from the road, he is the one who is on the road and yet does not stay away from the house. Is he an ordinary man or a great sage? No one can tell. Even the devil does not know where to locate him. Even the Buddha fails to manage him as he may desire. When we try to point him out, he is no more there, he is on the other side of the mountain.[55]

The bodhisattva, as a mystical figure, has the facility to carry an abstract form out of which emerges the expressions of a theme. It is that mythological format that is the occasion for the emergence of the hero/heroine, the human/god, the promised self. It is a framework within which our expectations are made possible and meaningful. As a figure in literature, it offers the advantage of perspective. One can view it at a distance and therefore witness more clearly the dynamics of its drama. At the same time, I can know that it not only acts for me, but it is my most intimate nature.

In Jungian terms, the bodhisattva figure was not originally invented as a means to entertain us or to solve our awkward problems. To the extent that it captures our attention and imagination—to that extent it is native to our preconscious origin, emerging as an overt expression of our covert questions. The occasion for its appearance and all its characteristics are created by our most private fears and hopes.

We respond to the drama of the bodhisattva figure because we respond to our inner needs. Because of fear or ignorance, we are tempted to project all of this inner dynamic onto the outer drama. It is often more dramatic and always safer. The task of maturation or individuation is to recognize and own one's projections; to allow one's own inner image to emerge; to give a conscious form to that image so that it is neither inhibited nor preconditioned. I propose that the bodhisattva, as metaphor, is a valuable tool in that work.

T. W. Organ relates the following story from the Vedantic tradition:

Ten men were once fording a swift river. Upon reaching the other shore, they counted themselves to see if all had arrived safely but alas . . . each man could count but nine men. A passerby, hearing their wailing over the loss of a comrade, counted the men and discovered they were ten. He then asked each man to count, and when the counter counted but nine, the stranger touched him on the chest and said, "Thou art the tenth."[56]

I suggest that the passerby is the bodhisattva. As an historic figure, it stands for the conceptual model of self. As a metaphorical figure, it points to the experiential self. But as bodhisattva self, it is truly a passerby, appearing only to disappear, but not before it touches those of us who count and wail and informs us, "Thou art the tenth."

Notes

1. Chang Chung-yuan, *Original Teachings of Chan Buddhism* (NY, 1969), p. 60.
2. Jung, C. G., *Two Essays on Analytical Psychology* (NY, 1970), p. 250.
3. Jung, *Memories, Dreams and Reflections* (Vintage Books, NY, 1963), p. 208.
4. Jung, *Psychology and Alchemy*, Bollingen Series XII (Princeton, 1968), p. 20. Bollingen Series referred to hereafter as CW (Collected Works).
5. Jung, *Answer to Buber* (NY, 1957), p. 3.
6. CW XII, p. 21.
7. Ibid., par. 44.
8. *Psychology and Religion*, CW XI, par. 956.
9. *Two Essays*, CW, Vol. VII, par. 201.
10. Onley, James, *Metaphors of Self* (Princeton, 1972), pp. 31–32.
11. Rhoades, Donald H., *A Faith of Fellowship* (Philadelphia, n.d.), p. 82.
12. Onley, p. 34.
13. Ibid, p. 267.
14. *Civilization in Transition*, CW, Vol. X, par. 304.
15. *Memories, Dreams and Reflections* (NY, 1963), p. 4.
16. *On the Psychology of Eastern Meditation* (NY, 1949), p. 18.
17. Robinson, Richard H., *The Buddhist Religion* (Belmont, 1970), p. 54.
18. Ibid., p. 55.
19. Evans-Wentz, W. Y., *Tibetan Yoga and Secret Doctrine* (Oxford, London, 1935), p. 233, n. 2.
20. Campbell, Joseph, *The Hero with a Thousand Faces* (NY, 1967), p. 161.

21. Hutchison, John A., *Paths of Faith* (NY, 1969), p. 155.
22. Suzuki, D. T., *Studies in the Lankavatara Sutra* (London, 1930), p. 129.
23. Goddard, D. A., *A Buddhist Bible* (NY, 1938), p. 352.
24. Chang, pp. 98–99.
25. Suzuki, p. 221.
26. Lin Yutang, *The Wisdom of China and India* (NY, 1942), p. 493.
27. Suzuki, pp. 219–220.
28. Ibid., p. 221.
29. Ibid., p. 229.
30. *Memories, Dreams and Reflections*, p. 279.
31. *Psychology and Religion*, CW, Vol. XI, par. 953.
32. Ibid., par. 953.
33. Suzuki, *Essays in Zen Buddhism*, Third Series (London, 1934), p. 65.
34. Jung, in D. T. Suzuki, *An Introduction to Zen Buddhism* (Rider, NY), p. 13.
35. Nietzsche, Friedrich, *Thus Spake Zarathustra* (Chicago, 1957), p. 6.
36. Erikson, Erik H., *Young Man Luther* (NY, 1962), pp. 260–262.
37. Deutsch, Eliot, *Humanity and Divinity* (Honolulu, 1970), p. 116.
38. Extensively detailed in Suzuki, *Studies in the Lankavatara Sutra*, pp. 222 et passim.
39. *Two Essays*, CW, Vol. VII, par. 282.
40. Conze, Edward, *Buddhism: Its Essence and Development* (NY, 1951), p. 30.
41. *Structure and Dynamics of the Psyche*, CW, Vol. VIII, p. 90.
42. *Psychological Types*, CW, Vol. VI, p. 460.
43. Suzuki, pp. 65–66.
44. Conze, p. 128.
45. Zimmer, Heinrich, *Philosophies of India* (NY, 1951), p. 545.
46. Ibid., p. 544.
47. Suzuki, p. 63.
48. Ibid., p. 120.
49. Jung, *Aion*, CW, Vol. IX, Part II, p. 204.
50. Chang, p. 201.
51. *Mysterium Coniunctionis*, CW, Vol. XIV, par. 129, n. 66.
52. Whitmont, Edward C., *The Symbolic Quest* (NY, 1969), p. 236.
53. Suzuki et al., *Zen Buddhism and Psychoanalysis* (NY, 1960), p. 25.
54. Ibid., p. 32.
55. Ibid., p. 70.
56. Organ, T. W., *The Self in Indian Philosophy* (The Hague, 1964), p. 22.

Frederick J. Streng

Mechanisms of Self-Deception
and True Awareness

Spiritual and psychotherapeutic cultivation is done within culturally distinct languages, social organizations and images of selfhood. Our conscious awareness gives focus, and our unconscious processes give structure, to experienced freedom, power and love. The images of the self, self-transcendence, soul or spirit that are used in connection with social behavior and personality structure are both causes and effects of mental and emotional processes of imaging. The salvific goal in religious effort and the model of true self-awareness in psychotherapy are intrinsically connected with some ultimate value(s), which also must be related to one's understanding of "the way things really are." This ultimate value-cum-reality may be apprehended through quite different psycho-mental procedures. For example, the ideal may be perceived as a state of freedom through total non-attachment, or liberation through the communion with a supreme (personal) reality. The formulation of the goal, therefore, is intrinsically related to a manner, or way, of achieving this goal; and this "way" requires retraining of the heart and mind so that self-deception can be avoided (at least to some extent). To know the truth about oneself, then, requires our participation in the procedures which form the tacit context in which the truth is known.

The philosopher of science Michael Polanyi (1951; 1967; 1975) has pointed out the significance of "tacit knowledge" in any activity of knowing. He asserts that any intentional action, even focused perception, includes some level of a skilled performance. When we focus on some object of knowledge, whether it is a concrete physical object, or a non-material object such as a comprehensive value—e.g. a fully functioning personality, comprehensive peace, or metaphysical reality—we have a focus of perception which requires a cultivated skill. Our awareness of the cultivated procedures is tacit, or

232

implicit; but it is as much a part of the awareness of the object of knowledge as the object itself. This tacit knowledge is necessary as a condition for perceiving the significance of the object. Thus, this tacit knowledge is an immediate experience; likewise, it is—on reflection as we "stand off" perceptually from the processes of cultivation—recognized to be one of several ways of apprehending the object of knowledge. The cultivated awareness is an interpreting framework, a procedure for making judgments, which allows the object of perception to come into focus.

The recognition of tacit knowledge is important for understanding the integration of sensations and other psychological processes because it highlights the lived presuppositions in human awareness (Hall, 1977). Within the large and complex question of the character of the most appropriate processes of self-awareness, I want to focus in this analysis on the tacit assumptions which can be used to understand the shift from self-deception to true awareness. The procedure is to examine two expressions of this shift from widely different cultural settings: the work of C. G. Jung and the second century B.C.E. Indian Buddhist text *The Eight-Thousand Line Perfection of Wisdom Sūtra* (*ELPW*). By looking at these alternatives we may be able in a limited way to expose some of the conditioning assumptions found in each of these approaches, which, in turn, may stimulate self-reflection on contemporary therapeutic procedures.

Cross-cultural comparisons in therapies for true self-awareness as I am proposing are intellectually exciting and fraught with problems. Such studies are exciting in that they seek to locate and elucidate perennial problems in human self-awareness and in the understanding of one's social and physical environment. Comparisons can provide heuristic devices for probing different cultural imagery and definitions and for constructing analytic tools to examine the coherence and assumptions found in general claims about human experience. By specifying similarities and differences one can clarify issues that may provide the basis for new constructive formulations of recurrent human efforts at understanding and life enhancement. At their best they help to distinguish structural elements from incidental form, the typical from the culturally accidental.

The dangers arise from oversimplification of important distinctions in vocabulary, assumptions, and structural approaches. The difficulties in determining "original" meanings, in assuming the relative importance of concepts in a more comprehensive structure of understanding, and in intuiting the intention of (especially religious or salvific) claims are legion. Nevertheless, I will try to highlight a few assumptions in the procedure of true self-awareness in order to explore the tacit knowledge implicit in each of these differently formulated approaches to self-awareness.

The specific issue in the shift from self-deception to true awareness can be formulated as the awareness of the self as it lets go of the attachment to the ego-image. That is, we are focusing on the experience of the nonego as a process that frees one from attachment to the ego. One of the most interesting aspects of this comparison is the difference in understanding the character or nature of selfhood and of nonego according to an early Indian Buddhist text and a contemporary psychoanalyst in the light of two assumptions common to both. The first common assumption is that both understand the self as a dynamic process, as an expression of energy in flux. The second is that both acknowledge a deeper awareness of reality that is already inherent in existence but that is hidden within unexamined conventional, often compulsive, personal behavior. This deeper awareness is the true awareness, which is not simply a descriptive proposition about oneself but a *mode* of awareness or even a deepening skill in becoming aware of oneself in relationship.

Nevertheless, the descriptions of the process for transforming self-deception to true awareness provide quite different definitions of selfhood and nonego. The different understandings of selfhood and nonego lead Jung to affirm the importance of an intense projection of the self in the experience of divinity, or *numinousum*, while the *ELPW* describes the emptying process of an empty ego in relation to an empty nonego, or empty dharma, or no-path. The differences, I suggest, are intrinsically related to different assumptions about the psycho-ontological power of symbols, concepts, and the quality of consciousness. The fundamental differences, according to this analysis, are not simply different notions of selfhood and nonego, but two different modes or ways of "becoming aware" at the most profound level of human experience.

I hope to show that different types of religious knowing condition different experiences of the self. In both cases the self experience is "intrinsically guided by impersonal standards [i.e., generally applicable standards] of valuation set by the self for itself" (Polanyi and Prosch, 1975, p. 42). To note different types of self-awareness both affirms and intends to move beyond the recognition that a functioning self has an ego-center, a coherence of awareness and action, that can survive the tension of incompatible experiences. Insofar as this ego-center selects pragmatically what is valid and invalid for its sense of selfhood it has an implicit set of evaluative standards, or a tacit integration of experienced options, that incorporate some and discard other sensory, imaginal, and emotional perceptions. This essay is concerned to analyze alternative ways to integrate a self-awareness in the light of the implicit evaluative sense of the relation between an ego-image and an experienced ultimate context of life. The analysis will show that the principle of integration according to Jung's statements is a symbolic representational content that pivots on an awareness of unconscious archetypes and conscious archetypal images, while the principle of integration according to the claims of the *ELPW* is an attitudinal fusion that pivots on a quality of consciousness.

When Carl Jung gave the three Terry Lectures of 1937 at Yale University, he considered the relation of religion to psychology. Interestingly, he gave two definitions of religion. One of them expresses a perspective common in the Western theological tradition. Early in the first lecture, on the anatomy of the unconscious mind, he says, "Religion . . . is the term that designates the attitude peculiar to a consciousness which has been altered by the experience of the *numinousum*" (Jung, 1938, p. 6). The other definition comes in the third lecture, entitled "The History and Psychology of a Natural Symbol," in which he discusses the mandala. Here religion is related to the unconscious dimension of the human personality. He says:

> Religion is a relationship to the highest or strongest value, be it positive or negative. The relationship is voluntary as well as involuntary, that is, that you can accept consciously the value by which you are possessed unconsciously. That psychological fact, which is the greatest power in your system is the god, since it is always the overwhelming psychic factor which is called god. (Jung, 1938, p. 98)

These excerpts indicate Jung's recognition of a transcendent dimension of the human condition as well as the dynamic power of consciousness in creating the world of our experience. Both aspects of his vision of the human condition make possible a comparison with the Indian Buddhist vision of the human situation. *ELPW* provides a basis for comparison in that it also emphasizes the quality of consciousness as a basic condition for true awareness of one's self and the world. In contrast to Jung's analysis, however, it emphasizes that the basic character of the self, including the deepest aspect of consciousness and all perceived things in the world, is empty of any essential, a priori, or self-existent reality. Even the *numinousum*, the divinity, is empty—as is the self, in both conscious and unconscious functions.

In comparing Jung's version of the human condition with that found in the *ELPW*, we focus on one of the most dramatic claims made by Jung in his final lecture: namely, that the mandala, found in the contemporary world, as expressed by many of Jung's clients, had an empty center. This was important for Jung since he was well aware, through his study of historical sources, that traditionally the mandala had a divine figure, a god or a goddess, at the center of this great circle. He says:

> A modern mandala is an involuntary confession of a peculiar mental condition. There is no deity in the mandala, and there is also no submission or reconciliation to a deity. The place of the deity seems to be taken by the wholeness of man.
>
> When one speaks of man, everybody means his own ego personality—that is, his personality in as much as he is aware of it—and when one speaks of others one assumes that they have a very similar personality. But since modern research has acquainted us with a fact that an individual consciousness is based upon and surrounded by an indefinite extended unconscious psyche, we must revise our somewhat old fashioned prejudice that man is his [individual] consciousness. This rather naive assumption must be confronted at once by the critical question: Whose Consciousness? Is it his consciousness or the consciousness of other people around him? (Jung 1938, p. 99)

Jung answers his own question by saying that the individual consciousness is partially a collective unconscious:

> It is a remarkable fact that this replacement is a natural and spontaneous occurrence, and that it is always essentially unconscious.

If we want to know what is going to happen in a case where the idea of God is no longer projected as an autonomous entity, this is an answer of man's unconscious mind. The unconscious produces a new idea of man in loco dei, of man deified (or divine), imprisoned, concealed, protected, usually dehumanized and expressed by abstract symbolism. (Jung, 1938, p. 106)

This recognition that the religious factor is identical to one's psyche is for Jung and for many other readers awesome. One's own psyche, says Jung, *is* the divinity:

The gods in our time assemble in the lap of the ordinary individual and are as powerful and awe-inspiring as ever, in spite of their new disguise—the so-called psychical functions. Man thinks of himself as holding the psyche in the hollow of his hand. He dreams even of making a science of her. But in reality she is the mother and the maker, the psychical subject and even the possibility of consciousness itself. The psyche reaches so far beyond the boundary line of consciousness that the latter could be easily compared to an island in the ocean. (Jung, 1938, p. 105)

Jung warns, however, that this is a psychologically dangerous situation for most people. It is safer to keep the intensity and power of the beyond in an image of an external autonomous power. He says, "The experience formulated by the mandala is typical of people who cannot project the divine image any longer. They are in actual danger of inflation and dissociation" (Jung, 1938, p. 105). A person who denies the reality of the unconscious psychic forces, or assimilates his own ego into that psychic energy, becomes the victim of "inflation" whereby the personality is dissolved and one acts psychotically. Jung writes:

Since the idea of God represents an important, even overwhelming psychical intensity, it is, in a way, safer to believe that such an autonomous intensity is a non-ego, perhaps an altogether different or superhuman entity, "totaliteraliter." Confronted with such a belief, man must need to feel small, just about his own size. But if he declares the tremendum to be dead, then he must find out at once where this considerable energy, which was once invested in an existence as great as God, has disappeared to.

Since it is a matter of tremendous energy, the result will be an equally important psychological disturbance in the form of dissociation of personality. The disruption can produce a dual or multiple personality. It is as if one single person could not carry the total amount of energy, so that parts of the personality which were hitherto functional units instantly break asunder and assume the dignity and importance of autonomous personalities. (Jung, 1938, p. 104)

In another writing, Jung explains the problem of being absorbed into psychic powers beyond the capacity of one's ego:

It must be reckoned a psychic catastrophe when the ego is assimilated by the self. The image of wholeness then remains in the unconscious so that on the one hand it shares the archaic nature of the unconscious, and on the other, finds itself in the psychically relative space-time continuum that is characteristic of the unconsciousness as such. . . . Hence it is of the greatest importance that the ego should be anchored in the world of consciousness and that consciousness should be reinforced by a very precise adaptation. For this, certain virtues like attention, conscientiousness, patience, etc., are of great value on the moral side, just as accurate observation of the symptomatology of the unconscious and objective self-criticism are valuable on the intellectual side. (Jung, 1968, pp. 45–46)

Jung warns his readers about the danger of identifying the ego with its extended unconscious totally. We can ask ourselves, however, whether there is a way to understand the tremendous psychic power at the root of the human selfhood as a neutral and integrable capacity rather than as the source of a psychic catastrophe. Jung himself says that one can and must know the hidden, the "shadow" side of one's personality, and reconcile the conscious and unconscious aspects of the self. At the same time the autonomous collective unconscious always stands in tension with the ego. One's true self moves between the archetype and ego-individuality without locating oneself in either. This is the process of ever-deepening self-awareness.

Another way to understand the empty center in the deepest human awareness is found in the *ELPW*, which claims that the enlightened person knows the emptiness of both the ego and any absolute reality, whether this is termed "God," "nirvana," the "Self," a "dharma," or even "Buddhahood."

To be aware of oneself and the world as "empty," from the Buddhist viewpoint, requires a shift in the mode of apprehending the human situation. It is a shift from the conventional or habitual way to one expressing the perfection of wisdom and compassion. True compassion, however, requires knowing that awareness of any idea, any perceived object, or oneself is possible only without attachment to that idea, to the object, or to the self. In chapter 9 of the *ELPW*, the manner of knowing emptiness in an empty manner is described as follows:

> The perfection of the bodhisattva has no mental attitude, because it is imperturbable. This perfection is unshakeable, in consequence of the stability of the realm of dharma. This perfection is quieted because no sign is apprehended in all dharmas. This perfection is faultless, as the perfection of all virtues. This perfection is undefiled, because imagination is something that is not. No living being is [ultimately] found in this perfection, because of the reality limit. This perfection is unlimited because of the manifestation of all dharmas does not rise up. (Conze, 1973, pp. 151–52)

For the skillful perceiver of emptiness, the world, self, and interpersonal relations do not disappear into a nihilistic void.

Granted, there is a psychological danger when one pursues the empty way of knowing. The person training in the empty manner of experiencing life is warned not to realize emptiness as a goal itself or as reality in itself. This is accomplished by focusing on caring for all beings in existence. Such caring or compassion for all beings is understood in the profound sense that there is an intrinsic relationship between oneself and all existing beings already. This is explained by the Buddha in the twentieth chapter of the *ELPW* in the following words:

> Since [the bodhisattva] has not abandoned all beings, he is thus able to win full enlightenment safely and securely. At the time when a Bodhisattva has made all beings into an objective support

for his thought of friendliness, and with the highest friendliness ties himself to them, at that time he rises above the factiousness of the defilements and of Mara [the Evil One, Death], he arises above the level of the Disciple and Pratyeka-buddha, and he abides in that concentration [on friendliness]. (Conze, 1973, p. 224)

The nature of emptiness as manifested in the perfection of wisdom is a very complex topic. I want to make only three points regarding emptiness in *ELPW*. The first is the claim that the self and its constituents are empty, or without self-existent reality. The experienced self, as an empty self, is a process of interactive energies identified as the five *skandhas:* materiality, feelings or sensations, perceptions, impulses or unconscious predispositions, and consciousness. This flow of material, sensory, mental-emotional, perceptual, and unconscious energy is without self existent power, just as each of the constituents arises only in relation to mutually dependent conditions (Streng, 1982, 1975). In chapter 1 of the *ELPW*, the venerable adept of perfect wisdom, Subhūti, says that despite the talk of "a bodhisattva," there is really nothing outside the verbalizing process that corresponds in a one-to-one way with the idea of a "bodhisattva." One who does not become fearful when hearing this is at the irreversible stage of the bodhisattva path; he stands well (*suṣṭita*) while not having stood anywhere (*asthānayogena*) (Vaidya, 1960, p. 4). In chapter 2, Subhūti instructs the god Śakra on the deepest value of life, perfect wisdom, and how to achieve it. He says that having abided (*tiṣṭatā*) in emptiness (*śūnyatām*) a bodhisattva "is stayed" (*sthātavyam*) in the perfection of wisdom. Then he continues by contrasting "abiding in emptiness" with other possibilities that one should avoid. For example, the bodhisattva should "not be stayed" (*na sthātavyam*) in form and the other four *skandhas*, not in any of the five senses or mind (*manas*), not in sensory or mental objects, not in the elements, not on "the pillars of mindfulness, right efforts, roads to psychic power, faculties, powers, limbs of enlightenment and limbs of the path" (Conze, 1973, p. 97), not on the fruits of different levels of spiritual attainment, even arhatship.

The second point is that the experienced world has various dimensions or levels of quality. One of the most important variations is between the compulsive personal identification with projected images of oneself and the world, on the one hand, and the freeing, spontaneous (or empty) manner of interaction of self and one's environment, on the other. A person's awareness includes thoughts and images, but more fundamental than the directional organizing and constructive power of specific symbols themselves for determining either self-deception or true awareness is the mode or quality of becoming conscious. The *ELPW* speaks of the freeing, or empty, manner of awareness as "not being stayed" (*na sthātavyam*) in things or ideas. In two subsequent sections of chapter 1, the text delineates several possibilities of what one should not be stayed in, for example, the idea that form is empty, that it is to be apprehended as something, not even in the idea that "this is Buddhahood."

Further, a bodhisattva should not "be stayed" in the notion "that the fruits of the holy life derive their dignity from the Unconditioned," or in the stage of a Buddha, or in the recognition that he has done a Buddha's work (Conze, 1973, p. 97). This list of negations by Subhūti leaves another disciple, Śāriputra, with a question: If one should "not be stayed" even in the highest level of enlightenment, *how* then should one abide in emptiness and train oneself (*śikṣitavyam*) (Vaidya, 1960, p. 19)? Subhūti responds with a question: Where did the Buddha abide (*stitha*)? Śāriputra answers: The Tathāgata, the completely enlightened one, (*samyaksambuddha*) abode (*stitha*) nowhere. On what grounds is this claim made? Because the completely enlightened one has "not stationed" (*apratiṣṭita*) his mind anywhere (Vaidya, 1960, p. 19).

The third point regarding emptiness in the *ELPW* is the claim that to live in an empty manner is enlightenment. Enlightenment is the freeing of one's thoughts, emotions, or psychic energy from inappropriate restrictions due to attachment or compulsive identification with them. In the conversation between Subhūti and Śāriputra mentioned above regarding where the Buddha "abode" in his attainment of perfect enlightenment, Śāriputra correctly says that the Tathāgata did not abide (*na stitah*) in the conditioned realm or in the nonconditioned realm, nor did he abandon (*vyutthita*) them both. Subhūti then affirms Śāriputra's statement and summarizes the view of the *ELPW* by saying:

Even so, Śāriputra, a bodhisattva, a great being, is stayed [*sthātavyam*], is trained. [He thinks:] As the Tathāgata, the highest (completely) enlightened one, so I am not anywhere stayed [*sthatah*], not non-abiding [*nasthitah*], not fixed [*vistitah*], not non-fixed [*nāvistitah*]. Being stayed [*sthasyam*] in this way, one is trained [*śikṣitavyam*, i.e., trained correctly]. As the Tathāgata, so I 'stand' [*sthāsyami*]; thus I am trained. As the Tathāgata has stood [*sthānam*], thus, I stand [*sthāsyami*]; thus I train . . . well placed [*suṣṭitah*], not having stood anywhere [*asthānayogena*]. Even so a bodhisattva, a great being, is stayed [*sthātavyam*], is trained. Thus trained the bodhisattva, a great being, abides [*viharati*] in the perfection of wisdom and does not lose his attentiveness to it. (Vaidya, 1960, p. 19)

Thus to train, or to stay in the course of perfect wisdom, a person should avoid being "fixed" or "stayed" in any object of perception or mental ideal.

Our language and the way we use language in a habitually symbolic way disposes us to think that there are units of reality that exist in themselves. Insight shows—says the *ELPW*—that such a view is not true. The point of meditating on the perfection of wisdom is not simply to construct a new system or image for understanding but to allow insights into the kind of verbal fallacies and emotional afflictions that human beings easily slip into. The formulations and imagery are, at best, expedient means. According to this perspective neither the ego nor the archetype—to use Jung's terminology—is a final determinate. They are determinates of selfhood only to the degree that a person gives them power.

The attachment to the concept or image of the "I" can be called a type of narcissism; however, it is a narcissism that pervades all existence, and is based on the habitual division between oneself and others. It can be eliminated only by actualizing a sense of oneself in relation to others; while selfhood is not an eternal reality, it is a complex of physical, emotional, and mental interactions even before an "I" is specified. Narcissism, as a precognitive tendency to define reality from the standpoint of the ego, is—from the standpoint of the *ELPW*—based on a dualistic mode of perception. It is a fabrication looming into a fantasy because it misappropriates the experience of becoming.

From the perspective found in the *ELPW*, any talk of a self, ego, or archetype is a mental construction. If one wants to talk about them, one should do so with the recognition that they are simply concepts that direct one's perception but do not represent (or re-present) entities outside the language system in a one-to-one relationship. The fact that all ideas and symbols are fabrications does not mean that all imagery is totally useless in attaining enlightenment. Indeed, some notions are said to be more useful than others for actualizing true awareness. To say that things are empty is more useful than to say that they refer to an essential self-existent entity; but one should not get caught in thinking that therefore there must be something that is essentially empty and something that is essentially self-existent. This would exemplify a dualistic orientation. The thought process about oneself and others that is conventional and symbolically powerful tends to keep one bound to one's own projections and obstructions. Symbolical image construction participates in the same reality of dependent coarising as the freeing actualizing of emptiness, but it is without the awareness of the empty character of that in which one is actually participating.

How do these two visions of the condition of the human situation contribute to an understanding of the emptiness at the center of the deepest human self-consciousness? The answer, I suggest, is related to an understanding of how people know the truth about themselves. This, in turn, is related to the way one finds one's own deepest values—that is, the way one valorizes experience. The Jungian approach places an emphasis on the symbolic power of images and dispositions for constructing an experienced world. The bodhisattva in the *ELPW* emphasizes shifting from a symbolic mode of consciousness to a different quality of consciousness, which we might call here an "emptying consciousness." Despite many overlapping concerns, a difference is reflected in the way that each orientation understands the possibility and danger of identifying the conscious individual or the conventional self with the deepest or most comprehensive dimension of that self.

From the Buddhist perspective in the *ELPW*, letting go of a mythic consciousness as a valorizing process is the highest goal in the most radical form of emptiness meditation. On the other hand, Carl Jung warns that inflation of ego necessarily attends the identification of oneself with an archetypal motif. The fears of identifying oneself with an archetypal motif arise, to a significant degree, because of a common Western assumption, suggested in his first definition of religion. While Jung recognizes that the Collective Unconscious is part of the self, he follows the advocates of mainline Christianity who are trained to perceive ultimate values by locating (projecting) them outside of the self. The classical manner by which ultimate values are identified by the worshipping Christian community begins with an assumption of a radical distinction between the sacred and the secular, between the holy and profane. The sacred is the incomprehensible, the wholly other source of everything, the creator who is never to be confused with the creature.

According to Jung, people need to maintain a balance between the archetype and ego by avoiding the integration of all possible archetypes into the ego. If the ego is absorbed into the archetype, the ego loses contact with the conditioned world. This model depends on the assumption that there is an ultimate value expressed in the archetype and the ego, and that there is some autonomy in each, such that each must stand over against the other in a mutually dependent tension. God is an autonomous psychic complex. Similarly, for Jung, a mandala is an expression of how one views one's awareness through a symbol, a psychic construct, or a constructed world of experience. A mandala is a true image of an experienced world. An empty center is dangerous because total absorption into the nonego requires the loss of the conditioned ego.

The Buddhist view in the *ELPW* suggests that the mandala, as any symbol, may function not only as a way of constructing a world of order and meaning. It may, at a more profound level, be a tool or expedient for shifting one's mode of consciousness from a concern to construct a meaningful world as a process of self-realization to a concern to dissipate attachment to an empty self-image as a process of self-realization (or no-self realization). In the latter process, the value given to a particular symbolic form is transcended by a process that recognizes all symbolic forms as conditioned mental-emotional processes. It is a process of letting go of a mythologizing process of valorization.

On the last page of her lucid discussion of symbolic projection, *Projection and Re-Collection in Jungian Psychology*, Marie-Louise von Franz (1980) notes that when a Zen Buddhist master lives "in complete accord with the rhythm of psychic energy and with its regulator, the Self, he has no projections anymore" (p. 199). It is such a shift that the Perfection of Wisdom advocates as necessary for overcoming self-deception. Von Franz goes on to say how unusual such a centered person is:

> [O]nly a person with the most highly reflected concentration can achieve this. We average human beings, by contrast, will hardly be able to avoid the necessity, for the rest of our lives, of again and again recognizing projections for what they are, or at least as mistaken judgments. (von Franz, 1980, p. 199)

Here von Franz recognizes that projection of an inflated ego-image need not be the *necessary* result of a loss of ego. This is possible when ego is not seen as a separate entity forming its relation to an overwhelming external energy through an emotionally toned symbolic structure, and when the centering *process*—as expressed in her understanding of the Jungian notion of *unus mundus* (von Franz, 1980, pp. 91–92)—in which all mental and physical acts, the ego and Collective Unconscious appropriately interact, is emphasized. Such a practical expression of the self is genuine self-knowledge. The degree to which both archetype and ego are recognized as intrinsically relative to each other, and to the degree that ego-consciousness can no longer be distinguished from all other psychological and physical factors—to that degree it functions as the no-mind (nonego) in the principle of integration according to the *ELPW*.

References

Conze, E. (1973). *The perfection of wisdom in eight-thousand lines and its verse summary*. Bolinas, Calif.: Four Seasons Foundation.
von Franz, M-L. (1980). *Projection and re-collection in Jungian psychology* (W. H. Kennedy, trans.). LaSalle, Ill.: Open Court.
Hall, J. (1977). *Clinical uses of dreams: Jungian interpretations and enactments*. New York: Grune and Stratton.
Jung, C. G. (1938). *Psychology and religion*. New Haven: Yale University Press.
——— (1968). Read, H., Fordham, M., and Adler, G. (eds.). Aion: Researches into the phenomenology of the self. *Collected works*, 9. Princeton: Princeton University Press.
Polanyi, M. (1951). *Personal knowledge*. Chicago: University of Chicago Press.

———— (1967). *The tacit dimension.* London: Routledge and Kegan Paul.

————, and Prosch, H. (1975). *Meaning.* Chicago: University of Chicago Press.

Streng, F. J. (1975). Reflections on the attention given to mental instruction in the Indian Buddhist analysis of causality. *Philosophy East and West* 25/1, January, pp. 71–80.

———— (1982). Realization of *Param Bhutakoti* (ultimate reality-limit) in the *Astasahasrika Prajnaparamita Sutra. Philosophy East and West,* 32/1, January, pp. 91–98.

Vaidya, P. L. (1960). *Astasahasrika Prajnaparamita with Haribhadra's commentary called Aloka.* Buddhist Sanskrit Texts, No. 4. Darbhanga: Mithila Institute of Post-Graduate Studies and Research in Sanskrit Learning.

Harold Coward

Jung's Commentary on the
Amitāyur Dhyāna Sūtra

Jung's Commentary on the *Amitāyur Dhyāna Sūtra*, a Mahāyāna Buddhist text, forms the main body of his lecture "The Psychology of Eastern Meditation" delivered in Zurich, Basel and Bern during March–May 1943.[1] Originally composed in Sanskrit in India, the *Amitāyur Dhyāna Sūtra* was translated into Chinese by Kālayasas in the fifth century A.D. and introduced to Japan in the seventh century A.D.[2] Along with the *Larger Sukhāvatī Vyūha* and the *Smaller Sukhāvatī Vyūha*, the *Amitāyur Dhyāna* is one of the three principal *sūtras* of the Jodo Shinshu sect of Japanese Buddhism.[3] Jodo Shinshu or Pure Land Buddhism was founded by Shonin Shinran in Kyoto in the twelfth century A.D. and has flourished in Japan ever since. With the emigration of Japanese people to North America and Europe during the last century, Jodo Shinshu Buddhism has become known worldwide.[4] Therefore it was most appropriate for Jung to direct his attention to one of Jodo Shinshu's basic texts. The fact that Jung selected this as a Buddhist text upon which to comment elicited criticism from those who felt that the Pāli Hinayāna texts were much better representatives of Buddhist doctrine. But, as was frequently the case in his encounter with other religions, Jung had an intuitive sense of what was spiritually important for the psychological experience of devotees. He responds to his critic as follows:

> ... in Japan and the Mongolian areas of Buddhism this *Sūtra* enjoys the highest authority and is far better known than the Pali Canon. For me, therefore, it was much more important to comment on this *Sūtra* than on the undoubtedly more correct views of the Canon.... I am concerned with the real man here and now....[5]

It is interesting that Jung selects this text as a representative of yoga or meditation. In his introduction Jung describes "yoga" as "the disciplining of the instinctual forces of the psyche, which in Sanskrit are called the *kleśa*."[6] He distinguishes this kind of yogic meditation from *hatha yoga* which he describes somewhat unfairly as "a sort of gymnastics consisting chiefly of breathing exercises and special body postures."[7] Although correctly seeing this text as presenting an approach to yogic control of the *kleśa* through visualizations on the Buddha Amitābha, Jung does not clearly recognize that what is presented in the text is a form of *bhakti* yoga (yoga of devotion).[8] Ultimately it is through devotional surrender, via the visualizations of the text, that the *kleśa* or instinctual forces (as Jung calls them) are overcome and liberation realized. Here again Jung perhaps errs in referring to this text as representative of "theistic Buddhism."[9] Although it is clear that the text uses forms and appearances of the Buddha as a focus for meditation, this should not lead one to think that, for Jodo Shinshu, Amitābha Buddha ultimately exists as a separate entity over and against the devotee. Indeed, the self-declared goal of the Eighth Meditation of the text is to help the devotee discover Amitābha to be no different from the structure of the devotee's own mind.[10] With these caveats in mind, let us proceed to consider: I. Jung's Commentary on the text; and II. A comparison of Jung's psychological categories with those of Yogācāra Buddhism, of which this text is an example.

I. JUNG'S COMMENTARY ON THE TEXT

The main theme of the *Amitāyur Dhyāna Sūtra* is a sermon which Śākyamuni delivers to Vaidehi, the Queen who has been wrongly imprisoned by her son. The son has seized power by imprisoning his father the King and leaving him to starve to death. The Queen has been arrested because in visiting her husband she has been smuggling food to him. Now imprisoned by her son and unable to help her husband, Queen Vaidehi in her agony prays to Śākyamuni, who is in residence on a nearby mountain. In response to her plea Śākyamuni Buddha and his two disciples Mahāmaudgalyāyana and Ānanda go to Queen Vaidehi through the sky and appear before her in her room of imprisonment in the palace. The Queen asks the

Buddha to preach to her "in detail of all the places where there is no sorrow or trouble, and where I ought to go to be born anew."[11] India, she says, is full of depravities and she longs for rebirth in a world that is pure. In an act of devotional contrition the Queen throws herself upon the ground before the Buddha, confesses her sins, and begs for his mercy and instruction. The Buddha responds to her devotion by projecting from his forehead a visualization of "the pure and admirable countries of the Buddhas in the ten quarters" for Vaidehi to see and choose from.[12] From all the radiant Buddhas and their heavenly countries arrayed before her Queen Vaidehi declares that she wishes herself "to be born in the realm of Buddha Amitāyus (or Amitābha), in the world of Highest Happiness (*Sukhāvatī*)," and asks for the instruction that would enable her to obtain the right vision of that pure land.[13] Śākyamuni Buddha then teaches her sixteen meditations in all. In the first thirteen meditations he describes and has her perceive in detail Amitābha Buddha and his Pure Land of Bliss (*Sukhāvatī*). The last three meditations focus on the three grades of people and the corresponding three different ways for each to attain rebirth in Amitābha's Pure Land.

The above setting and interaction between Śākyamuni Buddha and Queen Vaidehi has been described in some detail because Jung, in his Commentary, virtually ignores it. Aside from one brief paragraph (para. 913) in which he simply sets the stage, all of Jung's attention is focused on an analysis of the first thirteen meditations. Yet from the perspective of the psychological experience of Pure Land Buddhist devotees, it is the *bhakti* approach of Queen Vaidehi to Śākyamuni Buddha, characterized by her complete faith (*śraddha*) and surrender, correlated with her low spiritual state (described in meditation sixteen) that provides a pathway to the Pure Land that even the most sinful can follow. We will come back later to the significance of Jung's failure to attend to the devotional faith perspective which enabled Queen Vaidehi, and perhaps most Jodo Shinshu Buddhists, to realize the Pure Land.

Another section of the text which Jung ignores comes at the very beginning of the first meditation in the form of three prerequisite requirements for entering the meditation. These prerequisites are: (1) to act filially toward parents and support them, serve and respect one's teachers, be compassionate of mind and abstain from injury; (2) to take the vow of seeking refuge with the three jewels, fulfill all moral precepts and ritual ceremonies; and (3) to give one's whole mind to the attainment of *bodhi* or enlightenment, deeply believe in dependent origination, study and recite the Mahāyāna sūtras.[14] Jung's omission of this material is most unfortunate, for it serves to foster the common Western misconception that Eastern meditation is detached from ethical considerations. Certainly the first two of these three precepts are almost wholly ethical in their content and these ethical requirements are clearly joined to the visualization exercises that follow as prerequisites for the realization of the Pure Land of Amitābha. Like many other Western scholars Jung was not sensitive to this strongly ethical aspect of the text.

Unlike the meditation technique of Zen Buddhism, which aims at an absence of appearances in the mind, this text adopts the opposite technique of using the designated appearances of Amitābha and his Pure Land as the means for meditation. While Jung naturally searches the objects present in the visualizations for evidence of archetypal content, the Jodo Shinshu devotee sees the gem objects of the visions as symbols of the immutables (*asamskṛta*) of Amitābha's Pure Land and consequently as embodying Mahāyāna teachings. As Ryukyo Fujimoto puts it,

> These gems and other objects which are felt by the senses and extol the teachings of Buddhism are all symbols of the realm of the *Dharmakāya* (Body of Truth). As such, the entire realm of the Pure Land is nothing more than the *Dharmakāya* which is, by word definition, the congregation of the eternal dharmas and virtues.[15]

It would be as if Jung had written an insightful Commentary on the "Revelation or Apocalypse to John" from the New Testament, discovering the presence of much archetypal material but missing the Christian content of symbols. Jung would not be wrong, but Christians would say that he had missed a major aspect of the text's meaning. Pure Land Buddhists feel the same way about Jung's psychological analysis of the visualizations presented to Queen Vaidehi by Śākyamuni Buddha. They are grateful for his recognition of the importance of the text, and find that his psychological comments add a new dimension to their experience of the text, but, overall, they feel that he has not been sufficiently sensitive to the rooting of the visualizations in Mahāyāna Buddhist doctrine.[16]

The strengths of Jung's Commentary become evident when we move to the visualization exercises themselves. The meditations begin with concentration upon the sun, when it looks like a suspended drum, as it is setting in the West toward the Pure Land of Amitābha. Jung notes that in southern latitudes the intensity of the setting sun is such that a few moments of gazing at it are sufficient to create a strong after-image which will last for some time. This, Jung suggests, produces a hypnotic effect which allows the devotee to fix the sun in one's mind and clearly examine it from all sides. The round shape of the sun prepares the way for subsequent circular visualizations, and its brightness for the resplendent visions that come afterward.[17] The sun is the symbol of warmth and light, the central point of our visible world. "As the giver of life it is always and everywhere either the divinity itself or an image of the same."[18] For the Buddhist devotee, says Jung, the sun is an allegory of the immortality-dispensing Amitābha,[19] while in the Christian world the sun is a favorite allegory of Christ.[20]

Now, as the thirteen meditations proceed, the adornments that make up Amitābha's Pure Land gradually emerge in the devotee's consciousness. All are objects of the senses that for the Buddhist extol the teachings of Buddhism, and, for Jung, have psychic significance. There is the perception of water clear and pure, of ice shining and transparent, of lapis lazuli, the ground beneath which is seen a golden banner with jewels and diamonds. The reflected brilliance of all this is so great it is like a thousand million suns. Superimposed over its surface is a network of golden ropes. This dazzling image is to be kept front and center in the devotee's consciousness at all times except when asleep. This exercise, it is claimed, gives one a dimly seen perception of the Pure Land of Amitābha.[21] A Buddhist analyst would note that the rays emitted from gems located at the crossings of the golden ropes construct in the sky (in lazer beam fashion) towers with musical instruments which play the sounds of Buddhist doctrine: "suffering," "non-existence," "impermanence," and "non-self."[22] Jung passes over this "doctrinal singing" but observes that water, the basis of this meditative exercise, is, like the sun, a second source of life. Water also has power as a spiritual symbol, says Jung—witness Christ's allegory of "living water" with the Samaritan woman at the well. Meditation on these two symbols of sun and water are especially powerful for aiding the process of individuation by which sense perceptions of the outer world are united with archetypal contents of the unconscious. Reflection on the sun and water in this ancient Buddhist text trigger one of Jung's most powerful and penetrating passages:

> A meditation on sun and water evokes these [spiritual] associations without fail, so that the meditator will gradually be led from the foreground of visible appearances into the background, that is, to the spiritual meaning behind the object of meditation. He is transported to the psychic sphere, where sun and water, divested of their physical objectivity, become symbols of psychic contents, images of the source of life in the individual psyche. For indeed our consciousness does not create itself—it wells up from unknown depths. In childhood it awakens gradually, and all through life it wakes each morning out of the depths of sleep from an unconscious condition. It is like a child that is born daily out of the primordial womb of the unconscious. In fact, closer investigation reveals that it is not only influenced by the unconscious but continually emerges out of it in the form of numberless spontaneous ideas and sudden flashes of thought. Meditation on the meaning of sun and water is therefore something like a descent into the fountainhead of the psyche, into the unconscious itself.[23]

Turning back to the symbols of the text Jung remarks that the blue stone of the ground, the lapis lazuli, is transparent enabling the gaze of the meditator to penetrate into the depths of the psyche's secrets. The banner, which is seen through the transparent floor, represents the unconscious which has now taken on form. Before it was invisible (unconscious). Now, through deepening meditation (*dhyāna*), the unconscious has taken on form and become visible. Jung then makes a critical evaluation of the nature of Eastern meditation as exemplified by the visualization exercises of the *Amitāyur Dhyāna Sūtra*. The great difference between the Eastern and Western mind, says Jung, is that when the East turns inward in meditation, the external world of the senses is completely left behind. "It is as if the light of consciousness had ceased to illuminate the objects of the outer world of the senses and now illumines the darkness of the unconscious."[24] This critique of Eastern meditation cannot be accepted. Zen and certainly the *Satipatthāna* (mindfulness) meditations sharpen one's consciousness of the world of the senses rather than, as Jung suggests, "leaving it behind." And even in this Jodo Shinshu text, where subjective images are used, the meditation begins with concrete images of nature (water and the setting sun), adds elements of Buddhist doctrine perceived through the sense of hearing, and seeks to put one in touch with a Buddha nature which is at once the true form of one's own consciousness and simultaneously the true form of nature (the *Dharmadhatukāya*) as it occurs everywhere around us.[25] Jung's contention that Eastern meditation seems to completely extinguish the world of the senses simply cannot be accepted.

This mistaken conclusion causes Jung to create yet another caricature of Eastern meditation, namely, its experience of the *kleśa* or instinctual defilements. Jung says, "Here the Eastern text skips over a phenomenon that is a source of endless difficulties for the European."[26] Thinking that Eastern meditation causes one to lose contact with the external world, Jung notes that this opens one to being caught up in one's own subjective fantasies. Such fantasies, says Jung, are not dealt with in the Amitāyur text and are considered cheap and worthless. They are the *kleśa*, the disorderly and chaotic instinctual forces which Eastern yoga seeks to control by avoidance. Psychic progress, maintains Jung, occurs only when one comes to grips with the dark forces of the psyche, rather than seeking to avoid them—as he thinks Eastern meditation does. This is one of the reasons Jung strongly counsels Westerners against following yoga practices, because, says Jung, Europeans already have a tendency to avoid the dark corners of their psyches. This tendency will only be fostered by Eastern meditation techniques which Jung thinks also ignore the *kleśas*. Such meditation, concludes Jung, is entirely meaningless and worthless.[27]

Ryukyo Fujimoto, however, thinks that Jung is quite mistaken. The very fact that yoga has coined the term *kleśa*, of which Jung is so fond, indicates the Eastern familiarity with the darker forces of the unconscious. Fujimoto comments, "A glance over the synonymous words for defilement would be suggestive of the great many ways in which the Buddhist spiritual therapists have gone into the problem."[28] He goes on to list words such as *avidya* (ignorance), *asrava* (eruption), *mraksa* (oppression), *mara* (obsession), *avaraṇa* (obstacles), *granthah* (fetter, especially in relation to egoism) and *oghah* (the rapid flood of passion) as evidence of the awareness by Buddhists of the darker forces of the unconscious. In fact such forces are strongly in evidence in the sixteenth meditation of the *Amitāyur Dhyāna Sūtra,*[29] a section of the text which Jung ignores in his Commentary. It is precisely for persons of a low nature (that is, heavily weighed down with *kleśa*) that the sixteenth meditation prescribes a form of *bhakti* or devotional yoga as being most suitable. Queen Vaidehi, as it turns out, is such a person. Jung, unfortunately, misses all of this, and consequently misses aspects of the text which deal with the dark forces of the psyche, not by avoidance, but by recognition, and a yoga of devotional surrender to the grace of Amitābha Buddha.

Jung correctly attaches great importance to the eighth meditation in which it is revealed to the devotee that his or her mind is indeed the Buddha. In this meditation the imaginative reconstruction of the image of Amitābha in his Pure Land, taught to Queen Vaidehi by Śākyamuni Buddha, evokes the realization that Amitābha is nothing other than the psyche of the meditator. As Jung puts it, "It is not only that the image of the Buddha is produced out of 'one's own mind and thought,' but the psyche which produces these thought-forms *is the Buddha himself.*"[30] The image of Amitābha sits in the round lotus in the center of the octagonal Pure Land receiving all beings, including the meditator, with great compassion. Jung comments:

> This means that the inmost being which is the Buddha is bodied forth in the vision and revealed as the true self of the meditator. He experiences himself as the only thing that exists, as the highest consciousness, even the Buddha. In order to attain this final goal it was necessary to pass through all the laborious exercises of mental reconstruction, to get free of the deluded ego-consciousness which is responsible for the sorrowful illusion of the world, and to reach that other pole of the psyche where the world as illusion is abolished.[31]

In Jung's view this is a good example of what happens when the darkness of the personal unconscious grows transparent and the supra-personal God or Self archetype of the unconscious appears to the meditator. The form and content taken by the Self archetype in its manifestation is supplied by the myths of the tradition to which the devotee belongs—in this case Jodo Shinshu Buddhism.[32] Jung finds images of Christ enthroned in similar round and outwardly extending images to be present in Western medieval art, alchemy and in the experiences of his modern patients. Jung employs the Sanskrit term *maṇḍala* for this universal form taken by manifestations of the Self archetype. A Sanskrit word meaning circle, a *maṇḍala* is a circular image which is drawn, painted, danced, or, in this instance, visualized for the purpose of assisting meditation. The enacting of *maṇḍalas*, says Jung

> ... are nothing but projections of psychic events, which then exert a counter-influence on the psyche and put a kind of spell upon the personality. Through ritual action, attention and interest are led back to the inner sacred precinct, which is the source and goal of the psyche and contains the unity and life of consciousness.[33]

The ritual meditation, prescribed in the *Amitāyur Dhyāna Sūtra*, has served to lead Queen Vaidehi through the layers of her personal unconscious to the individuation of the self archetype of the collective unconscious in the Amitābha symbol of the Pure Land.

Jung completes his Commentary by adding some comparative comments on the differences (from the perspective of his psychology) between the individuation of the Self archetype via the Buddha sitting in the Lotus *maṇḍala* of this text and the enthroned Christ of the Christian *maṇḍalas*. In comparing the two *maṇḍalas* Jung finds a subtle but enormous difference. "The Christian during contemplation would never say 'I am Christ,' but will confess with Paul: 'Not I, but Christ liveth in me' (Gal 2:20). Our sutra, however, says: 'Thou wilt know that *thou* art the Buddha.' "[34] Both confessions require the transcending of one's initial self-identity with ego-consciousness to a greatly enlarged awareness of identity with the Self archetype. But whereas for the Buddhist the identity with the Buddha nature discovered within is complete, the Christian can never equate himself fully with God or Christ. Individuation is achieved not by a loss of one's ego but by a surrender of it to Christ, so that "Christ liveth in me." For Jung this is the subtle but enormous difference between Eastern and Western meditation.

While we can agree with Jung's point about the difference in terms of the amount of ego-loss and the degree of identity with the divine, we cannot accept Jung's view that the Eastern approach produces a result which is cut off from the concrete world of sense experience, and lacking in ethical content. While the meditations of the *Amitāyur Dhyāna Sūtra* may appear to transport Queen Vaidehi to an idealistic and unreal Pure Land, its aim is not escapism, as Jung seems to suggest, but rather a deeper insight into the true nature of reality—an insight which will allow her to successfully grapple with and live through the agony and stress of her daily life. Nor does it free her from the obligation of ethical actions. As the Śākyamuni makes clear to Queen Vaidehi (especially the parts Jung omits) living a life of full moral compassion is both a prerequisite for entering the meditation and an integral part of the final vision of the Pure Land— the true self of the devotee which is to be actualized in daily life.[35]

II. JUNGIAN AND YOGĀCĀRA CATEGORIES COMPARED

Commentaries such as Jung's have invited Buddhist scholars to compare the categories of traditional Buddhist psychology with those employed by Jungian theory. Ryukyo Fujimoto has done this with regard to Yogācāra categories assumed in the *Amitāyur Dhyāna Sūtra*.[36] The Yogācāra notion of *Ālaya*, or a store of repository consciousness, is seen to parallel Jung's notion of the collective unconscious. The *Ālaya* contains all the *bīja* or memory traces of actions or thoughts which the individual has stored up throughout innumerable lives. This *Ālaya* repository of past and present *karmas* (actions) contains some *karmas* which are purely individual and others which are common to all human beings—thus creating the uniformity of human nature. Jungian theory of the collective unconscious agrees with the latter contention but is uncertain about the former. Jung vacillated between viewing *karma* as individual or collective. In his early thinking there is no personally inherited *karma* (no individual rebirth as Yogācāra suggests); there is only the collective inherited *karma* of one's ancestors, the archetypes, which one creatively individuates in one's own personality development.[37] However, in his last years, Jung comes close to accepting the Yogācāra notion of personal *karma* and its psychological function in rebirth.[38]

According to the Yogācāra thought, in the *Ālaya* the *anāsrava* karmic seed lies dormant with the potential to bloom into or allow the realization of Buddhahood.[39] This is the doctrine of the

Tathāgata-garbha which claims that all beings have the seed of Buddha realization hidden in the depths of *Ālaya* consciousness. The visualization meditations prescribed in the *Amitāyur Sūtra* are designed to uncover this undefiled seed of Buddhahood (*anāsrava-bīja* or *Tathāgata-gotra*). The ultimate goal of the meditation is to see our true self as nothing but the Buddha Nature within, once our external *persona* has been dropped. This potential Buddhahood within is influenced (*vāsanā*) to grow through hearing the words of the Buddha.[40] Jung's parallel to all of this is his notion of a God or Self archetype within the collective unconscious of all beings, which is realized or made present through the process of individuation.

There is also some correspondence between Yogācāra and Jung as to the details of the individuation process. In Yogācāra thought *Manas*, the persona consciousness, is described as having the qualities of ignorance (*avidyā*), self-arrogance (*māna*), egoistic view (*ātmadṛṣṭi*) and self-love (*ātmasukha*). Because of these four qualities the *Manas* may be designated as paralleling Jung's notion of ego consciousness. Yogācāra Buddhism, however, never uses the term "unconscious" in the way that Jung does. Fujimoto explains:

> . . . *Ālaya* and *Manas* have each a characteristic function of thinking in their own ways. In this sense, they are not unconscious in the sense of *acitta*. Rather, their functions are so much more subtle and delicate (*sūksma*) that we cannot differentiate and bring them into the sixth consciousness to exercise analytical reflection through meditation.[41]

Within the range of awareness there is only sense-consciousness. *Ālaya* and *Manas* lie buried deep below. *Vijñapti* is the sixth consciousness and is in the realm of awareness. In our ordinary state *vijñapti* is found together with the seventh consciousness of Yogācāra which is ego-thinking creating what Jung calls our "persona."[42]

In order to achieve *Bodhicitta* or mind of enlightenment, all seeds of obstructing states must be rooted out through meditation. In technical Yogācāra terms, the two hindrances of evil desires (*kleśāvarana*) and conceptualization (*jñeyāvarana*) need to be removed for the perfect realization of *Bodhicitta*. Although Jung would agree that psychic processes such as over-attachment to thinking as opposed to intuiting and ignorance of contents of the unconscious are obstacles to individuation of the archetypes, he would never agree that the *perfect enlightenment* implied by *Bodhicitta* is humanly attainable. This is one of those points where Jung draws the line in his acceptance of the claims of Eastern Yoga.[43] In Jung's theory the process of individuation brings many of the contents of the unconscious into conscious awareness and shifts the center of gravity of the personality from the Ego to the Self. But although the Self may extend its awareness down to enclose the archetypes and outward to include much of the sense and conceptual content of the external world, the Self can never become exhaustive or omniscient in either direction. The limitation of an individual ego as the knower of the Self means that there will always be both external and internal contents left unknown. The idea of a Self so completely individuated that all internal and external contents of the psyche are exhaustively known—the Yogācāra *Bodhicitta* concept—is simply not possible in Jung's psychology. From the Yogācāra perspective, however, it is not only possible but, indeed, that is the end goal set forth for Queen Vaidehi to achieve. When her mind becomes a perfectly pure stream of consciousness (*vijñana*) like a mirror perfectly reflecting the *Dharmakāya*, then she realizes that her true self is nothing but the Buddha Nature. Thus, through the long process of devotional meditation, the *mahābodicitta* (the Enlightenment Mind) has realized itself.[44]

III. CONCLUSION

Although one of the first major Western psychologists to seriously read Buddhist texts, Jung read them through the concepts of his own psychological theory excluding Eastern material when it did not fit. This is clearly in evidence when we examine the sections of the *Amitāyur Dhyāna Sūtra* which Jung simply leaves out of consideration in his commentary. What Jung does appreciate in this Buddhist scripture is the way in which spiritual realization results from a recognition of the true nature of the inner psyche. The meditation technique outlined in the text provides a functional parallel to the process of the individuation of the Self/God archetype in Jungian psychology. Attention has also been drawn to the degree to which Yogācāra concepts are compatible with Jung's concepts, and to places where Jung draws the line in his acceptance of these Buddhist views.

Notes

1. "The Psychology of Eastern Meditation," *The Collected Works of C. G. Jung* (hereafter *CW*). Princeton: Princeton University Press, 1969, vol. 11, pp. 558–575.
2. F. Max Müller, "Introduction" to The Amitāyur Dhyāna Sūtra in *The Sacred Books of the East*. Delhi: Motilal Banarsidass, 1972, vol. 49, pp. xxi–xxii.
3. *Seiten*, edited by S. K. Ikuta. Vancouver: British Columbia Young Buddhist League, 1968, p. 15.
4. For a study of the practise of Jodo Shinshu in North America see "Sacred Language, Sacred Ritual: Jodo Shinshu Religious Forms in Transition," by Harold Coward and David Goa. *Studies in Religion*, 12, 1983, pp. 363–379.
5. *C. G. Jung: Letters*, ed. by Gerhard Adler. Princeton: Princeton University Press, 1974, vol. 2, p. 417.
6. *CW* 11, p. 560.
7. Ibid. To accomplish these postures however requires a mental as well as a physical discipline. See *The Hathayogapradīpikā of Svātmārāma*. Sanskrit text with English translation by Tookaram Tatya. Adyar: Adyar Library and Research Centre, 1972.
8. Ryukyo Fujimoto, *An Outline of the Triple Sutra of Shin Buddhism*. Kyoto: Hyyak-en Press, 1960, vol. II, p. 158.
9. CW 11, p. 561.
10. *The Amitāyur Dhyāna Sūtra* (hereafter A.D.S.), translated by J. Takakusu. *The Sacred Books of the East*. Delhi: Motilal Banarsidass, 1972, vol. 49, p. 178.
11. Ibid. p. 165.
12. Ibid. p. 166.
13. Ibid.
14. Ibid. p. 168.
15. *An Outline of the Triple Sutra of Shin Buddhism*, p. 156.
16. For example, see the whole response of the Pure Land Buddhist scholar Ryukyo Fujimoto to Jung's Commentary (as cited above, pp. 147–158).
17. CW 11, pp. 565–566.
18. Ibid. p. 569.
19. Ibid. p. 562.
20. Ibid. p. 569.
21. A.D.S. p. 171.

22. Ibid.
23. CW 11, pp. 569–570.
24. Ibid. p. 571.
25. *An Outline of the Triple Sutra of Shin Buddhism*, p. 154.
26. CW 11, p. 571.
27. Ibid.
28. *An Outline of the Triple Sutra of Shin Buddhism*, p. 157.
29. A.D.S., pp. 196–199.
30. CW 11, p. 567.
31. Ibid. p. 568.
32. Ibid. p. 578.
33. CW 13, pp. 24–25.
34. CW 11, pp. 574–575.
35. *An Outline of the Triple Sutra of Shin Buddhism*, p. 158.
36. Ibid. pp. 148–158.
37. *C. G. Jung: Letters*, vol. 2, p. 548.
38. C. G. Jung, *Memories, Dreams, Reflections*, edited by A. Jaffé. New York: Vintage Books, 1965, p. 319. See also my discussion of this issue in "Jung and Karma," Chapter 5 of *Jung and Eastern Thought* by Harold Coward. Albany: SUNY, 1985.
39. *An Outline of the Triple Sutra of Shin Buddhism*, p. 150.
40. Ibid.
41. Ibid.
42. Ibid. p. 151.
43. *Jung and Eastern Thought*, Chapter 3.
44. *An Outline of the Triple Sutra of Shin Buddhism*, p. 152.

Harold Coward

Jung's Commentary on
The Tibetan Book of the Dead

The Tibetan Book of the Dead or *The Bardo Thödol* is one of a series of instructions on six different types of liberation from rebirth: liberation through wearing, liberation through seeing, liberation through remembering, liberation through tasting, liberation through touching and *The Bardo Thödol* or liberation through hearing. This text is designed to be read to the dying person to help keep the mind focused on the teachings received from one's spiritual master or *guru* during one's lifetime. The teaching focuses on three kinds of events: those occurring just before death, those occurring during the possible intermediate state of up to forty-nine days following death, and those accompanying the cessation of the intermediate state and rebirth in a new life. The teaching was ascribed to Padmasambhava and written down by his wife Yeshe Tsogyal. Tradition has it that Padmasambhava buried the text in the Gampo hills in central Tibet where it was later discovered by Karma Lingpa, an incarnation of one of Padmasambhava's disciples.[1] This teaching has been passed down through the years in both the Nyingma and Kagyü traditions of Tibetan Buddhism. Occasionally it is taught to young lamas at around the age of eight years. These young lamas not only learn the text by heart but also meditate on it while visiting dying or dead people several times a week. Thus the events dealt with in the text are given existential reality for the student, and the basic Buddhist teaching of the impermanence of life is constantly reinforced.

The term "Bardo" means "gap." It is "the interval of suspension" that occurs at the moment before death, in the period of up to forty-nine days after death, and at the moment of conception into the womb. Although the text is ostensibly written for the dead, it is in fact about the psychological forces that engage us as well throughout life. It is this particular aspect of the text that Carl Jung especially appreciated. Although the text discusses reincarnation, a doctrine that for the most part Jung rejected,[2] its discussion of various kinds of psychic existence greatly interested Jung—especially in relation to its use as a focus for meditation in this life. In the Tibetan tradition the meditation on this text, in company with visits to the dead and dying, begin as early as eight years of age, continue throughout adult life, and form the focus of one's thought at the moment of death. In this sense *The Bardo Thödol* provides, for the Tibetan, a blueprint for living as well as for dying such that there will be ultimately an opportunity for final liberation from the cycle of birth, death and rebirth.

Jung's "Psychological Commentary" on the text was written in German in 1935, and played a major role in first bringing this text to the attention of the modern West. Jung wrote this Commentary in response to a request by W.Y. Evans-Wentz, an American authority on Tibetan Yoga and philosophy then living in Cairo.[3] Working together with Kazi Daiva-Samdup, Evans-Wentz first introduced *The Tibetan Book of the Dead* to the Western world in an Oxford University Press publication of 1927. The request from Evans-Wentz came in the midst of the period of Jung's life (1920–1940) when he was looking East for independent and parallel support for many of his own psychic discoveries.[4] Jung was particularly bothered by the tendency in Western religion to project its unconscious psychological needs onto the cosmos in the form of a mediating God or Messiah.[5] In *The Tibetan Book of the Dead* Jung found confirming evidence for this insight. In it clear demonstrations are offered showing how our psychological needs and fears are projected in the forms of divine beings both good and evil. Jung was so intrigued by these ancient Buddhist insights into the workings of the psyche that, at the outset of his "Psychological Commentary" on the text, he says, ". . . *The Bardo Thödol* has been my constant companion, and to it I owe not only many stimulating ideas and discoveries, but also many fundamental insights."[6]

There is a difficulty with the Evans-Wentz translation from the Tibetan—a difficulty of which Jung was likely unaware. The Evans-Wentz version is often more a paraphrasing than a translation of the original text. As such it is marred with numerous misunderstandings as, for example, the disregard of the difference between Hindu tantra and Buddhist tantra. This tendency to read the Tibetan text through Hindu rather than Buddhist eyes was heightened by the fact that

Evans-Wentz took advice from Sir John Woodroffe, an authority on Hindu tantra.[7] Indeed Woodroffe also adds a Foreword to the text which is printed along with Jung's "Psychological Commentary" in the Oxford publication of Evan-Wentz's version of the text. Evan-Wentz's references were mainly to Woodroffe's works on Hindu tantras which have little relevance for the Buddhist tantric tradition of Tibet. Thus Jung is sometimes led astray because he relied on a source text which is often inaccurate. For readers today there is fortunately a new English translation available by Francesca Freemantle and Chögyam Trungpa which relies on the Tibetan tantric tradition for its sources.[8] For another trustworthy English presentation of this Tibetan Buddhist tradition, readers are directed to *Death, Intermediate State and Rebirth in Tibetan Buddhism* by Lati Rinbochay and Jeffrey Hopkins.[9] With these reservations in mind, let us now turn to a consideration of Jung's "Psychological Commentary" on *The Bardo Thödol.*

JUNG'S COMMENTARY

At the outset Jung's attention is arrested by the fact that in *The Bardo Thödol* not only the "wrathful" but also the "peaceful" deities are conceived as projections of the human mind—an idea which has a very recent advent in the West with European thinkers such as Sigmund Freud.[10] But while the modern European explains away such deities as illusory projections, *The Bardo Thödol* makes the surprising, and, in Jung's view, completely correct move of maintaining that these psychic projections are also utterly real. This it accomplishes by regarding metaphysical statements, i.e. statements about deities, to be statements of the psyche. Jung put it as follows:

> It is the psyche which, by the divine creative power inherent in it, makes the metaphysical assertion; it posits the distinctions between metaphysical entities. Not only is it the condition of all metaphysical reality, it *is* that reality.[11]

For the Tibetan, the projected deities of the mind are "*only* psychological" (as the modern European would put it) but also *real*, since the process of the mind is real. This claim appealed greatly to Jung. He comments, "The background of this unusual book is not the niggardly European 'either-or,' but a magnificently affirmative 'both-and.' "[12] It provided Jung with independent confirmation of his own view that all the contents of the psyche are objectively real. That is why for Jung, the study of the subjective contents of the psyche is an empirical science.

However, there are specific points where Jung draws the line in his acceptance of the ideas in *The Bardo Thödol*. He alerts us to two of these at the beginning of his Commentary. First there is what Jung refers to as the idea of "the supratemporality of the soul"—a most unhappy choice of terms as one of the fundamental tenets of Buddhism is *anātman* or the "no-soul" doctrine.[13] This does not mean that there is no rebirth for the individual in Buddhism—only that there is no substantive essence called *ātman* or soul that is reborn. But that there is rebirth over and over again until one finally achieves release or liberation is a fundamental Buddhist teaching. Here again, as in most of his writing, Jung rejects this Buddhist doctrine. A 1940 lecture entitled "Concerning Rebirth" cites the Buddha's experience of a long sequence of rebirths but then goes on to say, "it is by no means certain whether continuity of personality is guaranteed or not: there may only be a continuity of *karma*."[14] Jung's dominant view is that this *karma* or motive force accruing from past actions and thoughts is collective rather than individual in nature. At the end of his life, however, Jung comes close to accepting the Eastern notion of a personal *karma* which, in its psychological function, causes a personal rebirth.[15] But in his 1935 *Psychological Commentary on the "Tibetan Book of the Dead,"* Jung clearly rejects any notion of personal rebirth. In response to the Buddhist notion of reincarnation, Jung observes that neither scientific knowledge nor reason can accept the hypothesis of personal rebirth assumed in the Tibetan understanding of Bardo *karma*.[16] In his reading of *The Bardo Thödol*, Jung simply excludes the notion of rebirth, and, instead, heuristically places himself in the position of the dead man[17]—a move which bespeaks a certain logical inconsistency.

But as soon as Jung puts himself in the dead man's shoes and begins reading the text, a second point arises where Jung draws the line. This point relates directly to a difference of views between West and East over the perfectibility of the person.[18] The Bardo text, in line with Eastern thought in general, assumes that not only is the person perfectible in theory, but that such an exalted state is a necessity if liberation from birth, death and rebirth is to be realized. The example of the Buddha and of countless Buddhist saints demonstrates the truth of this assertion. *The Bardo Thödol*, in describing the dying person's experience of the *Chikhai Bardo*, says this: In the moment before death, a luminosity of clear light may be seen and will last for a long time in a person who has practiced much meditation and perfected the state of tranquility. The perfected person will have a direct perception of the Buddha nature in the form of a pure and all encompassing light. This perception can be aided by reading the following lines clearly and distinctly into the ear of the dying person:

> O son of noble family, (name), listen. Now the pure luminosity of the dharmāta is shining before you; recognise it. O son of noble family, at this moment your state of mind is by nature pure emptiness, it does not possess any nature whatever, neither substance nor quality such as colour, but is pure emptiness; this is the dharmāta. . . . But this state of mind is not just blank emptiness, it is unobstructed, sparkling, pure and vibrant. . . .
>
> These two, your mind whose nature is emptiness without any substance whatever, and your mind which is vibrant and luminous, are inseparable; this is the dharmakāya of the Buddha. This mind of yours is inseparable luminosity and emptiness in the form of a great mass of light, it has no birth or death, therefore it is the Buddha of Immortal Light.[19]

The Dalai Lama's comment on this state is that it is one in which ignorance is eliminated, the attachment and grasping resulting from the predispositions of previous actions cease to operate and the cycle of uncontrolled rebirth is ended.[20]

Jung finds this notion of a perfectly clear mind, one empty of all obscuring ignorance and in which there is only the steady radiance of the clear light of pure reality (the *dharmakāya*), a very challenging notion to us in the West. To equate the identity of the dying person with the divine reality itself, the *dharmakāya*, is, from a Western perspective, downright dangerous. Theologically it is blasphemous in that it equates the individual with the Divine. Psychologically, says Jung, it suggests that one who claims to have such an experience is suffering from a theosophical inflation of the psyche.[21]

But in spite of his rejection of the Tibetan claim of the perfectibility of the person, Jung does see an important lesson that the West
needs to learn from this portion of *The Bardo Thödol*—namely, that
the radiance of the Divine comes to us through its reflection in the
psychological processes of our own psyches. Here, of course, Jung
has in mind his notion of the Western experience of God through
the individuation of the God or Self archetype.[22] While this can lead
to a mystical experience of great luminosity—an experience in
which one is taken out of one's limited ego and identified with the
larger universe without and the collective unconscious within—yet
it is still the finite ego that is having this experience of the enlarged
Self. Thus finite limitation of the personality remains. There is always an "I" that is having the experience. Consequently, for Jung,
there can never be the complete identity between the individual and
the Divine of the sort that *The Tibetan Book of the Dead* describes as
the goal of the *Chikhai Bardo*, the Bardo of death. It is to aid in the
attainment of this goal that *The Bardo Thödol* is read to the dying lama
by his *guru* or by one of his colleagues. As Evans-Wentz puts it, the
purpose of *The Bardo Thödol* is "to restore to the soul the divinity it
lost at birth."[23]

For those who do not realize liberation as a result of having *The
Bardo Thödol* read to them at the moment of death, the text goes on to
a detailed description of the following states: the *Chönyid Bardo* or
"Intermediate State" and the *Sidpa Bardo* or "Rebirth State." Since
both of these states involve our normal psychological processes of
conceptualization and projection, Jung finds none of the difficulty
associated with the supra-normal claims of the first state. Indeed,
Jung finds the descriptions of these last two states quite fascinating.
In his mind they parallel the analysis of the various layers of consciousness recently pioneered in the West by Freudian psychoanalysis. This, Jung thinks, is especially true of the final state or *Sidpa
Bardo* where a kind of sexual projection results in the selection of the
mating couple as the "vehicle" for conception and rebirth. But first
let us examine the *Chönyid Bardo* or Intermediate State.

For the person who does not reach liberation at the time of
death, karmic ignorance in the form of attachment to the self and fear
of becoming extinct serves as a connecting link to the Intermediate
State between lives. According to the Tibetan Buddhist texts the
intermediate being has all five senses, clairvoyance, the ability to

move about freely regardless of obstacles and to arrive immediately wherever he or she wants. During the Intermediate or *Chönyid Bardo*, the being has the form of the person who he or she had been in the past life. He or she sees other intermediate beings of his or her own type ranging from "hell-beings," hungry ghosts, animals, humans, demi-gods or gods. If a place of birth appropriate to one's karmic predispositions is not found within seven days, a small death occurs and one is born into another state of transformation. This can occur up to six times for a total of forty-nine days.[24] These texts also offer a detailed description of the physiology involved in the passing over from the earthly life just finished to rebirth in an intermediate state and eventually to rebirth in human form. The description offered by Buddhist texts is based on a theory of winds (currents of energy) that serve as foundations for different levels of consciousness. "Upon the collapse of the ability of these "winds" to serve as the basis of consciousness, the events of death—internal and external—unfold."[25] When the young lama is commanded to sit with dying persons and meditate upon them, it is the process of the collapsing winds that is being observed. Through meditations such as this the lama not only learns to observe these processes at work but to cause these "winds" or currents of energy in their coarse and subtle forms to dissolve into a very subtle life-bearing wind at the heart. This yogic meditation is thought to mirror the process which takes place at death. For the technical details of this meditation the reader is directed to *Death, Intermediate State and Rebirth* by Lati Rinbochay and Jeffrey Hopkins.[26] Suffice it here to say that this sophisticated theory of Buddhist Tantra envisages 72,000 wind channels with three main ones running from the forehead down along the spinal column to the sexual organ. The channel-centers along these three main channels are visualized as "wheels" with varying numbers of spokes located at the forehead, top of the head, throat, heart, solar plexus, base of the spine and the sexual organ. Rinbochay and Hopkins describe the interrelation of these wheels and channels as follows:

> At these wheels, the right and left channels wrap around the central one, constricting it and lessening or preventing the passage of wind.
> At death, the winds that serve as the foundations of consciousness dissolve into the winds in the right and left channels.

These in turn dissolve into the wind in the central channel, whereupon the constrictions are loosened, in the sense that the outer channels become deflated, thereby loosening the central channel and allowing movement of wind inside it. This induces manifestation of subtle minds, which ordinary beings fear since they feel they are being annihilated. Yogis of the Highest Yoga Tantra [Tibetan Yoga], however, put these same states to use in the spiritual path.[27]

Now all of this was quite fascinating to Jung, not so much for the "channel" and "wheel" theory, but for the contents revealed in the *Chönyid Bardo*—contents which Jung equated with his slowly developing notion of archetypes. One thing the "channel" and "wheel" theory of Buddhism did provide was a mechanism which allowed psychic contents to be transmitted from one life to the next just as are the archetypes of the Collective Unconscious. While Western genetics had demonstrated physical inheritance, Jung found himself alone in the contemporary West with his notion of a collective psychic inheritance. But here in *The Tibetan Book of the Dead* he found confirmation in the form of a parallel description of both a mechanism for psychic inheritance and of the contents inherited. This led Jung to boldly affirm the existence of archetypes for the first time in his writings.[28] Jung writes:

> The *Chönyid* state is one of karmic illusion—that is to say illusions which result from the psychic residua of previous existences. . . . Among these inherited psychic factors there is a special class which is not confined either to family or to race. These are the universal dispositions of the mind, and they are to be understood as analogous to Plato's forms (*eidola*), in accordance with which the mind organizes its contents. One could also describe these forms as *categories* analogous to the logical categories which are always and everywhere present as the basic postulates of reason. Only in the case of our "forms," we are not dealing with the categories of reason but with categories of the *imagination*. As the products of the imagination are always in essence visual, their forms must, from the outset, have the character of images and moreover of *typical* images, which is why, following St. Augustine, I call them "archetypes."[29]

What so impressed Jung about the Buddhist description of the *Chönyid Bardo* is that here we were dealing with inherited forms presented as visual images of a good or evil nature—hungry ghost, hell being, animal, human, demi-god or god—all of which Jung had found in the individuated forms of archetypes. Thus there was evidence in *The Tibetan Book of the Dead* for his view that archetypes with specific contents, both good and evil, were inherited. Where Jung drew the line was in the Buddhist view that such forms and contents were a direct karmic inheritance from one's own actions in a previous life. For Jung, at this point in his life, psychic inheritance could only be accepted in a collective sense; there was no individual reincarnation of the kind described in *The Bardo Thödol*.[30]

In his Commentary on the third state of *Sidpa Bardo* or the Bardo of rebirth, Jung makes two kinds of observations. Commenting on the suggestion of the text that it is even possible at this stage for the person to give up the desire to be reborn and to reach the pure state of the *dharmakāya,* Jung notes that what this would require is nothing less than the complete giving up of the ego and capitulation to the objective powers of the psyche. In short, says Jung, what it amounts to is "the end of all conscious, rational, morally responsible conduct of life, and a voluntary surrender to what *The Bardo Thödol* calls 'karmic illusion'."[31] It equates to a deliberately induced psychosis.[32] What Jung misses in the Buddhist analysis is that the cause of the psychotic terrors that worry him so much is nothing other than the "grasping," "desiring" ego. To transcend ego, in the view of *The Bardo Thödol*, is not to leave the psyche defenseless in the face of its competing urges. Rather, it is to remove their cause from the psyche completely, thus making possible the realization of the *dharmakāya.* Rooted in his Western conception of the absolute necessity of the ego for any conscious discriminating experience, Jung simply cannot put himself into the Buddhist perspective of seeing the ego as the root of desire, and thus the obstructor of the *dharmakāya.*

Jung's second comment on the *Sidpa Bardo* centers on the rather graphic descriptions in the text of how the being in the Intermediate State selects a womb to be born into. According to *The Bardo Thödol* what happens is that a being in the Intermediate State (the *Chönyid Bardo*) sees a future mother and father lying together. Due to one's own previous sexual activity, and the memory traces still in the psyche, one is attracted to the act of copulation and this desire causes the cessation of the *Chönyid Bardo* and initiates conception and rebirth in a new life. The mechanism involved is important for Jung.

When certain conditions are present,[33] the intermediate being sees the mother and father lying together. It desires the mother (if it is to be reborn as a male), or the father (if it is to be reborn as a female) and this desire causes the intermediate being to enter the womb. Then a reverse evolution of the "winds" and "wheels" takes place until the birth of a fully developed person occurs.[34] It was, of course, the sexual basis of the rebirth selection process that caught Jung's eye. It reminded him of the claims of Freudian psychoanalysis stated in terms of the Oedipus complex: the young boy is sexually attracted to the mother, the young girl to the father. It is unfortunate, suggests Jung, that Freud did not pursue the development of this complex backward rather than forward into the problems created in adolescence and adulthood. Had Freud pursued these desires back into the intra-uterine experiences of the womb and still further back before that, he might have come upon the *Sidpa Bardo*—but from the other direction. Jung draws this "tongue in cheek" line of theoretical speculation to a close by noting that such a bold attempt to follow psychic evolution backward is doomed to failure, however, because it is impossible to find even some trace of an experiencing subject at the intra-uterine and pre-uterine stages.[35]

CONCLUSION

All of this leads Jung to conclude that if Westerners are not to give up their philosophical and scientific assumptions, the only way they can read this text is backward—as if one were engaging in Freudian psychoanalysis.[36] One would start with the *Sidpa Bardo*, the state of rebirth, since as living humans that is the one we are all obviously in. Freudian investigation backward into the beginnings of the *Sidpa Bardo* gave some insight into our biological drives but was unable to go further. To go further into the *Chönyid Bardo* requires that we give up Freud's uncritical assumption that everything psychological is subjective and personal and also the assumption of Buddhist yoga that psychic contents are a manifestation of personal reincarnation. Using his own theoretical assumptions regarding the psychic reality of the collective unconscious, Jung is able to read backward into the *Chönyid* state. For him it is not an Intermediate State between death and rebirth, but a valuable mythic description of the archetypal forms and contents of the collective unconscious.[37] For both Jung and the *Chönyid Bardo*, these are not mere fantasies or speculative metaphysical forms but psychic realities—psychic data that is real in itself. But when Jung's "backward reading" of the text comes to the *Chikhai Bardo* and its possibility of direct experience of the *dharmakāya*, Jung remains silent. He can do nothing else, for in his view if ego has been transcended, then, to the extent that one is still alive, one is unconscious. Jung's comment on a similar claim made in *The Tibetan Book of the Great Liberation* would apply to the intuitions of death described in the *Chikhai Bardo:*

> The experience of "at-one-ment" [e.g. at one with the *dharmakāya*] is one example of those "quick-knowing" realizations of the East, an intuition of what it would be like if one could exist and not exist at the same time. . . . But for my part I cannot conceive of such a possibility. I therefore assume that, in this point, Eastern intuition has overreached itself.[38]

In his reading of *The Tibetan Book of the Dead* Jung never manages to "step outside" the "conceptual glasses" of his own psychological theory. This fact causes him to interpret the text by "reading it backward" and in the end to dismiss its highest goal (the realization of the pure light of the *dharmakāya*) as Eastern intuition overreaching itself. Consequently Jung grasps the Buddhist viewpoint of the text mainly through his rejection of it. Yet it must be admitted that Jung's thought reaches out and engages this Tibetan Buddhist text in a critical dialogue that few Westerners have been able to duplicate.

Notes

1. *The Tibetan Book of the Dead: The Great Liberation Through Hearing in the Bardo* by Guru Rinpoche according to Karma Lingpa. Translation by Francesca Freemantle and Chögyam Trungpa. Berkeley: Shambala, 1975, p. xi.
2. See my summary of Jung's lifelong struggle with the Eastern notion of reincarnation in Harold Coward, *Jung and Eastern Thought*. Albany: SUNY, 1985, pp. 95–107.
3. See Jung's letter to Evans-Wentz dated 8 December, 1938 in *C.G. Jung: Letters*. London: Routledge & Kegan Paul, 1973, Vol I, pp. 248–249.

4. See C.G. Jung, "Psychological Types," *Collected Works* (hereafter CW), vol 6. Princeton: Princeton University Press, 1971; also Jung's autobiography, *Memories, Dreams, Reflections,* ed. by Aniela Jaffé. New York: Vintage, 1965, p. 197; and in the 1957 Preface which he wrote for *Psyche and Symbol.* New York: Doubleday Anchor, 1958, p. xiii: ". . . we must ask whether our experiences are the only ones on record and, if not, where can we find comparable events. There is no difficulty in finding them; plenty of parallels exist, for instance, in the Far East. . . ."

5. *Psychological Types,* CW 6, p. 194.

6. *Psychological Commentary on "The Tibetan Book of the Dead,"* CW 11, p. 510.

7. *The Tibetan Book of the Dead,* compiled and edited by W.Y. Evans-Wentz. London: Oxford University Press, 1960, p. xx.

8. *The Tibetan Book of the Dead: The Great Liberation Through Hearing in the Bardo,* op. cit.

9. *Death, Intermediate State and Rebirth in Tibetan Buddhism* by Lati Rinbochay and Jeffrey Hopkins. Valoris, N.Y.: Snow Lion, 1981.

10. See, for example, Sigmund Freud, *Moses and Monotheism.* New York: Vintage, 1958; and *The Future of an Illusion.* New York: Anchor, 1964.

11. *Psychological Commentary on "The Tibetan Book of the Dead,"* CW 11, p. 512.

12. Ibid. p. 511.

13. See, for example, Edward Conze, *Buddhism: Its Essence and Development.* New York: Harper Torchbooks, 1959, pp. 18–23.

14. *Concerning Rebirth,* CW 9, Pt. I, p. 113. See also a letter to E.L. Grant Watson dated February 1956 where Jung clearly distinguishes his view that our actions may have an impact on future generations (a kind of collective *karma* or collective rebirth) from the Indian understanding of the passing on of one's *karma* through the mechanism of personal rebirth. *C.G. Jung: Letters,* vol. 2, p. 548.

15. *Memories, Dreams, Reflections,* op. cit. pp. 318–319. For a complete summary and analysis of Jung's changing views on karma and rebirth see Harold Coward, *Jung and Eastern Thought.* Albany: SUNY, 1985, pp. 99–106.

16. *Psychological Commentary on "The Tibetan Book of the Dead,"* CW 11, pp. 518–519.

17. Ibid. p. 512. Jung's problem with the Buddhist concept of rebirth seems to be based upon an inadequate understanding of what "person/personal" means within a Buddhist context. The Buddhist notion of "rebirth" always incorporates stimuli from the previous context (life situation). Thus the individual in the Buddhist view is not a defined entity

but an intertwining of energies, potencies and forces which become manifest in the individual but which reverberate far beyond what we in the West would call "the individual."

18. For a summary of the Western view see, John Passmore, *The Perfectibility of Man*. New York: Charles Scribner's Sons, 1970.
19. See the Freemantle and Trungpa translation, op. cit. p. 35.
20. *Death, Intermediate State and Rebirth in Tibetan Buddhism*, op. cit. p. 11.
21. *Psychological Commentary on "The Tibetan Book of the Dead,"* CW 11, p. 513.
22. For a summary of Jung's view of this process see Harold Coward, *Jung and Eastern Thought*, op. cit. pp. 127–134.
23. *The Tibetan Book of the Dead* by W.Y. Evans-Wentz, op. cit. p. xiv. See also *Death, Intermediate State and Rebirth*, op. cit. p. 29.
24. The above is taken from a summary by the Dalai Lama in *Death, Intermediate State and Rebirth*, p. 10.
25. Ibid. p. 13.
26. Ibid.
27. Ibid. p. 15.
28. While he had cautiously moved in this direction three years earlier in his 1932 lectures on Kundalini Yoga, it is not until his Commentary on *The Tibetan Book of the Dead* that he becomes explicit and fully confident regarding the inheritance of the archetypes. (See *Jung and Eastern Thought*, op. cit. p. 97).
29. *Psychological Commentary on "The Tibetan Book of the Dead,"* CW 11, pp. 517–518.
30. Ibid. pp. 517–519. In *The Tavistock Lectures* Jung remarks about the archetypal contents of the dreams of young children: "Therefore you find with many children an awareness of the contents of the collective unconscious, a fact which in some Eastern beliefs is interpreted as reminiscence of a former existence. Tibetan philosophy, for instance, speaks of the 'Bardo' existence . . ." CW 18, p. 95.
31. Ibid. p. 519.
32. Ibid. p. 520.
33. The required conditions include: the mother must be free from disease and not menstruating; the intermediate being must be nearby and must wish to enter; the male and female must desire each other and meet; the womb must be free from disease and open; both mother and father must be fertile; the intermediate being must have accumulated a karma for being born as a child of that male and female, who must also have accumulated a karma for being its father and mother. See *Death, Intermediate State and Rebirth*, op. cit. p. 58.

34. Ibid. pp. 58–60.
35. *Psychological Commentary on "The Tibetan Book of the Dead,"* CW 11, p. 515.
36. Ibid. p. 517.
37. Ibid. p. 525.
38. *Psychological Commentary on "The Tibetan Book of the Great Liberation,"* CW 11, p. 505. Jung remained in a basically Cartesian presupposition by ruling out the possibility of a "mind" beyond the individual's mental activity—the Buddhist assumption.

Radmila Moacanin

Tantric Buddhism and Jung:
Connections, Similarities, Differences

INTRODUCTION

In this chapter I propose first to discuss the conceptual and methodological equivalents between the two systems, and identify the points where they meet, where they are similar or parallel, and where they differ. Next, I intend to examine Jung's view of Eastern traditions in terms of their relevance to the Western world, and his as well as the Tibetan Buddhists' view regarding the possible dangers inherent in practicing Tantra. Finally, I should like to comment on the issues of ethics and their potential impact on the world community, which are an important and integral aspect of both systems.

CONSCIOUSNESS AND THE UNCONSCIOUS

The basic concepts of consciousness and the unconscious in the Jungian system and in Buddhism have a variety of connotations and therefore are subject to much misunderstanding and distortions. To compound the problem, Jung's concepts are often confused with those of Freud, which are vastly different. I shall try to review some of them, being well aware that my survey is grossly inadequate. A whole lifetime—or as Buddhists would say, several lives—of study and practice would hardly enable anyone to comprehend fully these concepts in both systems.

Jung views consciousness and the unconscious as being of equal importance.[1] Consciousness, however, is a 'late-born descendant of the unconscious psyche,'[2] which means that the former emerges out of the latter. In one instance Jung equates consciousness with ego.[3] He postulates that:

Consciousness needs a centre, an ego to which something is conscious. We know of no other kind of consciousness, nor can we imagine a consciousness without an ego. There can be no consciousness when there is no one to say: '*I* am conscious.'[4]

Jung believes that consciousness, 'that most remarkable of all of nature's curiosities,' exists and has an urge to be widened for the simple reason that without it 'things go less well.'[5] On the other hand Jung talks about 'higher consciousness' which is a deeper and more receptive consciousness that relates to the transpersonal realm.

And in paraphrasing a sentence by Ignatius Loyola, putting it into psychological terminology, Jung states:

Man's consciousness was created to the end that it may (1) recognize . . . its descent from a higher unity . . . ; (2) pay due and careful regard to this source . . . ; (3) execute its commands intelligently and responsibly . . . ; and (4) thereby afford the psyche as a whole the optimum degree of life and development. . . .[6]

According to Jung, the symbols of wholeness, which resolve and transcend opposites, could be called 'consciousness,' as well as 'self,' 'higher ego,' or anything else. To him, 'all these terms are simply names for the facts that alone carry weight.'[7]

The development and extension of the sphere of consciousness is what Jung calls individuation.[8] But he postulates that the conscious mind occupies only a relatively central position while the unconscious psyche surrounds it.[9]

The unconscious is the psychic area with an unlimited scope. It is the 'matrix of all potentialities,'[10] and it is best imagined as a fluid state which has a life of its own, and whose activity is autonomous and independent. 'The unconscious perceives, has purposes and intuitions, feels and thinks as does the conscious mind.'[11] Jung defines the contents of the unconscious as follows:

. . . everything of which I know, but of which I am not at the moment thinking; everything of which I was once conscious but have now forgotten; everything perceived by my senses, but not noted by my conscious mind; everything which, involuntarily and without paying attention to it, I feel, think, remember, want, and do; all the future things that are taking shape in me and will sometime come to consciousness. . . .[12]

Thus the unconscious includes future contents of the conscious psyche, and anticipates future conscious processes. But in addition, the unconscious contains ancestral deposits accumulated since immemorial time. To Jung therefore the unconscious has a Janus face: one side of it points back to prehistory, the world of raw instincts, and its other side points toward man's future fate.[13] This is a paradox for 'the unconscious is seen as a creative factor, even as a bold innovator, and yet it is at the same time the stronghold of ancestral conservatism.'[14] Like Mercurius—the personification of the unconscious—it is dualistic and contains all aspects of human nature: dark and light, evil and good, bestial and superhuman, demonic and divine.[15] One can conceive of the unconscious as a treasure-house, which is the source of all inspiration, creativity and of wisdom. As an autonomous psychic system which speaks in the language of symbols, one of its roles is to correct the biases of the conscious mind and compensate its one-sidedness with a broader, imaginal, non-rational perception that restores the balance and reveals a more comprehensive meaning. Unconscious motives are often wiser and more objective than conscious thinking. Therefore the unconscious may be a valuable guide pointing the way to one's true destination, a destination that is true to one's self and not falsified by prejudices of the conscious mind.

At the basis of separate individual consciousness and the unconscious behind it, there is the collective unconscious, the common heritage of all mankind and the universal source of all conscious life. In the depth of the collective unconscious there are no individual or cultural differences, no separation. It is the realm of primordial unity, nonduality, and through it each person is connected with the rest of humanity.

Tibetan Buddhists say that the conscious mind when it is clear, unobscured, free from projections—the pure consciousness—is the root of happiness and liberation, and is experienced as a state of bliss. This is the highest state of consciousness known as clear light. However, there are various kinds and degrees of consciousness and they are described in different terms. Similarly, there are various levels of consciousness and the unconscious in the structure of the psyche as conceptualized by Jung.

In the view of one school of Buddhist tenets there are six kinds of consciousness: those of sight, hearing, smell, taste, touch, and the mental consciousness. Then there is the afflicted, or deluded, consciousness responsible for the misconception of the ego. And underlying all of it is the 'store consciousness' (*alaya-vijnana*), the source of all consciousness, the Universal Mind, in which primordial forms and all experiences since beginningless time are stored. Its latent contents appear to the other kinds of consciousness when aroused by the corresponding conditions and associations.[16]

The notion of store consciousness clearly corresponds to Jung's concept of the unconscious. Like Jung's description of the unconscious, Lama Govinda argues that *alaya-vijnana*

> . . . contains demonic as well as divine qualities, cruelty as well as compassion, egotism as well as selflessness, delusion as well as knowledge, blind passion and darkest drives as well as profound longing for light and liberation.[17]

And in discussing the Tantric experience Lama Govinda states:

> It is not sufficient to identify ourselves with the oneness of a common origin or a potential Buddhahood, unless we take the decisive step toward the transformation and reintegration of the divergent tendencies or elements of our psyche.[18]

When we try to compare, as Jung did, the Buddhist concept of enlightened mind with the collective unconscious or the higher consciousness, we encounter enormous obstacles due to the fact that all these concepts have many different aspects, and are ambiguous and controversial. Furthermore we are dealing here with two different categories: philosophical and metaphysical on one hand, and psychological on the other hand, and consequently no real comparison could be made. Yet, in either system, Buddhist or Jung's, these categories represent only abstract knowledge, and do not and cannot express the profound experience that is the aim of both, namely individual transformation, achieved by transcending the mundane existence, and thereby attaining liberation or self-realization. In that moment of

transcendence the knowledge ceases to be philosophical or psychological: it is the indescribable, direct, immediate knowledge beyond
words and thoughts, the experience of the void (sunyata), the numinous, the Self, oneness of man and God.

Jung referred to this experience, in one way or another, through
much of his writings, but he articulated it most eloquently in his
Septem Sermones ad Mortuos—Seven Sermons to the Dead—written
during the period of his confrontation with the unconscious. This
brief but extraordinary work, replete with paradoxes, is strikingly
reminiscent of Buddhist thinking. In fact it echoes the words of *The
Heart Sutra*, 'form is emptiness, emptiness is form,' or from *The
Lankavatara Sutra*, the statement that 'space is form, and . . . as space
penetrates into form, form is space.'[19]

And now this is Jung speaking:

> Nothingness is the same as fullness. In infinity full is no better
> than empty. Nothingness is both empty and full. . . . A thing that
> is infinite and eternal hath no qualities, since it hath all qualities.[20]

Jung names this nothingness or fullness 'pleroma,'[21] which he distinguishes from 'creatura,' the principle of distinctiveness. In pleroma
'both thinking and being cease, since the eternal and infinite possess
no qualities. . . . In the pleroma there is nothing and everything.'[22]
And in a further passage Jung writes:

> Everything that discrimination taketh out of the pleroma is a pair
> of opposites. To god, therefore, always belongeth the devil.
> This inseparability is as close and, as your own life hath
> made you see, as indissoluble as the pleroma itself. Thus it is that
> both stand very close to the pleroma, in which all opposites are
> extinguished and joined.[23]

One recognizes in pleroma the Buddhist concept of emptiness,
as well as the most important Tantric concept of polarity and its
integration, which is at the very heart of every Vajrayana meditative
practice. At the same time Jung's concept of the 'transcendent function' is a development and practical application of the principle of
pleroma. It should be noted that Jung wrote *Septem Sermones ad*

Mortuos at the time when he had not yet discovered the Eastern traditions.

SPIRITUAL TRANSFORMATION

The ultimate goal of Jung's psychology and of Tibetan Buddhism is spiritual transformation. Jung refers to it as self-realization, wholeness, while for Tibetan Buddhists it is Buddhahood, enlightenment, for the sake of all beings. According to the latter every single individual has the potential to become a Buddha, to achieve the supreme transformation. The urge for light, for a higher consciousness, according to the Buddhists as well as Jung, has been always present and is ubiquitous. As Jung says:

> . . . within the soul from its primordial beginnings there has been a desire for light and an irrepressible urge to rise out of the primal darkness . . . the psychic primal night . . . is the same today as it has been for countless millions of years. The longing for light is the longing for consciousness.[24]

For the Buddhist there is pressure towards Buddhahood, which is man's quintessential nature, and for Jung it is the urge towards wholeness. In both instances it entails a long, and for Jung a never-ending journey, which is unique to each individual and which can be accomplished only in the mind. In Tantric Buddhism in particular, the mind is the king whose power is unlimited. Just like the alchemist who can change metal into gold, the mind can transform any event into transcendental wisdom and use it as a means to attain enlightenment. And that majestic power lies within us, nowhere else, and not apart from us, but to recognize it we need the key of consciousness.

According to the teaching of Tantric Buddhism, enlightenment, liberation, can be attained in the present life. It consists of a fundamental change in our perception of reality, 'the turning about in the deepest seat of consciousness,' when the 'I' or self-consciousness has turned its attention towards the universal consciousness. It is the 'intuitive experience of the infinite and the all-embracing oneness of all that is.'[25] The experience can also be described as a discovery of a world beyond the ordinary world of appearances, in which all opposites no longer exist. In this open space, one abandons all limitations; there is no exclusiveness, no this or that, but this and that, everything is included, nothing rejected. This is the world of nonduality, pleroma, from which everything originates, and into which everything disappears. Buddhists call it sunyata, emptiness, the open space which contains both the principle of causality and synchronicity.

> In its deepest metaphysical sense, it [sunyata] is the primordial ground, the ever-present starting point of all creation. It is the principle of unlimited potentiality. . . . On the intellectual plane *sunyata* is the relativity of all things and conditions, insofar as no thing exists independently but only in relationship to others— and ultimately in relationship to the whole universe. This relationship is more than a mere causal, time-space relationship; it is one of a common ground and a simultaneous presence of all factors of existence. . . .[26]

From the Tantric point of view each being contains the whole universe. There is no separation of the individual and universal mind, the mind not being subject to time and space limitation. Today the discoveries of modern physics reveal the basic view of the world as one of unity, interrelation, and interpenetration of all things and events.[27] And according to *The Avatamsaka Sutra,*

> All the Buddha-lands and all the Buddhas themselves, are manifested in my own being. . . .[28]

This parallels Jung's conviction that the macrocosm manifests itself in the microcosm of the human psyche. He talks about

> . . . that unknown quantity in man which is as universal and wide as the world itself, which is in him by nature and cannot be acquired. Psychologically, this corresponds to the collective unconscious. . . .[29]

The collective unconscious is the realm of the psyche where non-duality prevails, but which contains, like sunyata, the principle of unlimited potentiality. Thus to Jung the principles of the universe are reflected in the psyche.

THE UNION OF OPPOSITES

The fundamental concept in Tantra is recognition of polarity, and its integration is the core of Tantric practice: the union of male and female energies, matter and spirit, active and passive principles, wisdom, the discriminating principle (personified by Manjushri, the Buddha of wisdom), and compassion, the unifying principle (personified by Avalokiteshvara, the Buddha of compassion).

The principle of opposites is equally of primary importance in Jung's psychology. For Jung, opposition is inherent in the structure of the psyche, as it is in the cosmos: the cosmological is reflected on the psychological level. Within the framework of his psychology, the basic pair of opposites are consciousness and the unconscious. One could say that on the cosmological level, the former represents creatura, individuality, and the latter pleroma, non-duality.

On the psychological level, the significance of the principle of opposites lies in the fact that the psyche is a dynamic unity, a self-regulating system in which consciousness and the unconscious are complementary to each other. To deny one or the other results in one-sidedness, disequilibrium and hence a loss of wholeness. 'There must always be a high and low, hot and cold, etc . . .' says Jung. However, 'the point is not conversion into the opposite but conservation of previous values together with recognition of their opposites.'[30] Nothing is rejected, and nothing is accepted as an absolute. In Jung's view:

> It is . . . a fundamental mistake to imagine that when we see the non-value in a value or the untruth in the truth, the value or the truth ceases to exist. It has only become *relative*. Everything human is relative because everything rests on an inner polarity. . . .[31]

To Jung 'the *union of opposites through the middle path*' is a 'most fundamental item of inward experience.'[32] The resolution of opposites ends conflict and brings wholeness. But wholeness cannot be achieved through suppression or negation, which is always one-sided, but only by raising one's standpoint to a higher level of consciousness. This is the basic premise of Jung's psychological method.

'Individuation, or becoming whole,' he says 'is neither a *summum bonum* nor a *summum desideratum*, but the painful experience of the union of opposites.'[33] I should like to suggest though, that the realization of the union of opposites *is* the *summum bonum* because it brings with it spiritual freedom, experienced in the integrated and unified personality.

Buddha on his journey to Enlightenment abandoned asceticism, as he must have realized that by practicing it one rejects part of oneself and consequently wholeness cannot be attained. Instead he adopted and later taught the Middle Way.

THE MIDDLE WAY AND THE MADHYAMIKA

Buddha's way, the middle way, was reformulated and systematized in philosophical terms by the third century Indian philosopher Nagarjuna in his Madhyamika (Middle Way) system of thought, which is considered to be the central philosophy of Mahayana Buddhism. While Buddha maintained his 'noble silence' when asked philosophical and metaphysical questions, Nagarjuna, a brilliant dialectician, applied the dialectic method and argued that truth is not to be found in any view or concept, in any system of understanding. The truth, the Absolute, which is inexpressible, can only be comprehended in rising above any kind of exclusiveness. The conflict produced by reason and contending positions can be resolved by attaining a higher standpoint—that is, by the awareness of the total rather than the separate parts. One goes beyond to intuition, considered to be a higher faculty: the non-dual knowledge, the knowledge of the Real, the Absolute.

And here is Jung's view of intuition:

> In intuition a content presents itself whole and complete, without our being able to explain or discover how this content came into existence.... Intuitive knowledge possesses an intrinsic certainty and conviction....[34]

The central point in the philosophy of Nagarjuna is the rule of the Middle Way, which in practice means: "to see things as they are, to recognize the possibility of determining things differently from

different standpoints and to recognize that these determinations cannot be seized as absolute."[35]

Equally basic to the philosophy of Nagarjuna is the distinction
between the mundane and ultimate truth, which is actually one of the
foundations of Buddha's teaching, and is always emphasized in
Mahayana Buddhism. But this does not mean a separation between
the worldly and the transcendental. It is rather the realization of the
relativity of the mundane, and a consequent deepening of inward
awareness in the process of which the mundane, the superficial, is
not destroyed but is transformed and then seen in a new light.[36]

The Madhyamika teaches that

> ... to realize the ultimate is not to abandon the mundane but to
> learn to see it 'with the eye of wisdom'. . . What needs to be
> abandoned is one's perversions and false clingings. . . . This ap-
> plies not only to actual life but to words, concepts, understand-
> ing, systems of understanding.[37]

EGO AND NON-EGO

In the Tantric system, any worldly pleasure, any experience of
the senses, any occasion in this world can become an opportunity for
enlightenment when wisdom is applied. We have seen that wisdom
(*prajna*) implies non-exclusiveness, non-attachment, the principle of
relativity, sunyata.

The greatest obstacle is the ego. Ego—or rather one's *view* of
one's 'I'—is at the root of all problems and sufferings, according to
Buddhist thought. When Buddhists talk about ego they refer to the
illusory belief in a solid, concrete, separate entity, independent and
disconnected from any other phenomena. In that sense naturally the
ego becomes an insurmountable barrier between oneself and the rest
of the world, with no possibility of true communication and communion, not only with others but also with the depth of oneself. That
barrier has to be demolished, and that is the chief problem in the path
to liberation.

The aim, then, is not so much the dissolution of the ego as the
dissolution of the false view of the ego; and what is to be achieved is
an openness to all possibilities that present themselves, and above all,

a realization that we are infinitely more than we believe we are when identified with our concrete little ego. We have limitless potentials, once we are free from the bondage of our egocentric world: the Buddhist would say, we can become a Buddha.

Indeed, according to Jung, the ego, full of distortions and projections, needs to be dissolved before the Self can emerge. The Self, however, which is the totality of the psyche, includes the ego. In the process of individuation one does not destroy the ego, rather one places it in subordinate relation to the Self. The ego is no longer the center of the personality; the Self, the mandala, which unites all opposites, is its center. What is dissolved is the inflated, concrete ego, pursuing its exclusive selfish purposes, just following its own impulses. The individuated ego, in relation to the Self, is not only needed for adequate functioning on what the Buddhists refer to as the mundane level of reality; it is also of crucial importance in the encounter with the transpersonal, in order to preserve the integrity of the psyche.

For Jung, transformation is the goal of psychotherapy, and the disappearance of egohood is the only criterion of change. But he maintains that frequently for Westerners 'a conscious ego and a cultivated understanding must first be produced through analysis before one can even think about abolishing egohood.'[38]

However in the alchemical sense of *solutio*, the dissolution of a dry, hard soil of ego-consciousness through a confrontation with and fertilization by the fluid unconscious is a necessary prerequisite for transmutation to take place. This is another way of viewing the sacrifice of the personal ego to the transpersonal Self, the ongoing process of death and rebirth. The experience of non-duality, the mystical experience, or every creative act must go through that process.

The illusion of a permanent, separate ego does not mean there is no individuality. Our essential oneness with the universe, in the view of Lama Govinda,

> . . . is not sameness or unqualified identity, but an organic relationship, in which differentiation and uniqueness of function are as important as that ultimate or basic unity.
>
> Individuality and universality are not mutually exclusive values, but two sides of the same reality, compensating, fulfilling, and complementing each other, and becoming one in the experi-

ence of enlightenment. This experience does not dissolve the mind into an amorphous All, but rather brings the realization that the individual itself contains the totality focalized in its very core.[39]

Universality and individuality, unity and diversity, pleroma and creatura, nirvana and samsara, the 'two sides of the same reality'; there could not be one without its opposite.

SUFFERING AND METHODS OF HEALING

Both Buddhism and Jung have as their primary concern relief of suffering. In fact the whole Buddhist system has evolved around that core idea initially formulated by Buddha in the Four Noble Truths that all life is suffering, but there can be an end to it. In Mahayana Buddhism the ideal of the Bodhisattva, the symbol of compassion, is the ultimate expression of the underlying concern to lead every being to freedom from suffering, to enlightenment.

Jung too tells us in his autobiography and throughout his writings that he is concerned with the healing of human suffering. 'We do not profess' he says,

> . . . a psychology with merely academic pretensions, or seek explanations that have no bearing on life. What we want is a practical psychology which yields approvable results—one which explains things in a way that must be justified by the outcome for the patient.[40]

But unlike Buddha, Jung does not perceive the possibility of an end to suffering. In his view happiness and suffering represent another pair of opposites, indispensable to life, and one cannot exist without the other. He states:

> Man has to cope with the problem of suffering. The Oriental wants to get rid of suffering by casting it off. Western man tries to suppress suffering with drugs. But suffering has to be overcome, and the only way to overcome it is to endure it. We learn that only from him [the Crucified Christ].[41]

At another time, Jung discusses the double-edged possibility of the consequences of suffering: it can be a discipline 'needed for the emotional chaos of man, though at the same time it can kill the living spirit . . . it remains forever an unresolved question whether suffering is educative or demoralizing. . . . Man's fate has always swung between day and night. There is nothing we can do to change this.'[42] Thus suffering has the potential of becoming a 'psychic mover,' a prelude to the process of healing and individuation or it can lead to pathology. The painful symptoms of a neurosis often are the expression of the psyche's urge towards wholeness. They contain seeds of potentials to be actualized, and when they are worked with rather than avoided or suppressed they become sources of new achievements, new integration—'the dark night of the soul' turns into illumination. Jung experienced that throughout his life. On the other hand excessive, overwhelming suffering, particularly in an individual whose inner constitution is weak and the ego disconnected from the Self, can lead to diametrically opposite directions: madness, criminality, and other kinds of pathology.

The path leading via the underworld to illumination, to the Self, is by no means an easy one. It requires the sacrifice of our most cherished possession, our ego, so that the Self can emerge. Similarly Buddhists say the root of all suffering is attachment to ego, and they urge us to relinquish it, so that our true nature, our Buddha-nature, can be revealed. But this can only come about spontaneously; it cannot be forced, either with Jung's therapeutic methods, or any Buddhist methods.

In both systems the path differs with each individual, and it is always carried on within individuals as their own unique inner work. Jung's process of individuation, his journey to wholeness, is a very individual pursuit. Jung was even opposed to the use of groups as a psychotherapeutic method. The path of the Buddhist adept is likewise very individual, although it makes use of group practice, recognizing the powerful energy that is generated from it, and especially from participation in rituals.

It is invariably, in both systems, a non-dogmatic, empirical method aimed at the living inner experience, a dynamic way of going inward towards the center, where the seed of enlightenment, of the Self, is contained in each of us. 'No textbook can teach psychology; one learns by actual experience'[43]—says Jung. And in another passage he writes: 'In psychology one possesses nothing unless one has experienced it in reality. Hence a purely intellectual insight is not enough, because one knows only the words and not the substance of the thing from inside.'[44]

The cognitive function, though, is not minimized in Jung, or in Buddhism. According to the Tibetans, 'Intellectual understanding increases the power of the rational mind and this increases the power of formal meditation.'[45] After listening to the teaching disciples must try to understand it through reason before they can transform it into living reality. And then if it does not correspond to their experience of living reality they should abandon it. Is that not what Jung tells us when he maintains that a conscious understanding must precede the disappearance of egohood? And furthermore, is he not in his psychology primarily concerned with practical results that must be justified by the subjective experience of the patient he is treating?

The First Noble Truth, which is that the nature of life is suffering, must first be clearly understood before anything else can be done. It has been said that the path leading to liberation is completed through intellectual, as well as moral and spiritual perfection. In the Buddhist practice of mindfulness one is closely attentive to the activities of the mind, ideas and thoughts, sensations and feelings. And in Tantra especially, all the hidden tendencies, projections, must be known and experienced before they can be transmuted into wisdom.

In Jungian analysis one must deal with one's shadow, the dark rejected part of the psyche, detect projections and egocentric aims. The intensity of the emotional turmoil is not repressed or devalued, but the energy that is contained there is utilized in the process of change. Similarly in Tantric practices the energy of the emotions, like anger, desire, aversion, etc., is mobilized to transmute the passion. Both systems fully recognize the potential destructiveness of hidden unconscious tendencies. For that reason the total psyche must be approached, its dark as well as its light aspects, personified in Tantra by peaceful and wrathful deities, repeatedly constructed and dissolved in one's visualization. One is continually facing the conflict of opposites in the effort to transcend them. This is the purpose of the *sadhanas* (meditation exercises), which are based on a profound understanding of depth psychology.

In Jungian analysis, the transcendent function is the comparable principle that is aimed at in the dialectic process between analysts

and analysands. The latter on their way to individuation are reconciling the conflicting parts of their psyche, the split between the
conscious ego and the unconscious and reaching beyond all pairs of
opposites.

In both systems the adept, or the analysand, must eventually
become independent from outside support. The methods used in
working on inner growth vary infinitely, depending on the person,
the time, and the circumstances. Buddha used a different language to
teach the same truth to different people, being aware of the importance of individual characteristics and needs. 'Since individuality . . .
is absolutely unique, unpredictable, and uninterpretable,' Jung
stresses, 'the therapist must abandon all his preconceptions and techniques. . . .'[46] The integrity of the psyche of the other is highly re-
spected and never to be violated by imposing one's own definitions
and preconceived ideas. In this manner true communication can be
established. This is Jung's view, but it is also in the spirit of the
Madhyamika philosophy.

Transformation comes about through the vehicle of symbols.
Jung recognized that 'any imagination is a potentiality,'[47] and
through his method of active imagination found a way of healing and
transforming the personality. Similarly in Tantric meditation the initiate becomes impregnated with the symbols visualized, the deities—
all different symbols of Buddha—and is transformed into Buddha.

In the Tantric model Jung discerned an analogy to his psychology of the unconscious. He points out that Tantra deals with contents which are 'constantly reproduced by our unconscious in this
form or another. . . . This is not mysticism, this is psychology.'[48]

Note should be made of the powerful symbology that Tibetan
Buddhists use in their iconography (*thangkas*), their sacred texts, and
their rituals, all designed to express the inexpressible and to evoke
certain experiences that transport the individual to higher levels of
consciousness beyond mundane reality. The teachings are done in a
style that is poetic, imaginal, and often repetitive. In his writings
Jung also makes abundant use of repetition, circumambulation, paradoxes, and avoids a language and style that is purely rational. He tells
us that,

> . . . in describing the living process of the psyche, I deliberately
> and consciously give preference to a dramatic, mythological

way of thinking and speaking, because this is not only more expressive but also more exact than an abstract scientific terminology. . . .[49]

REDEMPTION OF GOD

The idea of psychic transformation is fundamental to Tantra, Jung, and alchemy. In Tantra adepts identify with the divine qualities, in the process of which they become aware of their own divine essence. The Buddhist, we are told,

> . . . believes in the divine principle in man, the inborn spark of light (*bodhi-citta*) embodied in his consciousness as a yearning toward perfection, toward completeness, toward Enlightenment. To put it paradoxically, it is not God who creates man, but man who creates God in his image, i.e., the idea of the divine aim within himself, which he realizes in the fires of suffering from which compassion, understanding, love and wisdom are born.
>
> The unfoldment of individual life in the universe has no other aim apparently but to become conscious of its own divine essence, and since this process goes on continuously, it represents a perpetual birth of God or, to put it into Buddhist terminology, the continuous arising of Enlightened Beings, in each of whom the totality of the universe becomes conscious.[50]

Here we find an extraordinary parallel to Jung's thought that 'the creator . . . needs Man to illuminate his creation'[51] and that this work can be accomplished only in the individual psyche, which is the carrier of the divine spark.

Let us listen to Jung speaking on this subject:

> Although the divine incarnation is a cosmic and absolute event, it only manifests empirically in those relatively few individuals capable of enough consciousness to make ethical decisions, i.e., to decide for the Good. Therefore God can be called good only in as much as He is able to manifest His goodness in individuals. His moral quality depends upon individuals. That is why He incarnates. Individuation and individual existence are indispensable for the transformation of God the Creator.[52]

The Mahayana Bodhisattva—who has attained the highest state of consciousness and through his actions and attitudes, his wisdom and compassion, is an active force in furthering 'the transformation of God'—he is, it seems to me, in Jung's terms, the most fully accomplished individuated person on whom God depends to illuminate His creation. Both Jung and Buddhists affirm that only human beings can perform that task in the universe—therefore the necessity for human existence, or as Tibetan Buddhists would say for 'the precious human rebirth.' This is perhaps the true meaning of the Mahayana ideal of the Bodhisattva whose sole and unique purpose in this world is to work for the benefit of all beings. And when Bodhisattvas are teaching and inspiring those on the path to liberation continuously and progressively to expand their consciousness, they are leading them towards those inward experiences intimated by Jung, and alluded to in his statement that:' . . . it can be expected that we are going to contact spheres of a not yet transformed God when our consciousness begins to extend into the sphere of the unconscious.'[53]

However, the difference between the Mahayana Buddhist and Jung is that in Jung's thought the unconscious can never be totally conscious and the process of individuation is never completed, whereas to the Buddhist it is possible to know all of the unknowable and become fully enlightened. We should be reminded here, that in his entire work Jung is only considering psychological experiences that can be established empirically and is not dealing with metaphysical categories. Therefore, Jung states,

> . . . when God or the Tao is named an impulse of the soul, or a psychic state, something has been said about the knowable only, but nothing about the unknowable, about which nothing can be determined.[54]

In Jung's view, although it is man's task to reach maximum levels of consciousness, any increase of it brings an additional burden. This is diametrically opposed to the view of Mahayana Buddhists that consciousness is at the source of liberation, and it is bliss. The actual process in reaching the goal is by no means free from tortures. The advanced disciple may be put to all kinds of tests, and the experiences endured are not unlike the frightful and tormenting visions of the alchemist Zosimos.[55] But the end result is nothing short of bliss. Bliss is consistently emphasized in Tantric meditation, and it is an experience that comes even to the less advanced meditator. The cheerfulness and infectious laughter of Tibetan lamas, their exuberance coupled with calm and peacefulness, their exquisite spontaneity, warmth and openness reflect the state of mind of human beings unencumbered by problems and burdens of daily life, material or psychological, nor by fear of death. This is the very first impression invariably gained by anyone who has had the good fortune and privilege to meet them. By their attitude and behavior it is as though they want to convey to us, in a wordless but clear, unequivocal language, that it is indeed possible to transcend suffering, as their first Master had taught them.

In contrast to it, Jung does not propose to help his patients end their suffering. He believes that: 'Life demands for its completion and fulfilment a balance between joy and sorrow.'[56] While he contends that suffering is a natural, not unhealthy aspect of life, and happiness an impossible state to attain, Tibetan Buddhists claim that suffering can be transmuted into happiness.

However, Buddhists, as well as Jung, and the alchemists, perceive that the major task to accomplish is the redemption of the divine spark within. To the Tantric Buddhist it means finding the deity hidden in the unconscious and suffocated by the ego. To Jung it is the conscious realization of the Self, and its separation from the ego. To the alchemist it is the redemption of the *anima mundi* imprisoned in matter.

JUNG'S VIEW OF EASTERN TRADITIONS

One can find many paradoxes and inconsistencies in Jung's writings, and his views of Eastern traditions are a good example of this. At times Jung is speaking in favor of Eastern traditions, praising their ways of approaching the psyche and their intuitive wisdom, which the West lacks, and at other times he warns Westerners against the dangers of embracing a system that is foreign to their culture.

Personally I am amazed at Jung's penetrating understanding (despite occasional misconceptions) of the Eastern systems, including the Tibetan tradition, without having had the benefit of direct contact with the latter and without experiencing their meditative practices. I am just as amazed today at some of the Tibetan lamas' keen perceptiveness and sensitivity to the West and its lifestyle. I have often pondered over it, and I suggest that in both cases this is due to the intuitive wisdom of a clear, unprejudiced mind which is capable of transcending historical and cultural barriers and reaching valid conclusions.

Jung sees vast differences between the Eastern and Western standpoints and raises the question of the possibility and advisability of imitating each other.[57] Along with this contention, he also tells us that in the human psyche the collective unconscious 'possesses a common substratum transcending all differences in culture and consciousness.'[58] This unconscious psyche, by virtue of being common to all human beings, contains 'latent predispositions towards identical reactions.'[59] Indeed Jung is aware of the close parallels between Eastern and Western psychology.[60] His concern, though, is that Westerners will adopt Eastern values from their usual extroverted position, and make dogmas out of them, rather than seek those values within themselves, in their psyche. He finds that the core of Eastern teachings consists in inward looking of the mind, which in itself has a self-liberating power. He is very critical of the Westerners who merely attempt to imitate and whose endeavors remain superficial and therefore useless, and more than that, even damaging to their psyche.[61] Jung remarks:

> One cannot be too cautious in these matters, for what with the imitative urge and a positively morbid avidity to possess themselves of outlandish feathers and deck themselves out in this exotic plumage, far too many people are misled into snatching at such 'magical' ideas and applying them externally, like an ointment. People will do anything, no matter how absurd, in order to avoid facing their own souls.[62]

Jung says that the basic problem, whether in the Eastern or Western world, 'is not so much a withdrawal from the objects of desire, as a more detached attitude to desire as such, no matter what its object.'[63] In this respect he fully understood one of the principal postulates of Tantra, that it is not desire as such, but lack of control, possessiveness, and attachment to desire that brings about a confused state of mind, and consequently suffering. Hence the need to see all phenomena as impermanent and empty.

Jung cannot conceive of the possibility of achieving total non-duality, a state of at-onement. 'One cannot know something that is not distinct from oneself. . . . I therefore assume that, in this point, Eastern intuition has overreached itself.'[64] In making this statement Jung seems to forget that his own concepts are often irrational and paradoxical, and besides that, non-duality on a transpersonal level does not exclude individuality on a conventional level of existence. Furthermore experiences of non-duality are not unknown in the Western tradition too. I am referring here to the disciplines and contemplative exercises of medieval monastic life, when the individual for a moment felt in unity with God, or rather *was* God,[65] like the Tantric meditator who becomes the deity he visualizes.

In many ways Jung comes closer to Eastern systems than to Western traditions despite his insistence that Westerners should stay with their own traditions, their symbols and mythology. Along with the Buddhists, he rejects dogmas and in his psychology, like in Buddhist teaching, it is only the subjective, inner experience that validates the theory. Jung himself had profound inner experiences, and it is from the depth of his soul that he gained direct immediate knowledge which he then translated into his work. In that respect he was following the gnostic tradition. The latter had inspired and influenced him before Eastern traditions came to his attention. Scholars have suggested that Hindu or Buddhist traditions influenced gnosticism, although there is no conclusive evidence.[66] It may be that the human mind independently produced similar or identical ideas in two different parts of the world. This would only confirm Jung's concept of the common structure of the psyche, transcending cultural differences. But whatever its origin, gnosticism has more than superficial parallels with Buddhism.

In comparing these two systems one finds many analogies. Some of the most salient of these include the idea of human liberation through internal transformation; of the psyche carrying within itself the potential for liberation; of the emphasis on the primacy of immediate experience; and of the need for initial guidance but the eventual freedom from any external authority. Both systems also see the disciples' own minds as their guide and it is there that they must discover the truth. A further similarity is the belief that not sin but ignorance, lack of self-knowledge, is the source of suffering and enslavement by unconscious impulses: the one who remains ignorant lives in illusion and cannot experience fulfilment. And, of course, the discovery of the divine within is central to each: the one who achieves gnosis is no longer a Christian but becomes Christ.[67]

Here is a passage from the Gnostic Gospel of Philip that is remarkable in its similarity to the fundamental Tantric view:

> ... You saw the spirit, you became spirit. You saw Christ, you became Christ. You saw [the Father, you] shall become Father ... you see yourself, and *what you see you shall [become]*.[68]

And now another passage implying that the Kingdom of God is but the symbol for a transformed state of consciousness:

> Jesus said ... 'When you make the two one, and when you make the inside like the outside and the outside like the inside, and the above like the below, and when you make the male and the female one and the same ... then you will enter [the Kingdom].'[69]

It appears obvious that Buddhist and Gnostic Christian symbols express the same inner experiences and, whether the disciple adopts one or the other, the essential quest for meaning and spatial and temporal transcendence is the same. Therefore when Jung penetrated the depth of his psyche and thereby gained access to direct knowledge arising out of his own transformative experience, he became a link in the chain of ancient mystical traditions, Buddhist and Christian. Or to put it differently, in the depth of the collective unconscious—or the height of his supra-consciousness—Jung met the consciousness of the medieval Christian mystic, a Master Eckhart, and that of the Tantric master. The words expressing the ineffable experience, the union with the One Mind, or with God (which is beyond words anyway) and the tools used in the process may differ, but the core of the experience does not: in the heart of it, for the briefest moment, the gap between various traditions is closed. And it is precisely there that I am looking for parallels between Jungian and Tantric systems. The methods and techniques that Jung developed in the context of, and to conform with, the Western tradition and mythological images, and with the socio-cultural conditions of contemporary Europe and America, are less important. They reflect only the necessity to remain rooted in one's own culture, which

Jung recognized, and which Tibetan Buddhists would acknowledge too. And most of all, every Buddhist would be in perfect agreement with Jung's statement that 'We must get at the Eastern values from within and not from without, seeking them in ourselves. . . .'[70]

DANGERS

Both Jung and Tantric Buddhists are aware of the latent risks inherent in the practice of their respective methods. Jung repeatedly warns us of the possible dangerous effects when releasing unconscious contents without proper safeguards and precautions, as it may overwhelm consciousness and cause its collapse, resulting in serious consequences, even psychosis. He compares the potential explosive power of the archetypes to that of the released atom, and he says:

> The archetypes have this peculiarity in common with the atomic world, which is . . . that the more deeply the investigator penetrates into the universe of microphysics the more devastating are the explosive forces he finds enchained there.[71]

For this reason, as already noted, it is of crucial importance to have a strong, well-developed psychic structure before confronting the unconscious so mental equilibrium can be maintained.

Tantric masters issue very similar warnings, namely, that the methods they teach are profound but also extremely powerful and therefore hazardous unless the proper preparations are made and the disciple is led into the practice gradually under the guidance of a qualified teacher. They furthermore stress the importance of relating at all times to the actuality of one's experience, to the solid, earthy aspect of it.[72] This is where Jung would agree: he knew so well how crucial it was for him to keep on with his daily work, maintain close contact with his family, and fulfil his other obligations while in the midst of his own confrontation with the unconscious.

Tibetan Buddhists urge Westerners not to abandon the values of their own culture. In fact a proper understanding of one's own culture and being deeply rooted in it—they would say—is a prerequisite for venturing into and benefiting from practices of a foreign tradition. There is also always the danger of grasping the literal rather than the intrinsic meaning of symbols and rituals, and thereby going astray and getting lost in one's practice.

Tantric images visualized in meditation represent archetypes and therefore particular caution is needed in dealing with them. As every archetype has a double aspect—a light and a dark one—the power of its dark side when it suddenly emerges from the depth of the unconscious may cause delusional fantasies and loss of touch with reality. For example, the archetype of the Great Mother contains such paradoxical aspects as nurturing and creative, as well as devouring and destructive. A fragile individual whose consciousness is not well developed may become disoriented by the emergence of the archetype in its unexpected terrifying aspect.[73] I have been a witness to this unfortunate effect on Western students, on more than one occasion, at intensive meditation courses.

ETHICAL ISSUES

Atisha, the eleventh century Indian sage, responsible for a revival of Buddhism in Tibet, said: 'When the container and its contents are filled with wrongs, change this adverse circumstance into the path to full awakening.'[74] This admonition could just as well be made to the people of the twentieth century. Tibetans today recognize that since we are living in an age of degeneration when both the environment—the container—and its inhabitants—the contents—are polluted and afflicted with enormous and dangerous problems, this is especially the time to use the prevailing situation as an encouragement to cultivate our minds, transform our outlook, or as they say, to change the adverse circumstances into the path to liberation.[75]

Jung on the other hand was also extremely concerned, in this time of confusion, with the fate of our civilization and the danger of humanity destroying itself. He discerned, however, that

> We are living in what the Greeks called *Kairos*—the right time —for a 'metamorphosis of the gods.' . . . So much is at stake and so much depends on the psychological constitution of modern man.'[76]

According to Jung—and this is the same idea that Tibetan Buddhists are proposing—the change must begin with individuals, in their own psyche, their greatest instrument. To Jung that implies self-knowledge, knowing the dark side of the psyche, the unconscious as well as its conscious aspects, and to reconcile the polarities. Without this knowledge, unconscious contents cause projections and illusions that falsify our relations with others, and that is where the wars begin. 'Right action comes from right thinking, and . . . there is no cure and no improving of the world that does not begin with the individual himself,'[77] says Jung. The right action and right thinking, is that not what Buddha taught 2500 years ago?

The more conscious we become of our unconscious drives and act accordingly, the less contaminated with projections are our relations with the world, and the more open we are to enter into communication, yes, even communion with it. Jung talks of society's need for an affective bond, the principle of *caritas*, the Christian love of the neighbor. He warns us that: 'Where love stops, power begins, and violence, and terror.'[78]

Compassion is the basic element in Buddhist philosophy and psychology, and in Tibetan Buddhism it is inseparable from wisdom, the enlightened state of mind. Today the Dalai Lama, who is regarded as the incarnation of Avalokiteshvara, the Buddha of compassion, is teaching and bringing to the Western world, wherever he goes, the ideal of compassion as a means to achieve harmony in the world, and as the principle of universal responsibility.

The Buddhist concept of voidness (sunyata) is sometimes misinterpreted in the West as implying annulment of ethical considerations. Jung suspected that Westerners' attempt at detachment as a way of liberation, which they learned from yogic practices, was only a way of liberation from moral responsibilities.[79]

Buddhism is one of the most highly developed ethical as well as psychological systems. Ethical issues and individual responsibility are always and without exception an integral part of its philosophy and practice. The rule applies to all schools and of course to Tantric Buddhism as well.

And Jung, a psychologist and physician, in all his multidimensional work, and his entire life, has consistently reminded man—the only carrier of consciousness—of his responsibility and ethical obligation to transform himself, or shall I say, to transform God.

Notes

1. Jung, *The Structure and Dynamics of the Psyche*, p. 256.
2. *Ibid.*, p. 350.
3. Jung, *Mysterium Coniunctionis*, p. 109.
4. Jung, *The Archetypes and the Collective Unconscious*, p. 283.
5. Jung, *The Structure and Dynamics of the Psyche*, p. 361.
6. Jung, *Aion*, p. 165.
7. Jung, *The Practice of Psychotherapy*, pp. 319–320.
8. Jung, *Psychological Types*, pp. 449–450.
9. Jung, *Psychology and Alchemy*, p. 137.
10. Jung, *Mysterium Coniunctionis*, p. 197.
11. Jung, *The Structure and Dynamics of the Psyche*, p. 349.
12. *Ibid.*, p. 185.
13. Jung, *The Archetypes and the Collective Unconscious*, p. 279.
14. Jung, *The Practice of Psychotherapy*, p. 34.
15. *Ibid.*, p. 192.
16. Govinda, *Foundations of Tibetan Mysticism*, pp. 71–77.
17. Govinda, *Creative Meditation and Multi-Dimensional Consciousness*, p. 30.
18. *Ibid.*, p. 31.
19. *The Lankavatara Sutra*, p. 48.
20. C. G. Jung, *Septem Sermones ad Mortuos*, in his *Memories, Dreams, Reflections*, p. 379.
21. Pleroma is the Greek word for 'plenitude.'
22. Jung, *Septem Sermones ad Mortuos*, p. 379.
23. *Ibid.*, p. 382.
24. Jung, *Memories, Dreams, Reflections*, p. 269.
25. Govinda, *Foundations of Tibetan Mysticism*, p. 77.
26. Govinda, *Creative Meditation and Multi-Dimensional Consciousness*, p. 105.
27. Fritjof Capra, *The Tao of Physics* (Boulder: Shambhala, 1975), p. 99.
28. Quoted in Beatrice Suzuki, *Impressions of Mahayana Buddhism* (Kyoto: Eastern Buddhist Society, 1940), p. 48.
29. Jung, *The Practice of Psychotherapy*, p. 312.
30. Jung, *Two Essays on Analytical Psychology*, pp. 75–76.
31. *Ibid.*, p. 75.

32. *Ibid.*, p. 205.
33. Jung, *The Archetypes and the Collective Unconscious*, p. 382.
34. Jung, *Psychological Types*, p. 453.
35. Ramanan, *op. cit.*, p. 50.
36. *Ibid.*, p. 258.
37. *Ibid.*, p. 329.
38. C. G. Jung, 'Foreword to Suzuki's *Introduction to Zen Buddhism*,' in his *Psychology and the East*, p. 154.
39. Govinda, *Creative Meditation and Multi-Dimensional Consciousness*, pp. 48–49.
40. Jung, *The Structure and Dynamics of the Psyche*, p. 351.
41. C. G. Jung, *Letters* (Princeton: Princeton University Press, 1973), Vol. 1, p. 236.
42. *Ibid.*, Vol. 2, p. 248.
43. Jung, *Man and His Symbols*, p. 81.
44. Jung, *Aion*, p. 33.
45. Dhargyey, *op. cit.*, p. 92.
46. Jung, *The Practice of Psychotherapy*, pp. 7–8.
47. C. G. Jung, *Psychological Analysis of Nietzsche's Zarathustra*, Vol. 3 (Winter 1935), p. 23.
48. *Ibid.*, p. 4.
49. Jung, *Aion*, p. 13.
50. Govinda, *Creative Meditation and Multi-Dimensional Consciousness*, p. 141.
51. Miguel Serrano, *C. G. Jung and Hermann Hesse; A Record of Two Friendships* (New York: Schocken Books, 1966), p. 88.
52. Jung, *Letters*, Vol. 2, p. 314.
53. *Idem.*
54. Jung, 'Commentary on *The Secret of the Golden Flower*,' p. 56.
55. Jung, *Alchemical Studies*, pp. 59–64.
56. Jung, *The Practice of Psychotherapy*, p. 81.
57. Jung, 'Psychological Commentary on *The Tibetan Book of Great Liberation*,' p. 111.
58. Jung, 'Commentary on *The Secret of the Golden Flower*,' p. 13.
59. *Idem.*
60. Jung, 'Psychological Commentary on *The Tibetan Book of Great Liberation*,' p. 134.
61. Jung, *Psychology and Alchemy*, pp. 99–101.
62. Jung, 'Psychological Commentary on *The Tibetan Book of Great Liberation*,' p. 120.
63. *Ibid.*, p. 125.
64. *Ibid.*, pp. 132–133.

65. Ira Progoff, *The Cloud of Unknowing* (New York: Dell Publishing Co., 1957), pp. 23–38.
66. Elaine Pagels, *The Gnostic Gospel* (New York: Vintage Books, 1979), pp. xx–xxi.
67. *Ibid.*, pp. 149–161.
68. Quoted in Pagels, *op. cit.*, p. 161. (Italics added).
69. Quoted in Pagels, *op. cit.*, p. 155.
70. Jung, 'Psychological Commentary on *The Tibetan Book of Great Liberation*,' p. 112.
71. Jung, *The Archetypes and the Collective Unconscious*, p. 224.
72. Guenther and Trungpa, *op. cit.*, p. 89.
73. Erich Neumann, *The Origins and History of Consciousness* (Princeton: Princeton University Press, 1954), p. 322.
74. Geshe Rabten and Geshe Ngawang Dhargyey, *Advice from A Spiritual Friend* (London: Wisdom Publications, 1984), p. 65.
75. *Ibid.*, pp. 65–66.
76. Jung, *The Undiscovered Self* (New York: The New American Library, 1959), p. 123.
77. Jung, *Two Essays on Analytical Psychology*, p. 226.
78. Jung, *The Undiscovered Self*, pp. 117–118.
79. Jung, 'Psychological Commentary on *The Tibetan Book of Great Liberation*,' p. 135.

Nathan Katz

Ḍākiṇī and Anima—On Tantric Deities and Jungian Archetypes

It was no accident that when Oxford Orientalist W. Y. Evans-Wentz brought to Western awareness some obscure ritualistic and yogic translations from Tibet in 1927, he asked the great Swiss psychiatrist, Carl Gustav Jung, to provide introductions and psychological commentaries for two of the four volumes he published. There are, on the surface at least, striking similarities between Jung's psychological theories and Tibetan Buddhist thought. It shall be the purpose of this article to see if these similarities, intuitively apprehended by Evans-Wentz, are merely superficial resemblances, or if they go deeper.

Although most scholars of Tibetan Buddhism today would find Jung's a dubious hermeneutic indeed, it is our intention to take up these questions again. In order to do so, we shall not concern ourselves overmuch with Jung's own attempts at interpreting Tibetan Buddhism for Western audiences; we are not so concerned with Jung as a hermeneutic for Tibetan texts as we are with comparing two more or less systematic images of what it means to be human, as taken from Jung's and Tibetan Buddhist writings. Our sources, therefore, shall be Tibetan hagiographical texts and Jung's specifically psychological writings, leaving his ventures into Eastern thought more or less to the side. Our purpose in so doing is to avoid fitting Tibetan thought into Jungian categories, which tends to become a rather monological methodology. Rather, by treating each as systems in their own right, and not merely applying the categories of one onto the other, we would hope to develop a dialogue between them, thereby avoiding superficial or prejudiced comparisons, and to arrive at some fundamental issues with which both Jung and our Tibetan authors are concerned.

The focus of this article shall be the phenomena of anima (Jung's "female within the male") and *ḍākiṇī* (Tibetan, *mkha' 'gro ma*), the demoness-like beings who magically inspire and initiate Vajrayāna adepts to whom Herbert V. Guenther has applied Karl Jaspers' term, "ciphers of transcendence."[1] After delineating the basic concepts involved in understanding both the anima and the *ḍākiṇī*, we shall consider three areas in which they appear to overlap: (1) their function of inspiration; (2) their position in the subject/object (or conscious/unconscious) dichotomy; and (3) the symbolic concreteness (in this case, of contrasexuality) of which both Jungians and Tibetans are fond.

THE RATIONALE FOR A DISCUSSION OF JUNG AND TIBETAN BUDDHISM

For Jung and all schools of Buddhism, over-identification with the ego is the fundamental human problem. Ego as a reference point for relation with the external world is flatly denied by Buddhism; Jung would have us recenter our personality at a point which ". . . no longer coincides with ego, but . . . midway between the conscious and unconscious."[2] When there is an unwarranted identification of self with the persona (personality as presented to the world), which by its nature excludes the unconscious, the unconscious intrudes upon the consciousness and neurotic symptoms develop. Jung's solution would be to break down the narrowly-defined persona, with its insistence upon ego as its center, thereby expanding and restructuring its notion of self to include unconscious archetypal materials and relocating its center as separate from the conscious ego. Thus our problem, according to Jung, is not ego per se, but the erroneous identification of self with ego, the former uncontainable in the latter.

Buddhism would accept Jung's analysis of the problem insofar as it goes. Buddhism agrees that humans falsely identify with ego; yet, upon closer analysis, it finds ego to be totally lacking. Unlike for Jung, the problem is not, as has been said, that humans have an ego; the problem is ego itself. Buddhism does not speak of the destruction or relocation of ego; rather, it asks us to see that one may be in the world without continual reference to some fixed point of relation between self and other. Whereas the individuated person, according to Jung, becomes conscious of archetypal materials in relation to the conscious ego, the Buddhist ideals (*arahant, bodhisattva, mahāsiddha*) deny the possibility of such relation entirely and speak rather of a spontaneity of cognition-action without reference to self and other. In the famous *Diamond-Cutter Sūtra*,[3] for example, the *bodhisattva* (the ideal of Mahāyāna Buddhism) is admonished to produce the cognition-action of non-abidingness; that is, in leading all sentient beings to *nirvāṇa* (the goal of the *bodhisattva*), no thought of beings, *nirvāṇa*, or self may arise. This seemingly paradoxical statement means that once the category of relation is existentially negated, one may be in the world without fixed reference points to relate self and other. This mode of cognition-action is at the same time the perfection of wisdom (*prajñā-pāramitā*) and the generation of the great compassionate heart (*mahākaruṇācitta*), indicating that the possibility of spontaneous cognition-action arises when the fiction of self has been left behind. In Buddhist terms, this is called the generation of *bodhicitta*, or thought of enlightenment, and is the starting point for the practice of Vajrayāna Buddhism, the form to be considered in this article. Thus, whereas for Jung cognition must always be intentional and referential (i.e. for there to be cognition of the unconscious, the ego must become aware of an archetype), Buddhism, by claiming ego to be purely fictitious in the first place, offers the possibility of a spontaneous cognition-action without fixed reference points.

Despite these very important differences in assumptions, we feel that there remains a rationale for a comparison of Jung and Buddhism, particularly in the realm of inspiration and symbolism. Jung does not seek merely to restructure the ego to a more balanced accommodation with the external world; he indicates that there is a fundamental problem in identifying oneself with ego, a notion which Buddhism would second. (This does not mean that the term "ego" means the same for Jung and Buddhism. In fact, it does not.) We hope to elucidate just where the similarities and differences occur by a phenomenological investigation of the anima and the *ḍākiṇī*.

ANIMA

In Jungian psychological theory, the anima is the most accessible of the archetypal contents of the unconscious. It is a multivalent and multifunctional image. At times she is a counterbalance to the persona to the extent that the individual identifies himself with the persona:

> The anima is an unconscious subject-imago analogous to the persona. Just as the persona is the image of himself which the subject presents to the world, so the anima is the image of the subject in his relation to the collective unconscious, or an expression of unconscious collective contents unconsciously constellated by him. One could also say: the anima is the face of the subject as seen by the collective unconscious.[4]

And at other times the anima is the ". . . personification of the unconscious"[5] in its entirety. She functions as a source of neurotic symptoms when there is over-identification with the persona.

> To the degree that the ego identifies with the persona, the anima, like everything unconscious, is projected onto the real objects of our environment. She is regularly to be found, therefore, in the woman we are in love with. . . . The more normal a person is, the less will the daemonic qualities of the anima in the objects of his immediate environment . . . the more sensitive a person is, the closer these daemonic projections will come, until in the end they break through the family taboo and produce the typical neurotic complications of a family romance.[6]

And she is also a psychic helpmate, a wisdom imago:

> My psychological experience has shown time and time again that certain contents issue from a psyche more complete than consciousness. They often contain a superior analysis or insight or knowledge which consciousness has not been able to produce.[7]

As with any archetype, the anima cannot be known in itself, but only as it presents itself to consciousness. She appears always as a contrasexual image, although Jungian psychiatrist James Hillman[8] has taken Jung to task on this point, claiming that it is just as likely for the anima to appear to a woman (rather than the animus) as to a man in certain cases.[9]

The anima is relatively accessible because she is everything the conscious self is not. In Jungian therapeutic practice, the anima is the first of the archetypal (i.e. collective) images to come to consciousness, following the shadow, which is personal (i.e. not collective). As such she plays the role of mediator between consciousness and the unconscious, as well as being the most likely culprit in the genesis of psychopathology. The anima is an autonomous complex and, as such, a dissociation of the conscious self is required for it to become known. This dissociation may be pathological, as Jung describes:

> The forces that burst out of the collective psyche have a confusing and binding effect. One result of the dissolution of the persona is a release of involuntary fantasy, which is apparently nothing else than the specific activity of the collective psyche. This activity throws up contents whose existence one had never suspected before. But as the influence of the collective unconscious increases, so the conscious mind loses its power of leadership. Imperceptible it becomes the led, while an unconscious and impersonal process gradually takes control. Thus, without noticing it, the conscious personality is pushed about like a figure on a chess-board by an invisible player. It is the player who decided the game of fate, not the conscious mind and its plans.[10]

Or it may be a deliberate, constructive aspect of Jungian therapy, wherein the therapist and patient work toward a form of dissociation:

> The psyche not being a unity but a contradictory multiplicity of complexes, the dissociation required for our dialectics with the anima is not so terribly difficult. The art of it consists only in allowing our invisible partner to make herself heard, in putting the mechanism of expression momentarily at her disposal, without being overcome by the distaste one naturally feels at playing such an apparently ludicrous game with oneself, or by doubts as to the genuineness of the voice of one's interlocutor.[11]

When one becomes aware of the anima, either by neurotic disturbances or by deliberate therapeutic dissociation, her autonomy becomes apparent because she is truly archetypal or, put differently, because she cannot be identified with the personal, conscious self. James Hillman makes this point:

> "*My*" anima expresses the personalistic fallacy. Even though anima experiences bring with them a numinosity of person, the

feeling of a unique inwardness and sense of importance (exaggerations and mythologization of mood, insight, or fantasy), to take these experiences literally, as literally personal, puts the anima inside "me." The heightened subjectivity of anima events is "anything but personal" because it is archetypal ... [and] to take the archetypal literally as personal is a personalistic fallacy. So, when under the domination of anima our soulfulness makes us feel most uniquely "me," special, different, called—this is precisely the moment when, as Jung goes on to say in the same passage, "we are most estranged from ourselves and most like the average type of *homo sapiens*."[12]

The most common response to the discovery of the anima is fear because the existence of autonomous complexes within one's psyche is inherently frightening, because one can no longer imagine consciousness to be the master of the self, and "it is normal for man to resist his anima because she represents ... the unconscious with all those tendencies and contents hitherto excluded from conscious life."[13] These contents have been excluded because the conscious self, or ego, finds them generally unpleasant and they become "partial personalities [that] have the character of an inferior woman or an inferior man, hence their irritating influence."[14]

The anima exists in relation to the persona or self as consciously presented to the world. The relationship between anima and persona is compensatory,[15] and when the disparity between conscious and unconscious becomes inflated, pathological projection of the unconscious ensues. These projections can lead to psychotic conditions, as Jung writes:

> The effect of projection is to isolate the subject from his environment, since instead of a real relation to it there is now only an illusory one. Projections change the world into a replica of one's own unknown face. In the last analysis, therefore, they lead to an auto-erotic or autistic condition in which one dreams a world whose reality remains forever unattainable. . . . The more projections interpose themselves between the subject and environment, the harder it becomes for the ego to see through its illusions.[16]

However, these projections are also potential teachers, mirrors which reflect to us our true psychological condition, useful friends on Jung's path to individuation. As Emma Jung tells us:

> One function of the anima is to be a looking glass for a man, to reflect his thoughts, desires, and emotions. . . . That is precisely why she is so important to him, whether as an inner figure or projected to an actual, other woman; in this way he becomes aware of things about which he is still unconscious.[17]

Thus the anima could ". . . function [as guides to the depths of the unconscious] if only man and woman can learn to relate to them within themselves in an open and constructive way," as Jungian psychiatrist June Singer[18] writes. As such, the anima is a wisdom imago, as well as a psychologically disturbing character. In herself she is neutral; all that remains in question is our relation to her, our refusal to identify the totality of our psychic being with the persona, which according to Jung is the negation of egocentricity.[19]

The anima is also an image of power. Precisely because she has such capabilities for disturbing us, she has the potential for healing us. Jung very perceptively writes:

> The thing that cures a neurosis must be as convincing as the neurosis; and since the latter is only too real, the helpful experience must be of equal reality. It must be a very real illusion, if you want to put it pessimistically. But what is the difference between a real illusion and a healing religious experience? It is merely a difference in words.[20]

The healing process then becomes a reappropriation of the power of the anima into the image of the self. This is done, as has been noted, by the therapeutic dissociation of the persona and the recognition of the anima as an autonomous, powerful complex. Thus the anima is recognized:

> "She" [a literary anima figure] is a mana-personality, a being full of some occult and bewitching quality (mana), endowed with magical knowledge and power. All these attributes naturally have their source in the naïve projection of an unconscious self-knowledge.[21]

After the anima is so recognized, her power can be appropriated:

> Through this process the anima forfeits the daemonic power of an autonomous complex; she can no longer exercise the power of

possession, since she is depotentiated. She is no longer the guardian of treasures unknown . . . but a psychological function of an intuitive nature.[22]

Jung then points to a very interesting phenomenon after the power of the anima has been appropriated:

Well then: who is it that has integrated the anima? Obviously the consciousness, and therefore ego has taken over the mana. Thus the ego becomes a mana-personality. But the mana-personality is a dominant of the collective unconscious. The well-known archetype of the mighty man in the form of a hero, chief, magician, medicine man, the ruler of man and spirits, the friend of God. This masculine collective figure who now rises out of the dark background and takes possession of the conscious personality entails a psychic danger of a subtle nature, for by inflating the conscious mind it can destroy everything that was gained by coming to terms with the anima.[23]

The anima always appears as a concrete image. She is not something which, at depth, can be known; rather, she is known as she presents herself to consciousness, formal and concrete. This could be said of any of the archetypes, since to be conscious means, for Jung, that an image appears to the conscious self: consciousness is always intentional and referential. The reference of the consciousness of anima must therefore be a concrete image of the anima and never the anima herself. Ira Progoff makes this point when he writes that ". . . on the question of what they [the archetypes] are in themselves, Jung states that we must remain silent."[24] The concreteness of the anima is extended to include actual women when they function as an anima.[25]

One's encounter with the anima brings about a recentering of the personality, a readaptation to life. This process either may be psychotic degeneration, when one's private reality is projected upon the public reality indiscriminately, or it may involve a non-egoistic mode of being. This transformation is described thus:

If we picture the conscious mind, with the ego at its center, as being opposed to the unconscious, and if we now add to our mental picture the process of assimilating the unconscious, we can think of this assimilation as a kind of approximation of conscious and unconscious, where the center of the total personality no longer coincides with the ego, but with a point midway between the conscious and unconscious. This would be the point of new equilibrium, a new centering of the total personality, a vital center which, on account of its focal position between conscious and unconscious, ensures for the personality a new and more solid foundation.[26]

This idea of a non-egocentric recentering of the total personality, in which Jung goes beyond his psychoanalytic colleagues who would rather attempt to affirm the readjusted ego's centeredness, indicates that a fundamental problematic involved in all neurotic pathology is the identification with ego (or persona, of which ego is the center) itself. As Jung writes, "Reality sees to it that the peaceful cycle of egocentric ideas is constantly interrupted by ideas with a strong feeling-tone, that is, by affects,"[27] which have their origin in the unconscious. This journey toward non-egocentrism is called by Jung the process of individuation, wherein the persona is not so rigidly defined as in a neurotic condition, and the unconscious is allowed into dialogue with consciousness. This individuated person is able to integrate the contents of the archetypes, to gain their power thereby, and learn from their wise perspective. It is somewhat paradoxical that the individuated person feels himself or herself to be the least "individual," because such a person is able to appreciate that the psyche is truly collective at bottom and in no sense personal. It is the substratae of consciousness and not merely repressed personalistic contents, as other depth psychological schools believe. As Jung writes:

[The archetypes] personify those of its contents which, when withdrawn from projection, can be integrated into consciousness. To this extent both figures represent *functions* which filter the contents of the collective unconscious through to the conscious mind. . . . The reason for their behaving in this way is that though the *contents* of anima and animus can be integrated, they themselves cannot, since they are archetypes. As such they are foundation stones of the psychic structure, which in its totality exceeds the limits of consciousness and therefore can never become the object of direct cognition. The effects of anima and

animus can indeed be made conscious, but they themselves are
factors transcending consciousness and beyond the reach of perception and volition.[28]

The point to be noted is that Jung does not intend his archetypes to
be "*merely* psychological." He writes that ". . . the archetypes . . .
have a nature that cannot with certainty be designated as psychic."[29]

Jung here has opened up two very crucial questions, with which
we shall conclude our discussion of the anima: (1) the question of
private and public realities generally, and how it relates to the psychotic or the yogi; and (2) the dilemma of means of knowledge of
psychic substructure: obviously one cannot know the ground of consciousness in the same way that one knows an external object.

Jung only hints at a solution to the first question in his later and
more speculative writings. In his introduction to the Chinese alchemical text, *The Secret of the Golden Flower*,[30] he indicates that it is
perhaps the fundamental bifurcation of reality into private and public
sectors which is, at bottom, the root cause of all psychological disorders. However, this remarkable notion is nowhere systematically
incorporated into his psychological theory.

Jung is aware of the problems involved in treating the psyche as
an ordinary object of investigation. He writes:

> Man thinks of himself as holding the psyche in the hollow of his
> hand. He dreams of making a science of her. But in reality she is
> the mother and the maker, the psychical subject and even the
> possibility of consciousness itself. The psyche reaches so far
> beyond the boundary line of consciousness that the latter could
> easily be compared to an island in the ocean. While the island is
> small and narrow, the ocean is immensely wide and deep, so that
> if it is a question of space, it does not matter whether the gods are
> inside or outside.[31]

Thus Jung is aptly raising the question of the very possibility of
the scientific (i.e. "objective") investigation of the psyche, which has
been the task of the psychologists of the West. Some of the implications of this question shall be drawn out in our comparison with
Tibetan notions of the mind and the means of knowing it. It seems,
however, that Jung is aware of the shortcomings of his own method-

ology for resolving questions as to the nature of the psyche itself. His conclusion, therefore, has been to avoid making claims about its fundamental nature, a position in which we find a refreshing honesty.

ḌĀKIṆĪ

We shall be dealing with the phenomenon of the ḍākiṇī largely as it appears in the hagiographies (Tibetan, *rnam thar*) of the *mahāsiddhas* (Tibetan, *grub chen*), the "saints" of Vajrayāna Buddhism, traditionally eighty-four in number. We shall be working with canonical texts,[32] their modern adaptations,[33] and some of the few hagiographies which have been translated into Western languages.[34] These hagiographies are from a relatively early period of Vajrayāna literature, wherein the ḍākiṇīs are depicted fiercely. In later purely Tibetan writings, they often take on a more pacific character. Also, whereas in the early writings the ḍākiṇīs usually appear spontaneously, in later *sādhana* texts one finds instructions for their visualization and worship. We have thus limited our scope because we find stronger parallels for comparison with the anima in these early writings, most of which are of Indian origin.

The hagiographies are "introductory" tantric texts, as they can be read by all without specific empowerments, and are vastly popular as homiletic as well as meditatative texts in Tibet. They are accounts of the spiritual evolution of the adept. They are written in an encoded language called in Sanskrit *sandyābhāṣā*, "twilight language," richly symbolic and multivalent in meanings. As Lama Govinda writes:

> In the symbolic language of the Siddhas, experiences of meditation are transformed into external events, inner attainments into visible miracles and similes into factual, quasi-historical events. If, for instance, it is said of certain Siddhas that they stopped the sun and the moon in their course . . . this has nothing to do with the heavenly bodies . . . but with the "solar" and "lunar" currents of psychic energy, and their unification and sublimation in the body of the yogin.[35]

The *mahāsiddha* is the image of human perfection of Vajrayāna Buddhism, and as such holds a similar position as the *arahant* in

Theravāda Buddhism and the *bodhisattva* in Mahāyāna Buddhism.[36] They indicate a convergence of the Apollinarian and Dionysian trends in Indian religions, of the ecstatic and the ascetic, of the *upāsaka* (layperson) and the *bhikṣu* (monk), of intellectual and popular religions. Rebelling against the formalism of *bodhisattva* practices at the great monastic universities of India of the fourth to eleventh centuries C.E., the Vajrayāna sees in the *mahāsiddhas* the highest ideal of Buddhism, a going beyond the monasteries into the world, yet remaining aloof from it.

The word *siddha* (Tibetan, *grub pa*) comes from the root *sidh*, "to be successful," as in Siddhārtha. Thus *mahāsiddha*, of which *grub chen* is the Tibetan translation, means "great successful one," translated in early scholarship as "great sorcerer" or "great magician." Their practices, or *sādhana* (from the same root), lead to certain "accomplishments," or *siddhi* (*dngos grub*), many of which seem magical in nature, while others, such as *mahāmudrasiddhi* (Tibetan, *phyags rgya chen po*), are clearly spiritual. A "typical" hagiography of a *mahāsiddha*, to the extent one exists, would include the following motifs: (1) birth in varied castes: brahmin (Saraha), kingly (Indrabhūti), thief (Nāgabodhi), dancing-girl (Sahajasiddhi); (2) unusual accomplishments in early career: abbot at Nālandā University (Nāropa), translator of Buddhist Sanskrit texts (Marpa), powerful sorcerer (Mila Raspa); (3) turning point involving renunciation of previous vocation (Nāropa, Mila Raspa, Tilopa, Indrabhūti, etc.); (4) initiation into Vajrayāna practices, usually by a *ḍākinī*; (5) meeting the guru; and (6) attainment of the highest *siddhi* and the working of miracles.[37] We shall outline the role of the *ḍākinī* through these and some other hagiographical motifs, where the influence of the *ḍākinī* is virtually universal.

Probably the most famous encounter with a *ḍākinī* is interpreted by Herbert V. Guenther in his account of the life of the *paṇḍita* Nāropa, who occupied the prestigious and learned position of gatekeeper (analogous to dean) of Nālandā, the greatest of the Buddhist monastic universities of medieval India.

> The vision which induced Nāropa to resign from his post and to abandon worldly honours was that of an old and ugly woman who mercilessly revealed to him his psychological state. Throughout the years he had been engaged in intellectual activities which

were essentially analytic and thereby had become oblivious to the fact that the human organ of knowledge is bifocal. "Objective" knowledge may be entirely accurate without, however, being entirely important, and only too often it misses the heart of the matter. All that he had neglected and failed to develop was symbolically revealed to him as the vision of an old and ugly woman. She is old because all that the female symbol stands for, the emotionally and passionately moving, is older than the cold rationality of the intellect which itself could not be if it were not supported by feelings and moods which it usually misconceives and misjudges. And she is ugly, because that which she stands for has not been allowed to become alive, or only in an undeveloped and distorted manner. Lastly she is a deity because all that is not incorporated in the conscious mental make-up of the individual and appears other-than and more-than himself is the old, ugly and divine woman, who in the religious symbolism of the Tantras is the deity *rDo-rje phag-mo* (Vajravārāhī) and who in a psychological setting acts as "messenger" (*pho-nya*).[38]

A similar account of the *ḍākiṇī* presenting an adept with that which is psychologically most abhorrent to him is found in the hagiography of Abhyāharagupta:

> Once, as he was sitting in the temple cloister, there appeared a young maiden who dropped a piece of beef near to him which was dripping in blood, shoved it to the *ācārya* [teacher] and said: "I am a *Caṇḍālā* [outcaste] maiden, but eat what is slaughtered for you." But he answered: "I am a *Bhikṣu* of pure order; how shall I eat meat which is extraordinarily offered to me?" But she sank back and disappeared in the court below. That was . . . Vajrayogiṇī [a popular *ḍākiṇī*] who gave him the beef.[39]

Not only do the *ḍākiṇī* reveal to the adept his state of mind, which is neurotic because of the defilements of attraction and/or aversion (as to the bloody beef), rooted in ignorance, but they also positively direct the adept in his journeys. We read of the brahmin Rāhulabhadra (later called Saraha, or mDa' bsnun in Tibetan) who is directed by four brahmin girls offering cups of beer to leave his caste position and live with an arrowsmith woman.[40] Three beautiful visionary women tell Marpa that he must make a third arduous trip across the Himalayas to India to complete his training under Nāropa.[41] Marpa is also told that although he mastered the *mahāmudrā* teachings, he has neglected the *drong 'jug* practices and had better attend to them.[42] Mila Raspa is advised by the *ḍākiṇī* as to his disciples.[43] This advice comes in the form of direct visions, as with Nāropa and Abhyāharagupta, or in dreams.[44]

The Tibetan term for *ḍākiṇī, mkha' 'gro ma,* is composed of the syllables *mkha',* or "space" (Sanskrit, *ākāśa*), *'gro,* meaning "to go," and the feminine particle *ma.* Guenther[45] explains the etymology thus:

> The Tibetan explanation for the word is that "sky," "celestial space," is a term for "no-thing-ness" (*stong pa nyid,* Sanskrit *śūnyatā*) and "to go" means "to understand." The *Ḍākiṇī* is therefore an understanding of no-thing-ness. It is a fine example of "embodying" language.

Govinda[46] explains the term by telling us that since *mkha* means space or ether, or that which makes movement possible, *'gro* means "to go" and *ma* is a feminine particle, therefore *mkha* 'gro ma means a "heavenly being of female appearance who partakes of the luminous nature of *ākāśa.*"

The role of "the feminine" in the lives of the *mahāsiddhas* is enormous. The *Grub thob brgyad cu rtsa bzhi'i gsol 'debs* is a poem by rDo rje gdan pa which contains entreaties (*gsol 'debs*) to the eighty-four *mahāsiddhas,*[47] and in it fully fifty-six of them are praised for keeping company with women. Two *mahāsiddhas,* Saraha[48] and La-vapa,[49] are said to be born of the *ḍākiṇī.* We find Kukuripa[50] living with a *ḍākiṇī* who appeared to the world as his pet dog. The attainment of *mahāmudrā* by Vaidyāpāda is dependent upon his taking up residence with a *caṇḍālā,* or outcaste woman.[51] rDo rje dril bu pa is instructed by his guru, Dārikapa, to study the Cakrasaṃvara cycle of teachings with a hideous female swine-keeper, and later becomes guru to a beer-seller girl.[52] We hear Saraha singing his *dohā,* or Bengali mystical song:[53]

> Oh, I am a brahmin.
> Together with a magician-girl I enjoy.
> I don't see caste or no-caste.

As one who lives as a *bhikṣu* with shaved head,
I wander together with my consort.
There is no difference between attachment and non-attachment.
Impurity is simply a mental fabrication,
And this is not known by others.

Dārikapa, a king, becomes the servant of a harlot.[54] Putaloki in the very same verse " . . . won the harlot and perfection."[55]

The most important roles for the *ḍākinī* in the *mahāsiddha* tales are those of inspiration, as discussed, and of teaching and initiating the *mahāsiddhas*. In some cases this is done indirectly, as in the story of Biwapa of the Sa skya lineage, to whom a *ḍākinī* in the form of a common woman appears and admonishes him for even considering giving up his Vajrayāna practices,[56] or in the case of Kāṇha who is directed by a *ḍākinī* to a place where spontaneous initiation occurs.[57]

An account of a more direct initiation by a *ḍākinī* is a motif in the hagiography of Tilopa, as found in the *Chos 'byung* of Padma Karpo, and as recounted by Helmut Hoffmann.[58] Seeing an ugly crone on the road, Tilopa recognizes her to be a *ḍākinī*. She tells him to give up his *bodhisattva* practices, the exoteric Mahāyāna, and study the esoteric Vajrayāna. After he accepts her as his guru, she gives four major empowerments to Tilopa: (1) the Cakrasaṃvara-maṇḍala empowerment, after which time Cakrasaṃvara became the *yi dam* (tutelary deity) of the bKa'brgyud lineage founded in part by Tilopa; (2) the *utpattikrama* (Tibetan, *bskyed pa'i rim pa*) method for transmuting the five poisons into the five wisdoms; (3) the *sampannakrama* (Tibetan, *rdzogs pa'i rim pa*), or the attainment of *mahāsukha* (mystical "great bliss"; Tibetan, *bde chen*); and (4) the initiation of how to act like a "mad drunkard" (*smyon pa*), the highest Vajrayāna empowerment.[59] The *ḍākinī* then tells him to seek further teaching from the "queen of the *ḍākinī*."

After long trials and tribulations, he finally made his way to the court of the *Ḍākinī* queen, whose palace walls of metal gave forth tremendous heat and brilliance. But neither this nor other terrors dismayed him, and he forced his way into the enchanted palace, passed through an endless succession of splendid apartments until finally he reached the queen of the *Ḍākinīs*, who sat on her throne of superb beauty, loaded with jewels, and smiling gently at the gallant adept. But he kept repeating his magic formula [which had been given him by his guru *ḍākiṇī*], ripped off the jewelry and clothing of the queen and raped her. . . . [I]n the end he was seen in a lonely place in an aura of light surrounded by twelve lamps and twelve women. With this the master was recognized, and he now disseminated secret teachings in certain mystic verses (*Vajra-Dohā*), and from that time on he is said to have been able to walk in the heavens. With this he had become equal to the *Ḍākas* and the *Ḍākiṇīs*.[60]

Such potent symbolism lends itself to the danger of misinterpretation, as the great modern teacher, Lama Mipham, said that those who take tantric texts too literally end up only with too many children![61] The *Hevajra Tantra* clearly tells us that mind produces and maintains the *ḍākiṇī*,[62] and that the "homes" of the various *ḍākiṇī* are the various *cakras*, psychophysical energy centers along the spinal column.[63] Thus we may speculate that when Tilopa is said to rape the queen of the *ḍākiṇīs*, the reference is to the arousal of spiritual energies. Govinda explicates a similar passage:

In one of the most controversial passages of Anangavajra, it is said that all women should be enjoyed by the *sādhaka* (practitioner) in order to experience the *mahāmudrā*. It is clear that this cannot be understood in the physical sense, but that it can only be applied to the highest form of love which is not restricted to a single object and which is able to see all "female" qualities, whether in ourselves or in others, as those of the Divine Mother [a symbol for the "perfection of wisdom" or *prajñāpāramitā*].[64]

We find other *mahāsiddhas* receiving teachings directly from the *ḍākiṇīs*. In the hagiography of Padmasambhava, we find tales of his receiving the empowerment of Avalokiteśvara in the stomach of a *ḍākiṇī*.[65] Tilopa received teachings directly from the *dharmakāya* ("truth-body") of Jñāna-ḍākiṇī (Tibetan, Ye shes gyi mkha' 'gro ma).[66] Nāgārjuna receives alchemical teachings from a *ḍākiṇī*.[67] Kasoripa:

. . . conjured up Vajrayoginī [*yoginī, rnal 'byor ma* in Tibetan = *ḍākiṇī*[68]] and saw her face. On her inquiry what he wanted, he said that he wished to reach her stage, whereupon she lowered herself into his soul and he at once obtained the *Siddhi*.[69]

The *ḍākiṇī* are multivalent symbols. They appear in many different forms. We find Stephen Beyer citing the *Tse dbang kun khyab lo rgyus:*

> I the Lotus *Ḍākiṇī* instantaneously change my state and become the Lion-Faced *Ḍākiṇī*, very fierce, holding aloft a chopper and a skull bowl, my body embraced by the Father, the Black Slayer of Death (gshin rje gshed), who holds a copper-iron wheel.[70]

As well as offering empowerments, teachings, and magical powers (as we shall see), Beyer notes that, "In ritual invocations, it is recognized that *ḍākiṇīs* can be evil as 'pollutors and demons of madness' or as 'misleading demons'."[71]

Ḍākiṇīs may also take different forms to teach the adept equanimity and non-discrimination. We read:

> [Buddhasānti and Buddhaguhya] went to Potala mountain (equated with the spinal cord in yogic treatises), at the foot of which the goddess Tārā was reciting the Dharma before the Nāgas (sea-serpents). She appeared to them as an old woman looking after a herd of cattle. In the middle of the mountain, Bhrutī was preaching the Dharma to a number of Asuras (antigods) and Yakshas (nature spirits). She appeared to them as a girl looking after a flock of goats. On top of the mountain both of them saw a stone image of Avalokiteśvara. Buddhasānti was of the opinion that they had not yet developed ability to visualize Avalokiteśvara in his godly form.[72]

Ḍākiṇīs may also be actual women. In the hagiography of King Indrabhūti,[73] he is inspired by the religious accomplishments of his sister, Lakṣmiṅkārā, who was also a *mahāsiddha*. We read of Buddhaśrījñāna who studies with a *caṇḍālā* girl named Jatijālā.[74] Two of the female *mahāsiddhas*, Sahajasiddhi and Mandāravā, become *ḍākiṇīs*.[75] Mila Raspa is able to see in a young farm girl all the qualifications of a *ḍākiṇī*, and he takes her as his disciple.[76] In one case, that of the *mahāsiddha* Kukuripa, the *ḍākiṇī* is a dog.[77]

The *ḍākiṇī* also play such roles as: (1) sources of magical and

spiritual powers; (2) testers of the *mahāsiddhas;* (3) guardians of esoteric "hidden texts" known as *gter ma;* and (4) biographers of the
mahāsiddhas.

As sources of power, the *ḍākiṇīs* enable Nāgārjuna to provide
for the entire monastery at Nālandā by magical means.[78] They also
assist Padmasambhava in his sorcery duel with non-Buddhists at
Buddha Gaya by giving him " . . . a leather box with iron nails containing instructions for feats or sorcery to defeat his opponents."[79]
When the *mahāsiddha* Vyāli was unsuccessfully practicing alchemy,
a *ḍākiṇī* knocks some chemicals into his potion. When he then becomes successful, he tells him: "The essence of life and nature, the
secret of immortality, cannot be found in dry intellectual work and
selfish desire, but only by the touch of undiluted life in the spontaneity of intuition."[80]

As testers, a *ḍākiṇī,* incarnated as a girl, Ras chung ma, tests the
power and motives of Mila Raspa.[81]

The *ḍākiṇīs* are also guardians of *gter ma,* texts hidden by Padmasambhava and other tantric authors until humanity is ready for
these esoteric teachings. Padmasambhava entrusts some of these hidden treasures to the *ḍākiṇīs* for safekeeping.[82] The *ḍākiṇī* Ye shes
mTsho rgyal holds the texts of the legend of the great *stūpa* of
Bouddhanātha in the Kathmandu Valley, also composed by Padmasambhava.[83] The same *ḍākiṇī* also records the hagiography of Padmasambhava,[84] much as the *ḍākiṇī* Ras chung ma is the author of the
hagiography of Mila Raspa.[85] The role of the *ḍākiṇīs* in the quests of
the discoverers of these hidden esoteric treasures, the *gter ton* ("discoverers of *gter ma*"), is discussed by Hoffmann.[86]

An interesting phenomenon is that when a *mahāsiddha* has attained great spiritual heights, his relationship with the *ḍākiṇīs* under-
goes a reversal. Rather than being compelled, inspired, and em-
powered by them, he now becomes their teacher. Padmasambhava
spends several time periods teaching the *ḍākiṇīs,*[87] and they choose
him as their tutelary rather than vice versa.[88] Mila Raspa is sustained
by the *ḍākiṇīs* during periods of fasting and meditation.[89] The great
Tibetan historian, Padma dKarpo, described Mila Raspa as "king of
the *ḍākiṇīs,*"[90] indicating this new relationship between the adept and
the *ḍākiṇīs,* much as Hevajra is described as "rejoicer of the
ḍākiṇīs."[91]

Certain yogic practices are the special province of some of the *ḍākiṇīs.* The Tibetan rite of *gcod,* which involves psychic dismemberment and self-sacrifice and has thus been likened to a deliberate, self-induced schizophrenic episode, was founded by Machig Labdron, who ". . . is pictured as a naked white *ḍākiṇī,* beating a drum and blowing a thighbone trumpet, one leg raised and turned in the posture of a yogic dance."[92] One of the six yogas of Nāropa, *gtum mo,* or the generation of psychic heat, is called "the warming breath of the *ḍākiṇī.*"[93]

Summarizing, the major functions of the *ḍākiṇīs* in the hagiographies of the *mahāsiddhas* are: (1) inspiring and directing the *mahāsiddha;* (2) directly or indirectly bestowing empowerments to the *mahāsiddha;* (3) the patron of the *mahāsiddha,* and in cases of very great spiritual achievement on their part, this relationship is reversed; (4) the source of power of the *mahāsiddha;* (5) guardians of the *gter ma;* and (6) biographers of the *mahāsiddha.* The *ḍākiṇīs* may appear in visions, dreams, meditations, and as actual women. They are revered as preceptors of particular yogic practiced (i.e. *gcod* and *gtum mo*), and may be demonical as well as beneficent.

Their role in the lives of the *mahāsiddhas* is enormous, as the Bengali teacher Saraha sings in his *Dohā-kośa:*[94]

> There how should another arise,
> Where the wife without hesitation consumes the householder?
> This *yoginī's* action is peerless.
> She consumes the householder and the Innate shines forth,
> There is neither passion nor absence of passion.
> Seated beside her own, her mind destroyed,
> Thus have I seen the *yoginī.*
> One eats and drinks and thinks what occurs to be thought.
> It is beyond the mind and inconceivable,
> The wonder of the *yoginī.*
> Here Sun and Moon lose their distinction,
> In her the triple world is formed.
> Oh know this *yoginī,*
> Perfecter of thought and unity of the Innate.

COMPARISONS AND CONCLUSIONS

Our comparisons of the phenomena of the anima and the *ḍākiṇī* reveal striking similarities, both in the appearance of "the feminine" and in their psychological function in the lives of those on Jung's path to individuation or of practitioners of Vajrayāna Buddhism. As tempting as it might be to delve into how Jungians and tantrikas conceptualize these phenomena, that would be well beyond the scope of this phenomenological study.[95]

From the descriptions we have seen, the first striking parallel between anima and ḍākiṇī is their contrasexuality. Jung speaks of animus and anima; Tibetan texts speak of dpa'bo (Sanskrit, vīra, "spiritual hero," or ḍāka) and mkha' 'gro ma (Sanskrit, ḍākiṇī). Jung is much more specific in claiming that this function must be symbolized contrasexually, whereas Tibetans would be just as content with a ḍākiṇī inspiring a yoginī (female yoga adept) as a yogi (male adept).[96] However, our Tibetan authors would insist upon sexual symbolism for this function, as we read in the Vyaktabhāvānugatatattvasiddha of Sahajayoginī Cintā (one of the mahāsiddhas): "That man may wake up to his true nature, pure in itself and without duality, (this invisible point) manifests itself in the shape of a man and a woman."[97] Or as we read in the Hevajra Tantra:[98]

> Therefore twofold is the Innate (sahaja), for Wisdom (prajñā) is a woman and Means (upāya) is the man. Thereafter these both become twofold, distinguished as absolute (vivṛti) and relative (saṃvṛti). In man there is this twofold nature, śukra (relative) and the bliss arising from it.

Or, as the mahāsiddha Kāṇha sings: "How can enlightenment be attained in this bodily existence without thine incessant love, oh lovely young girl?"[99]

One of the major functions of the anima and the ḍākiṇī is that of inspiration. Much has been made of Jung's adaptations of the literary motif called the "Beatrice figure," the feminine which inspires and leads men through various travails. The parallels here to the function of the ḍākiṇī in the hagiography of Nāropa, for example, is most striking. In so inspiring men to begin their symbolic journeys, the call of the anima or ḍākiṇī may be shrill or beatific. Just as the ḍākiṇī who summons Nāropa from his comfortable position at Nālandā University is terribly ugly, revealing to him the state of his mind and the qualities which he has neglected, so the anima, Jung claims, is responsible for many neurotic disturbances in life. It is these disturbances which lead one to psychotherapy; it is the *ḍākiṇī* that leads one to a guru. We find that the analogy may be carried further: after one has become individuated, the anima becomes a guide to the unconscious; after successful training with the guru, the *ḍākiṇī* becomes one's patron and initiator. So we find in both Jung and Tibetan materials an image of a disturbing female figure, leading one to a guru or a psychiatrist (or in less fortunate cases, to a mental hospital), who, by the process of psychotherapy or meditation, becomes beneficent.

In one of Jung's excursions into the non-European area, he finds the anima as a mana-personality, powerful and awesome, but somehow conquerable. After such conquest, her power becomes reappropriated and oneself becomes the mana-personality—as a magician, sorcerer, or what have you. Analogous to this motif, we find the *ḍākiṇī* as exceedingly powerful, and the *mahāsiddha* may call upon her power for magical or other purposes. If the *mahāsiddha* is exceptional (as in the hagiographies of Padmasambhava and Mila Raspa), he gains power over the *ḍākiṇī*, becoming in turn her patron and teacher.

We also find the image of ongoing relationship carried through in Jung's writings and Tibetan texts. Several *mahāsiddhas* are said to take up residence with a woman; the majority of them are depicted in iconography with women. Jung tells us that since the anima is unknowable in herself, we must, as an individuated person, remain in dialogue with her—as with the other archetypes.

The *ḍākiṇīs* appear to the *mahāsiddhas* in dreams (which could also be said of Jung's anima), real women such as Lakṣmiṇkārā and Sahajayoginī (Jung speaks of "anima women"), and even a Kukuripa's dog (for which we find no analogy in Jung's writings).

The inspiration of the anima or the *ḍākiṇī* is a call for one to look inward. As such, she is the link between the conscious and unconscious. In appearing to consciousness, the anima calls its attention to what has remained hidden; she is the door to the unconscious.

In Buddhist terminology, one does not come across such a term as "unconscious," although the notion of *ālaya-vijñāna* (Tibetan, *kun gzhi*) comes close. One difficulty involved is the highly personalistic nature of the unconscious as understood in classical psychology. However, Jung's unconscious is not nearly so personal as is Freud's. Jung wants to reorient Western psychological thinking so as to become less personalistic. "Whenever a Westerner hears the word 'psychological', it always sounds to him like *only* psychological," he writes in commenting on some of the difficulties in a Western approach to psychologically-oriented Buddhist texts.[100]

In considering the *ḍākiṇī*, we find the Buddhist taking a similar position. The *ḍākiṇīs*, though psychic, are readily identifiable—they are well-known actors in the drama of Tibetan spiritual life. We have observed a Buddhist describe a "private" (i.e. psychic) vision to a lama, which was at once identified and pronounced to be the devotee's tutelary deity, or *yi dam*. If one elects to speak in such categories as "private" and "public" realities, undoubtedly the *ḍākiṇī*, like Jung's archetypes, would be in the public domain, notwithstanding the notion that their basis is psychic. However, it is this very basic bifurcation of reality into private and public sectors which would be seen by Buddhism as an expression of the problem of self: belief in an objectifiable, external world is a corollary to belief in an abiding reference point of its relation to consciousness, or ego. Such categories must break down somewhere along the Buddhist path, as Guenther observes:

> The *yoginī* who effects the integration of man is not an "object" but a participant in the drama of man's development that is enacted within and portrays itself as taking place without, so that it is often difficult to decide which is within and which is without. No wonder that this experience is spoken of as magical.[101]

In summary, then, when approaching the anima and the *ḍākiṇī* from a phenomenological perspective, we find more than accidental analogies. For example, the following ten attributes could as well be predicated of one as of the other:

(1) contrasexual appearance (much more emphasized by Jung than by the Tibetan texts)
(2) function of inspiring and leading
(3) appearance in dreams, visions and actual women
(4) source of power
(5) teacher and guide
(6) preliminary to therapy or meditation instruction
(7) wrathful and peaceful appearances; multivalence of image generally

(8) concreteness of image
(9) leading to transformation of the individual, and
(10) psychogenic origins.

However, when one considers how these phenomena are reflected upon, one runs up against enormous gaps. Furthermore, when Jung attempts to explicate Buddhism, or Eastern religions generally, we go even further afield. For example, at one place Jung writes:[102] "In the Eastern view the concept of the anima, as we have stated it here, is lacking, and so, logically, is the concept of the persona. This is certainly no accident for, as I have already indicated, a compensatory relationship exists between persona and anima." One might be so charitable as to attribute such a claim to Jung's lack of familiarity with Buddhism and Buddhist texts. One might also attribute it to a pernicious "Orientalism" in the sense of wanton over-generalization.[103]

Such problems aside, we are left with a compelling, cross-cultural portrait of a phenomenon of great import for human growth. It becomes obvious that both Jung and our tantric authors wished to call our attention to this phenomenon with great urgency. Such a phenomenon is sufficiently subtle to warrant its study from as many perspectives as possible, so there is no need to either bifurcate human thinking into irreducible "Eastern" and "Western" modes that cannot meet, even in dialogue, nor to assume that Jung was struggling to articulate something which classical Buddhists had said better centuries earlier (or vice versa). We would offer that this phenomenon, called anima or ḍākiṇī, could be treated as a paradigm for comparative religio-psychological study which neither reduces one perspective to another, nor sees the discourses of Buddhist and Jungian psychology as rigidly and artificially compartmentalized.[104]

Notes

1. Herbert V. Guenther, *Treasures on the Tibetan Middle Way* (Berkeley: Shambhala, 1971), p. 103, fn. 1.
2. Carl G. Jung, *Two Essays in Analytic Psychology* (Princeton: Princeton University Press, 1972), p. 221.
3. *'Phags pa shes rab kyi pha rol tu phyin pa rdo rje gcod pa zhes bya ba theg pa chen po'i mdo bzhugs so (Vajracchedikā Prajñāpāramitā Sūtra)* (Dharamsala: Tibetan Press, n.d.), fasc. 8a.

4. Jung, *Two Essays*, p. 304.
5. Carl G. Jung, *Psyche and Symbol*, ed. Violet de Laszlo (New York: Anchor Press, 1958), p. 9.
6. Jung, *Two Essays*, p. 299.
7. Carl G. Jung, *Psychology and Religion* (New Haven: Yale University Press, 1972), p. 40.
8. James Hillman, "Anima I," *Spring* (1973):97–132; and "Anima II," *Spring* (1974):113–146.
9. There are obvious dangers in confusing any male-defined notion of "femininity" with actual women. It is not my purpose here to expunge Jung's thought of sexist elements, of which there are many. Issues involved in such an effort have been indicated by Naomi R. Goldenberg, "Jung After Feminism," in *Beyond Androcentrism: New Essays on Women and Religion*, ed. Rita M. Gross (Missoula: Scholars Press, 1977), pp. 53–66.
10. Jung, *Two Essays*, pp. 160–161.
11. Ibid. p. 201.
12. Hillman, "Anima I," p. 123.
13. Jung, *Psychology and Religion*, p. 91.
14. Ibid. p. 15.
15. See Jung, *Two Essays*, p. 192.
16. Jung, *Psyche and Symbol*, p. 8.
17. Emma Jung, *Anima and Animus* (Zürich: Spring Publications, 1974), p. 65.
18. June Singer, *Boundaries of the Soul: The Practice of Jung's Psychology* (New York: Anchor Press, 1973), p. 231.
19. See Jung, *Psychogenesis in Mental Disease* from *The Collected Works of C.G. Jung*, vol. 3 (New York: Pantheon Books, 1964), p. 41.
20. Jung, *Psychology and Religion*, p. 114.
21. Jung, *Two Essays*, p. 227.
22. Idem.
23. Ibid. p. 228.
24. Ira Progoff, *Jung's Psychology and its Social Meaning* (New York: Anchor Books, 1973), p. 63.
25. See Jung, *Collected Works*, vol. 17, p. 339; vol. 9, p. 335; and Hillman, "Anima I," p. 115.
26. Jung, *Two Essays*, p. 221.
27. Jung, *Psychogenesis in Mental Disease*, p. 41.
28. Jung, *Psyche and Symbol*, p. 19.
29. Jung, *Collected Works*, vol. 8, p. 439, and cf. 964, 419, as cited by Hillman, "Anima I," p. 114.
30. Richard Wilhelm, trans., *The Secret of the Golden Flower: A Chinese*

Book of Life (New York: Harcourt, Brace and World, 1962), pp. 111–113.

31. Jung, *Psychology and Religion*, p. 102.

32. For one, the *Grub thob brgyad cu rtsa bzhi'i lo rgyus (Caturaśīti Siddhi Pravṛtti)*, by Mi 'jigs pa sbyin pa dpal (Abhayadattaśrī), *bsTan 'gyur*, Peking ed., *rGyud 'grel*, vol. lu, fascs. 1-68a, Otani number 5091, in an edition published as *The Eighty-Four Saints of Buddhist* (sic), (Varanasi: E. Kalsang, 1972). We shall also be using the *Grub thob brgyad cu rtsa bzhi'i gsol 'debs (Caturaśīti Siddhābhyarthanā)*, by rDo rje gdan pa (Vajrāsana), *bsTan 'gyur*, sNar thang edition, *sNgags*, vol. nu, Otani number 4578.

33. Especially the modern work by Khetsun Sangpo, *rGya gar paṇ chen rnams kyi rnam thar ngo mtshar pad mo'i 'dzum zhal gsar pa (Biographical Dictionary of Tibet and Tibetan Buddhism)*, vol. 1, *The Arhats, Siddhas and Paṇḍitas of India* (Dharamsala: Library of Tibetan Works and Archives, 1973).

34. Herbert V. Guenther, trans., *The Life and Teachings of Nāropa* (London: Oxford University Press, 1963); Bhupendranath Datta, trans., *Mystic Tales of Lama Tārānātha* (Calcutta: Ramakrishna Vedānta Math, 1957); Jacques Bacot, trans., *La Vie de Marpa le 'Traducteur'* (Paris: Libraire Orientaliste Paul Guenther, 1937); W. Y. Evans-Wentz, ed., *Tibet's Great Yogi, Milarepa* (London: Oxford University Press, 1969); Keith Dowman, trans., *The Legend of the Great Stūpa and the Life Story of the Lotus Born Guru* (Emeryville: Dharma Publishing, 1973); and Helmut Hoffmann, *The Religions of Tibet* (London: George Allen & Unwin, 1961).

35. Lama Anagarika Govinda, *Foundations of Tibetan Mysticism* (New York: Samuel Weiser, 1972), p. 53.

36. See Nathan Katz, *Buddhist Images of Human Perfection: The Arahant of the Sutta Piṭaka Compared with the Bodhisattva and the Mahāsiddha*, 2nd edition (Delhi: Motilal Banarsidass, 1989 [1982]).

37. I am indebted to Professor Steven Goodman of Swarthmore College, who developed this typology for me as an independent study project at Temple University in 1975.

38. Guenther, *The Life and Teachings of Nāropa*, pp. viii–ix. See also pp. 24–25 for the textual account wherein the *ḍākiṇī* terrifies and abuses Nāropa and admonishes him to give up the pretense of his learning and seek his Vajrayāna guru. Reading this compelling tale, it is not difficult to see why the first accredited Buddhist college in the Western world was named for this *mahāsiddha*.

39. Datta, *Mystic Tales*, p. 65.

40. Sangpo, *rGya gar paṇ chen rnams*, p. 161.

41. Bacot, *La Vie de Marpa*, p. 33.
42. Evans-Wentz, *Tibet's Great Yogi, Milarepa*, pp. 144–145.
43. Garma C.C. Chang, trans., *Hundred Thousand Songs of Milarepa* (New York: Harper Colophon, 1962), pp. 35, 64.
44. Evans-Wentz, *Tibet's Great Yogi, Milarepa*, pp. 88, 305.
45. Guenther, *Treasures on the Tibetan Middle Way*, p. 103, fn. 1.
46. Govinda, *Foundations of Tibetan Mysticism*, p. 192.
47. rDo rje gdan pa, *Grub thob*, passim.
48. Sangpo, *rGya gar paṇ chen rnams*, p. 159.
49. rDo rje gdan pa, *Grub thob*, p. 3.
50. *Grub thob brgyad cu rtsa bzhi'i chos skor* (Tibetan wood block text, Library of Tibetan Works and Archives), fascs. 154–157.
51. Datta, *Mystic Tales*, pp. 54–55.
52. Sangpo, *rGya gar paṇ chen rnams*, pp. 384–385.
53. Ibid. pp. 161–162.
54. rDo rje gdan pa, *Grub thob*, p. 4.
55. Ibid. p. 7.
56. Sakya Geshe Thukjey Wangchuk, *A Short Historical Outline of the Sakyapa Sect* (Dharamsala: Imperial Printing Press, n.d.), p. 5.
57. David L. Snellgrove, ed. and trans., *The Hevajra Tantra: A Critical Study*, 2 vols. (London: Oxford University Press, 1959), p. 9.
58. Hoffmann, *The Religions of Tibet*, pp. 142–144. See also Sangpo, *rGya gar paṇ chen rnams*, pp. 586 ff.
59. The *smyon pa* teaching is not restricted to Tilopa by any means. The *mahāsiddha* Mekopa is held by the tradition to be among the foremost of these "mad drunkards." See Sangpo, *rGya gar paṇ chen rnams*, pp. 695–696, where Mekopa sings:

To one's mind, the wish-fulfilling gem,
Worldly and transworldly are seen as particular aspects,
As apprehension and nonapprehension are not two.
Steadfastly look at the state of that mind.
How comes the notion of dualistic apprehension?
As there is no inherent existence in that state,
None of the *dharmas* are formed,
The nonapprehension of which is found
By desireless deception.

60. Hoffmann, *The Religions of Tibet*, pp. 143–144.
61. From a discussion with Herbert V. Guenther.
62. Snellgrove, *The Hevajra Tantra*, I.i.9.

63. Ibid. II.iii.67. For a lengthy discussion of the psycho-physical nature of female and sexual symbolism in the tantras, see Snellgrove's introduction to the text, pp. 33–39.

64. Lama Anagarika Govinda, "Principles of Buddhist Tantraism," *Bulletin of Tibetology* 2, 1 (March 1965):9–16.

65. W.Y. Evans-Wentz, ed., *The Tibetan Book of the Great Liberation* (London: Oxford University Press, 1968), pp. 131–133.

66. Sangpo, *rGya gar paṇ chen rnams*, pp. 587–589.

67. Mi 'jigs pa sbyin pa dpal, *Grub thob*, pp. 51–57, trans. Nathan Katz and Kelsang Yeshi, "The Hagiography of Nāgārjuna," *Kailash: A Journal of Himalayan Studies* 5, 4 (1977):269–276.

68. On the equivalence of these terms, see Stephen Beyer, *The Cult of Tārā: Magic and Ritual in Tibet* (Berkeley: University of California Press, 1973), p. 47; and cf. Snellgrove, *The Hevajra Tantra*, p. 135.

69. Nalinaksha Dutt, "Synopsis of Taranatha's History," *Bulletin of Tibetology* 6, 2 (July 1969):26.

70. Beyer, *The Cult of Tārā*, p. 314.

71. Ibid. p. 342.

72. Dutt, "Synopsis of Taranatha's History," p. 19.

73. Mi 'jigs pa sbyin pa dpal, *Grub thob*, trans. Nathan Katz, "A Translation of the Biography of the Mahāsiddha Indrabhūti with Notes," *Bulletin of Tibetology* 12, 1 (February 1975):25–29.

74. Datta, *Mystic Tales*, p. 51.

75. Ibid. pp. 18–19; and Evans-Wentz, *Tibetan Book of the Great Liberation*, p. 165.

76. Chang, *Hundred Thousand Songs of Milarepa*, pp. 50–63.

77. *Grub thob brgyad cu rtsa bzhi'i chos skor*, fascs. 154–157.

78. Katz and Yeshi, "The Hagiography of Nāgārjuna," p. 274.

79. Evans-Wentz, *Tibetan Book of the Great Liberation*, p. 171.

80. Govinda, *Foundations of Tibetan Mysticism*, p. 56.

81. Chang, *Hundred Thousand Songs of Milarepa*, p. 126.

82. Evans-Wentz, *Tibetan Book of the Great Liberation*, p. 179.

83. Dowman, *The Legend of the Great Stūpa*, p. 17.

84. Evans-Wentz, *Tibetan Book of the Great Liberation*, pp. 188–189.

85. Evans-Wentz, *Tibet's Great Yogi, Milarepa*, p. 309.

86. Hoffmann, *The Religions of Tibet*, pp. 59–60.

87. Evans-Wentz, *Tibetan Book of the Great Liberation*, pp. 130, 142.

88. Ibid. p. 177.

89. Chang, *Hundred Thousand Songs of Milarepa*, pp. 13, 118.

90. W.Y. Evans-Wentz, ed., *Tibetan Yoga and Secret Doctrines* (London: Oxford University Press, 1967), p. 146.

91. Snellgrove, *The Hevajra Tantra*, I.x.36.

92. Beyer, *The Cult of Tārā*, p. 47.
93. Govinda, *Foundations of Tibetan Mysticism*, p. 194.
94. Saraha, *Dohā-kośa*, v. 84–87, trans. David L. Snellgrove in *Buddhist Texts through the Ages*, ed. Edward Conze (New York: Harper Torchbooks, 1964), pp. 235–236.
95. Although I did attempt something of the sort in "Anima and mKha' 'gro ma: A Critical, Comparative Study of Jung and Tibetan Buddhism, *The Tibet Journal* 2, 3 (Autumn 1977): 13–43.
96. See Evans-Wentz, *Tibetan Book of the Great Liberation*, p. 121.
97. Quoted in Herbert V. Guenther, *Yuganaddha: The Tantric View of Life*, 2nd ed. (Varanasi: Chowkhamba Sanskrit Series, 1969), p. 87.
98. Snellgrove, *The Hevajra Tantra*, I.viii. 27–29.
99. Quoted in Guenther, *Yuganaddha*, p. 43.
100. Carl G. Jung, "Psychological Commentary" to *The Tibetan Book of the Dead*, ed. W. Y. Evans-Wentz (London: Oxford University Press, 1960), p. xxxviii.
101. Herbert V. Guenther, trans., *The Royal Song of Saraha: A Study in the History of Buddhist Thought* (Berkeley: Shambhala, 1973), p. 50.
102. Jung, *Two Essays*, p. 192.
103. Edward W. Said, *Orientalism* (New York: Vintage Books, 1979), pp. 31–72.
104. This is the third go-round in print for this essay, and I am pleased with the attention it has attracted. It first appeared in 1977 in *The Tibet Journal* (see note 95 for full citation), and a revised edition appeared in Nathan Katz, ed., *Buddhist and Western Psychology* (Boulder: Prajñā Press, 1983), pp. 241–262. The present article is further revised, based on discussions at professional meetings and in private. I want to thank Lucy Bregman of Temple University, Reginald A. Ray of Nāropa Institute, Robert A. F. Thurman of Columbia University, Roger T. Corless of Duke University, and Robert A. Clark, a Jungian psychiatrist at Friends Hospital, Philadelphia, for useful comments and criticisms.

Notes on the Contributors

MASAO ABE has been the leading exponent of Zen and Japanese Buddhism in the West since the death of D.T. Suzuki. As a member of the Kyoto School of Philosophy, he is also deeply involved in the comparative study of Buddhism and Western thought, and in the Buddhist-Christian dialogue. A graduate of Kyoto University in Japan, Abe studied and practiced Buddhism, especially Zen, with Shin'ichi Hisamatsu while also studying Western philosophy. As a Research Fellow of the Rockefeller Foundation, he studied Christian Theology at Union Theological Seminary and Columbia University from 1955–57. In Japan he was Professor of Philosophy at Nara University of Education from 1952–80. He holds a Doctor of Letters from Kyoto University, and since 1965 has served as Visiting Professor at many universities in the U.S.A., including the University of Chicago, Columbia University, Princeton University, Claremont Graduate School, the University of Hawaii, Pacific School of Religion, and Haverford College.

Abe's recent book, *Zen and Western Thought*, published by Macmillan and the University of Hawaii Press, is a collection of his important essays on Zen in relation to Western thought. This book was selected in 1987 by the American Academy of Religion to receive an award for excellence. Abe has also edited *A Zen Life: D.T. Suzuki Remembered*, published by Weatherhill.

PETER BISHOP is currently lecturing at the South Australian College of Advanced Education. He has a Master's degree in sociology and is currently completing a Ph.D. in the psychology of religion. He has published widely in the field of depth psychology and its relation to spirituality and contemporary social issues. His works include "Archetypal Topography: The Karma-Kargyudpa Lineage Tree," *Spring* 1981, "The Imagination of Place: Tibet," *Spring*

1984, "The Mysticism of Immensity," *Colloquium*, Vol. 18, No. 2, 1986. Forthcoming from Athlone Press (London) is *Tibetan Religion: Western Imagination (An Archetypal Study)*.

HAROLD COWARD is Professor of Religious Studies and Director of the Humanities Institute and the University of Calgary, Calgary, Alberta. In addition to numerous articles and edited books, he has published *Bhartrhari* (1976), *The Sphota Theory of Language* (1980), *Pluralism: Challenge to World Religions* (1985), *Jung and Eastern Thought* (1985), and *Scripture in World Religions* (1988). His articles on Carl Jung have appeared in *The Journal of Analytical Psychology*, *The Humanities Psychologist*, and *Philosophy East and West*.

RICHARD J. DEMARTINO studied Zen Buddhism with Daisetz T. Suzuki and Shin'ichi Hisamatsu, both in America and in Japan. He received his Ph.D. from Temple University in 1969. In Kyoto he taught at Otani University, and in America at Temple University. His publications include "On My First Coming to Meet Dr. Daisetz T. Suzuki," in *A Zen Life: D.T. Suzuki Remembered*, Masao Abe, editor (Tokyo: Weatherhill, 1986); "The Human Situation and Zen Buddhism," in *Buddhist and Western Psychology*, Nathan Katz, editor (Boulder: Prajna Press, 1983); "On Zen Communication," in *Communication*, Vol. 8, No. 1, 1983; "The Zen Understanding of the Initial Nature of Man," in *Buddhist and Western Philosophy*, Nathan Katz, editor (New Delhi: Sterling Publishers, 1981); "On My First Coming to Meet Dr. Shin'ichi Hisamatsu," in *The Eastern Buddhist*, Spring 1981; "Three Conversations Between Paul Tillich and Shin'ichi Hisamatsu," *The Eastern Buddhist*, October issues of 1971, 1972, 1973; and *Zen Buddhism and Psychoanalysis* (New York: Harper and Brothers, 1960) with Erich Fromm and D.T. Suzuki.

THOMAS P. KASULIS is Professor of Religion and Chair of the Division of Humanities and Arts at Northland College in Ashland, Wisconsin. His publications include *Zen Action/Zen Person* (University of Hawaii Press, 1981) and his editing and co-translating of YUASA Yasuo's *The Body: Toward an Eastern Mind-body Theory* (State University of New York Press, 1987) as well as numerous articles on comparative philosophy in a variety of scholarly journals. He is currently the president of the Society for Asian and Comparative Philosophy and is writing a book on the development of Japanese values.

NATHAN KATZ is Professor of Religious Studies at the University of South Florida. He is author of *Buddhist Images of Human Perfection: The Arahant of the Sutta Piṭaka Compared with the Bodhisattva and the Mahāsiddha* (Delhi, 1982; 2nd ed. 1989), co-author of *The Lost Jews of Cochin: Jewish Identity in Hindu India* (Berkeley and Los Angeles, 1990), and editor and contributor to *Buddhist and Western Philosophy* (New Delhi, 1981), *Buddhist and Western Psychology* (Boulder, 1983), and *Ethnic Conflict in Buddhist Societies: Sri Lanka, Thailand and Burma* (London, 1988). He has been awarded two Fulbright research grants (Sri Lanka, 1976–78; India, 1986–87), an A.C.L.S. travel grant, and a Florida Endowment for the Humanities project grant. He is Editor of *The Tibet Journal* and Director of USF's Graduate Program in Religious Studies. He previously taught at Nāropa Institute and Williams College.

MOKUSEN MIYUKI holds a B.A. in Indian Philosophy and Sanskrit Philology from the University of Tokyo, an M.A. in Philosophy from U.C.L.A., and a Ph.D. in Asian Studies and Research from the Claremont Graduate School. In addition to numerous articles on Buddhism and Jungian psychology in both English and Japanese, Professor Miyuki is author of *Kreisen des Lichtes: Die Erfahrung der Goldenen Blute* (West Germany), and co-author with Dr. Marvin Spiegelman of *Buddhism and Jungian Psychology*. He is Professor of Religious Studies at California State University, Northridge; faculty member of the C.G. Jung Institute of Los Angeles; and on the advisory board of the Institute of Buddhist Studies, Berkeley. He is a graduate of the C.G. Jung Institute in Zurich, Switzerland, and practices as a Jungian Analyst in the Los Angeles area.

RADMILA MOACANIN was born in Belgrade, Yugoslavia. She studied in Geneva, New York, and Los Angeles, and earned a diploma in Languages, an M.A. in United Nations and World Affairs, another Master's degree in Social Service, and received her Ph.D. in Psychology. She was a recipient of a Fulbright fellowship to Italy. Dr. Moacanin has worked as a psychotherapist at the University of Southern California Medical Center. At present she is engaged in private practice in Los Angeles, and serves as consultant in the National Intensive Journal Program. Over the past two decades she has been a student of Zen and later Tibetan Buddhism. Her publications include *Jung's Psychology and Tibetan Buddhism: Western and Eastern Paths to the Heart* (Wisdom Publications, 1986).

FREDERICK J. STRENG is Professor of History of Religions, Perkins School of Theology, Southern Methodist University. His extensive publications include a study of Nagarjuna, *Emptiness: A Study on Religious Meaning.* Professor Streng is a frequent contributor to Christian-Buddhist dialogue.

JAMES D. THOMAS studied at Phillips University and Earlham College and took his Ph.D. at Claremont Graduate School in California. For many years he taught philosophy at Mt. San Antonio College in California. He has worked in East Africa, Sri Lanka and Japan. He has studied with Professor Masao Abe. He considers himself a Quaker/Buddhist. Currently he teaches at Pendle Hill, a Quaker Center for Study and Contemplation near Philadelphia.

ISSHI YAMADA is a professor in the Department of History and Literature of Religions at Northwestern University. He is Editor of the sanskrit editions of the Mahayana Buddhist texts, the *Karuṇā-puṇḍarīka* and the *Sarva-tathāgata-tattva-saṅgraha.*

* * *

Note: A biography of SHIN' ICHI HISAMATSU appears on p. 100.

Index

Abe, Masao, 102, 119–20, 121–22, 124–25
Ādi-Buddha, 33
Alaya, 256
Amitābha, 33–36, 39, 40, 45, 181, 248, 251, 254
Amitāyur Dhyāna Sūtra, 33, 247–60
Anātman, 128, 264
Anattā, 214
Anicca, 214
Anima, 7, 48, 158, 302–03, 304–12; *dākinī* compared, 321–24
Arahant, 312–13
Archetypes, 139, 178, 185, 235, 243–44, 245, 254–55, 258, 268, 269, 296–97; gods as, 66; *see also* Anima
Atisha, 297
Ātman, 112, 128, 264
Augustine, St., 33, 89, 216, 268
Avalokita, lord, 213
Avatamsaka Sutra, 281
Avidyā, 57

Bardo Thödol. See Tibetan Book of the Dead, The
Beyer, Stephen, 318
Bhakti yoga, 248, 249
Bishop, Peter, 5
Bodhicitta, 257–58, 290, 304
Bodhimandala, 45
Bodhisattva, 202, 239–43, 291, 313, 316; as metaphor to Jung's concept of self, 6, 211–31; stages of spiritual progress, 199; as symbol of compassion, 286, 291
Böhme, Jakob, 13
Brahman, 128
British Medical Journal, 206
Buber, Martin, 223
Buddha, 20–21, 33–38, 45, 47, 54, 120, 129, 212; -body, 93; Gautama Buddha, 134; as image of wholeness, 172; laughing Buddha, 201–02; -nature, 182, 183, 257–58; Sākyamuni Buddha, 254
Buddhi, 57

Buddhism, 17; Four Noble Truths, 286, 288; Middle Way, 130, 283–84; "sinified" Buddhism, 183; *see also* specific headings, e.g.: Meditation; Yoga; Zen

Ch'an. *See* Zen
Chang Chung-yuan, 227
Chih-yen, 185
Chikhai Bardo, 81, 86, 93, 265, 266, 271
Ch'ing-t'u. *See* Pure Land Buddhism
Chögyam Trungpa, 169–70, 263
Chonyid Bardo, 81, 86, 87, 88, 91, 92, 93, 266–69, 270–71
Christ. *See* Jesus Christ
Cobb, John, 3
Cognitive function, 288
Collective unconscious, 46, 71, 104–05, 111, 117–18, 121, 135, 137, 140, 236–37, 243–44, 268
Compassion, 217, 286, 298
Consciousness, 17–22, 53, 56–58, 60–62, 105–09, 275–80; detached consciousness, 74–75; unity of, 172–73
Contemplation, 46–47; *see also* Meditation
Conze, E., 240, 241
"Creatura," 279
Cutting Through Spiritual Materialism (Chögyam Trungpa), 170

Dākinī, 303, 312–14; anima compared, 321–24
Dasabhumi-sutra, 199
Death, fear of, 109; *see also* Suffering
Death, Intermediate State and Rebirth in Tibetan Buddhism (Rinbochay and Hopkins), 263, 267–68
Defense mechanisms, 143–48, 155, 158
DeMartino, Richard, 102, 119, 120, 123, 125
Descartes, René, 128
Deutsch, Eliot, 221
Dewey, John, 126
Dharma, 76, 239

Dharmadhātu, 93
Dharmakāya, 84, 90, 258, 265, 269
Dhyana, 32, 43, 252
Dhyāni-Bodhisattvas, 33
Dyhāni-Buddhas, 33
Diamond-Cutter Sutra, 304
DKarpo, Padma, 319
Dōgen, 120–21, 122, 123, 124, 126, 144, 160
Dohās, 177–78
Dunne, J.Y., 74

Eckhart, Meister, 13, 15, 19, 295
Edinger, Edward F., 184, 196
Ego, 24, 56–57, 145–46, 234, 245, 258, 284–86, 303–04, 309–10; anxiety and, 92; self and, 14, 15, 73, 107, 112, 117, 121, 132–33, 139, 196–201, 234–35; Tantric Buddhism, 284–86
Egyptian Book of the Dead, 81, 82
Eight-Thousand Line Perfection of Wisdom Sutra, 233, 234, 235, 236, 238–45
Eightfold Path, 35
Enlightenment, 11–13, 14, 15, 84, 241, 258, 280–81; *see also* Satori
Erikson, Erik, 219–20
Evans-Wentz, W.Y., 48, 74, 81, 86, 94, 213, 262–63, 266, 302
Exercitia spiritualia (Loyola), 42, 43, 59, 67, 94
Extraversion, 53–54, 58, 59–60, 63, 64–65, 68, 71, 157, 168

Faith, 49, 50
Fantasy, 169; *see also* Imagination
Faust (Goethe), 25, 26
Feminine, The, 315, 320–21; *see also* Anima
Fen-yang, 215
Four Noble Truths, 286, 288
France, Anatole, 83
Freemantle, Francesca, 263
Freud, Sigmund, 44, 155–56, 159, 263; defense mechanisms, 4, 143–48, 155, 158; ego, 92; individuation, 155–60; intrauterine experiences, 86–87; introversion, 53; split with Jung, 166; therapeutic analysis, 145–46; transference, 4, 148–55; unconscious, 121, 125, 126
Fromm, Erich, 125, 126
Fujimoto, Ryukyo, 250, 253–54, 257
Fushin, 101

Gautama Buddha, 134
Gnosticism, 85, 166, 295
Goethe, Johann Wolfgang von, 25, 26

Govinda, Lama, 278, 285–86, 312, 315
Great Doubt, 138–39, 151
Guenther, Herbert V., 177–78, 303, 313–14, 315

Hakuin, 138
Hall, J., 245
Hatha yoga, 33, 57
Heart Sutra, The, 177, 279
Heisig, J., 175
Hevajra Tantra, 317
Hillman, James, 170, 178, 305, 306–07
Hisamatsu, Shin'ichi, 132; dialogue between Jung and, 101–27, 132–40
Hoffmann, Helmut, 316
Hopkins, Jeffrey, 263, 267–68
Hua-yen Buddhism, 183
Huang Shan-ku, 12
Hui Ming Ch'ing, 74
Huxley, Aldous, 175
Hyakujo, 11–12

I-Ching, 1, 172
Id, 145, 146
Ignatius Loyola. *See* Loyola, Ignatius
Imagination, 16; active imagination, 67; categories of, 89
Individuation, 4–5, 139, 155–60, 181, 184, 198, 258, 283, 310; *Oxherding Pictures* and, 202
Interpretation of Dreams (Freud), 156
Introduction to Zen Buddhism (Suzuki), 1, 2, 4, 218; Jung's foreword to, 1, 2, 4, 11–27, 218
Introversion, 53–54, 55, 56, 57, 59, 62, 64–65, 157, 168, 173
Intuition, 283
Ishin of Seigen, 125

Jaffé, Aniela, 101, 102
Jaspers, Karl, 303
Jesus Christ, 42, 50, 134; as image of wholeness, 172
Jodo Shinshu sect, 247, 248, 250, 253, 254
John of Ruysbroeck, 17
Joshu, 138
Jung, Carl Gustav: dialogue between Hisamatsu and, 101–27; foreword to *Introduction to Zen Buddhism*, 1, 2, 4, 11–27, 218; image of wholeness, 172–73, 276, 280, 282, 287; intuition, 283; mythical style, 175–79; psychological types, 157–58; split from Freud, 166; Terry Lectures, Yale University, 1937,

235; *see also* specific headings, e.g.:
    Individuation; Self
Jung, Emma, 307–08

Kagyü, 261
Kaku-an. *See* Kuo-an
Kālayasas, 247
"Kamma," 11
Kant, Immanuel, 75
Karma, 87, 88, 90–91, 93, 256, 264
Karma Lingpa, 261
Kasulis, Thomas, 4–5
Kataoka, Hitoshi, 119, 120, 122, 123–24,
    125
Kathakali dancers, 31–32
Kazi Dawa-Samdup, Lama, 81, 262
Kawai, Hayao, 121, 126
Keller, Gottfried, 31
Kierkegaard, Søren, 55
Kleśa, 33, 43, 105–106, 111, 248, 253–254
Koans, 13, 19–20, 22, 137, 138
Koichi, Tsujimura, 135–36
Kozankoku, 12
Kundalini yoga, 91, 168
Kuo-an, 181, 182–85, 191–96, 197, 198
    200–01
Kwan-yin, 219

Lankavatara Sutra, The, 279
Lao-tzu, 66
Larger Sukhāvatī Vyūha, 247
Levy-Bruhl, Lucien, 74
Lin Yutang, 215
Lin-chi, 202
Loyola, Ignatius, 42, 43, 59, 67, 94, 276

Madhyamika, 283–84
Mahābodcitta, 258
Mahabuddha, 33
Mahāsiddha, 312–13, 315–20, 321, 322
Mahāyāna Buddhism, 211–15, 250, 284,
    286, 313; *see also Bodhisattva*
Makyō, 139
Manda d'Hayye, 85
Mandaeans, 85
Mandala, 93, 197, 236, 244, 255, 285;
    Christian and Buddhist mandala
    distinguished, 46–47; as image of
    wholeness, 172, 173; as metaphor, 209
Mañjuśrī, 215, 223–24
Meckel, David, J., 101
Meditation, 20–21, 31–47, 173–75, 249–56;
    see also Yoga; Zen
Memories, Dreams, Reflections (Jung), 184
Metaphor, 208–09
Middle Way, 130, 283–84

Mind, 51–55, 120; as Mental Self, 72; names
    given to, 72–73; nature of, 71–72; No
    Mind, 104, 117, 122–24, 138, 139;
    non-creation, 75; Original Mind, 138;
    timeliness of, 73–74; Universal Mind
    (One Mind), 48, 49, 52, 62, 64, 67–68,
    75, 83, 278, 281; *see also* Self
Mind-ox Pictures, 182
Mipham, Lama, 317
Miyuki, Mokusen, 5–6

Nāgār juna, 214, 283–84, 317–18, 319
Narcissism, 242
Nāropa, 313–14, 315, 321
National socialism, 53, 59
Nicholas, of Flüe, 46
Nien-fo, 181
Nietzsche, Friedrich, 18–19, 25, 26, 66, 76,
    219
Nirvana, 111, 118, 135, 211–12, 214, 216–
    17, 219; samsara and, 69–70, 214–15
Nukariya, Kaiten, 12–13, 14
Nyingma, 261

Ohazama, Shuei, 13
One Mind. *See* Universal Mind
Onley, James, 208, 209
Organ, T.W., 229–30
Otto, Rudolf, 13
Oxherding Pictures, 181–205

Padmasambhava, 261
Pai-chang Huai-Lai, 11
Pali Canon, 11, 247
Pan Shan, 14
Paul, St., 17, 47, 199
Penguin Island (France), 83
Piaget, J., 176
Plato, 89, 128
"Pleroma," 279
Polanyi, Michael, 232, 234–35
Progoff, Ira, 309
*Projection and Re-Collection in Jungian
    Psychology* (Von Franz), 244–45
Prosch, H., 235
Psyche, 53, 54, 56, 58, 83, 105, 298;
    transcendent function, 61, 62–63, 70–
    71, 159, 288–89; *see also* Self
Psychoanalysis, 86–88, 93–94, 103, 143,
    161–63; Zen compared, 143–54
Psychologia, 101, 102
*Psychological Commentary on "The Tibetan
    Book of the Dead"* (Jung), 81–97, 168,
    174, 263–71

Psychological Commentary on "The Tibetan Book of the Great Liberation" (Jung), 148–80
Psychological types, 157–58
Psychological Types (Jung), 166
Psychotherapy, 22, 24–25, 110, 134–36
Pu-ming, 181–82, 185–90, 196, 198
Pure Land Buddhism, 174, 177, 181, 183, 247, 249, 250, 251, 254, 256

Rahula, Walpola, 128–29
Rebirth, 86, 88, 168, 261, 264; *see also Tibetan Book of the Dead, The*
Redemption of God, 290–92
Reincarnation. *See* Rebirth
Religion, science and, 49–50, 52
Rhoades, Donald, 208
Rinbochay, Lati, 263, 267–68
Rinzai, Master, 124, 130–31, 228–29
Robinson, Richard, 213
Rogers, Carl, 126–27

Sākyamuni Buddha, 254
Samādhi, 35, 57, 64, 183
Samsāra, 54, 64, 69–70, 82, 140, 216; nirvana and, 214–15
Sankhya, 69
Saraha, 177, 178, 320
Sāriputra, 241
Sato, Koji, 101, 119, 120–21, 122, 123, 124
Satori, 5–6, 12, 13, 14, 16–17, 19, 133, 178; *Ten Oxherding Pictures* and, 181, 182–83, 198, 199, 202
Scheler, Max, 88
Schizophrenia, 60, 61
Schopenhauer, Arthur, 18, 110
Science, religion and, 49–50, 52
Secret of the Golden Flower, The (Wilhelm), 1, 93, 166, 169, 174, 178, 206, 311–12
Self, 72–73, 106–13, 116–17, 119–40; as agent, 224–26; as archetype, 226–27; *Bodhisattva* as metaphor to Jung's concept of, 6, 211–31; as center of opposites, 222–23; ego and, 14, 15, 73, 107, 112, 117, 132–33, 196; Formless Self, 113; as goal, 221–22; no-self, 129–31, 133–34, 136, 139; Original self, 111, 112, 135; as superordinate system, 227–29; as uniting symbol, 223–24; *see also* specific headings, e.g.: Ego, Unconcious
Self-awareness, 242–46
Self-realization, 280–81; *Ten Oxherding Pictures*, 181–205
Septem Sermones ad Mortuos (Jung), 279–80
Shākyamuni, 33

Shin Buddhism, 173; *see also* Jodo Shinsu sect
Shingon Buddhism, 172
Sidpa Bardo, 81, 86, 87, 88, 90, 91, 266, 269–70
Silesius, Angelus, 19
Singer, June, 308
Six Oxherding Pictures, 202
Smaller Sukhavati Vyuha, 247
Spiritual transformation. *See* Enlightenment; Self-realization
Streng, Frederick J., 6, 240
Studies in Hysteria (Freud), 153
Subhūti, 240, 241–42
Suffering, 40, 107–11, 118, 134–40, 286–90; fear of death as, 109
Sūnyatā, 130, 281, 298
Superego, 145
Suzuki, Daisetz Teitaro, 116; *bodhisattva*, 216, 218, 223–24, 228–29; identity between nirvana and samsara, 214–15; Jung's foreword to *Introduction to Zen Buddhism*, 1, 2, 11–27, 218; *Ten Oxherding Pictures*, 181, 202–05
Swastika, 46
Swendenborg, Emanuel, 13, 89
Symbols of Transformation (Jung), 166

Tabula smaragdina, 69
Tantric Buddhism, 7, 87, 275–301; compassion, 298; consciousness and the unconscious, 275–280; ego and non-ego, 284–86; enlightenment, 280–81; ethical issues, 197–99; Four Noble Truths, 286, 288; Middle Way, 283–84; redemption of God, 290–92; spiritual transformation, 280–81; suffering, 286–90; union of opposites, 282–83; yoga, 94; *see also* Anima; Dakini
Tao Teh Ching (Lao-tzu), 66
Taoism, 172
Tathagāta, 40, 241–42
Tathagata-gotra, 257
Tathāgatagarbha, 5, 182–83, 257
Ten Oxherding Pictures, 5–6, 181–205
Terry Lectures, Yale University, 1937, 235
Tertullian, 54
Theologica Germanica, 14–15
Theravāda Buddhism, 211, 313
Thomas, James D., 6
Thus Spake Zarathustra (Nietzsche), 18–19, 25, 26, 219
Tibetan Book of the Dead, The, 25, 66; Jung's commentary on, 81–97, 168, 174, 263–71
Tibetan Book of the Great Liberation, The, 48, 168, 174; Jung's commentary on, 48–80

T'ien-tai, 183
Toyomura, Sachi, 119
Training of the Zen Buddhist Monk (Suzuki), 19
Transference, theory of, 4, 148–55
Ts'u-yuan, 182
Tsu-te, 202
Tsujimura, Kōichi, 101, 102

Unconscious, 21–23, 26, 56–57, 66, 275–80; collective unconscious, 46, 71, 104–105, 111, 117–118, 121, 135, 137, 140, 236–37, 243–44, 268; knowledge of, 68; mind as, 56–72; No-Mind distinguished, 138; One Mind as, 67–68, 75, 104; personal unconscious, 104–05, 117, 236–37; psychoanalysis and, 93–94, 117–18; psychology of the unconscious, 44, 45–46, 60, 61–62; *see also* Anima
Universal Mind (One Mind), 48, 49, 52, 62, 66, 83, 278, 281

Vaidya, P.L., 240, 241, 242
Vajrayāna, 3, 172, 174, 303, 304, 313, 316
Vimaliakīrti Sūtra, 213
Von Franz, Marie-Louise, 244–45

Whitmont, Edward, 228
Wilhelm, Richard, 93, 206
Woodroffe, John, 263

Yamada, Isshi, 101
Yoga, 17, 20, 31–47, 59, 63, 71, 94, 248, 258, 321; *bhakti* yoga, 248, 249; *hatha* yoga, 33, 57; *kundalini* yoga, 91, 168; Tibetan yoga, 168
Yogācāra Buddhism, 248, 256–59; *see also Amitāyur Dhyāna Sūtra*
Young Man Luther (Erikson), 219–20
Yüeh-shan, 144

Zaehner, R.C., 1, 3
Zarathustra. See Thus Spake Zarathustra (Nietzsche)
Zazen, 137, 138
Zen, 103–04; defense mechanisms, 143–48, 155; individuation and, 5, 155–60; Jung's foreword to *Introduction to Zen Buddhism*, 11–30; psychoanalytic theories compared, 143–65; transference, 148–55; *see also* Satori; Self
Zimmer, Heinrich, 31, 225–26
Zosimos, 291